THE JEALOUS

A SUFI MYSTERY

LAURY SILVERS

Published by Laury Silvers

Cover art by Ali Jafri

This is a work of fiction based on historical places, circumstances, and, in some cases, historical persons as read through the primary sources of the period and the secondary scholarship concerning it. All historical places, persons, and interpretations are ultimately the product of the author's imagination.

Limited selected quotes adapted from secondary and primary sources fall under "Fair Use." Alexander Knysh kindly gave his permission for the use of quotations adapted from his translation of al-Qushayri's *Epistle on Sufism*. Th. Emil Homerin kindly gave his permission for the use of his translation of a selection from Aisha Ba`uniyya's poems in *The Principles of Sufism*.

ISBN 978-1-7775313-2-4

✸ Created with Vellum

For my mother
(1933-2020)

She taught me that love is my religion.

ACKNOWLEDGEMENTS

My mother, Evelyn Silvers, was here for every moment of writing both books. She was the cheerleader every child wishes for herself. I am blessed beyond words. What thanks could I possibly offer to meet the freedom she gave me as a child to become my own person and her pride in me, no matter what I did? I am only sorry that she did not live to know that I had dedicated the book to her. I wanted her to hold the book in her hands and see it in print.

My partner, Michael, did hours and hours of careful editing, debating story points, reminding me of my characters' motivations, and pointing out gaps. He also wrote all the fight scenes. I relied on him every step of the way. There would be no book without him.

Layla Abdullah-Poulos gave me her time and expertise as she does to so many writers who are just starting out. She is an unsung hero, so let me sing her praises. More than showing me where my writing could improve, she walked me through the characterization of Mu'mina and other characters who are either affected by racial prejudices or who are the instigators of it. She made sure that I did not give in to stereotypes or tropes, and most importantly, that I pulled no punches. If I've erred, it is on me.

The academic and primary sources I relied on for the writing of this book are detailed on my website. Here, I would like to thank those who were generous in sending me published and unpublished works that helped me build this world as richly as possible and also answered my questions when I got stuck or confused.

Mathieu Tillier's work was essential to my account of the distinct justice systems. But he also gave me his valuable time over many emails, suggesting how Mu'mina's case might work through the secular and religious legal system and saving me from several fatal errors in my fictional account of the religious court system. Where I break with the historical evidence for the sake of drama, and I do that in a number of ways, I break with his scholarship and guidance.

On slavery, race, and consent, Peter Gray, Rachel Schine, Saadia Yacoob, and Yasmin Amin helped me navigate the primary and secondary sources, and shared their own works. Peter Gray helped me address the ethical questions in the book without risking anachronism. Much of the dialogue that touches on attitudes towards race in the book come from Rachel Schine's hard-hitting scholarship on depictions of black people in classical Arab literature. Saadia Yacoob's work on al-Sarakhsi demonstrates that some legal scholars did have a concern for female consent and experience during this period. Yasmin Amin gave me sources on Muhammad's record on consent in his family relations. Ash Geissinger pointed out some crucial insights in this vein that find their way into the narrative. Although it does not make an appearance in the book, Maryam Alkandari shared with me her helpful work on elite slaves in the Abbasid period.

Wes Snyder guided me in my characterization of Tansholpan by answering questions and sharing source materials that helped me understand how she would experience her abilities and her place in society. She is a complex character and I have Wes to thank for it.

Sarah Munawar and Michael Arnowit guided me in my characterization of the blind seer. They made sure she was not a stereotype and suggested where I could offer better depictions of diverse attitudes towards the blind elsewhere in the book.

Aun Hasan Ali educated me on all the details on the Shia of Baghdad. Sara Shah directed me to the story of Hurr upon which I built a major character arc. She and Zishan Syed also advised me on all the passages in which Shia characters express their experiences. Raha Rafii gave me insight into Shia law in the period.

Sara Abdel-Latif and Zahra Ayubi helped me think through historical articulations of ideal masculinity in early Sufism. Saliha DeVoe, Michael Quinsey, and Dubois Jennings talked to me about how Tein and Ammar would work through the challenges that face them as men. In particular, Dubois discussed with me how black men navigate the racism they encounter from their non-black male friends. I would also like to acknowledge the work of Pernilla Myrne and Marion Katz on masculinity and jealousy, and the sayings of Abu al-Husayn al-Nuri on self-sacrifice, which became the heart of this discussion in the book.

Nahyan Fancy checked Dr. Judah's medical opinions for me. Jennifer Bryson advised me at the outset on what medical conditions might fit the plot best. reneé mercuri provided me with crucial details on women's medical concerns. Shamseldin Rogers, Marion Katz, Nakia Jackson, Shabana Mir, and a number of women on Facebook gave me great insight into women's sexual health.

Ali A. Olami shared his detailed knowledge of the world of jinn and answered questions whenever I asked. Imran Khan, the journalist, inspired one of the jinn scenes based on something I read in his book, *In Truth, Madness*.

Rana Mikati shared her work on swearing and oaths. Rachel Schine advised me on period-specific racial insults. I have lost another citation for insults, whoever you are, forgive me. Others are taken from al-Jahiz's *Book of Misers*.

Talha Ahsan generously answered questions, offered sources, and suggested a scene in the book for Mustafa. Noor Naga gave me early and essential encouragement. Kristian Petersen helped me build YingYue's character. Katrina Daly Thompson found Mu'mina's birth name, Mwana. Joumana Medlej answered questions on inks and pens. Nadeem Ahmed of Eran and Turan, a Central Asian living history group, helped me dress Yulduz and Tansholpan. Jonathan Parkes Allen advised me on waterclocks. Nasrin Mahdavieh provided me with Yulduz's song. Rich Heffron gave me a source for Abbasid era sermons and Soad Mansory helped me find just the right line. Ash Geissinger answered many questions about hadith, Qur'an, and legal matters whenever I asked.

I also want to thank the many people on Twitter who piped up when I had a quick question, helping round out small matters in the book such as Syed Ziryab, @Basicbebeı, and Zainub of @chittyochitty, and Zainab Halipoto. There were many more, forgive me for leaving you out!

Rosemary Quinsey was more than a proofreader, she was also a writing coach. I am grateful for her contribution to my growth as a writer. Kathleen Self read a final draft of the book and pointed out where a little more explaining would do at crucial junctures. Sara Abdel-Latif gave me some proofreading help, as well. But I especially want to thank Shaheen Ali who, after my mother died in the weeks before the release of the book, graciously gave the draft an extra careful last read because I was not in any shape to do so.

I want to thank again Michael Mumisa and Alan Godlas whose mentorship in the writing of *The Lover* continued to feed my growth as an author in *The Jealous*. Also, I want to thank all my friends who supported me when *The Lover* was released. They shared the book, they talked it up, and they guided me in reaching out to people in real life and online. In this regard, I want to particularly thank Mo Zabian and Kristian Petersen. Likewise, Adam Gaiser stuck his neck out for me in getting *The Lover* in the hands of professors who have been, because of him, using it successfully in classrooms since.

My love to my family, Michael, Kaya and Ryan, Mishi and Ben, Eleonore, Tracey, Nancey, Catherine, and Candace and all the Quinseys for their support in the writing of this book. My thanks to my neighbours Bev, JoAnn, Claire, Cathal and the kids for cheering me on, and Billie Girl, as always, for being the very best dog. My sincerest gratitude goes to my teacher, Murat Coskun, for his guidance, and our community for their constant support and companionship.

Finally, thank you to the Department for the Study of Religion at the University of Toronto for providing me with a research fellowship allowing me to do the research that brought this story to life.

ON HISTORY AND FICTION

While the background, some storylines, and even some of the dialogue are adapted from historical and literary accounts of Abbasid Baghdad and its inhabitants, this is a work of fiction. I have taken liberties, most especially in how an Iraqi religious court in the ninth and tenth centuries might have adjudicated a murder case. The book takes up some of the uncomfortable realities of life at that time. Social norms such as slavery, racism, shadism, gender divisions, marriage, drinking habits, mosque attendance, and class divisions are all grounded in historical sources. Interested readers may want to read al-Jahiz's delightful satire *The Book of Misers*, which accurately depicts the social life and material details of the Abbasid period. Both The Lover (al-Muhibb) and The Jealous (al-Ghuyur) are not among the traditional ninety-nine names but were commonly used during this period.

The prologue contains a reference to a pomegranate tree. It is a reference to Sinan Antoon's exquisite *The Corpse Washer*. If your interest in reading my novels is to understand Iraq and the experience of the Iraqi people, please close this book and turn to the work of Iraqi writers such as those found in Hassan Blasim's Iraq + 100 collections, Shakir Mustafa's anthology, or *Baghdad Noir* collection of short stories, and the works of Shahad Al Rawi, Sinan Antoon, Dunya Mikhail, Leilah Nadir, and Ahmed Saadawi. Also see the online journal, "Arab Lit Quarterly." My novels do not assume to speak for or about the Iraqi people nor the nation of Iraq. They are an exploration of an Abbasid past and, ultimately, the way that past is remembered in the Muslim present.

If you want to know more, there is a glossary and character catalogue at the end of the book. I have also posted historical resources, a teaching guide, and book club questions on my website www.llsilvers.com. Follow me on Twitter @waraqamusa and @laurylsilvers on Instagram.

Allah

The Jealous

The Merciful The Compassionate The Lover The Holy The Peace
The Guardian of Faith The Protector The Firm The Compeller The
Dominating The Creator The Crusher The Praiseworthy The
Forgiver The Evolver The Bestower The Provider The Dishonouring
The Knower The Constrictor The Expander The Abaser The King
The Forbearing The Exalter The Honouring The Hearing The
Seeing The Everlasting Refuge The Opener The Subtle The Aware
The Great The One The Trustee The Grateful The Most High The
Most Great The Preserver The Wise The Restorer The Embracing
The Glorious The Resurrector The Light The Responsive The Strong
The Mighty The Friend The Reckoner The Accounter The
Originator The Unique The Life Giver The Slayer The Alive The
Equitable The Finder The Noble The Avenger The Powerful The
Expediter The Delayer The Most Exalted The First The Last The
Outward The Inward The Governor The Accepter The Pardoner The
Patient The Nourisher The One Who Forms The Revered The
Generous The Clement The Gatherer The Distresser The Possessor
of the Sovereignty The Lord of Majesty and Bounty The Self-
Subsisting The Sufficient The Enricher The Withholder The
Incomparable The Everlasting The Open-Handed The Right Guide
The Supreme Inheritor The Watchful The Able The Wise The Good
The Truth The Judge The Just The Witness The All Forgiving

THE FIRST DAY

Baghdad, 295 Hijri (907 CE)

PROLOGUE

"Raise her back, Saliha."

The woman's head was safely cradled against her chest. Saliha made sure her grip under the woman's arms was steady, bent her knees just a bit more, and lifted with her legs. As strong as she had become from washing people's clothes and hauling baskets of laundry to dry on roof terraces, she felt weak now turning the bodies of the dead for ritual washing and wrapping to ready them for the grave.

Usually they washed the bodies in their care while they were lying on their sides. The right side first, head to toe, then the left side, head to toe, three times. This woman was different. Saliha was careful not to lift her so high that the cloth covering her would slip down and expose her naked body, swollen with a tumour as big as a baby and trapped in her womb. Saliha's legs were screaming from holding still in that position, but she did not make a sound, not even a sharp exhale from the strain escaped her. The dead woman could still hear them. Her soul would remain within her body until the dirt covered her grave and until then, she shouldn't think she was causing anyone any trouble.

Once Saliha had got the woman's back high enough, Shatha

pressed gently on her stomach. Her hand swept down and away, tracing a path around the tumour that had had taken the woman's life. Finally, the excrement and urine left in her came out between her legs onto the table. Saliha was careful not to make a face, nor alter her breathing, despite the smell.

Shatha held one of the copper basins filled with water and powdered lotus leaves and poured it over the woman. She lifted the cloth covering her just enough to make sure the water reached between her legs, but not enough to expose her, even to their eyes, expertly rinsing the waste from the body without touching her. The water and waste flowed through the grooves carved into the bench-table and down to a lime-plastered gutter cut into the floor, and from there out under the wall toward a small garden where a pomegranate tree flourished, watered from the washing of the dead.

Following a glance from Shatha, Saliha slowly laid the young woman down onto the table. Together, they turned her on her left to wash her right side. Using another pan of water with ground lotus leaves, Shatha washed her right leg down to her toes.

Saliha tried to concentrate as she filled more water into jugs from the tap to be ready to fill the basins. Each time she had to use it, the tap from the cistern did nothing but distract her. Instead of keeping her mind on caring for their bodies, she took conscious pleasure in the luxury of not having to walk a bucket back and forth, over and over, to the closest public fountain. As her thoughts drifted, she nearly lost her hold on the copper jug as it became heavy with water, catching it just before it clanged against the sink basin. *Keep your mind on your work, woman!*

She was careful to make as little noise as possible as she emptied the water from the jug into a copper basin, adding nothing this time. They washed the woman again on each side with fresh water until all the pans were empty and nothing but fresh water had flowed out to the foot of the pomegranate tree, soaking the waste into the soil to feed its roots. One last time, she filled the basins. This time she dissolved a small amount of camphor into each, giving the water a clean, even sweet scent, and set them out. Saliha moved back to stand at the head of the woman as Shatha poured the scented water over every inch of her body through the cloth that covered her.

The undissolved camphor no longer stung Saliha's nose, but its scent lingered on her after work. Zaytuna complained of it to her regularly. At the lightest whiff, she would remind Saliha that her hands never carried the scent of death when they washed clothes together. *Uff!* Saliha thought, *Her complaints aren't about camphor anyway, are they?* But she would not quit this job for their friendship's sake. She would not go back to washing clothes. It took so much out of her; even if the body were that of an old woman who'd lived a full life, she felt the weight of the work in her bones. It was work most would say was unlike her. Serious. Gentle. Quiet. Respectful. Definitely not good for a laugh. But it suited her sense of life and death. You live. You find some joy. You die. You don't make a fuss.

Under no circumstances would she tell Zaytuna that the work made her think about what it would be like for her once she was in the hands of the corpse washer herself. Not even if it made Zaytuna accept that the job was good for her. She had never cared a whit what the preachers yelled in the streets, or the imams from the minbars, threatening a tight grave for free souls like her, the filthy rags of her missed prayers thrown in her face, and the bit of love she'd sought with men choking her throat. *Yell all you like, preacher,* she thought. *I am not yours to have a say. I belong to myself and God alone. And what God will do with me, God will do.* What Saliha could see, what she learned from washing these bodies, was that God took His creatures with care and sorrow for what must be endured in this world. That realization alone had returned her to prayer and her hand held out to God to grasp and pull her to Him.

The woman's eyes were sunken deep in their sockets. Her skin was ashen and slack, tugging on the delicate bones of her face. Alhamdulillah, at least, this one was whole. The beaten bodies of women and children made her flinch as if her dead husband Ayyub were behind her again, ready to strike. She owed them kindness in death that they had never got in life. She washed their brutalized bodies as if she were touching her own, by the grace of God alone, not here on the washing bench being turned by others' hands.

Saliha had been here long enough to see every sort of death. Here, the hospital's corpse washers accepted the bodies of the indigent and the unclaimed, whether they died alone in the streets or after the doctors had done all they could. They washed those whose families could not afford to pay a corpse washer to prepare their loved ones in keeping with the rulings of their own school of law, or those who died in the hospital but had no family to care about the legal particulars of how they found their way to the grave. Since she began this work, Saliha had washed and wrapped the bodies of unclaimed, unknown women or children who had washed up on the shores of the Tigris but whose bodies bore the indelible mark of long neglect.

Her thoughts strayed. Poor Tein, carrying the memory of bleeding and broken bodies from his days as a ghazi, fighting on the frontier. He faced similar tragedies every day now, solving grave crimes for the police. Saliha imagined him near her. His tall, muscular body wanting to touch her, his beautiful deep red-brown skin, the battle scar that snaked along the curve of his bicep and over his shoulder nearly reaching his throat, his high cheekbones and full lips, that scruff of beard on his pointed chin, and his eyes, his eyes with those long lashes. *Subhanallah!* In her mind, he was looking over her shoulder, watching her work and admiring her for it. Knowing brutality and death the way the two of them do now, she thought, *He should be even more willing to have a little fun with me. Don't we both deserve some comfort? Some life in so much death?*

Thoughts of Tein inevitably drew her back to Zaytuna. She sighed inwardly at Zaytuna's insistence that her twin brother was no good for her. This job was no good for her. This, that, and the other thing was no good for her. Look at this woman, her hollow face. Zaytuna was not far off! She looked like death in life, nothing like her brother, who was life itself. Saliha suddenly felt guilty and scolded herself at comparing this dead woman's face to Zaytuna's own. *It was rude, but walla, she did need to put more weight on.* She was eating now, but not enough. *Oh Zaytuna,* she thought, *you only have yourself to blame!*

It was Zaytuna who had brought her to this work, by dragging her along in her investigation into the death of a young servant boy. *Poor Zayd, may God have mercy on his soul. So, Zaytuna,* she thought, *I don't want to hear any more of your complaints!* Saliha finally did huff aloud, moving one of the basins too quickly sending it clattering against another, and shattering the peace of the room. She called herself to account, *God protect me from evil things!* Shatha's quiet voice followed her thought. No one except her apprentice would know that Shatha's tone, infinitesimally changed, was scolding, "Saliha, bring the camphor for rubbing."

Saliha did not apologize; she knew better now than to speak unnecessarily. She brought Shatha the small jar of camphor. She knew her master in this work didn't want apologies, only that she do her work properly. She watched as Shatha took a tiny amount of camphor on her finger and rubbed the woman's forehead, her palms, her knees, and her feet, all the places where she would touch the ground in prostration during the ritual prayer. Saliha collected the basins and jugs, putting them in their places on the shelves by the tap. Then she went to the cabinet at the back of the room where they kept the stores of ground lotus, camphor, and the winding cloth for the shrouds and took out three long sections of cloth, placing them on a side table near Shatha.

The woman lay on the table before them now, washed and scented, covered to her shoulders by a piece of white sheeting. Shatha laid the woman's long, brown hair out so it hung down from the edge of the table and gently combed it. It was wet but still held its wide, round curls. Her hair must have been glorious when dried and oiled, each curl perfectly defined. Saliha sighed. Shatha held each piece firmly near her head, so as not to tug on the woman's scalp and cause her pain. Then she separated the woman's hair into three pieces, then each piece into three again, and braided them, tying each off with thread. Each of the three braids was three fingers thick. *So beautiful.* Shatha gestured to her. They turned and lifted the woman again, over and to the side and back again, wrapping the winding cloth around her in three layers until they had her swaddled like a baby. Saliha thought, *You are free of the pain now, my sister.* She sighed aloud and Shatha twitched at the noise.

Shatha went out to let the family know their woman was ready for them to carry to the mosque for her funeral prayer. Sometimes the women of the family came in the room for the washing. Some even took turns pouring the water or holding the hand of their loved one while whispering soothing prayers in the ears of their mothers, daughters, sisters, and little children. Some stood to the side, watching and praying. Others sat on the bench outside the room waiting for the men in the family to carry out the wrapped body. But other times, no one was there to wait. Then orderlies would carry the body to a donkey cart, the driver alone accompanying it to the mosque for the funeral prayer.

Saliha moved to the side as four men came into the room with a pallet. Shatha directed them to lay the pallet on the second bench-table, and showed them how to lift the woman onto it, so that her body would not bend awkwardly, and so that they would not touch her in any way that was disrespectful.

They draped the body with the blanket they'd brought. It was clean but slightly moth-eaten with frayed edges. Such small holes, who would see? The little things caught her out and broke her. She knew it was likely their best from home. It would do until they could get to the mosque. There it would be switched out for a fine drape used to cover the believers first, for their funeral prayer and, then, for the walk to the graveyard carried on the shoulders of men.

The men would walk the streets with the body lifted on their shoulders, with family, friends, or maybe only strangers following behind. Saliha soothed herself with the thought that those they passed, as the body was carried through the streets and alleyways, might lift their hands and say a prayer for her. Then the men would lay her in her grave, on her side, with a brick for a pillow, facing Mecca, as they covered her with dirt and then left her alone with the angels to question her in her grave.

1

After the family had left with the woman's body, Saliha shook off the tension from Shatha's scolding for clanging the basins in her distraction and looked for signs that the old woman was not happy with her. Shatha unwound her thick linen wrap from under her arms and hung it on a peg by the door. Carefully taking her good wrap down, she pulled it over her shoulders and kerchiefed head so that it fell loosely around her, covering her completely. She took a wide, black sash off another peg, smoothed it out, and tied it around her thick waist to hold the wrap in place. She pulled the voluminous fabric just enough at her shoulder so she could easily tug it to cover her face as she walked in the street. Looking back before leaving, Shatha said, "You'll have your own black sash to wear when I think you are ready." Saliha let out a slow breath. She wasn't angry with her. *Alhamdulillah, the job is still mine.*

The sash, though. She wouldn't wear that every day, like Shatha did with such pride. Oh certainly, she would when they attended the funeral prayers of the women and children they had washed themselves. But a black sash around her waist marking her as a corpse washer would hardly impress potential lovers. Even so, she replied to Shatha, "Inshallah," as she continued putting the room in order.

Judah ibn Isa didn't seem to mind her being a corpse washer. But he was training to be a doctor, so she guessed he wouldn't. She smiled, remembering how he had tried to impress her by saying he was studying under someone important, someone ar-Razi. She rolled her eyes with pleasure at his efforts. What did she care about that? There was never going to be a marriage, even if he became Muslim himself. No man would ever have a say over her again. And men having a say was at the heart of marriage. Tein wasn't biting, despite Saliha's efforts to charm him into her bed. She'd have to look elsewhere. She wiped down the table, swept the room, careful not to raise any dust, checked to make sure she had stored everything correctly and whether the lotus leaves or camphor needed restocking.

Satisfied, she took her wrap down from the peg. She held it out to the light, admiring the design. No one could mistake this for a rag pulled from the old clothes left for the washer women to take away. No, she had bought it with the good money she was earning now. Her neighbour, Yulduz, had picked it out with her, drawing Saliha into a shop piled high with fabrics from all over the empire and beyond.

Yulduz inspected the Turkmen prints, sucking her teeth at each folded length of cloth that the shopkeeper pulled down from his shelves. "We've better than these back home." This would be the first new clothing Saliha had chosen for herself. Even her small trousseau from her marriage to Ayyub, *God show him the justice he deserves*, was picked out by his family and approved by her mother without her even seeing them. This. This would be hers.

When the shopkeeper had pulled down the brilliant blue and white wrap, bound-dyed like Yulduz's precious red and purple robe, Saliha nearly leapt in pleasure. Yulduz had to tap her lightly to control herself. Saliha should know better than to tip her hand to the shopkeeper, really, but it was so beautiful. Yulduz clucked at him in her Turkmen-accented Arabic, rounding every vowel beyond recognition, and clipping her words like a Baghdadi street urchin.

"Giv'er those Sindi ones." The shopkeeper laid out several more, stunning in their intricacy. Tiny birds, peacock feathers, and flowers played across the fine cotton and silk wraps. "More like it," Yulduz had said, her hand assessing the fabric as she went back and forth with the shopkeeper until finally she got the man to accept what she was willing to pay for the "cheap rag" that was now Saliha's dearest possession. It even had an embellished border of twisted brown threads sewn into curling vines around every edge, not just where it would cover her head.

Shatha had taken her off the unpaid apprenticeship period sooner than she had expected. As she pulled an edge of the wrap over her head across her deep blue kerchief, covering her thick, black braid hanging down to the small of her back, she felt pride in having impressed her master so quickly. She drew the wrap loosely around herself, so that it was open in front, suggestively showing too much of her long river-green qamis and sirwal, and let it hang over her arms like a great shawl. Her face, like most working women, went uncovered, and all to the good. What use was a niqab in drawing men except for prostitutes who plied their trade from behind face veils, using a discreet cough to identify themselves to potential customers? She wondered if she left work by way of the front of the hospital rather than the side door to the alleyway, she might run into Judah.

Saliha was tired, but still eager for a small flirtation to take home with her. She made her way through the passage past the surgery, oculist, pharmacy, then the bonesetters until she reached the airy main courtyard at the centre of the hospital that opened onto the arches of the wide front entrance. The leaves of the lemon and bitter orange trees clicked and hushed with the breeze, her wrap fluttering along with them. She took pleasure in how it must look but shivered from the cold. The change of season was coming. The weather was beginning to cool, although they'd likely see another spate of heat before the rain and cold weather settled in on them. There was time yet to save for quilted underclothes, maybe even a new woolen wrap. She glanced through the wide arched doorways of the wards as she passed, but she didn't see Judah. He could be found sometimes sitting in the shade under one of the trees, taking a break, or instructing the medical students beneath him. He must be making rounds right now. She sighed. Another day, then.

As she reached the end of the courtyard, a woman's low howl of pain echoed through the entrance hall. Without thinking, Saliha ran toward it, and then Judah, out of a men's ward. Orderlies got to the woman first and were lifting a writhing man out of a donkey cart, then carrying him through the doors to the nearest bed. A woman, surely his wife, was now screaming in terror, "She's killed him! She's killed him!" The man was not dead. He was in great pain, but not dead. His face was twisted with terror staring at something that was not there, looking at the space just over his chest, grasping at his left arm as if to pull the grip of some unseen force off of it.

Saliha gasped, "A jinn! God protect us from evil things!"

Judah directed the orderlies to take the man into the nearest ward. He saw Saliha and indicated to her to take hold of the woman and get her out of the way. Saliha rushed forward to her and took her arm. "Auntie, quiet, the doctor has him now."

The woman tried to pull her arm away. "Let me go to him! He's dying! She's killed him!"

Saliha held onto her more firmly and pulled her toward the courtyard. "The doctor has him now. We can see into the ward from here. Come."

The woman's eyes were wild, the delicate fabric of her niqab moving from the force of each word, "That whore of a slave! She's cursed him! An ifrit has taken hold of him!"

Saliha felt real fear at the word 'ifrit'. It was the worst sort of creature, a powerful jinn, who could kill or lead people to their worst selves so they did whatever ugly business the jinn had planned for them. She pulled the woman to sit and commanded her, "Tell me now what has happened. I must tell the doctor. This will affect your husband's care."

"His slave! Mu'mina, the slut! I saw her! She bought a talisman and forced him to wear it around his neck!"

"What happened? What did you see?"

"He was bruised but he didn't know how it happened! His eye blackened, his rib broken, and he didn't know how! He wouldn't believe me that it was her and he wouldn't take that cursed talisman off." The woman choked on the words, "That talisman drew an ifrit into our household to kill him."

"Can you sit here while I go speak to the doctor? Take a deep breath with me."

The woman sucked in a breath with her, then another. She nodded and pushed Saliha to get up and go to the doctor.

At the doorway, she saw Judah and a medical student speaking calmly by the bed, paying no attention to their patient. She stopped short. The woman's husband must be dead. She reached the bed and saw that the life that animated his body was gone. His skin was slack on his face, his mouth agape, one corner sagging down. Judah had closed his eyes, but one had come open again. One dead, milky eye staring.

She whispered, "The wife."

Judah asked, "How is she?"

"She says his slave forced him to wear a talisman that called on an ifrit to kill him."

A look of concern crossed his face, then settled into what looked like disappointment with her.

She retorted, "I'm telling you what she said."

He shook his head. "That is what he said, too. He was able to tell us before he died. An ifrit was sitting on his chest and had him by the arm. He could see it. He did not know why we could not see it too."

"She said there were bruises. It'd been beating him."

"You can see for yourself," he instructed. "There is a bruise nearly healed just below his eye." He leaned over the man and pulled up his qamis slightly. There were old and new bruises, yellow, green, and purple, layered on each other, across his chest. Judah pressed his fingers flat against the man's ribs feeling each carefully. "He has had at least one broken rib."

A piercing scream came from behind them. They spun around. The woman stood staring at her dead husband, then sank heavily to the ground. An orderly got to her first. He picked the woman up just enough for Saliha to move in behind. The woman's body fell against her, tugging Saliha's wrap from her head and shoulders, pooling around her on the floor. Saliha knew exactly how it looked and she did not move to cover herself. Instead, she put an arm around the woman to hold her up against her chest, laying the woman's head against her shoulder. *Walla*, she thought, *she's heavy like the dead.*

Judah came and crouched before the woman, but first he stole a look at Saliha uncovered before him. She did not look away. She heard him gasp, then whisper, "You are so good." She could sense that he wanted to pull her face to his own and kiss her full lips. He smiled at her, trembling, as if he *had* kissed her and lowered his eyes. "Thank you for caring for her."

Saliha almost laughed but bit her lip to hold it back. *What does he imagine I'm doing? Let him imagine, let him imagine whatever he likes.* Her face flushed, and she felt the warmth spread throughout her body. She wanted nothing more than to prop this heavy, emotional woman against one of the cabinets along the wall and find a quiet place to be alone with this dark-eyed man.

Judah rocked back to put more space between them and turned his attention to the dead man's wife. He lifted her niqab back over her head so that she could breathe more easily, muttering to himself, "She has lost her colour and she is in a cold sweat." Then he felt for her pulse in the crook of her arm. He said to Saliha, looking at her openly now, without trembling, "Her pulse is quick and shallow."

Saliha suppressed a smile, nearly teasing aloud, *Mashallah, the expertise! As if fainting were some extraordinary state!*

Judah called to one of the orderlies, "Go to the pharmacy and ask Firdaws ibn Ali for a cup of *khaya senegalensis*."

Saliha felt her stir and flicked the woman's niqab down over her face.

Judah nodded to her, then whispered, "I can get one of the female orderlies to replace you."

She shook her head. "No, I'm fine." It wasn't that she wanted particularly to sit with the woman. She felt for her, of course, but she had never been a good mourner. Even as a young girl she would escape the throngs of women who would gather around a grieving woman to wail with her. Inevitably, a cousin or her mother would drag her back in and prod her to cry. *Uff!* She thought, *If Auntie Basma were here, she'd pinch me to make me cry.* But she had always found a way to squirm out of their hands and run out into the walled courtyard of the woman's house to hunt lizards until it was time to go. She and Zaytuna were the same on this, at least. They stood up under grief and hardship. *How did so much noise make anything easier?* She smiled, assuring him she would stay. Having Judah so close without inviting hospital gossip, this was an opportunity she would not miss.

The orderly returned with a glass. Saliha put her hand out. "Give it to me." He looked at Judah, who nodded, and then gave it to her. She whispered in the woman's ear, "Come now, Auntie, have a sip of this."

The woman lifted her head, looking at Judah for help.

He said, "You've fainted. Saliha has a drink for you. When you feel you can, we will talk."

Saliha asked quietly, "Can you take the glass?" The woman reached up but her hand was still trembling. Saliha brought the glass up to the woman's mouth, easily flicking it under her short niqab with one finger and bringing it to her lips. The woman slowly sipped, her strength returning. Her body became less of a dead weight. She lifted herself, but at the sight of her husband, she began to moan and let herself slump back against Saliha. Afraid the woman would begin screaming again, and this time in her ear, Saliha comforted, "Shhhh, come now. We have to talk to the doctor."

The woman only moaned louder to say that the time for wailing was not under her control. She called out, "Where is my family? Send for my family!"

"Auntie." Saliha asked, "Where do you live? We'll send someone there."

"Go to Ajyad Road in Nahr Tabiq! Tell them Imam Hashim has died. Tell them that Hanan is here. Alone! Alone to bear up under this pain!"

Judah indicated that he heard. He began to walk toward the front hall to find someone to get the family but then turned back to them after a few steps. Saliha felt her wrap move from where it had pooled around her and she looked up at Judah over her shoulder. His gaze stayed with her as he gently lay the wrap over her head and shoulders so that she would not be so exposed to the men in the ward, then turned and left. Saliha lowered her head, placing her cheek against the woman's own and rocked her in her arms, but Hanan was getting heavy against her again, and the floor was only getting harder underneath her.

Saliha whispered into Hanan's ear, "Let's get up off the floor and find you someplace more comfortable," but she would not move. Her grief needed to be let go right there in the middle of the room, on the floor, before her husband, who was now lost to her in this world. Saliha sighed and gave in to the woman's grief, shifting her body behind her as best she could. She did as she should and moaned with her, softly echoing her grief. The men of the ward were watching the spectacle from their beds. But they grieved with her, silently, as men do. No doubt they prayed that their own wives and family would show them this loyalty and love when their time came.

She snorted without realizing at the thought that she was supposed to have mourned like this for Ayyub when he died. Hanan shifted underneath her at the sound. Saliha raised an eyebrow, thinking, *That's not for you, Auntie.* There were tears when Ayyub died, but they were tears of relief at being finally released from the living hell of him. Her own family scorned her for not lamenting his death. She expected it from his people. But her own mother? Her own aunts? Her cousins? She should have known. They dragged her back to him even after she showed them the bruises and after taking her to the bonesetters for a broken arm. "Rebellious woman," they called her. "Have some shame." When she turned to the men in her family, they did nothing to protect her. "You need a firmer hand than the one you're getting," they told her. When Ayyub burnt to death inside that pit of a house, he got what he deserved. She walked away from them all that day, never to speak to them again. *Shame be damned, if shame is being under the hand of a man!* Her back shot up at the thought of it, nearly pushing her burden out of her lap. Hanan shrieked. Saliha corrected quickly, stroking her shoulder, cooing, "I'm sorry. Your husband must have been so good to you." A sharp cry rose from the woman in return.

Saliha pulled her head back quickly so the scream wasn't directly in her ear. *That's it*, she thought. *She's going to have to move.* Saliha did not consult the woman this time, but rather pulled herself away from behind Hanan. She inched back to allow her to sit forward on her own power and waited a moment until the feeling returned to her legs so she could stand. She kept a hand on the woman to comfort her as she stood, then bent over to help her, saying, "We need to talk to the doctor." But Hanan got up on all fours and began crawling towards her husband's bed. Her wrap got caught under her knees and fell off her, pulling against the kerchief she wore underneath, and, in the process, nearly dragging her niqab off her face.

Saliha bent over to help her stand. "Come now, get up." She supported Hanan until she was up on one knee, then stood. The woman only took the few steps necessary to throw herself onto the bed where her husband lay. She began moaning, her voice rising to a wail, and saying over and over, "Oh God, what has happened to my love? What has happened to me?" Saliha picked up her wrap to cover her completely. She sat down at the edge of the bed, placing her hand on Hanan's back, waiting for this to end and for Judah to return.

Finally, Hanan's breathing became more even, and her moans became murmurs sighed with every breath. Saliha patted her back. "Are you ready to talk to the doctor?"

The woman pushed herself up saying, "Yes." Her eyes, red-rimmed and swollen from crying, were now hard and intent. Hanan's back was straight where it had been collapsed. She said with jarring clarity and contained fury, "And we must bring the police. That filthy slave will be executed for murdering my husband."

Saliha called over an orderly and asked him to find Judah, then turned to Hanan. "Auntie, let's go sit in the courtyard and wait for the doctor there."

The woman turned on Saliha, "I will not leave my husband until he is in the care of the washers! And why are you calling me 'Auntie', I am 'ma'am' to you!"

Saliha held her tongue and looked at the men in the ward. Some had returned to sleep; one man moaned lowly from his own pain, but another was sitting up and staring at them. She decided not to try to force Hanan. The woman had a right to be with her husband. But Saliha worried about the effect it would have on her husband's soul. She turned to her, saying gently, "Don't forget, he can still hear you. Remind him of God and his Messenger. Do not give him reason to worry." The woman looked to her in shocked realization and leaned over to whisper in his ear. Saliha could hear her repeating the shahada over and over, "There is no god but God, and Muhammad is God's Messenger," and interspersed with that, "Habibi, habibi."

Judah was crossing the courtyard to them and Saliha went to meet him. They stopped together at the thick archway to the room, leaning against it, facing each other. They were standing too closely again, and they knew it.

"She wants the police."

Judah nodded. "I cannot say that the beatings killed him. But who knows what damage could have happened internally. Is she still insisting it was an ifrit?"

Saliha laughed at him, raising her eyebrows. "Christians don't believe in the jinn?"

A stroke of anger crossed his face at her laugh, but he collected himself quickly. Pulling back within herself, she wondered if it was his nervousness around her or a preening manhood that could not stand a tease. The answer to that would matter. She shook herself into awareness. *This can't go beyond a flirtation. He could ruin you at the end of it.*

He answered her question lightly, the anger gone. "Of course we do. We leave food out for the jinn and give them their due respect so they leave us alone like everyone else." Then he corrected her, "I am saying that I do not know that an ifrit killed him. Not when other, more material, explanations might make more sense." He looked for an orderly. "I'll send a guard to find a watchman."

At the word watchman, Saliha realized that Tein would be here before long. After all, the watchman would bring the investigators for Grave Crimes in Karkh. It could only be Ammar and Tein. Not that there weren't enough murders and assaults to warrant more investigators. Tein had explained that in most cases, the culprit stayed with the body, or so many had witnessed the killing, that they resolved the case within a day of the commission of the crime, sending it on to the chief of Police for judgment and sentencing. Few killings amounted to a mystery. Two investigators were enough, so Tein would surely come.

Judah's eyes were soft. "Would you stay here with her until her family arrives? There are female orderlies who could do it." He smiled. "But, well, it is good to have you here."

With that one look, she forgot her suspicion of him and wondered if they might find a private place for a kiss after all. If not, then, at least she'd see Tein and he'd see Judah. She thought, *Let's see what comes of that*, and replied, "I'll stay."

2

Zaytuna sat against a pillar in the nearly empty courtyard of Shaykh Abu al-Qasim al-Junayd's home waiting for him to come down from his family's rooms to the common areas where the Sufi community of Baghdad gathered each day. It was early still. She kept an eye on a man sleeping in the far corner between the kitchen and the alley door. He had turned in toward the wall and was wrapped in a patched woolen cloak, pulled over his head and body, exposing his leathery feet. She wanted to cross the courtyard and cover them with her own wrap, but she left him to Hilal who surely knew he was there.

She heard the clanging of pots in the kitchen, then a sharp knock on the alley door. Hilal ducked out of the kitchen and stepped over the sleeping man to answer it. A deliveryman stood outside breathing heavily, wearing only a short sirwal and a scrap of turban on his head. Zaytuna could see his ribs from where she sat. A large sack nearly half his size slumped on the ground next to him. Hilal nodded and gestured to him to wait. He turned behind him and called out, "Abdulghafur!" while leaning down to touch the shoulder of the sleeping man. Zaytuna watched as Hilal woke him gently and helped him get out of the way of the path to the kitchen. Abdulghafur came out of the kitchen himself and hurried to the door, wiping his hands on a square of sheeting tied around his waist like an apron.

Zaytuna smiled at the sight of the boy. *Alhamdulillah*, she sighed to herself. At that, the boy turned and looked towards her as if he could feel Zaytuna's tenderness for him from across the courtyard. He grinned and put his hand on his heart, bowing his head to her. She put her hand to her own heart, feeling it beat so strongly she thought it might burst from the force of the gratitude she felt seeing the boy so happy and in place. He turned his attention to the bag slumped by the door and grabbed it, lifting it easily to his great shoulders, and carried it to the kitchen.

Hilal was insisting on something with the deliveryman, who was shaking his head. He finally gave in to Hilal's urging and took a seat next to the man in the patched woolen cloak. Hilal went back into the kitchen, and before long Abdulghafur came out with two bowls and wooden spoons, then came back again with a red earthenware jug of water and clay cups. He sat down before them, his legs underneath him, poured water for them, then rose to get back to work as the men thanked him and tucked into their food.

If she sat quietly like this and allowed herself to see God as The Provider at work in the food before the men, God as The Caring in Hilal's generosity, and God as The Just in Abdulghafur's service, she could almost feel the old oceanic waters of divine love approach her, leaving her assured that all was well. But they no longer came easily to her as they had done when she was struggling to find her way to understanding Zayd's death. Every day the waters receded from her, bit by bit. Before, the waves would take hold of her, turning her upside down and over and over until her sorrow and loss was swept out of her by its force, leaving her gasping and grateful on new shores within herself. But when the waters returned now, they only came in so far or they reached her in cold, accusing slaps around her feet and ankles that left her trembling in fear.

Zaytuna roused herself from the scene, and the small peace she felt observing it, as she heard footsteps behind her. She immediately stood and turned just in time as Junayd came through the entrance hall into the courtyard. Putting her hand to her heart and bowing her head, she said, "Assalamu alaykum, Uncle Abu al-Qasim."

"Wa alaykum assalam wa rahmatullahi wa barakatuhu, my daughter. You are here early."

"Is it alright? I wanted to speak with you."

"I am your uncle, you can come anytime. You know that."

"It is just that...."

Junayd interrupted her, "Let's go sit down."

They walked to his spot against the side wall where he could see the kitchen and back door to his right and the entrance hall to his left. She rushed ahead a few steps. The sheepskins he usually sat on had not yet been put out and she took several from the pile nearby and laid them over the woven reed mat covering the pounded earthen floor. As he went to sit down, he placed his hand on her left arm. At his touch, the old water rushed over her, saturating her and turning her heart over and over such that she had to consciously suck in a breath and call to herself to remain standing. She tried to take his hand to kiss it, but he pulled it away so gently she barely felt the cool softness of his skin on her fingers. He placed his hand on his heart again to her and leaned over to bring a sheepskin for her to sit on next to him. She said, "God forgive me," and took it herself before he could, laying it near his feet, and sat down.

"Tell me, what did you want to discuss?"

"Uncle, you are my uncle. I mean," she stammered, "I mean, I grew up with you and you have guided me as you would your own daughter. But I think I am ready for more. I want you to guide me as your student on this path. After Zayd, I mean, after what you gave me, I felt that I gained so much peace. I felt that I finally understood and accepted all that had happened to me, Tein, and my mother. I accepted my mother's life and her death. I was different. Everyone said so. But now, it is slipping away from me. I haven't really changed after all."

"My daughter, knowledge that comes in times of extremity has to be put into practice or it is lost, little by little, as the old life and old habits return. Do not think that your path will be easy because I forced you to see the truth. That merely pushed you to this moment. Now you stand before us for guidance. If you do this work well, not a single vein will remain standing in objection, but will bow in submission to God."

The words of her dear Uncle Nuri, "You are standing before the gate," said after she had solved the mystery of Zayd's death, came back to her and she realized she'd got it all wrong. What a sickening shame. Where she had felt the peace of divine waters saturating her moments before, now her whole body burned and she could barely breathe. She had thought Nuri, the great Sufi guide, a man as good as a father to her and all the children who grew up in this community, had been praising her. She thought he meant that she had found the sacred ground upon which her mother had stood, that she stood beside her. She had thought he meant that her mother's hand held her own again. But he was warning her that her hand had only just touched something her mother's hand had held, and for less than a moment. *Woman, what made you think you were worthy of being in your mother's presence? She loved you as all mothers must love their children, but you share no ground. How stupid you are, how stupid!* Zaytuna turned in and folded in on herself, wishing there was someplace she could hide. She pulled her wrap over her face like a child who thinks if she cannot see the world out there, it could not see her in here.

She could hardly hear Junayd speak through the hiss and roar of her self-recrimination, "Stop. My daughter, stop."

Feeling his hand on her head, the voices soothed and quieted, retreating to their places of hiding within her. She lifted her head, then sat back up on her knees, but could not uncover her face.

"Zaytuna, let me see your face."

She pulled the wrap aside but kept her eyes down.

"I will guide you."

Looking up at him, her heart stammered with hope.

"Your spirit and your mother's spirit are one. You are no more separate from her than you are from yourself. That spirit is God's reality. How could you ever be apart when all that is, is One? But your soul is distracted by this world of pain, loss, and pleasure. Inshallah, if you do this work, you will know. Will you do this work?"

She nodded and dropped her head again.

"I will guide you as my teacher, al-Harith al-Muhasibi, guided me. The first step on the path is to prevent yourself from giving in to your worst inclinations. You must learn the ways of the lowest part of yourself. You will observe them. You will practice not falling for its tricks. Most begin this path by giving up excess in everything, food, sleep, all the pleasures of this world."

Her heart hung onto his last words. *I can do that*, she thought. *I've done that. I can do that.*

"You may feel that you have mastered this part of the path already. You starved yourself and spent long nights in prayer for years. But the lower soul is clever. While it prompts some to gorge on food and luxuriate in comfort, it prompted you to withhold the pleasures of this world."

She looked up at him. "But..."

He held up his hand. "This path is an art of learning the soul's parts and habits. Your lower soul does not gorge on food and luxuriate in comfort, but rather on pain and suffering."

She bit her tongue to keep from objecting, *Me!*

"I know you will not give in to excesses in the body, but you give in to emotional excesses. Moments before, you were consumed in loss and shame and now you are consumed by self-righteousness."

She shook, refusing to accept it.

His voice cut through her, "Uncle taught that each level of the soul has an outer and inner expression. It has always been easy for you to restrain your body's basest desires, the outer expression of your lower soul. It is far more difficult to restrain the desires of your emotions. You must watch for the inward ways in which your lower soul gets you to do what it wants."

Her objection, emboldened for having been held back, burst from her, "Being scrupulous with everything I eat and drink and praying all night, praying all night to God because I suffer, is luxuriating in it?" She stared at him defiantly, forgetting herself and that this man, whom she called 'uncle' was Abu al-Qasim al-Junayd ibn Muhammad al-Khazzaz al-Qawariri, a teacher sought out by other teachers on the Sufi path for his guidance, a guide of guides.

He did not respond immediately. Then he said, "Restraint is not swallowing your words and letting them fester until they find their way out again in even more harmful ways. Restraint is holding back those words and tracing them to their source in your lower soul's promptings. For now, you must accept that you give in to these promptings. God is your Lover and you must remain His faithful companion. You must turn toward Him, accepting your faults and asking for forgiveness. Only then will the wounds that lie underneath it begin to be exposed and heal. If you betray him by giving in to that which leads you away from Him, these wounds will only grow."

She turned her face away from him.

His voice lowered, even more gentle to her ear, but its tone gained in intensity, its underlying frequency vibrating in tune with her heart so that it grabbed hold of it and then pushed it outside the limits she had imposed on it. "You mimicked your mother's movements like a child learning to pray for the first time. But instead of following her with the love of a child wanting to do as her mother did and so bring you nearer to the truth she embodied, you indulged the pain of not having the mother you wanted with you."

She looked up, desperately wanting to turn away and unable to do so.

"You made the pain of this world your Kaaba. You still circle it and kiss its stone. You are like the women who chain themselves to the ramparts of God's House in Mecca so no one can tear them away from their Lover. But their Lover is God and yours is pain."

As he pushed, she shifted, and finally what she had done consumed her. Just a few months ago he had held her head under the surface of the oceanic waters of God's oneness. She died to herself in that singular moment and was revived to the knowledge that the only existence was God's existence, and that existence was love. He pulled her out, but it only left her gasping for her old life. She clutched at the shreds of herself wanting to unsee, to unknow, that she had been worshipping the god of her own pain. But the fact remained before her, wherever she turned, as she unravelled the mystery of Zayd's death; there was the face of God. She had begun to accept it. She looked up at him, questioning, how had she forgotten? How had she turned away?

"Zaytuna, my daughter, you are feeling God's jealousy. You are between pain and love. Once you have been alone with your Lover, even for just a moment, if you look away from Him, choosing your loss over His love, He gives you what you want in a way you never wanted. He is a jealous lover, guarding you from straying. You chose forgetting over remembering, and so you slipped away."

Shifting with the shame, she lost her balance, falling, somehow, while still sitting on the sheepskin, into a chasm that suddenly surrounded her. She looked up at Junayd, desperate. He threw her a rope. The rope wound around her body and into her palms for her to grasp and whispered to her, *Hold fast to the rope of God*. She held on and jerked to a sudden stop. But the weight of her soul kept tugging at her, pulling her down, bit by bit. Her hands, calloused as they were from washing clothes, burned against its fibres. She closed her eyes so she could not see the abyss below, and moaned, "Help me."

He called down after her, "Zaytuna, you will listen when I, or one of your Aunts or Uncles, speak to you. I love you and will always remain family to you, but you will not count me as your teacher should you continue to object."

She tried to say, "Yes," but could not. Her throat was dry. Her tongue was swollen. She said it again, silently, this time to herself, *Yes.* The rope dissolved in her hands and the ground became firm beneath her. Her eyes were still shut, afraid of the chasm that might still be around her.

"Zaytuna, look at me."

She forced her eyes open. She forced herself to lift her head. She forced herself to look in his eyes. A gentle wave washed through her, taking with it the thumping and rumbling, and the prickling sweat, but it left her in confused, grasping need.

"This is harder than you can imagine."

An objection rose from her again, even in agreement, saying, *I know!* Then, a voice from somewhere else within her scolded, *My soul, will you ever stop!*

"My daughter, you will fail again and again. Uncle al-Harith taught me to examine my soul each night. You remember that he was called al-Muhasibi, 'The Accounter', because his path demands this precise and difficult work. Before you sleep each night, go over your day and make an accounting of your impulses."

As she listened, her breathing began to calm.

"Do not turn away from what you find, rather turn to God with it and ask for forgiveness. To repent is to turn to God, my daughter, so turn and keep turning."

She repeated, breathing through the word, "Turn."

He said, "It gets easier with practice. As you begin to understand how your soul's lowest inclinations work on you, you will shrink from them while you grow in love and affection for God. That which bars you from God will begin to irritate you, and that which opens the way to Him will be more desirable. As you become more cautious about your soul, over time, your eyes will seek your Lover alone and you will grow in tranquility with Him and His will for you."

He paused. "Zaytuna?"

She nodded, wary of what would come next.

"Will you do this?"

She heard the question like a balm; each word soothed her with his love for her and his confidence in her. He would not ask if he did not think she could. Quieted, for a moment, like a child in his arms, she said, "Yes."

Junayd smiled, his eyes brightening at her choice.

She had only just rested in his smile when she was disturbed by shuffling behind her. They both turned to look. A young Chinese woman with her much older father had come in. Both bowed to Junayd with hands over their hearts in greeting, then to her, and sat down by the far wall to wait.

At the sight of the girl, irritation bit at Zaytuna's throat. She did not bow in greeting to them as well. She did not turn away, either.

She gave YingYue the hardness she suddenly felt, saying to herself, *Can't I be with my Uncle without your intrusions? You've taken my Mustafa. Must you have everything of mine?*

Zaytuna looked away from them, her irritation rising to anger. *My God! does she pinch those round cheeks to pink them like some vain fool? Not very becoming a woman on the path. Did my mother care about her looks? No,* she answered herself. *She cared only for God.* Zaytuna looked at the skin on her hands, calloused, ashen, wrinkled old woman's hands. She nodded to herself, *More fitting.* She looked up at Junayd.

He was looking at her without expression. It wasn't cold. It was impassive, giving her nothing.

She froze. She tried not to think of anything at all. If she just stopped thinking, maybe he would look away. He did not and said nothing, his silence an excruciating rebuke. She had never felt the brunt of his silence in all the years leading up to this day, no matter how she had acted in his presence.

Within herself she heard his words, "You will fail," and "Turn," and she scrambled to turn on her thoughts. She pushed up against them. *Turn! Turn!* But they would not retreat. They stood before her in a wide-legged stance, saying *You will fail. You will fail. You will fail.*

His voice broke through to her, "Turn to God, Zaytuna, not yourself. You will fail. God will not."

She nodded, then muttered, "God forgive me." She turned to God within herself and held her thoughts out to him like a squirming, screaming child she wished would be taken out of her hands and away from her until it could learn to behave. He did not take it. It didn't feel like He took it. *Did He take it?* She dropped her arms, exhausted, then, heard herself say, *Forgive you for what, Zaytuna? For disliking that pink-cheeked girl who has your Mustafa so tied up in knots? For elbowing in on your family?* Zaytuna said aloud again, "God forgive me."

Zaytuna could not read Junayd's expression. He looked from YingYue to Zaytuna and said, "Go to her. I want you two to get to know each other. Tell her father I would like to speak to him."

She stood, desolate, and faced YingYue. She made herself walk across the courtyard, leaving her uncle behind her, saying to herself, *I can't do this.* She turned toward God, again, pleading, *Help me now! I have to talk to this girl. What wrong has she done me other than love my Mustafa? I cannot have him. Why shouldn't they love each other? God, I resent her! Help me!*

She reached YingYue and her father having no idea if the turmoil inside her was on her face. She tried to pull herself together, saying as evenly as she could manage, "Assalamu alaykum. Shaykh Abu al-Qasim would like to speak to you, Uncle."

The old man nodded and got up awkwardly. She could see that his joints hurt him, but she did not step forward to ask if he needed help. She knew from Tein not to offer men a hand in front of others. But YingYue was staring at her with plain accusation as she herself scrambled up to help her father, putting her hand out to help him stand. But her father slapped her hand away. She pulled it back, hurt, and Zaytuna sniggered to herself, her turmoil easing with silent laughter. YingYue glanced at her. Zaytuna did not try to pretend she hadn't seen it and give the girl some peace. She looked openly at the pretty girl from Taraz who made Mustafa blush. Her father finally managed to stand on his own and bowed his head to them both before turning to walk stiffly to where Junayd was seated. Zaytuna, still staring openly at YingYue, said, "The shaykh suggested we talk."

3

J udah leaned against the archway of the men's ward, standing too close to Saliha, and she was enjoying every bit of the delicious tension between them. He was still talking, but she had stopped listening. She admired the arch of his eyebrows, the long line of his nose, the rich sesame tone of his skin against, the dark luxuriant waves of his beard until the word "police" broke through her reverie.

"They'll be here soon," he said, "I should complete my examination of the body so I can give them my full findings."

Tein, she thought, *He'll be here soon*. She sighed at the thought of him. Judah's eyes widened reading it as desire for him. She saw his mistake and let it go, stepping away from the archway to put some space between them. Straightening her wrap over her head and covering part of her face, she said, "I'll watch Hanan while you look him over."

They returned to Hanan who sat slumped over her husband's body. She sat down beside her, putting her arm around her. At her touch, the woman heaved out a quiet sob.

"We need to step away for a moment so Doctor Judah can examine your husband for the police."

Hanan looked distraught and did not move.

"It'll be for just a moment."

Judah gave Saliha a look as if to say, "Leave her," then said to Hanan, "Please. You can sit at the end of the bed."

Saliha helped Hanan move and leaned in to comfort her while Judah called over an orderly to help him turn the body.

It wasn't long before Saliha heard a booming voice coming through the front hall, "Where's the body?" Judah stood up, gave instructions to the orderly, and hurried to greet the police.

"Ma'am, the police are here." Saliha asked, "Can you sit up?"

Hanan jerked up, nearly hitting Saliha on the head with her own, tugged her niqab straight, and arranged her wrap. She held the wrap closed under her chin with one hand from underneath and moved back to her spot beside her husband, placing her hand across his chest again.

Saliha stood as they walked in, adjusting her wrap as well, but she let hers fall loose, just slightly, so she could pull one edge across her face and cover her body. Judah came in with Tein and a short, bull-faced man, red-cheeks spotting his pale almond skin, wearing a black turban and leather cuirass with a sword at his belt. *That must be Ammar.* Tein pulled up short on seeing her standing there. She smiled. "Assalamu alaykum, ya Tein."

He nodded his head, and she thought she saw a smile in return, but he replied curtly, "Wa alaykum assalam."

Ammar turned to Tein, without greeting Saliha first, "Who's this?"

Judah looked from Tein to Saliha and back again, his cheeks flushing. He asked Saliha with a tone that suggested he had a right to know why she was so familiar with this large and undeniably handsome black man, "You know each other?"

She watched as Tein raised one eyebrow appraising Judah, and hoped it would spark some jealousy in him. Tein turned away from Judah to answer Ammar, "She's my sister's friend, Saliha. They live in the same house."

Ignoring Judah, Saliha spoke directly to Ammar, "I am an apprentice corpse washer here at the hospital. I was here when the man was brought in." She put her hand on the woman's shoulder. "I stayed here with his wife, while Doctor Judah," nodding toward him, "cared for the man."

Ammar said to her, "We'll need your account of what you saw. Don't leave."

She mocked him lightly, eyebrows raised, "That's why I'm still here. I would have gone home long ago if not for that."

Ammar raised his eyebrows at her in turn and said to Tein, "Definitely your sister's friend."

Tein smiled this time and nodded to Saliha who tipped her head to him.

Judah tried to interject, "I...".

Ammar ignored him, walking past him to the bed, Tein right behind him. He placed his hand on his heart, bowing slightly. "Assalamu alaykum. May God have mercy on your husband's soul. I understand you think your husband was murdered."

Hanan nearly sprung off the bed in response to the word "think," and pushed her hand against her husband's chest as she did so. She suddenly pulled her hand back in horror, then just as quickly she turned on Ammar as if he had brought all this on, "Think! I know he was murdered. And I know who did it! That slut, Mu'mina, his slave."

Ammar lowered his voice to reassure her, "Thank you, ma'am. That is helpful. I will need to hear everything you know and how you know it. But I need to speak to the doctor first. I will be with you shortly. Is that alright?"

She tugged at her wrap, clutching it harder under her chin, and nodded firmly. "Yes. I will be here."

Tein watched Ammar for what he should do. Should he stay with the wife, and Saliha, or go with him to question the doctor? Ammar motioned to Judah and Tein to follow him to the courtyard. Tein walked just behind them, then stood too closely on the other side of Judah in a subtle but threatening gesture. Judah looked up at him awkwardly, alarm spreading on his face.

Ammar rolled his eyes and called Judah back to his attention, "You attended the man?"

Judah turned to him, "Yes. . .yes, I did."

"What happened?"

Judah looked up again at Tein, then back to Ammar, and said, "I'm sorry. Yes. His wife brought him here in great distress. He could no longer walk. He was brought in a donkey cart and died soon after he arrived. He presented with contradictory symptoms. His face was flushed, yet his skin was cool and clammy, a light sweat; his pulse was weak; his eyes dilated; he vomited as we were moving him and had great pain in his chest and left arm."

"What killed him?"

Tein watched Judah shoot a quick look over at Saliha, his face reddening. She was speaking with the man's wife and Tein could see the relief in the doctor's face. Did he not want her to overhear him? Tein shook his head and laughed under his breath, saying to himself, *Oh, she has this one well tied up.*

Judah turned back to Ammar and said more confidently, "I cannot say for certain. Overall, the signs presented as a deficiency of yellow bile. But there is something else. He was hallucinating. He said that there was an ifrit sitting on his chest causing the symptoms I described to you. Hallucinations would be an excess of yellow bile, rather than a deficiency. So you see, I cannot offer you a conclusive account."

Ammar interrupted, ignoring everything else, "An ifrit?"

Ammar's voice, ever so slightly betrayed his fear. Tein had known him since they were teenagers who had run off to war against the Byzantines. Ammar had always left a small piece of bread for the jinn under bridges or outside small caves near flowing water. Tein teased him about it, but jinn were serious business for everyone. Everyone except him.

Judah objected to Ammar's question. "The presence of a jinn is not a medical diagnosis. Some believe they cause certain illnesses; I understand that, but I can only tell you what symptoms I observed."

Tein considered Judah. Maybe he was not the only one who thought the jinn were not real. He waited to see how Ammar would handle it. He took note as Ammar replied defensively, "Our investigation requires gathering all the details."

Tein decided to redirect the line of questioning, and couldn't help bringing a small humiliation to his phrasing, "So, you mean to say, Doctor Judah, that you don't know why he died?"

Judah put his thumbs in his zunnar belt and threw his shoulders back, which Tein noted did not make him any taller. The doctor said, "He died too quickly for me to make a clear diagnosis. Some conditions are terminal. Nothing can be done. This was one."

"The wife thinks he was murdered."

Judah was curt, "Again, I can only tell you what I observed."

Tein shifted his body toward him just enough to make the doctor feel a touch of menace. Ammar noticed the move and stepped back, giving Judah some room to escape Tein. Judah gratefully stepped into the breach.

Ammar asked Judah, "Ifrit aside. What else could cause those symptoms? A poison? A scorpion or a spider?"

Judah's eyes widened.

Tein thought, *Hadn't the good doctor considered that?*

Judah recovered immediately, returning to his pedantic tone, "A widow spider bite would cause one's yellow bile to decrease. This would explain some of his symptoms, but not others. Hallucinations are a result of a burning yellow bile."

Ammar asked, shaking his head in confusion, "What are we supposed to take away from that?"

Tein interrupted, "And poison?"

Judah stepped back again to look up at Tein and answered, this time without looking away, "Yes, any number of substances could cause these reactions. Balancing the humours is not a simple matter of addition or subtraction, many factors come into play, including balancing the medicines or surgical techniques we bring to bear on the imbalance. We compound substances for their effect on the humours, to increase some just so, while decreasing others. It is complex work. All to say, yes, a grouping of substances could cause a decrease of yellow bile, followed by a sudden increase. I will consult the pharmacist on what may be at work here, and if necessary," he said with pride, "the head physician of the hospital, Doctor Abu Bakr ar-Razi."

Ammar nodded, but Tein knew he didn't understand this medical talk any more than he did. "When do you think you will have it?"

"I should have the information for you by tomorrow. But sir, there is one last thing. The man has been beaten regularly. His bruises are old and new. He has a broken rib that healed recently."

Ammar said, "We'll need to get his wife out of the way to see them."

Judah looked at the woman, lying over her husband's body and said, "That's not necessary." He added in a high tone, "My trained observations should be sufficient."

Tein pushed back, "We're ghazis, doctor. We've observed more injuries than you'll see in your lifetime."

Judah backtracked and stammered, "My apologies, Ghazi. I only meant to say that, as you know, these injuries are not complicated and my account of them is complete."

"How old are the oldest bruises do you think?" Ammar conceded the ground to him.

"As you know," he inclined his head, "it depends on his health. At his age, it could be over a month to several weeks."

"How many separate beatings does it seem like to you?"

"I would say three," Judah answered.

Ammar looked from Tein to Judah, saying, "With the wife, for now, let's work with the ifrit story."

Tein wondered if Ammar was just saying that so he would not have to admit that he was worried about an ifrit. The three men walked back to the bed where Saliha and the woman were seated. The woman was still tenderly protecting her husband.

"Ma'am, thank you for waiting for us." Ammar bowed again and asked, "Could you tell us your name and your husband's name?"

She sat up straight, Tein saw she was careful where her hands were this time and looked back at her husband. "My husband is the renowned scholar, Imam Hashim ibn Uthman al-Qatifi. I am his wife, Hanan bint Sharaf ad-Din."

Ammar bristled. She couldn't know Ammar had no love for the religious elite and this was not the way to impress him.

"How did this ifrit come to kill your husband?"

Shifted her body slightly, she held her back straighter. "My husband's slave, Mu'mina. She's been no end of trouble for him! I tried to persuade him to release her. If only he had listened to me. This woman has no shame! God curse the day he bought her!"

"The slave. What is her connection to the ifrit that killed him?"

"I was at the Fruit Seller's Gate in the Karkh Market with my sister. We saw Mu'mina outside the gate where the soothsayers and curse writers sell their services. She was with one of them for a long time. The woman was playing an instrument like our jooza. But the way she played it, it sounded nothing like ours. God protect us, it was terrifying. Everyone in the square turned to watch her. As she played, she swayed, slowly at first then she became frantic. Her braids were flying when she ran that bow back and forth across the strings! Then she stopped playing and took up a piece of paper, pen and ink, and wrote on it. She folded the paper and stitched it into one of those flat leather pouches used for paper talismans and threaded it through a thong. Later, I saw my husband wearing the very same thing around his neck! How Mu'mina got him to wear the talisman, I will never know. I tried to warn him. Walla!" She raised one finger in declaration. "I warned him of her from the start. Now look at what happened...." Her hand fell and she broke down into tears again.

Ammar looked at the body. "There's no talisman there now."

She turned on him. "I ripped it off his neck as soon as he fell to the floor in this attack. Ya Rabb! Not soon enough! I should have cut it off in his sleep as soon as I saw it."

Saliha interrupted, "You cannot blame yourself for this. Removing the talisman would not prevent the ifrit from attacking. Once called...."

Ammar stuck his hand out to quiet Saliha. Tein had to restrain himself from back-handing him for it. Her face exposed, she smiled blandly at Ammar and nodded in assent. Tein relaxed. She can handle Ammar just fine. Saliha's concession was no concession at all, but Ammar didn't know that.

Turning back to the woman, Ammar said, "Ma'am, tell us what the curse writer looked like."

"She was old and dark like a withered date. God protect us from these Turkmen mongrels. She was no more than an animal who had lived her whole life in harsh wind and sun."

"How did you know she was Turkmen? There are many kinds of people with dark skin in Baghdad."

She looked at Tein with disgust and back again at Ammar, "I know the difference between them and *him*."

A small wave of exhaustion washed through Tein, but he remained impassive. Ammar didn't look to Tein, and he was grateful for it.

"I meant Turkmen." Ammar asked, "How did you know she was Turkmen and not Mongol or Tatar, for instance? What I'm asking, ma'am, is how do we recognize her when we go looking for her?"

"Her clothes." She looked him up and down as if he were stupid. "One of those bound-dyed robes they all wear, with lapels, can you imagine such a thing! But not tied under the arm like the Mongol women. It had their embroidery, those thick bright designs around the collar and down the edges. Don't you know them? My God and you call yourself police? Listen to me! Her robe was black and red. And she wore a cap instead of a kerchief with her grey hair out for all to see in long thin braids."

Tein made a mental note to start paying more attention to what people from across the empire wore.

"How did you know the talisman was meant to call an ifrit to harm him? Talismans have many purposes." Ammar reflexively touched the base of his throat where his own talisman hung under his qamis and leather cuirass. "It could have been for protection or healing."

She threw her arms out, her wrap fell open, her eyes glaring. "He is dead! This is how I know!" Then she raised her hands, palms open and up and pleading, "God, how will his death be avenged if this is the fool you've sent me!" Hanan looked Ammar up and down, then drew her arms back under her wrap and pulled it around herself, then looked at him full in the face. "Now listen, you! When I saw the talisman around his neck, I warned him, but he would not take it off. Then he began to be beaten. There were bruises everywhere on his body. Just as they would heal, more would appear! He said he had no idea where they had come from! Despite my demands, he still would not take the talisman off." She began to weep again, "Oh God, have mercy on my man's soul. Why did he not listen to me?"

Ammar grunted.

They were both well used to the frustration families of the dead would hurl at them. Ammar even had a soft spot for the old women; Tein had heard him call a few of them "mother" or "grandmother." But this one had got off on the wrong foot with her high-handedness about her husband's station. Tein knew Ammar was restraining his tongue so he could get the interview finished. Ammar finally interrupted her weeping, "Why wasn't he concerned about the bruises?"

Sniffing, she wiped her nose and dabbed at her eyes under her niqab. "He said he thought he was sick. He said he knew a man who bruised easily and died of it. But I knew him as his wife. As old as we are, he had the same energy as he always did. His appetite was good in every way." She fixed her eyes on him. "He was not sick! I told him, 'You go to see one of these physicians if you think you are sick'. I don't know if he did. He wouldn't tell me anything. But then his rib was broken. How does an illness break a rib, I tell you!"

They heard a commotion toward the front hall of the hospital. Women's voices were raised, and a man was trying to control them. One of the gatekeepers rushed into the ward his voice echoing in the quiet space. "Doctor Judah!"

Judah hurried to meet him halfway, gesturing to keep his voice down. They could still hear him. "Their family is here. I told them that only the men are allowed in, but the women are trying to push us aside."

Putting his hand on the man's shoulder, Judah said something then pushed him in the direction of the door. He returned, saying, "I've told him to bring in one male family member and those who will carry him to the corpse washer." He shook his head at the guard's ineptitude. "They deal with these women all the time. He should know better what to do."

Ammar nodded. "Did Imam Hashim come here for treatment?"

Judah replied, "I've never seen him before. But he could have gone to anyone. There are twenty-three other doctors here. He could have seen a doctor privately at a clinic as well. There are also women healers." He bowed slightly to the woman, begging her pardon, then turned to Ammar, "If I could speak with you alone for a moment?"

Hanan glared as the three men stepped aside.

"I observed what I could of his symptoms before he died, and the state of his body after death. His bruises and breaks are not new. They did not happen as a result of his convulsions. Now, there are illnesses which would cause such bruising. And coughing can cause a person to break a rib. He may have been ill, not beaten. But now that he is dead, there is nothing I can do to tell the difference short of cutting him open to see if he bears the mark of these diseases."

"Can we do that?"

"It is possible. We do that when we can to understand the workings of the body, but the family must agree."

Ammar looked over at the wife. "Not likely in this case." Turning back to Judah, he said, "Look, there are almost always quick accusations and confessions with this sort of crime. If the girl does not readily confess to killing him, would you testify in a written statement that his cause of death is unknown, and likely an illness?"

Judah nodded. "Yes."

Tein looked at Ammar not believing what he was hearing. The 'Golden Boy' of Karkh's Grave Crimes Section had never once tried to shut down the investigation of a case. He followed them through to the end. But this was their first case involving a jinn. Ammar was scared. This was going to be a problem.

Tein said, "Can't we ask her if we can examine the body?"

Ammar shot back at him, "Why would that be necessary? You heard what the doctor said. We'll have this case wrapped up one way or another."

Tein started to object, then thought better of it.

Judah excused himself and walked to the rear of the hospital.

They all turned to see a man rush toward the bed. The man had left the house without his turban or even a skull cap. His fine robe was hanging on him at an odd angle with no sash holding it closed. His robe was edged in fine embroidery spelling out something in calligraphic letters. Tein thought, *For whose sake did he rush here?*

Two men followed, both in rough clothes. Tein gave them a look and they stopped at a distance from the bed. The wealthy man hurried past Ammar and Judah, didn't even look at the dead body on the bed before him, not even at Tein, and fell to his knees before the woman. Tein nodded to himself. *There you have it.* Hanan gasped as the man fell down before her, then said to him in a whisper, "Alhamdulillah, you've come." Tein saw that he wanted to reach out to her but held himself back. *Not her brother, then. A cousin, maybe her husband's brother. Maybe both.*

The man consoled her, "Let's take my brother to the washers and get you home." She looked for the rest of her family, and answered her glance, "They won't let them in. The hospital must have its quiet." He asked Saliha, "Can you help her outside to the women in the family?"

She asked Tein, "Can she leave?"

Tein looked over at Ammar who answered, "Yes."

Saliha nodded, and went to help her stand, but Hanan had turned toward her husband. She leaned over him, kissing him on the forehead, holding him one last time. Tein watched the brother-in-law as Hanan said her last goodbye. The man wept quietly and wiped his tears away with the edge of his sleeve, then looked to Saliha again to give Hanan a hand. Hanan pulled herself up from her husband's body and tried to stand, but her legs were weak. Tein could see she was shaking. Saliha said to her, "You need to be strong for a few moments more." Saliha helped her and they stood together.

She put her arm around Hanan's waist. The woman leaned on her and began to moan again as they walked slowly toward the front hall.

The brother-in-law indicated to the two labourers who came with him to come to the bedside, but Tein held him back. "Not yet."

A deep-throated scream came from the front hall. The brother-in-law turned toward Tein and said, "She's found the women to comfort her."

Tein didn't say anything, but to him Hanan's scream sounded more like rage. He looked to Ammar, but he did not indicate that Tein should go and check. *No worry, Saliha is there. She'll tell me and if there's any trouble, the hospital guard will sound the alarm.*

Ammar turned to the brother-in-law and introduced himself. The man replied, "I am Isam ibn Uthman al-Qatifi. This man is my brother."

"Your sister-in-law believes your brother's slave murdered him."

Tein expected him to deny it and apologize for her emotional state. Instead he shook his head. "So that slave of his finally killed him. I feared as much when the news reached us."

"Why?" Ammar asked.

Isam's head tucked back. "The girl had him cursed. She had him so infatuated with her that he willingly wore the curse around his neck. He refused to remove it no matter what we said."

"Is the girl at home now? We are going to need to speak to her."

"Speak to her? Arrest her! She's outside. We've got hold of her. Not weeping for him, no doubt. Likely gloating!"

"We'll take care of her," Ammar assured him. "Your sister-in-law told us that she took the talisman off him before they left for the hospital. Can you find it when you get home and put it aside for us?"

"Of course."

"We'll come to get it. We'll need to speak to you all again."

"Whatever you need," Isam replied.

"Do you live with your brother and his wife?" asked Ammar.

"Yes, we share a large home with separate apartments, our mother lives with us as well. You can find us there."

"But you weren't home when this happened? Excuse me, but you look like you just got dressed."

The man looked down and adjusted his robe, then felt his bare head, realizing he had forgotten to put his turban on when he left the house. He blushed, stammering, "None of us were there but the two of them and the slave. Poor Hanan. I spent the night at my sister's home and the servants came this morning to bring some gifts that Hanan had graciously put together for my sister. She is lying in with her fourth child and my mother has moved in with her for the time being to help. We were still eating breakfast when we heard the news."

"No household staff were with your brother and his wife at home? Other than the slave?"

"The housekeeper and the boy who does the heavy chores came this morning with gifts, as I said."

"How did you get the news?"

"The slave brought the errand boy from the hospital to my sister's house. My sister could not come, of course, and our mother has collapsed with the news. But our other nephews are just outside, the housekeeper and the boy, and some of the neighbours. Do you need to speak to them now?"

"No, not now. For now, you can take the body to the corpse washers. I assume you want to bring him to the washers in your neighbourhood?"

Isam nodded gratefully.

Ammar turned to Tein and said, "Go outside and get hold of the slave."

Tein looked at Ammar impassively, despite wanting to offer a strongly worded objection. He knew Ammar had believed in the power of curses and the jinn. And he'd want this case cleared fast, but he couldn't think the slave could have killed this man with a talisman. *If it is murder, anyone in that house could have poisoned him. The brother-in-law is obviously in love with his brother's wife! What about the beatings?* He couldn't help it, he muttered under his breath, "He's lost this case before it's started."

Ammar heard him. "What?"

Tein shook his head and headed to the front hall. Saliha was chatting with Judah, standing too closely to him. Here he had thought Judah walked to the rear of the hospital. He must have walked around through the women's wards on the other side just to see her. Judah looked up and saw him, his face bearing the mark of a boy who had been caught at something. Tein laughed to himself, *Don't bother with the guilty looks. She's a wild mare, that one, and I'm not interested in taming her.* Saliha looked at him quizzically and her smile fell. Tein nodded to the two of them as he walked out to the street.

He expected to see a crowd of women weeping and wailing as he got outside, but there were perhaps ten people huddled across the street. There were women standing or crouching around Hanan and comforting her. Moans rose and fell with Hanan's own. He heard her call out the name "Hashim," then the name was echoed by the women surrounding her. Several men stood around them, shielding the women from the curious looks of passersby, although one woman held up her hands in prayer for the dead and the living. Two of the men were young, likely the nephews, the eldest in his teens and the youngest, a small boy, no more than five.

But just outside of the group, a male servant stood wide-legged with a firm grip on the arm of a slight, barefoot, black girl. Not a child, but not a woman either. She was wearing nothing but a worn linen qamis and sirwal, and a wrap around her waist like an apron. As he crossed the street to her, he saw the scars on her face. Three parallel lines of small bumps in a pattern that traced over her nose to each side defining her high cheekbones. She was hanging off the man's grip, her knees buckled beneath her, with the terror of innocence in her eyes.

4

How could this woman be on the path and be so harsh? YingYue bowed her head. *Or is it me? Have I done something out of place?* She looked up at this tall, extraordinary woman and felt ashamed, her face prickling with embarrassment under Zaytuna's gaze. She raised her hands to her cheeks, her delicate fingers trembling. Zaytuna looked at her with even more frustration, but what had she done?

Zaytuna turned away and said, "I'll get dates from the kitchen."

She disappeared into the reception hall rather than walk across the courtyard. She emerged moments later carrying what looked like a large folded woolen wrap, and without a look or a nod to YingYue, walked past her to the two men sitting on the far side. *She does everything with so much confidence. But she grew up here,* YingYue reassured herself. *This is her home.* Zaytuna kneeled before one of the men, who had nothing on but a short sirwal and a bit of turban on his head and handed him the wrap. The man took it eagerly and let it unfold in his hands, then pulled it around himself, nodding to Zaytuna in thanks. She put her hand over her heart and bowed her head to him, then rose and entered the kitchen. YingYue shot a quick look at Junayd, then scolded herself, *Why did I not see what the man needed?*

YingYue could hear Zaytuna greeting Hilal and Abdulghafur. She was so loud. *Does she not realize the shaykh can hear her?* Zaytuna said something again. It sounded like she was teasing one of them about burning the hintiyya. Then Hilal's voice came clear and strong across the courtyard, threatening to slap her with the kitchen paddle. Zaytuna said, "Shhhh!" There was even more laughter from within. Hilal never teased YingYue. To her he was always only ever polite. She never raised her eyes to him, nor the boy. If she had to go into the kitchen, she stopped and waited until they noticed that she was there and asked what she needed. *Wasn't that the right thing to do? Or did it make her a stranger?* She didn't want to cry, but the tears came anyway.

She heard her before she saw her. Zaytuna was there holding a small red clay bowl of dates in her hand, saying, irritated again, "What's wrong?"

YingYue looked at her but did not answer. What could she say? *Look at her. Her skin browned so deeply from the sun. She had heard her father was an Arab, and her mother an African. The mother was one of the great ones. An ecstatic lover of God. The aunties and uncles still related stories about her standing up to men in the street who dared to criticize her for preaching to the people. They still recited the poetry that flowed out of her when she dissolved in the divine ocean.* YingYue could see her mother in her. Not her looks. No, she looked like an Arab. Her brother took after the mother. She blushed. *God forgive me,* she thought as her mind turned to Tein, *he is a handsome man. No,* she corrected herself, *he is beautiful.* The Prophet, God bless him and peace, said, "God is beautiful and He loves beauty." The Beautiful shone Its divine light everywhere, even through a man who refused to worship Him. And this woman, not beautiful in her face, but beautiful in her devotion. *She does not even try to keep her skin from darkening in the sun. She does not even care what she looks like.* YingYue thought of her own small vanities. How she protected her skin from the sun. How she oiled her thick hair. How she loved the chance to have it braided into thin strands in the Turkmen style, each one tied off with the brightly coloured threads. *Zaytuna would never fall into such petty worldliness. Who would dare cross her? She understood why Mustafa would love her, would likely always love her.*

YingYue looked over the empty courtyard but imagined it being busy with people as it was most afternoons. The Sufis gathered together to talk. The children came each day for their lessons. Who was she? A spiritual child. A nobody who knew nothing and needed everything. Some of the Sufis were refined in their manners, some rough, some mad. But there was one thing they all shared; they were all tough like this woman before her. Even the most refined, you might cross them without knowing what you were doing, and they would forgive you, some may even try to guide you with hints and nudges or, recalling the year she and her father lived in Marv with her shaykh, Abu Bakr al-Wasiti, with a spiritual slap to the head. But nothing you could do would hurt them.

She shook her head at herself. Shaykh Abu al-Qasim had ordered her to tell Zaytuna her story, but she did not trust this woman enough to tell her. Nevertheless, she pulled herself around to his command and said, "I am different, not like the rest of you. I cannot do this."

Zaytuna sat down next to her as she said it, grunting, and kept her eyes on the far side of the courtyard. YingYue searched her face, it showed nothing, but her words did. Zaytuna nearly spat them out, "What can't you do?"

She cannot even hide that she does not like me. YingYue looked at Junayd, then said, "Belong to you. How do I belong to you all who have been on this path for so long?"

"Mustafa said you had come here all the way from Taraz. That is a long way. Why would you come?"

YingYue wondered why she asked. *Maybe the shaykh told her to ask about my story? Are we both forcing ourselves?* She asked, "Do you truly want to know?"

She thought Zaytuna looked exasperated and readied herself for a "No," but she replied, "Yes."

Sitting up, she crossed her legs, and leaned in, looking at Zaytuna, searching her face to see if she was telling the truth. *How do I speak to her?*

"Yes. I want to hear," Zaytuna pushed.

YingYue said it, "My father, he made me leave." She paused, then said each word with great emphasis, "I fell in love."

Zaytuna's eyes opened just slightly at those last words. YingYue thought, *She will listen.* Then said, "When I was a child in Taraz something happened. My parents were not Muslim then. I was born healthy, but I became sick. I was only one year old, maybe a little more. I was hot and cold at the same time. I could not eat. I spit up my mother's milk and grew thin. The doctor could not help. The healer could not help. The shaman could not help."

"But you are still here." Zaytuna said.

YingYue said, "Yes! You have good eyes!"

Zaytuna held back a laugh, and YingYue dropped her head in embarrassment, realizing Zaytuna thought her stupid rather than teasing. She made herself say, "My father took me to see QuanYin in the temple."

Zaytuna interrupted, "Who?"

"Please listen. A goddess. She is like God's name *ar-Rahim*. She is kind and compassionate. She is gentle and caring."

Zaytuna's head tucked back in shock. "You believe in her?"

YingYue held out a hand to stop her. "Please listen. Please."

"Fine." Zaytuna raised her eyebrows.

"I was just a baby. Father lifted me up to her so she would cure me. But I turned my face away from her. Father was angry with me. He pushed my face back to her. I turned away again. He held me up to her even closer. I squirmed out of his arms and fell down to the floor. He was afraid. Maybe I had angered the goddess and cursed myself. Maybe I would die. He said he scolded me, 'What have you done!' He said, then, I spoke my first word, 'Allah'."

Zaytuna leaned toward her, nearly reaching out. "Subhanallah! What did he do?"

YingYue's heart expanded. *She will hear me!* "He went to the mosque. The imam said I was a Muslim. The imam whispered the shahada in my ear. I do not know how, but I remember it. I can feel his breath in my ear like it just happened. I can hear his whisper, *There is no god but God and Muhammad is God's messenger.* My father saw me grow fat again before his eyes."

"Right then and there?"

"Yes. Father said the shahada, too, right there for himself and our whole family. He brought me to my mother. She held her baby, fat again, and wept. It was a miracle. But she was angry about my father saying shahada. My brothers accepted becoming Muslim."

Zaytuna sat forward. "Why wouldn't she?"

"She hated Taraz. Father had a dream he would build a paper business there. Dream or not," she said defensively, "it was a good decision because of the trade route. But she and my brothers had to leave everything behind. She never saw her family again. She was so lonely for them. She never even tried to speak Turkmen. I was born in Taraz, so it was easy for me. Chinese at home. Turkmen outside. Arabic at the mosque."

"But who did you love?"

She did not answer the question directly, "I grew up in the mosque."

Zaytuna audibly sighed.

YingYue flushed with embarrassment, started to get up, and knocked over the bowl of dates. "I am so sorry. I am talking too much."

Zaytuna didn't reply, but looked toward Junayd. He did not look back at her. She turned back to YingYue and said in kind words that sounded false, "I apologize. I wasn't sighing at you, just something on my mind. I want to hear the rest of your story."

Looking away, tears coming up again, she said, "Another time."

Zaytuna reached out touching her on the knee. "You said you spent all your time in the mosque?"

YingYue knew how she must look. Her face would be flushed. Her eyes red-rimmed with tears. She took a breath and made herself speak, "I spent my days there because my mother abandoned me."

Zaytuna did not reply immediately. She looked at Junayd again and replied unkindly, "Oh, really?"

"Yes!" YingYue insisted.

Zaytuna closed her eyes. "Tell me, then."

"God became my Companion. I memorized Qur'an and hadith in the mosque with the imam. I learned their meanings." She reached out and took Zaytuna's hand, so rough in her own. Zaytuna pulled her hand back. She looked at her empty hand, and said, "It was so peaceful at the mosque. My father's paper and printing factory was so noisy. My brothers at home were so loud. And my mother yelled at me for every little thing. But at the mosque, I sat by the pillars and dreamt about God." She looked up at Zaytuna. "The mosques are so different from here. They are enclosed but they feel open. The pillars are made of wood, wide at the top and smaller at the bottom. I don't know the Arabic words to describe them. They are carved. The carvings were small. Careful."

"Intricate. But there are pillars like that here, but only in al-Mansur's Mosque."

"Oh? I want to see them. But 'intricate', what does that mean?"

"What you said. Small details. All tied together."

"Yes, the designs were *intricate*. I traced my fingers in the grooves. I rested my head against them. In my heart, I told my secrets to my Companion."

"So what happened, why did you leave?"

"Something happened to me."

Zaytuna exclaimed, "What! Get to the point!"

YingYue was stunned into silence. A few moments passed, then Zaytuna reached out to take her hand, but YingYue pulled it away. She said, "I don't want to say it now."

"Why bring it all up, then?" Zaytuna shot back.

YingYue looked across the courtyard. Abdulghafur was dragging one of the great pots used for the community meals out to the back. A few people had come in and were sitting against the wall after greeting the shaykh briefly. Junayd and her father were still deep in conversation.

"My mother found my letters."

Zaytuna was still unfriendly. "What letters, YingYue?"

"Love letters. I took scrap paper from my father's warehouse and wrote letters. Many letters, so many every day. I wrote them in Arabic so my mother could not read them. I kept them in a box. Once a week I took the box to the river. I put the paper in the water until the ink was gone. My words of love...*dissolved*?" She looked at Zaytuna for confirmation, but she gave her nothing. YingYue went on anyway, "My words of love dissolved into the water. I wanted to dissolve in the water with the words and rush through the water with them."

Zaytuna gasped.

YingYue thought, *She understands me now.* YingYue watched as Zaytuna grasped her hands in her lap, pressing her fingers hard together. Finally Zaytuna replied, "I see."

"Mother found them and took them to the mosque. The imam read them to her, translating the words. He went straight to my father with them, mother right behind him. But father knew Whom I loved. He told them. They would not believe him. That night when father left, she beat me. I could not leave the house for a long time. I was broken," she touched her ribs, "and my skin was purple."

Zaytuna seemed angry now. "Bruised."

"Purple from beating. *Bruised*?"

Zaytuna nodded. Her hands were still clenched in her lap, she looked down at them and said, "Your letters were to God."

YingYue continued, "When my father came home, he beat my mother. She had no shame, so beating her did no good. The next day when he went to the factory, she covered herself like you all do. She had a big wrap. She covered her head and face. She hid the marks. She went to see the women in another Chinese family. My father said she asked them to take me away without him knowing and return me to her family in Lanzhou to marry one of my cousins."

Zaytuna was still looking down. "I'm sorry."

She reached out to Zaytuna, but Zaytuna only looked up at her and released her clenched hands and put them beside her, out of reach of YingYue's touch. YingYue's heart sank, she said quietly,

"Father found out and he kept me with him at all times. He even slept on the floor of my room. Alhamdulillah, he had a dream. This is the dream. I was walking on a wide road. It was a great road between cities. He said there was a city ahead of me with high red brick walls. It was three cities, each one built over the last. Each one older than the other. There was a minaret at the centre of the third city that soared into the clouds. He said that I opened the great gates of the city with my own hands. I found the minaret and lay at its feet."

"So you left for this city?"

"Yes. He told my brothers to take the business and watch over mother. He told her no man would ever marry me. He would only give me to God."

Zaytuna looked up at her suddenly. "How old were you?"

"I was fifteen. I never saw my mother again."

"Did you want to?"

"She is my mother."

"So where did you go?"

"Marv."

Zaytuna said, "The minaret in your dream was my Uncle Abu Bakr."

YingYue's eyes widened at the woman calling her shaykh, 'uncle'. She said, "He was my teacher."

"How is he?"

"He was hard on himself."

Zaytuna said, her voice soft for a moment, "May God protect him. I miss him."

YingYue said softly, "I miss him, too."

"So what did he teach you?" Zaytuna sounded frustrated again.

"I was sad and forgot about God. I was thinking about my mother. I missed her." She turned to Zaytuna, "She is my mother."

Zaytuna looked at Junayd again and said plainly, "I understand."

"I asked Shaykh Abu Bakr to help me find my Beloved again. So he told me that my feelings are not real. I should not be pushed by them this way and that way. My feelings cannot make me sad or happy."

"Sounds like Uncle Abu Bakr."

"He told me that all is One. There is no finding God. There is no losing God. I have not lost my mother. I have not lost my Beloved."

"So do you think that, that your feelings are not real?"

"I feel them, but they are all from God. I kiss the face of each one because each one is my Lover."

Zaytuna pushed off her knees and stood up. YingYue looked up at her. "Zaytuna, I am sorry. What did I do?"

She looked down at her, her words clipped, "Nothing. You sound like my mother. You could be my mother, the way you talk."

YingYue looked up at her, asking, "Is that good?"

"For you, maybe." Zaytuna looked toward the reception hall, then down at YingYue. "Why are you here?"

"My father, he walks Shaykh Abu al-Qasim to his store in the market. My father's store is not much further. We come to get the shaykh every day."

"No here. In Baghdad. Why didn't you stay with Uncle Abu Bakr?"

"He said he had taken me as far as he could, I had to come here for more."

"As far as he could?"

"Yes."

"What? What was that?"

"He scolded me that I will not leave myself behind for my Beloved. I will not dissolve in the river with my words of love."

Zaytuna nodded.

YingYue thought, *Of course this woman knew what it was to leave her self behind. To know that there is no self, only God, loving and loved, through His creation.* YingYue said, "Shaykh Abu Bakr taught me to do that, but I am scared I will lose God if I let go."

"Shaykh Abu al-Qasim will bring you there whether you like it or not." Zaytuna seemed upset.

"Like he did your mother?"

Zaytuna jerked her head toward her, her eyes on fire. "My mother gave up herself to God from the beginning. Long before I was even born. Long before we came to Baghdad."

YingYue folded in on herself from the force of her words. "Forgive me."

Zaytuna took a deep breath. "YingYue."

She did not lift herself up to look at her. "Yes?"

"You said you were sad because you feel like you don't belong?"

"Yes."

Zaytuna said, her voice flat, "You belong."

YingYue looked up, unfolding herself to her, but Zaytuna had turned away from her toward Junayd and had caught his eye, bowing to him with her hand over her heart. Then Zaytuna walked away, saying nothing, leaving her sitting on the floor with the bowl of dates uneaten, alone. YingYue wanted to cry, but she held her tears back, taking up, instead, a hand that no one could see but her, pressed it to her face and kissed it, saying, "My Love, my Love."

5

The call to the afternoon prayer had come and gone by the time Saliha got home. In the poorest parts in the neighbourhood of Tutha, most of the houses were nothing but a few small rooms opening onto a central courtyard, if that. Some were only single rooms, their entrances a passageway carved through other houses and found in narrow, winding alleys leading out of hard-packed dirt streets that sprawled from square to square. Saliha was grateful she had the light and air of the courtyard since they had no windows in their rooms, crowded in as they were on all sides. And grateful that she had her friends.

She was exhausted and hoped Zaytuna would be home, but more that if she were, that they would not end up arguing. They rarely worked together washing clothes anymore. When they did, Saliha only joined her to make up for having quit on Zaytuna to be a corpse washer. The truth of it was, she missed those days sometimes, as hard as the work was and as bad as the pay was, because she missed Zaytuna. It had been just the two of them, every day, washing and hanging laundry on the roofs of the wealthier homes in Karkh and knocking on doors to find new customers. There was always time to talk. Every little thing could be teased out together, examined, laughed over, and sometimes fought over, in their own time, at their own pace.

Now Zaytuna washed all the clothes in those houses alone. She was busier than before and making less money because she could not even do half the work they had done together. Her friend was tough, but she was never as strong as Saliha, not with all that cursed fasting and praying all night so she never had enough sleep. Saliha had tried to help her find another woman to wash clothes with, but Zaytuna resisted, saying she preferred to be alone. *So like her. Donkey of a woman.*

The courtyard was empty. Even Yulduz's clay cooking pot had been brought inside, the brick stove taken apart and piled in the corner, and the dung ash from the fire swept up. Saliha crossed the small courtyard and pushed aside the curtain covering her door and slumped down on the thin bedroll on the floor. Zaytuna had scoffed at her for the indulgences, new clothes, and worse still, a bedroll to sleep on rather than a mat and blanket on the ground like the rest of them. She'd snidely asked when she'd be bringing in layers of sheepskins to cover her bedroll and sheeting to go between her delicate skin and the itchy wool blankets they used in the winter. "Soon you'll have so many things, you'll need to move to a bigger home in a better neighbourhood and leave us entirely!" Zaytuna had taunted.

Saliha had tried to buy a bedroll for her, but she wouldn't permit it. Zaytuna nearly spat on the ground in front of her, "Bring me one of those things and you'll find it under Yulduz and Qambar, not me. Walla, why would you think a gift like that would make what you've done any better?"

Yes, well, Saliha thought, *she was willing to eat the meat that the money went to instead, wasn't she? Fine then, if that is how Zaytuna wanted it. She can lie with nothing but her reed mat between her bony self and the cold hard earth if that is what she wants.*

Saliha wasn't making that much more money, but it was enough for these personal luxuries and enough to bring meat to the communal pot a few times a week. It was only beef, and not much of it, but it was more meat than the likes of them were used to eating. Her neighbours certainly never complained about the money she made washing bodies.

Zaytuna, Saliha sighed to herself, *why have you left me like this? Why have you left me without my friend?*

She heard movement outside and then Yulduz's voice, "Saliha, my daughter, is that you?"

"Yes, Auntie!" Saliha called from her bed.

Yulduz was at her door. "Are you tired? Many poor to wash today?"

Saliha laughed to herself, Yulduz would never stop prying even though she had told her she couldn't share the secrets of the people she washed or the grieving families who stood by waiting for their loved ones' bodies. "Two today, Auntie. But that's not why I'm more tired than usual...."

Getting up from her bed, she went out into the courtyard, grateful for the company. If Zaytuna would not be there, then she would unburden what she could to her neighbour, Yulduz, even Umm Bashir if she were around.

The old woman was waiting outside and had poured her a cup of cool water from her own jug, and they sat together along the wall where there was some shade. "Come now, you," Yulduz said. "Tell me all about it."

Saliha had just settled down against the wall and had taken the cup from Yulduz when she heard movement from Zaytuna's room. "She's home?"

"She'd a bite to eat after she got back, then went for a nap. I suppose she was tired. She was early at the shaykh's, then on to wash clothes. It's not easy for her, doing the work without you."

"There are people other than me who would work with her," Saliha snapped without meaning to, "but she chooses not to find someone regular, you know."

"Layla helps sometimes. But who could replace you?"

Saliha held her tongue, only letting slip the old woman's name, "Yulduz..." in a scolding tone.

"Although with you helping us with food for the pot, she's got more energy than she used to. We all have, and we're grateful for it."

Acknowledging the concession, Saliha said, "Alhamdulillah." She watched the curtain over Zaytuna's door, waiting for her to come out and finish off the difficulty of her day with a sharp word. But when the curtain opened and Zaytuna ducked out her door, she was smiling, happy to see her.

"Must have been a good nap." Saliha quipped to Yulduz in whisper.

Yulduz laughed by way of nudging Saliha's shoulder with her own, and asked Zaytuna, "Would you like some water, too?"

"Sit, sit, Auntie. I'll get it myself." Zaytuna disappeared into her room.

"There's food left over in the pot, Saliha. Did you eat? Go wash your hands." Yulduz didn't wait for an answer and got up to get whatever was leftover for Saliha's meal.

Saliha pushed herself up and went to the basin of water.

"I've got dates," Zaytuna came out with a small bag in one hand and a cup of water in the other.

Leaning over the basin, Saliha began to cry.

Zaytuna rushed to her. "My sister, what's wrong?"

"I'm tired. That's all." She shook it off and rinsed her face. "It was a rough day. I didn't realize how rough until now."

"Did you have children today? You always seem so tired after washing children."

"No, it wasn't the washing. Well maybe. Yes, that's part of it. You know I can't say. But it was something else, on top of that."

"Shhh, no, it's alright. No need to tell me. Can you talk about the other thing?"

Zaytuna put the dates down and used her cup to pour water over Saliha's hands as she rubbed them together.

Yulduz came back with the leftovers from the midday meal scraped out into a small yellow clay bowl and a wooden spoon.

Saliha wiped her hands dry on her wrap and they went back to sit by Yulduz.

"May it bring you good health." Yulduz said, handing her the bowl. Then said to Zaytuna, "Where are those dates?"

Zaytuna got back up to get them.

Saliha took the bowl and put it before her, answering Yulduz, "May you have good health." It was barley flour stew. Cold. The flour, browned in the grease from frying the meat and onions to thicken the broth, had turned into a jelly. The meat and onions had all but dissolved into it and it was a cold, jiggling, shiny brown mound in the pot before her. Saliha's stomach turned at the look of it, but she took a spoonful all the same. There was no refusing. She closed her eyes and said, "Bismillah," forcing herself to put some in her mouth. And then opened her eyes, relieved. It was delicious. Yulduz had added black pepper and the bite of it cut through the cold fat. "Alhamdulillah, it's good."

"Of course," Yulduz answered with a brisk nod of her head and took a bite out of one of Zaytuna's dates.

Zaytuna asked Yulduz, "Where is Qambar?"

"Y'know that husband of mine. I can't stop'im from working even with those swollen hands of his. We'll go out together tomorrow."

Zaytuna nodded, then recited God's words,

> Those who are patient,
> seeking the face of their Lord,
> who stand up in prayer,
> who give to others from what We have provided for them,
> in secret and openly,
> and who push back at ugliness with beauty,
> they will have the final abode.

Saliha wondered what was going on in Zaytuna's head. She was happy, for one. But verses breaking out of her like that? That usually meant something. She'd wait to ask later. Then she put her finger into the bowl and brought out the last of the stew, licking it with a smack and smiled with gratitude at Yulduz.

"Walla, you've a child's love of life." Yulduz laughed. "Don't lose it.

Now, tell us about your day. Has that Christian doctor fallen for your wiles yet? Marta has her heart set on it!"

Saliha was too tired to laugh but she smiled, assuring Yulduz. "You two old gossips. I feel like I live to give you something to chew on! Well, there's more of that to tell, but later. We'll wait for Marta." Zaytuna looked up at her, eyebrows raised. Saliha shot Zaytuna a look right back that said, *Nothing for you to worry about...yet!*

Yulduz slapped Saliha on her leg. "We'll have that man a Muslim before long and you two in your marriage bed!"

Zaytuna was still staring, unamused. "You think Shatha is going to keep you on that job if she hears about this flirtation?"

Until today, Saliha and Judah had only shared careful looks and, at times, polite words in the company of others. *Who would fault them for being so close today when that woman had collapsed in her arms and Judah was treating her? But the conversation in the archway? That conversation was enough to end her apprenticeship right there.* The realization gripped Saliha and she froze. Then it grabbed hold of what else she'd been doing and showed it to her. She put her hands up to her face, holding her cheeks. They were hot with shame. She'd also been thinking about Judah, Tein, and arguing with Zaytuna in her head, all while washing that poor woman's body. *Not just that woman's body. Others, too. This wasn't the first time. Her mind should have been on helping them to the grave, not on her petty thoughts.* She said out loud without realizing it, "God forgive me."

Zaytuna tucked her head back in surprise and reached out to her. Saliha took her hand, saying, "Can we go to the mosque together later?" Zaytuna hesitated. She realized immediately that Zaytuna had other plans and said, "It's alright, I'm fine on my own. I should get to sleep early."

"No. It is just that I am going to Uncle Abu al-Qasim's. There is a gathering tonight. Please come."

"Can't you not go?"

She didn't answer.

Saliha changed direction, hoping to hold her friend there with the news. "A man died today at the hospital. Some well-known scholar from Nahr Tabiq. His wife claims he was murdered."

Zaytuna sat up, a look of concern, but also naked curiosity on her face. Saliha thought, *She is so obvious. Thank God.* "His wife claimed that his slave killed him with a curse."

Yulduz and Zaytuna both exclaimed, "A curse!"

Here was her friend. Maybe Zaytuna would stay with her if she could drag out this story and get to talking through what was weighing on her. Saliha had settled in to tell them everything, slowly, when they heard footsteps running down the passageway and Layla ran in breathless.

So this is how the day will be. Saliha had forgotten Layla would come for her lesson. She was still covering herself up in her hand-me-down wrap just like the wealthy girls rather than the servant that she was. It was ridiculous, but they loved her for it. At least, she loved the little girl, but she suspected Zaytuna did as well. Layla plopped herself down beside Zaytuna laying her head on her shoulder, ignoring Zaytuna's discomfort with this gesture of intimacy. She greeted the women in her most dramatic tone, "Assalamu alaykum Auntie Zaytuna, Assalamu alaykum Auntie Yulduz, Assalamu alaykum Auntie Saliha."

All three laughed and replied together, just as dramatically, "Walaykum assalam Layla."

She sat up and turned to look up at Zaytuna. "I'm sorry I'm late for my lesson."

"How *are* your lessons going?" Saliha asked.

Layla exclaimed, jumping up, "I'll show you!" She had got to Zaytuna's door when she called back, "Auntie Zaytuna, may I enter your room to get the tablet and pen?"

Zaytuna called back to her, "Yes." Then she turned to Saliha and said as if she did not care one way or another, "She's coming along. We've moved on to sentences. If she didn't have to work during the day, she could go to school, or even to Uncle Abu al-Qasim's to study with the children there. I'd prefer that for her, rather than this," sighing slightly to indicate that she was put out by the girl.

Saliha nudged Yulduz. "Why don't you study along with them? It's never too late."

"What need do I have for reading and writing Arabic? I did my letters in my own language, that's enough. Look who's talking, what about you?"

Saliha put her hands up.

Smiling at them both, Zaytuna said, "There's not always a need for it."

Layla came out with the tablet under her arm holding the charcoal-ink pot and reed pen in her hands. She sat down on the floor next to Zaytuna again and placed the pot and pen down carefully before her, then tugged the wood tablet out from under her arm. Zaytuna saw there was still writing on it and said, "For shame, Layla, you didn't rinse your tablet from last class. Go wash it now."

"Not yet! I want Auntie Saliha to see what I wrote."

Zaytuna tried to take the tablet from Layla, but the girl growled at her playfully, and pulled it back, thrusting it at Saliha.

Saliha said, "Sweet one, you'll have to read it to me."

"There's no need, Layla, go wash the tablet."

Layla ignored Zaytuna and nearly crawled into Saliha's lap with it. She pointed at the first word, "*I*," then pointed at the second word, "*love*," then the third, "*Auntie*," then the fourth, "*Zaytuna*." She looked up, grinning. "*I love Auntie Zaytuna!*"

Zaytuna blushed, while Saliha and Yulduz exclaimed, "Mashallah! Well done!"

"Now, go wash the tablet," Zaytuna scolded her lightly.

Layla got up and went over to the large basin of water in the corner of the courtyard and called back, "There's no water. I'll go get some from the fountain, inshallah."

Saliha watched the girl go and muttered, "These children, abandoned by their parents to work for food and a place to sleep. They work so hard. They need so much love." Gesturing to Umm Bashir's room. "And here we have our little Bashir. He has everything sweet Layla does not and he won't do a cursed thing." She turned to Yulduz, "When *will* Umm Bashir make him help?"

"The boy is already ruined." Yulduz replied, with a disgusted shake of her head, "She means to keep him with her always, no doubt. One of those mothers who cannot stand to see their boys love another woman. The poor girl who has to marry him."

"Enough complaining about them." Zaytuna scolded.

Saliha bit her tongue. *How many times had she listened to Zaytuna detail her frustration with Umm Bashir and the boy?*

Yulduz didn't hold back, "The pious lady speaks!" She turned to Saliha, saying with mock gravity, "Let's be quiet now so that God does not become angry with us."

Zaytuna laughed despite herself, then she put her hand on Saliha's knee. "Quick, before she gets back, what happened at the hospital?"

"The wife says her husband was killed by an ifrit called in by a talisman." Saliha looked between the two of them. "His slave made him wear a talisman that she'd bought outside the Fruit Seller's Gate. He was beaten repeatedly by the ifrit and it finally took hold of him and killed him."

"God protect us from evil things! Do you know who made it?" Yulduz cried out.

"A Turkmen woman like yourself. The wife said she wore a Turkmen robe, with lapels, a red and black one."

"That's Hajja Tansholpan! May God protect her. Her talismans are powerful. Then he must've been a bad man." Yulduz said, "Marta and I often visit her for a chat after Marta sells out all her soaked chickpeas inside the Market Gate. I've seen her work. She'd not hurt a soul, not unless he deserved it. She's given talismans to me to set things right," nodding to Saliha, "when it got to that."

Zaytuna interrupted, "You say 'God protect us from evil things' then admit you've used them yourself?"

"Oh, pious woman control yourself!" Yulduz protested, "I've never asked for a person to die or to call the jinn. I've only asked for a good curse, something to teach the cruel ones of this world a lesson." She turned back to Saliha, "And let me tell you, no matter the problem, the issue is resolved."

"Do they really work?" Saliha's eyes were wide.

The three women looked up as Layla returned with the bucket, dumped the water from the leather bucket in the basin and ran out the passageway to get another.

"Well," Yulduz said, returning to her point, "It isn't that you see what happens, but you feel relieved, and the other person changes. If a woman's jealous of you, sniping at you, bringing the evil eye, she turns kind and generous." She finished with another brisk nod of the head. "Then you know she's been brought low somehow and taught a lesson just as you've requested."

Saliha sat back up with a snort. "That seems like a cheat! If I am going to pay for a curse, I want to see the person brought low before me. Walla, that seems only fair!"

Zaytuna asked Saliha, her eyebrows raised. "You've never bought a curse?"

"No! Not protection. Not a love potion. Nothing. God wills what God wills. What's it to me to steer things one way or another?"

"Oh please, sister, I have seen you do the steering myself! You steer this way and that and especially in the direction of handsome men!"

Saliha grinned at her, knowing exactly what she was doing. "If God saw fit to put a handsome man to the right of me and an ugly man to the left of me, and my two hands on the reins of the horse of my desire, why shouldn't I use those hands to pull to the right?"

"You do not turn! You ride straight past them!" Zaytuna yelled at her.

Saliha laughed. "Oh Zaytuna! It is so easy to bait you."

Zaytuna stood, angry. Layla returned and dumped another bucket of water into the basin. She was about to turn around for a third when Zaytuna called out to her, a bit roughly, "That's plenty! Wash your tablet now and let's get started."

Layla shrugged and put the bucket down.

Saliha thought, *Zaytuna's moods don't affect that girl and a good thing, too.*

Layla picked up her tablet and began to rinse it beside the basin, letting the water fall into the bricked depression beside it where it would soak into the earth beneath.

Saliha looked up at Zaytuna. "Zay, I'm sorry. Please sit."

Zaytuna sat back down, saying to Layla, "Come work over here."

"So what happened to the slave?" Yulduz asked.

Saliha replied, "This was the hard part. She is a tiny thing. I saw Tein take her in hand. They must have arrested her, and they'll be arresting Tansholpan as soon as they find out it was her who wrote the talisman."

Yulduz cried out, "Ya Rabb!" She pushed her old body off the ground in one motion. "I've got to get to the Fruit Seller's Gate right now and warn her. Lord, help her! She'll need to get away." She turned to Zaytuna, pointing at her, "And you! If you breathe a word of this to your brother Tein, I'll have Hajja Tansholpan write a curse against the two of you!" She turned and pushed aside the thin curtain to her room to grab her sandals and robe. Dragging it on over her qamis and sirwal, she belted it and strode out to the passageway.

Layla came over, tablet under one arm, as Yulduz pushed past her. "What's wrong with Auntie Yulduz?"

"A friend of hers may be in trouble with the police."

Layla took Zaytuna's hand and shook it. "She should let you take care of it, Auntie. You can set anything right."

Saliha said, "Layla, go into my room. There is a bag of coin in the box at the back, take a few fals and go get us some nuts, and a candy for yourself."

At the word "candy," Layla nearly set off but then held firm and asked Zaytuna, "May I?"

"Zay, I need to talk." Saliha said.

Zaytuna pushed Layla, "Go ahead and take your time." Layla smiled and ran into Saliha's room, then out again in a moment, and was out the passageway.

Zaytuna reached across to her. "Tell me."

"It's not only the murder, it's your brother."

"Is anything wrong!"

"No, no. I said he was there today. But, Zay, Tein *and* Judah were there."

Zaytuna grunted.

"Don't be mad! But I tried to make Tein jealous. I wanted to see if he loved me."

Zaytuna interrupted, "Love you! What are you playing at? You don't love him. And what good would it do you, if you did? He's a drunk. He still hurts from the death of our mother. He still hurts from the slaughter of his wife and child. He's no good for loving a woman."

"I know he hurts!"

"You think you can heal him? Saliha!" Zaytuna's voice rose.

Saliha retorted, "Well, you have nothing to worry about. He doesn't love me. He didn't react at all, no matter how I played Judah in front of him. But Judah, he reacted. He was jealous."

Zaytuna hit back, "Good, then go become a doctor's wife and live under his jealous protection! I thought you'd had enough of marriage and men showing they love you by controlling you. Do you even remember how it was between you and Ayyub?"

Saliha's eyes narrowed and her voice became firm, "I remember exactly how it was. I don't want to marry him. I don't want to marry either one of them."

But Zaytuna wasn't listening. Her objections became an angry flood, "How will it be for you when your doctor shows you he loves you by becoming angry if you look right or left? How is that going to work for you? You who cannot keep your eyes down!" She spat on the ground. "Must everything be possession for them? God is the Possessor of all things. This love is nothing but unbelief!"

Saliha shrieked, "Enough!"

"Enough? You..."

She put her hand out, her palm facing Zaytuna. "Enough!"

"When you show up here with a bruised face or arm from his loving jealousy, will you quote hadith that I'll never accept to make me believe that the Prophet would have said that enduring the jealousy of men is a woman's jihad? Is that how you want to gain martyrdom and paradise? Do you want to die at the hand of his 'love'?"

"You don't understand!"

"Fine then, Saliha. What don't I understand?"

"Tein saw me standing close to Judah. I saw him. He didn't care. But Zaytuna," her face fell, "I realized then that I cared."

Zaytuna muttered, "God protect you from your own foolishness."

6

The enslaved girl was still being held in Ammar's office. If Ammar had his way, she would have been in the cells beneath them by now. She had slept for a time curled up, her face buried in a rough linen pillow on the back of one of the wide low couches edging the room. Tein knew too well how terror wears its way through to exhaustion. Now she was awake, sitting up straight, her hands gripping the edge of the couch. She had unwound her wrap from underneath her arms and had pulled it around herself like a blanket. It was thin and faded with a deeply frayed embroidered edge, a long ago hand-me-down from her employer, no doubt, and not warm enough for the weather. Her head scarf was newer, but it was a short length of purple with barely enough to tie back at the nape of her neck. Tein didn't think she had much hair with the way it was pulled close around her head. Her skin was a deep, shining black, like obsidian, and adorned with small scars down her nose and across her cheekbones. Her eyes were on fire. Her mouth was a tight frown. Tein wanted to take her hand. He wanted to reassure her but he couldn't. He needed to know what she'd done. She wasn't the first person sitting on that couch trapped between fury and fear. He never knew what would come of it. Some burned in silence; others blew to pieces, falling apart and admitting everything or coming at them in one last desperate act of violence.

Ammar sat forward. "Tell us what happened."

"I killed him."

Tein felt sick.

"How did you do it?"

"I bought a talisman and put it on him. An ifrit came and killed him."

Tein shot up. The wife's superstitious claim repeated as if it were true! He threw his hand out in a gesture of objection at Ammar. "What's this story? That's not a confession; it's a fantasy!"

Mu'mina swung around on him. "You talk to me! I know what I did. I killed him."

"You don't understand," Tein objected. "You only put a talisman on him."

"I know what I did."

Ammar shot Tein a look, then asked the girl, "Why did you want to kill him?"

"He raped me."

"You're his slave," Ammar said. "He has the right to have sex with you."

"I killed him."

"That's it, then." Ammar stood. "I'm going to Ibn Marwan to let him know and get a scribe. Tein, you stay here."

Tein stood up and moved to get in the way of the door so he couldn't leave. "You can't take this to him yet. That's no confession!"

Ammar sighed at him but took a step back. "You just heard what I did. She confessed."

"I killed him," she said again, now almost pleading.

Tein looked past Ammar to Mu'mina, sitting on the couch, her hands still gripping its edge, and all the provocation drained from him. "You don't understand what you've done."

"Watch her, I'll be back." Ammar walked around him.

Tein looked down at her. "You may die."

"Alhamdulillah," she said, as if gratitude to be executed were a thing he should understand.

He replied, frustrated and angry, "You may not die. Sometimes they execute slaves. Sometimes they don't. In that case, you'll rot in prison. Is that what you want?"

She turned her face away from him.

Tein forced himself to step out of the room to keep from grabbing her and shaking her. He shut the door slowly and firmly to keep himself from ripping it off its hinges, and then leaned against the shut door, forcing himself to take hold of his anger and frustration. He wrestled his anger down, like Uncle Nuri taught him, keeping a tight grip on it. Once it stopped moving, he allowed himself a deep breath. Then another. It stayed down. He began to feel his muscles lose their readiness to fight. He pushed himself away from the door and looked down the arcade.

It didn't take long for Ammar to emerge from his sergeant's office. When Ammar caught sight of him standing there, Tein could see from his expression that the matter was closed. His anger rose up again. He stepped on the neck of it before it could get too far.

A short, fat man with a stubby black turban had followed Ammar out of the office. Ammar approached saying, "Ibn Marwan wants Ben Haddad here to get her confession down. Afterwards, you'll bring her down to the holding cells until we can get her before the chief of police's court for judgment and sentencing."

Tein objected anyway, "She's confessed to buying a talisman to curse him, nothing more."

"She admitted to killing him." Ammar stopped in front of the door. The scribe caught up to him, giving Tein a tired look. Ammar put his hand on the scribe's shoulder. "Now move aside so Ben Hadad can get in there."

Instead of stepping aside, Tein stepped forward to push the scribe back away from the door, but he did not move. The rigid little shit held his ground, allowing the uncomfortable space between them to remain.

The scribe said, sounding bored, "Let me by."

Tein gave it a moment longer, then moved, but just enough so Ben Hadad would have to walk around him to enter. The scribe sucked his teeth at him and went inside.

"You actually believe an ifrit killed him?"

"Tein, I don't know what killed him. She could have poisoned him and is calling it a curse from that talisman to scare the rest of the family. What do you care if it was an ifrit or not? She confessed."

"We don't know how he died. Shouldn't we find out if she could have killed him? She must have wanted him dead. I get that. But someone else could have killed him. Maybe she thinks her wanting him dead did the job. Wanting isn't a crime."

"The investigation was closed as soon as she confessed."

Not caring how Ammar took it, Tein said what he'd been thinking, "I was there. I saw you arranging with the doctor to claim it was illness if you couldn't get a confession out of her. You don't want to investigate this case. You don't care who did it or who pays for it. You just want the paperwork tied up and move on."

"You're imagining things. Why don't you ask yourself why you're defending her?" Ammar widened his stance.

"You know what you're doing." Tein shifted his body just slightly, his shoulders back, his arms loose, yet flexed at his side. "Coward."

Ammar took a step toward him, hand on the hilt of his sword. "Watch yourself."

"She's black, she's a slave. She's not important. The thought that she could call an ifrit scares you. She'll rot down there to cover your fear."

"You're right. She is black. She is a slave. No one cares about her. But tell me when you've ever seen me give up on a case because the person wasn't important. Have I?"

Tein wouldn't answer.

"Never, Tein."

"You are right now."

"I'm not going to accept or reject a confession because she's a black slave." Ammar relaxed his stance, giving Tein ground. "I'll admit that she scares me. Look at her face. The scars her people put on her. These Africans. You think she doesn't count spells on those to call up the jinn?"

Tein took a step back to keep from laying his hands on Ammar. He wanted a drink. He wanted a jug of wine. He felt the kind of shame and betrayal that leads a man to kill and that can only be staved off by sitting in a dark corner of a tavern and not coming out again. This man was his friend. As much a brother to him as his childhood friend, Mustafa. Maybe more. He turned his face away from Ammar so he wouldn't see how what he'd said had marked a friendship bonded in war over a decade ago. He silently demanded of him, *Why aren't you afraid of me? Am I so different? Does being half-Arab absolve me of being African, of being black? Is it because I have no scars?* He couldn't say it aloud. If he did, he didn't know if he could keep from hurting him. He held himself together, bound between fury and sorrow, and argued for Mu'mina's sake because that is all that could matter right now, "How are those scars any different from the tattoos of the Bedouin women? Are you afraid of them?"

"A man died because she either had a spell put on him or got him cursed." Ammar voice turned shrill, "What's she going to do to us before she's executed? What curses are going to come down on our heads? We have to finish this before she changes her mind and takes revenge on us, too."

Tein lost some of his grip on himself. "Nothing will fall on our heads! Talismans cannot kill people. They are paper with words folded over and sewn up in leather. Nothing more! Curses have no power. And there are no ifrit. Don't you see, she's innocent even if she believes she's guilty?"

"There we have it."

"Ammar, you are being irrational."

"Irrational? Because you don't believe in what we all know to be true, we are irrational? What you believe is not my business. Tein, you're a brother to me. But don't let your beliefs get in the way of your police work."

Tein pushed down hard on his anger and the urge to laugh at the irony. He only allowed himself to take one step towards Ammar. "I won't take her below."

Ammar stepped to the side away from him. "I'll do it."

Tein took one more step, increasing the threat.

Ammar sighed, took another step away. "What would it take to let this go?"

"Let me talk to her."

"You talk to her, then it's done?"

"If you listen, you'll agree the case is still open."

The scribe walked out, paper in hand, and held it up to Ammar, saying, "Got it. I left the jail intake on your desk."

Tein's anger gave way to fear as he watched Ben Hadad walk back to Ibn Marwan's office.

"It's too late, Tein. What could change Ibn Marwan's mind at this point? He, sure as God knows it, doesn't care about a girl like that."

Tein pushed, "Let me try."

"Fine. But we also have to find the woman who wrote the talisman."

"What? What does she have to do with this?"

"The talisman is the murder weapon. Ibn Marwan wants us to bring her in."

"You all are out of your minds, and a girl is going to be executed because of it!"

Ammar crossed his arms. "If you really care about her, you are better off not challenging this. You think raising doubts about her confession is going to do her any good? She's not going to be set free. She's going to be put down into that cell, and she's going to wait there until evidence comes to light that exonerates her. And Ibn Marwan has no intention of letting us investigate further."

"You can make it happen!"

"No. We already have another case waiting, a butcher was found standing over a dead body. He confessed to the night watchman, but someone else has come forward and said they did it instead. We've got to sort out that mess."

"Let me talk to her."

Ammar opened the office door. "Be my guest."

Tein pushed past him. Ammar followed and sat at the edge of the room looking at the girl.

Mu'mina looked right back and burned. Every cell in her body was on fire, screaming rage and fear. She held it in but wanted nothing more than to burn this place down. The Black One came in and sat so that he faced her. The Arab sat further away, watching her, but watching the Black One, too. *The Arab is his master and is going to let The Black One speak.*

"I need to ask you a few more questions."

She clenched her jaw. *She would not speak.*

"Your name is Mu'mina?"

She wanted to spit in his face.

"My name is Tein."

"I heard him call you that." She mocked him, "It is an insulting name. A man named Fig. A big man like you lets that little one there call you twat?"

The Twat laughed as if he didn't feel the insult. *But why would he? He can do with me as he likes.*

He smiled at her, trying to seem kind. As if she had not seen this before. "My mother gave me that name. It is from a verse in the Qur'an that she loved, *Wa at-teini wa az-zaytun wa tur is-sineen, wa hadha baladi'l-amin, la qad khalaqna al-insan fi ahsani taqwim…*We swear by the fig and the olive, by Mount Sinai, by this peaceful land, we certainly created the human being on the most beautiful form. My twin sister is named Zaytuna."

"Your mother named you Twat?" She asked, letting the fire of her rage play on her tongue. He winced, just slightly. *That hurt him. She wanted to hurt him more. Destroy him and that Arab.*

"Your accent. I can't place it."

"Why would you? You're African but are no better than an Arab."

"I'm Nubian, but my father was Arab."

"That is no excuse."

"Maybe not."

She held herself down, gripping the edges of the couch.

"Your parents, did they adorn you with that...," he traced on his own face the design of the scars across her cheeks and down her forehead and nose, "...before you left them? Or did you do it?"

He had no right to know. She kept herself from touching the marks her mother gave her before she was sold away from her parents and made so their people would know her as one of their own if she could free herself and find her way back home. She knew where to go. *South through Egypt*, she repeated to herself, *then hold fast to the coast.*

"When were you sold to Imam Hashim?"

"I killed him."

The Twat asked again, "How long has Imam Hashim owned you?"

She held her mouth shut tight and watched them.

He leaned into her. "If you want to die, I need to know. You must answer these questions. We cannot let you die without them. These are the rules."

She began to tremble like a seed on a hot skillet.

There was a soft touch, then arms surround her, holding her. A cool stream washed through her, but her fire tried to boil it away. It hissed, steaming, but the cool water kept flowing, replenishing what was lost. There was no end to it. She closed her eyes, reached up, and put her hands on the arms, leaning her head into the embrace, and heard a whisper in her ear, *Tell him, Mwana. You will find your way home.* She opened her eyes, lifted her head, and pushed away the arms holding her. She burned. "No."

"You must tell us. How long has Imam Hashim owned you."

The arms were around her again, comforting her, and the voice, *Tell him.*

She did as Lady Fatima instructed, saying through her teeth, "Two years, more."

He smiled. He should stop smiling. She nearly caught fire again, but Lady Fatima held on tight.

"When were you captured?"

Opening her eyes, she answered on her trust of Lady Fatima alone, "My parents are slaves."

"When were you sold away from them?"

"After I bled," she hissed.

"To Imam Hashim." He said it like it was a fact, as if he knew everything.

"Wrong." Her voice was tight, "My first master sold me to Imam Hisham when we were on hajj." Her throat opened with the words, "God curse them both."

The Arab Master interrupted, "Are you Muslim?"

Did she have to answer him, too?

There was a touch and her Lady answered, *Yes.*

She burned up against her touch despite everything. The touch became a hand laid flat against her back over her heart. She cooled again, but not enough to answer him without loathing, "Yes. I follow Muhammad, Fatima and Ali, and their blessed children. God curse the ones who killed them." She spat on the carpet. "None of you are any better than Yazid!"

The Twat and his Master exchanged looks.

"Are you Shia?" The Arab Master asked.

The hand pressed against her back, the voice whispered, *Tell him about when I first came to you.*

My most precious thing, why? She held onto it until she couldn't any longer. "Lady Fatima came to me my first night away from my parents. She took me in her arms and told me that she was my mother now. She said I must say shahada and go on hajj."

The Twat asked softly, as if by speaking softly she would make the mistake of trusting him, "What did your master say to that?"

The hand against her back pushed her lightly. She acquiesced, "I already said it in front of Lady Fatima. He made me say shahada again." She couldn't hold back; it shot out of her, "He was to be my witness! As if his witness were greater than the Prophet's daughter, the blessed mother of Hasan and Husayn, the wife of Sayyidi Ali!" She pressed her mouth shut and dug her fingers into the couch.

I am with you, Mwana.

The Twat turned to the Arab. "Now what do you think?"

"How did your first master treat you?" The Arab asked.

"You mean, did he rape me?" She sneered. "After I told him about Lady Fatima, he stopped. But he brought men to his house and made me stand in front of them and tell them my story."

"Did you go on hajj, as the Lady directed?" The Twat asked.

Tell him.

"He waited almost three years. Two years ago, I walked around the Kaaba. My mother Fatima took my hand in hers. Everyone left us. I looked around me for the people who had been crowding me just before. But they were gone. My mother Fatima and I circled the Kaaba alone."

The Arab asked, "Did you tell your master?"

Lady Fatima's hand pressed against her. "He saw me, but he couldn't see her." She leaned forward and said, "His heart is dead, like yours." She waited for him to cut her back, but his eyes were empty, like a man who has control of everything. "He asked whose hand I was holding so I told him. What did he say? Can you guess?"

The Twat shook his head.

"He thanked God for such a prize. A prize to have such a devoted slave. He told men all over Mecca what I had seen." She mocked his voice, "Look at my slave who holds the hand of the Prophet's beloved daughter!"

The Arab leaned forward and put his head in his hands.

"And Imam Hashim?" The Twat asked.

"My master made me stand in front of him and tell him my story. Right there, he offered my master more money than anyone has ever paid for any slave. My master went back to Damascus without me and I came to Baghdad with Imam Hashim."

The Twat turned on the Arab, looking like he would kill him. She moved away from them, backing slowly to the far end of the couch, watching the door. Maybe this is what her Lady wanted. They fight. She runs. She readied herself, her muscles twitching.

"And now?" He turned to The Arab. "Now, is she worth saving to you?"

The Arab lifted his head from his hands. "She worships Fatima, may God glorify her name, as if she were a Zanji god."

The Twat was standing over the Arab before she knew what was happening. Standing, she crept to the door so that they wouldn't notice. But the Arab looked at her and shook his head. She stiffened, unable to sit back down or run for the door. Lady Fatima took her hand and tugged her down to the couch beside her.

The Arab did not stand to meet the Twat's challenge. He leaned back against the cushions, relaxing in an exaggerated pose. "Yes?" He turned to her, ignoring The Twat. "He thinks I will save you now because I am Shia. He only wants to save you because he is black. He thinks he's black like you."

What was this man doing? Save me from what? Save me in this world only to be punished for killing the imam in the next! She reached out to Lady Fatima but could not feel her. She pleaded with her, *Let me die for what I've done!*

God knows what atom's weight of good or ill you have done. The Lady answered. *Do not suppose you know His justice.*

Looking at the Black One, she asked Lady Fatima aloud without realizing it, "Can I trust him?"

Lady Fatima's cheek was next to hers, nodding. *Yes.*

"Tein is an Arab like me. He speaks Arabic. His Nubian mother was a woman of great stature. A noble woman before God. Not like you. He is a ghazi who fought beside me on the frontier against the Byzantines. He is no more African than you are Muslim."

The Twat stepped forward, his hands open, his muscles ready. She felt herself standing against her will. Lady Fatima said, *Use his name.*

She heard herself saying, "Tein."

He turned to her. His hands were still ready to kill.

Lady Fatima's voice spoke through her own, "Who was your mother?"

He stared at her, not answering.

Now in her own voice, her chest tight from fear, she repeated, "Who was your mother?"

He stepped back from the Arab and faced her, saying with barely contained anger, "I am my mother's son, not my father's. She *was* a noble woman. I carry her name. I am Tein ibn al-Ashiqa as-Sawda al-Shuniziyya." His hands softened. "You can trust me."

She nodded, but her body clenched, unbelieving.

Tein sat. "Will you tell me what happened?"

The clenching gave over to trembling. Her voice shook, "I killed Imam Hashim."

"What do you mean when you say, 'I killed him'? How did you kill him?"

"I bought a talisman to curse him."

"Where did you get the money for that?"

"The imam would give me coin when he was pleased with me."

"And you think the talisman worked?"

"Why else would he be dead?"

"Did you ask for anything specific in the talisman?"

Looking at the Arab, she found her anger, saying with quiet venom, "To shrivel his penis."

He shrank back and touched the talisman at his neck.

"So he would no longer have sex with you," Tein said.

Turning back to Tein, she directed her anger at him. "Yes."

"But that's not a curse to kill. Why do you think he died?"

Her hands twitched with wanting to slap these men, but she laid her hands flat against her thighs. Lady Fatima placed a hand over her hands. "Her talismans are powerful."

"Who is she and where does she sell her talismans?" The Arab demanded.

Tell him.

She looked at Tein when she answered, "A Turkmen woman at the Fruit Seller's Gate in the Karkh Great Market."

Tein looked at the Arab sharply, then asked her, "What do you think happened to Imam Hashim?"

"An ifrit came to do the work of killing his manhood, then saw he was evil and took his case to a jinn court. They must have found him guilty. They have their own justice."

The Arab interrupted, saying to Tein, "If the jinn want to protect her, she's made a pact with them."

Turning on him, she spat, "You think my mother Fatima would permit such a thing!"

"How do you know that?" Tein broke in, "How do you know he was brought before a jinn court?"

"That's how things are. How stupid are you? After he wore my talisman, he was getting beatings. He was black and blue. He had broken bones. He did not know who gave them to him."

"The doctor who saw him at the hospital said some of those bruises could have come from an illness."

She replied quickly, without a shred of doubt, "No, an ifrit did it. Does a black eye and a bloody lip come from being sick?"

"Maybe someone, someone real, beat him up?"

"A real person!" She turned to the Arab despite herself. "He denies jinn!"

The Arab shrugged.

She lost touch with her Lady and said, burning with hatred, "He was an evil man. I cannot be the only one he forced himself on, and maybe she had someone beat him. He deserved it. Just like he deserved the ifrit who killed him."

"He might have died from those beatings."

"You did not see that an ifrit had a hold of him." She said with certainty.

"You saw the ifrit?"

"He could see it. He *said* there was an ifrit on him."

"Why didn't you see it too? If your talisman called it? You don't understand; it might have been a poison. A poison could cause him to see something that *wasn't* there. Even a spider bite could do it."

"Made him see what *was* there."

The Arab turned to Tein. "You see?"

"Let's say a talisman did do the job. You still didn't intend to kill him."

She didn't answer. She could not breathe to speak. *No, she had not. The curse writer had done it. But the blood was on her hands all the same.*

Tein rushed, "Don't you see, the jinn did it, not you. You are not guilty."

"The blood is on my hands," she said aloud.

He pleaded with her, "You are innocent." He turned to the Arab, "Don't you see, even if *you* believe a jinn did it, she did not do it. On your terms, Ammar. On your terms, she is not guilty. You can't let that confession go through."

This man did not understand. No matter what, Imam Hashim died because of what she had done. She struggled to trust this man. She struggled to trust her Lady. *Why wouldn't she let this end? Why wouldn't she let her just take her punishment in this world and return with her to find Paradise in the next? End all this? End her slavery?* The Arab did not speak. He wanted her to die. She pleaded with the Arab, "Tell him he is wrong."

The Arab ignored her and stood. "Maybe I can get the confession back and reopen the case. That doesn't make her innocent, Tein. It just weakens her confession."

"But we can investigate," Tein said eagerly.

The Arab went to the door, halfway in and halfway out. "Let's hope Ibn Marwan agrees with you. If we can't investigate, all that happens is that she'll rot under suspicion in the prison beneath us." He left, shutting the door behind him.

She found her voice, burning with helpless fury, "Stop!"

"I want you to live."

"I will still be a slave, and I will not have paid for what I've done."

"His family won't want you. They'll sell you."

"I will still be a slave. Let me die. Let me pay."

"No. I believe you are innocent," he said it like a master with the right to decide if she lived or died.

"Why are you doing this?" She was desperate. "Because you and I are African?"

He paused, then said, "I don't know." Then insisted, "I would do it for anyone." He looked toward the door. "So would he, despite all this."

Her head buzzed so loudly she could not hear anything but its noise. She slipped into darkness, but a hand grasped her and pulled her up. Lady Fatima had her. Her dress was made of folds of light.

Her hair was bound up in silken light. Her wrap enfolded her in light. The Lady pulled her up and into her arms. She held her, rocking her, humming in her ear like a lullaby, *Now, quiet, my daughter. They have what they need. You stay here with me.* With nothing left, she let go in her arms.

Tein rushed to the couch. He listened for her breath. She had fainted.

Ammar opened the door. The look on his face said that Ibn Marwan had not changed his mind.

"You've brought her confession into question but nothing more. We're to bring her down the cells."

"What did you say?"

"I told him if she did it, it was unintentional. She bought the talisman to unman him, not to kill him."

"Why didn't you say she couldn't have done it?"

"Because she could have done it, Tein."

"Weren't you..."

"Stop. Ibn Marwan doesn't accept that it was unintentional. Her first confession was certain. All he is giving me is putting the confession into doubt. He didn't even want to do that. He did it only to get rid of me."

Mu'mina moaned.

Tein said to her, "You've fainted. Are you alright?"

She opened her eyes, and tried to sit up, pulling away from him.

Seeing she was afraid he pulled back, too, and asked Ammar, "So she sits in jail until we find out who really did it?"

"No. Ibn Marwan had the scribe add at the bottom of her confession that there is doubt. He did it right in front of me, then he sent it with a messenger to the police chief's office. He's letting the chief decide."

"Can we investigate until then? Do we have time to give the chief more evidence?"

"If there's a backlog of cases at the court, you'll have time."

"She didn't do it. Not even unintentionally. I'll prove it."

"Ibn Marwan is insisting we get to work on the butcher's case. I'll follow that up. For you, Tein, I'll look the other way while you do this. For you, not for her sake," he said, tipping his head toward Mu'mina.

Tein stood stoically and touched her on the arm, saying to her, "Mu'mina, if you can, stand. I have to take you downstairs, to the holding cells."

She stood, unsteadily. Tein took her gently by the arm. "I will sort this out. Please trust me."

"Let me die," she moaned.

Ammar said, mocking her, "You should ask your god, the one you call 'Fatima', for her help."

Still weak, she said, "Her own children were attacked and slaughtered at Karbala. Those who lived were forced to walk across the plains in humiliation to submit to Yazid. I can only pray that she will let me die to pay for this."

Ammar shuddered, then shook it off, saying to her as he left, "If the chief doesn't think there is enough to decide on, he'll just send you back to jail and you'll be forgotten to die, little by little, under our feet."

7

---

*Z*aytuna's room was dark. Her woven fishskin mat crinkled under her feet as she bent her knees to break the stiffness in her legs from standing so long. She called the women back to mind, again, holding up to God the enslaved girl and the talisman maker Tansholpan. *God help them. God bring them justice. If Mu'mina killed him, forgive her, and make her way to you painless. If not, bring the truth to light.* But the slight girl kept turning into a long-boned woman, and Tansholpan's Turkmen cap and grey braids kept transforming into her red scarf wrapped around her matted hair. Zaytuna punched the air with her voice, reciting part of the verse, *Lord, do not blame us if we have forgotten or erred,* so loudly that she heard Yulduz say, "Shush!" from across the silent courtyard.

Zaytuna tried to collect herself, and then heard a sound from the passageway. It could not be Yulduz. She held her breath and listened, turning her head to the right, then to the left, closing out her prayer quickly, whispering to the angels on either side of her, "Assalamu alaykum." She grabbed the thick stick Tein had got her for protection and listened still.

Then, she heard the familiar gait, the slight drag in his step from his limp. Tein. She sighed in relief and put the stick down. But the relief gave way to desperate hope that he was coming to sleep there, like he used to, just the two of them. She suddenly wanted to cry. *Stop it, woman! He won't stay. He's here to talk about the case. Alhamdulillah. That's the answer to your prayers, not having that huge, stinking body taking up too much space.* But she wanted him there, the way he used to sleep just outside her door, watching over her, like the dog of the Seven Sleepers. She started to cry and slapped her hand to make the tears stop. The sound rang out in the silence. Pulling aside her curtain, Tein stood framed by the moonlight and the arch of her door.

She whispered, "Come, come. Alhamdulillah, you are here."

Tein stepped inside and reached out to her, stinking of the night. The curtain fell behind him and the room lost the little moonlight it had. He said too loudly, "My sister!"

Yulduz yelled out from her room, "Quiet!"

Taking Zaytuna in his arms, he laughed. He held her too tightly, awkwardly, one of her arms trapped between them and her jaw pressing against his collarbone. She pushed against him, trying to release herself, and whispered, "Sit down!" He held her for a moment longer and then let go.

She whispered, "What made you come? Is it about the slave?"

"What? How do you know?"

They both said at the same time, "Saliha."

He unbuckled his knife belt and let it fall to the floor, saying, "It's not that. I'm just tired. Can I sleep here?"

"But you need to tell me."

"I know I share case stories with you, Zay, but not tonight."

"It's God's..."

"Stop. No God's will tonight. Not tonight, I'm tired."

She snapped at him, "You stink. Not just wine, I smell women on you."

He replied, exhausted, "Like old times."

"You can have your old spot outside the door." She pointed beyond the door in the dark.

"It's cold, Zaytuna. Have some pity."

"Fine. You can stay in here, but you can't use my blanket." She heard him slump onto the floor, and she got down as well. She propped her hand on his leg, reaching over him to the box where she kept her dear things. She felt the edge of the small clay lamp. "I have oil for the lamp."

"You've given in to luxury, Zaytuna. God will be angry."

She ignored the comment and lifted the lamp, careful not to spill the oil, then realized. "Uff, ridiculous, what use is this? I've got no way to light it."

"No fire outside?"

"Did you see one?"

"How did you afford the oil?"

"Not with any money you've given me."

He blew out his nose, "Humph."

She gave a hard look into the darkness and said, "Saliha gave it to me. I only took it to make her stop trying to give me things." Then she added for good measure, "And I don't want your money, either."

"I know."

She heard the acceptance of her ways in his voice and it pulled her back. Could she not control her tongue? She turned inwardly toward God and said, "Forgive me," aloud, without realizing it.

He knocked one of his legs against her. "I accept."

She nearly blurted out that she was speaking to God, not him, but pulled herself back in time, saying instead, "I am sorry, Tein."

"I'm not sure what you are apologizing for now," he laughed, "but later, there will be something. I'll remember it for then."

She laughed with him and put her hand on his bent knee. "I'm glad you are here." She teased, "Was the tavern you ended up at closer to me than Barley Road?"

"It was the same distance, either way. I wanted to see you."

She pulled his bent leg against her and held it. "Tell me why you are so tired."

He felt her arm around his leg, the warmth of her body against him, even the bones of her ribs against his calf, and it felt like home. He said, "Let's sleep. I miss you."

"Not yet, tell me."

His tongue was loose from the wine. He said what he would not during the day, when he was sober and remembered how easily they fought, but rather what he was thinking right there and then, "I never should have moved away from you, Zay. I should have found us a place together."

"Habibi, come here."

His body was so heavy, he could barely move his limbs. He pushed against the reed mats, dragging against them, exposing the pounded earth floor below, raising dirt. She'd be angry with him. "I'm ruining your mats."

"Shhh, come here."

She pulled on him, trying to help and making it worse, but he got himself up against the wall next to her. She leaned into him and took his hand. Her long fingers, like their mother, laid flat against his own. Tein wanted to settle in, crawl under her arm, pull himself in and rest despite his size, but the wine hadn't done its work. His Mother. His wife, Ayzit. His infant son, Husayn. The men he'd failed in battle. The people whose cases he couldn't solve. The people he'd sent to lose their heads. Their bodies followed him everywhere, and all of them, huddled together, wouldn't fit. He sat up, his limbs stiff and heavy with fear and recrimination, and let go of Zaytuna.

"What, habibi?"

What could he say? So he asked instead, "Tell me, did you have a lot of houses to work today?"

"One house, but I went to go see Uncle Abu al-Qasim this morning."

"And?"

"I asked him to be my shaykh."

Tein squeezed her hand for a moment and she leaned against him. He asked, "So what comes next?"

She laughed uncomfortably. "I have to be good."

He pushed her shoulder with his own. "You'd better give up now, sister!"

"Maybe I should," she said resignedly.

"Zaytuna, I was just having fun with you."

"In the short time that he asked me to correct myself, before I even left him, I did everything wrong and ignored every correction."

Tein started laughing again, his body shaking off some of the sorrow that gripped him. He finally felt the wine with the release of it and wanted more. He said, "Oh Zaytuna, I'm sorry, but that is so you!"

She pushed him away. "What good are you!"

He lifted his hand like a poet poised to declaim and said with a flourish, "I am the one who has loved you, loved you since the womb."

Her voice sank, "That sounds like something that could have sprung from Mother, if God were the Lover speaking those words and not your drunk body."

The comment stung. "What's wrong?"

"YingYue was there."

The second it came out of his mouth, he regretted it, "Mustafa's girl."

She pushed herself up against him to standing. She spoke down at him, "I'm tired, Tein. Let's just sleep."

"I didn't mean it like that, sit down."

"What did you mean it like? What have you seen?"

Tein had seen the beautiful young Chinese girl stealing glances at him when he visited the aunts and uncles and blushing as she spoke to Mustafa. He answered, "Nothing, you told me that Mustafa was interested in her. What is this anyway? You don't want him."

She sat down against the wall across from him. "I can't have him, yet I don't want to give him up."

He turned hard on her, "Zaytuna, you kept him like a donkey on a rope all those years. Let him go."

"Maybe I can't let him go to her."

He shook his head. He told her that she'd turned their dearest childhood friend into no more than a pack animal for her whims, and she'd registered none of it. He wanted to drive the point home even deeper. She should know that who Mustafa married was not her choice. At least it better not be, who knows with Mustafa. But he held himself back. He wanted to sleep there tonight, not stumble into the nearby cemetery to sleep cold, huddled with the poorest of the poor who lived within its gates, so he asked instead, "Why not her?"

"She reminds me of Mother."

He repeated the name, "Mother," and the frustration he felt towards Zaytuna dissolved into the exhaustion that had driven him to a tavern, and then to her, for comfort. Comfort he could see now he was not going to get.

"She's a natural, like Mother." She added bitterly, "Not like me. You should have heard her talk about how she loved God. She wrote God love letters." Her voice became high and tight, "She took the letters to the riv...".

Tein let it out, "The girl we arrested, Mu'mina..."

"...er to dissolve..." She stopped cold with a sharp intake of breath.

"I'll tell you." He waited for some response, but Zaytuna held still.

She finally spoke, "Saliha said you had to arrest her. Did you charge her?"

"Ammar did."

"Not you?"

"I fought it."

"Tein, I'm sorry you had to arrest her. Of course, you had no choice."

He opened his mouth to speak, then shut it. What good would it be to try to explain to her that he had a choice? *A man always has a choice.*

She interrupted his silent recriminations, "What about Tansholpan?"

"Who?"

"The curse writer."

Tein could hear she was pleased with herself for knowing more than he did. He asked, because she expected it, "How do you know who she is?"

"Yulduz says Tansholpan is the only one who could write such a powerful curse."

He tried not to sound smug himself, "A curse didn't kill him."

"Well, that is good because Yulduz vowed she'd get a curse written against you and Ammar if Tansholpan is arrested."

"She may yet, if Ammar has his way."

"Why?"

"Because Mu'mina confessed to giving the imam the talisman made by Tansholpan and believes it killed him."

Zaytuna nearly jumped up. "But that's not the same thing at all! She only confessed to giving him a talisman. What she believes isn't evidence!"

He slapped his knee. "Thank you! I tried to explain that to Ammar! He took what she said as a plain confession of fact. I got him to let me question her and tried to make him see it wasn't a confession."

"So why wasn't she released?"

"He still thinks she did it. I reminded him there are other ways he could have died, but he's not interested in pursuing them."

"But I don't understand, Ammar's usually so thorough."

"All I succeeded in doing was getting her confession thrown into doubt. She'll be brought before the police chief as soon as possible. Once we find Tansholpan, that'll be that."

"May God open Ammar's eyes!"

"I'm doing my best."

That got her back up. "Oh, you are God, now?"

"Curse your moods!" He reached out to her quickly, hoping she'd not dig in at the insult, saying, "You know that's not what I meant."

She pushed his hand away. "Uff."

There was a movement outside, coming from within the courtyard. They'd woken one of the neighbours.

Zaytuna lowered her voice, turning her ire on Ammar, hissing, "What is wrong with that man?"

Tein met her emotion with his own, "He'd be relieved if she were executed. He's afraid of her."

"Why?"

Tein responded as if the answer were obvious, "She's African."

"But you're African."

"Am I?"

"You think because an Arab man raped our mother, we are Arab?"

Tein retorted, "But what do we have other than Mother's drum and a few of her beads? She never told us about our family, where she came from, or why she left. We've grown up in Arab lands. We speak Arabic, we dress like Arabs, we eat like Arabs. How are we not Arabs?"

"Fine, you be Arab. I am African. What we have is enough."

Tein snorted. "And you the one who looks like an Arab, and me the one who is called 'crow' and 'Zanji' everywhere he goes."

Her breathing changed and he knew what it meant. He pulled himself up to sit closer to her, one knee resting on her leg. He reached out to touch her face and wipe away her tears, saying, "My beautiful African sister."

She sniffed and brushed his hand away. But he raised his hand again, and lightly traced lines down her nose and across her cheekbones saying, "Mu'mina, has these small scars across her face. Ammar said she counts spells on them."

"Is she Muslim?"

"Yes. She had a vision of Fatima and is devoted to her."

"Doesn't that mean anything to him?"

"No," Tein said, "he says she worships Fatima as if she were an African god."

"Does she?"

"Oh, the piety! Why would it matter? She deserves justice either way. The imam raped her."

Zaytuna was certain. "I would have killed him, too."

"He deserved whatever he got."

"Tein, it sounds like she killed him, you just don't know how yet."

"Why wouldn't she just confess to what she actually did then? Why insist it was the talisman?"

"You don't know what's going on in her mind."

He huffed in reluctant agreement, "You should have seen her, Zaytuna."

"What should I have seen?"

He didn't realize it until that moment. "She reminded me of Mother."

"You said that."

He became impatient. "Listen to me. Maybe this is why Mother left to wander on her own. Was it just for God? Or was she trying to escape something?" Tein sighed and leaned forward heavily, putting his elbows on his knees, placing his forehead against his open palms. "I've been nothing but a useless burden. To you, to Ayzit, Husayn, my own mother, myself, and even Ammar, curse him. Curse it all! Curse this living!" He tried to hold back, but broke into uncontrollable sobs, his tears running down through his fingers.

Zaytuna reached forward to comfort him. She heard movements outside her room again. Someone must have come out to sleep in the courtyard, although why they would in this cold? She wondered if they could hear him weeping, too. He'd be mortified. "Tein," she said, brushing his cheek, then, using both hands, took the turban off his head, setting it down next to her box and their mother's drum in the corner. She pulled him to her. "Come here."

Folding over onto his side, he stretched out his legs as far as they would go and tugged his great body towards her. She pushed him to lay his head in her lap, and he wrapped his arms around her waist. Zaytuna covered him with her body, while he shuddered with sobs. She breathed quiet into him until it passed.

He reached out for the blanket underneath her and pulled an edge toward his face. She thought, *God he's going to blow his nose with that!* She said aloud, "Uff, Tein, how could you be so disgusting?" She found a clean square of folded cloth in her box, and tucked it into his hand saying, "Here, use this."

Sitting up and crossing his legs, Tein blew his nose. "I'm fine. It's just the drink."

She wanted to tell him to leave the past behind him, but who was she to talk? She couldn't put her own pain down for longer than a moment. He was stuck from the earliest moments in his life having to protect her and their mother. Tein had pulled a man off of their mother in the dead of night. He circled the graveyards where she preached to make sure no one attacked their mother in her ecstatic states. He had slept at their feet, always ready for anyone who might harm them. All of that, and he still couldn't keep their mother from dying. He fought back the Byzantines but couldn't protect his wife and child when their camp was raided. She realized in that moment, he was going to have to save this girl whether she was guilty or not. *I'll do my part for his sake. Alhamdulillah.*

She whispered, "So what can we do?"

He didn't answer. He laid down, pushing against her as he did, forcing her to make room.

"Tein, what are you doing?"

"Come here."

She realized then what he wanted. She lay down next to him and pulled the blanket over them both, curling up behind him tucking her arms in between them, as if he were carrying her like a baby tucked into a wrap on his back. It had been a long time since they had slept next to each other like this. Not since they were very young. Not since Mother died, when he stopped holding her at all.

He finally answered her question, "I don't know what we can do. Maybe first, can you keep Yulduz from cursing me?"

Zaytuna heard a stifled laugh outside, and then she realized who it was. Saliha. *My God, how long had she been listening?* Zaytuna laughed a little louder than she would have to cover what sounded like Saliha retreating to her room.

"Can you stand the stink?"

She laughed. "You smell fine. Just don't kick me."

"Don't let me oversleep, it's a long walk to the office in the morning."

"Yes, I remember it well."

THE SECOND DAY

8

"It's late." Zaytuna kicked Tein awake with her foot.

Every one of his muscles was sore and tight in the morning cold. His mouth was sticky. His head was throbbing. He prayed for her, "May your morning be like the light of a full moon dawning on a donkey's ass."

She laughed, "Amin!" Then she went into the still-dark courtyard leaving him thick-headed and slumped against the wall. He stuck his legs out and found the jug and cup that Mustafa had made for her many years ago and poured himself some water. *He never made one of these for me*, Tein thought, as he drank it down in one gulp and poured another, leaving the jug empty. *But then Mustafa was never trying to convince me to marry him. And now that was done.* There was a man for her somewhere, although whether she'd accept him was another matter. But he sorely wished someone would take her off his hands already so he wouldn't have to worry about her.

Tein reached up and felt around for the bag of dates hanging from the peg on the wall. Lifting it off, he opened it and shoved three into his mouth. He rolled them around until he had the seeds in his cheek, swallowed the meat, then spat them out to the other side of her room. Thwat, thwat, thwat. He felt around in the dark for his turban and shoved it on his head, then picked up his knife belt from where he'd let it drop, stood, straightened his woolen robe, and strapped the belt around it.

Stepping out into the courtyard, he realized it was later than he thought. A faint dawn light illuminated the courtyard. Ammar wouldn't like it. He corrected himself, *What does it matter what Ammar likes?*

Old Qambar sat in the far corner of the small courtyard near the water basin, whispering his morning supplications. Yulduz was shaking out one of the reed mats from their room and raising dust.

"It's a bit early for that," Tein grumbled. "Can't you do it in the alleyway like everyone else?"

Squinting one eye and grimacing as if the combination was some sort of magical mechanism, Yulduz said in the most formal Arabic she could manage, "May this dust keep you from seeing the innocent ones you persecute!"

He raised a finger, pointing at her, and said, "I'm coming for you, next!"

Qambar shifted to try to get up to challenge him, as he should. Tein raised both hands to him in humble surrender. "I'm sorry. I'm having a hard morning after a hard night. I shouldn't have spoken that way to your woman." He headed out toward the passageway so the old man would not have to get up and do what was right.

"Apologize to me! Not him!" Yulduz yelled behind him.

Zaytuna was coming back through the passage with a bucket of water as he was leaving. He grabbed her and kissed her roughly on the cheek. She laughed and pushed him off. He hurried past her through the lane, then went north towards the Round City, skirting the major markets, walking as fast as he could given his hangover and old leg injury.

The injury didn't hamper his strength, nor his ability to take on a man in a fight. But every limp reminded him that he'd not seen a Byzantine water carrier coming at him with a dagger as he raised his sword against a soldier before him. One moment of carelessness had led to him getting stabbed in the thigh. At least his sword made it through the soldier's shoulder before he fell himself. The water carrier stumbled beside him. Another ghazi was right behind him and thrust his sword through the water carrier's neck for his efforts. He helped Tein get far enough back from the fighting where one of the women following the camp tended his wound. The muscle had been severed, but it didn't bleed out to killing him. It healed into a gnarled lump that had bothered him ever since. He fought for another year despite the pain before he was sent back to Baghdad, kicked out of the military for good.

His head was still pounding, and he was visibly limping by the time he crossed through Solomon's Gates to the arcades where the police for Karkh had their offices. As he got closer, he saw that Ammar's door was open, and he swore under his breath. He called himself out, *If he gives you any grief, quit. Find Khalil. You can always beat up gamblers late on their debts. It'd be a far sight less ethically complicated than this cursed job.* He got to the door and saw Ammar wasn't there and looked down the arcade. Ammar stepped out of Ibn Marwan's office, head down, with documents rolled up in his hand. Tein hurried in to sit and try to look like he'd been there all day before Ammar got through the door.

Ammar said, "There you are."

"I slept at Zaytuna's last night."

"That's a long walk."

"I'm here." Tein shrugged.

Ammar went to the cabinet where he kept their case documents and placed the rolled-up paperwork in one of the diamond-shaped shelves. "I spoke with Ibn Marwan. We're to arrest the curse writer for performing black magic leading to murder. We're not to call it heresy. He doesn't want the Mazalim High Court hearing of it. No need to make the people think the caliph's coming down on their soothsayers and curse writers."

Tein sat up. "Why are we arresting her at all? It's a death sentence!"

"Ibn Marwan wants Imam Hashim's case wrapped up fast, so we can clear up the butcher's case. And there was another killing last night, but that one is easy." He laughed. "A stabbing in a tavern. The owner pinned the man who did it, breaking his arm. He's already in the cells, we just have to get witness accounts."

"And how are we supposed to provide evidence that it was black magic? We haven't got the talisman yet. Do we make that up, too?"

Ammar looked at him sideways. "We'll arrest her today, and maybe she'll admit to it. But we can get corroboration from the people down by the Gate. Someone down there will tell us what kind of talismans she writes."

"Ammar..."

"You heard Imam Hashim's wife describe what the Turkmen woman did." Ammar reflexively touched his own talisman of protection at his neck. "She played some instrument and went into a trance. Those Turkmen women out at the gate are barely Muslim. Mu'mina, she's still calling on her Zanji gods. God protect us from these two."

Tein shot up from the couch despite the pain in his leg. As he did, Ammar sat down in one smooth movement, putting his arm across the cushions behind him. Tein stopped himself before he got within striking distance. He forced himself to step backward to the couch where he had been sitting, then fell down hard onto it. He said slowly, biting every word, "There are leads we're not following up. Illness. Poison. Debts. The family."

"She confessed, Tein. There's doubt around it, but the curse writer can tell us if the talisman was meant to kill him."

"You're afraid."

Ammar stood up and adjusted his sword belt around the waist of his leather cuirass. "We're picking up the Turkmen woman. Let's go."

"There's no magic and no jinn." Tein stood to follow.

As he was walking out the door, Ammar raised his hand dismissively and pronounced, "Enough."

"Ashura? The Prophet's family slaughtered on the plain of Karbala?"

Ammar stopped cold and turned back, "Be careful."

"If magic worked, if talismans could kill, then why Ashura? You think that Husayn was ignorant of curses and talismans? You think he would not have made use of them, or, if not him, a woman among them? Someone would have invoked God's power or the jinn. Yet, they were still slaughtered."

Ammar put his hand on the hilt of his sword in warning.

Tein pushed anyway, "These women's lives are at stake because you're afraid of creatures that don't exist and leather pouches hanging around someone's neck."

"I've heard you. Let's go." Ammar stood aside and pointed to the door.

If Ammar wouldn't follow up other leads, he would. Tein walked out, cursing him under his breath.

Ammar caught up with him and passed him.

Tein nodded sharply, *Good. Better we walk in silence.*

Ammar turned around, "What did you say?"

"I didn't say a word." Tein pulled his head back. He'd not said it aloud.

Ammar looked past Tein. Tein turned around but no one was there.

Shaking his head at Tein, Ammar turned back to walking ahead a few paces. Ammar, for his short legs, kept a faster pace than he knew Tein could manage all the way to the Fruit Seller's Gate.

As they were approaching the square outside the yellow-bricked arched gate that led into the alleyways lined with produce stalls, they found their way was partially blocked. A crowd was gathering around a young woman standing on a block.

Ammar stopped. When Tein caught up to him, he said, "Ya Rabb, this better not turn into a riot." He tipped his head toward the crowd. "Let's keep an eye on this for a minute and see what direction it's taking."

The young woman's threadbare wrap was pulled around her closely, held shut under her chin in her fist. She was taking in the crowd, asking questions, listening. Tein could tell from the way her body moved with the energy of the crowd that she had them well in hand.

She was a slight thing, but her voice projected across the square. "Tell me where you are hiding something, and I will name it! If I surprise you, then leave a coin in the bag that our friend will pass around among you. Who will try?"

It was nothing but a Seer. Tein thought, *These fakes know no shame when it comes to stealing what little money the people have.*

An older woman in a clean, but faded and stained green wrap, frayed at all its edges, yelled out, "Tell me what's in the pocket of my sleeve!"

The Seer shifted to the left as if she were leaning in to hear an invisible someone whispering to her. She nodded, then stood up and called out, "May God, The Provider, help you and fill your pocket. I am sorry to say that you do not have even one fals. Not in your pocket. Not anywhere!"

Tein looked to either side of this Seer for an informant whispering to her but didn't see anyone. He moved closer, winding his way through the crowd. Only then did he realize that she must have been born without eyes. Her eye sockets were sunken in.

The crowd turned to the older woman for confirmation. "Subhanallah! She's right! My pocket's empty, and I've nothing to my name." The old woman pleaded, "My grandson and I don't know how we'll eat today."

The crowd gasped and dropped coins into the bag being passed around.

The Seer turned and spoke to someone behind her. Tein pushed past a tall man in a leather apron to see. There was another woman, and this one was wrapped more warmly in good wool. Quilted sirwal and boots stuck out from under her wrap. There was money being made here. Tein wondered what the Seer was wearing under her costume of poverty. The assistant called over a young man in a decent turban and robe standing nearby, and handed him a few coins. The young man pushed through the crowd to give the old woman the coins grandly with a "Bismillah" and a bow. Here and there, people nudged each other, saying, "Mashallah," at this gesture of generosity.

Tein's anger at Ammar spilled over onto this scam. He said loud enough for everyone to hear, "She pulls you in through this act of kindness. The woman asked what was in her pocket. It had to refer to money. Anyone could see that woman hasn't got a fals, her clothes are in tatters!"

"That's not what we're here for." Ammar got behind him. "Are you trying to create a riot?"

A woman nearby yelled at Tein, "She's blind! How could she know?"

Tein turned back to Ammar, ignoring the woman. "This is criminal. She has assistants who are passing the information back to her. Don't you see her listening to someone?"

"That's her re'ya, her personal jinn. They tell people's secrets!"

"That's her human assistant." Tein scanned the crowd. Poor and rich alike mingled, all moving in as close as they could to the Seer. A small cluster of rich women stood together in brightly hued and patterned woolen wraps, their gossamer-thin niqabs fluttering with their conversation as they gestured toward the stage. Their servants stood nearby, dressed in clothes as fine as their masters. Only one of the servants was keeping an eye on the women to see if they needed anything, while the others paid close attention to the Seer.

The Seer called out again, "Who else will ask me what they have?"

A boy in a good turban and a stiff robe raised his arm, his hand was balled into a fist. "Me! What have I got in my hand?"

The crowd gasped as the young woman leaned to the left.

Meanwhile, Tein picked out a young boy in a ratty scrap of turban and filthy short robe tied with rope over sirwal so long they dragged in the dirt, squirming past the wealthy women, one of them pulling her wrap away from him so he wouldn't touch it. He called out, "Mother!" as a ruse while keeping his eye out for purses to cut from the belts of those stupid enough to expose them in the marketplace. Tein didn't bother with him. Pickpockets were the Marketplace Inspector's job.

Off to one side, three men stood near the Seer, their heads together talking. They wore linen robes darkened from age and use, but bright white turbans, wrapped like Hanbalis with a twist under the chin. He wondered what their pious selves could be doing here, until one turned and looked toward him. He nudged Ammar. "Isn't that Hanbali over there, the one with the few beard hairs? Isn't he one of Barbahari's men who was taken into custody for harassing women in the street and destroying property?"

"You still angry that he smashed Salman's wine jars?"

Tein wasn't in the mood. "Why is he out on the street?"

"I thought he'd been jailed for good without a hearing." Ammar said, "Let's get a bit closer to them to keep an eye on them."

"They'll only be here to start trouble." Tein nodded.

The boy in the good turban called out again, "What have I got!"

The Seer said, "I'd tell you that you have a sticky candy in your hand, but there's a policeman here who thinks all I can do is say what is obvious."

"What?" Ammar looked at her.

With his eyes still on Barbahari's men, Tein answered, "I complained of her loud enough for anyone to hear. There's nothing clairvoyant about it."

"I do have a candy!" The boy opened his hand and showed a hardened brown lozenge covered in fibres from his pocket.

An old working woman in the crowd yelled at them, "You, police! Pay attention!"

Tein realized everyone was watching them.

The Seer called to the boy again, "Boy, how about I tell you what you had in your pocket this morning, but is no longer there?" The crowd murmured as she leaned toward the left to listen to an unseen voice. She nodded, then called out, "A lizard! You caught a lizard yesterday as it was sunning on a wall and put it in your pocket. But you crushed it by accident, so you threw it into a canal. You even said a prayer for it."

Everyone turned to look at the boy. His face had lost all its colour. He could barely get the words out. A man next to him bent over to hear him, then stood up and said, "It's true! The boy says it's true!"

Nearby them, they heard a woman hiss, "Didn't God warn us not to take allies other than Him? God protect us from evil things. Her sockets are sunk. Her jinn took them in payment for her soul! God told us that *the blind and the seeing are not the same!*"

Some whispered in assent, shifting uncomfortably, and saying, "God protect us from evil things."

A man called back to her over his shoulder, "You old bat! That's not what God means. God's talking about ignorant, unseeing fools like you! What are you doing standing out here watching the show if you are so afraid of a blind woman? Go home and complain to your poor husband!"

Her face turned bright red as laughing and jeers erupted. She swatted the air around her as if the insults were swarming flies.

Tein said loudly, "One of her informants saw a bloodstain on the pocket of his robe and told her. It's not too far to guess that a little boy would be chasing lizards. We all did!"

The Seer answered him, "The boy threw it into the Musa canal across the Tigris."

An old woman in a black wrap covering all but one eye turned to Tein and Ammar, taunting, "Are you disbelieving now?"

Tein put his hand on his heart and bowed to the woman as a gesture of conciliation, but had his eye on Barbahari's men, who seemed angered by the Seer's last answer.

Ammar had seen it, too. "This doesn't look good."

The man had one of his hands concealed inside his qamis. He yelled to the Seer, "You! Tell me what I am holding in my hand!"

The Seer remained silent. People called out here and there, "Tell him! Tell him!"

Ammar said to Tein, "Go to the front and stay with her in case anything blows up. I'll move behind them." Ammar skirted the crowd so the men would not see his approach. He came up close behind the man, but he couldn't see what he was holding and readied himself for it to be a weapon. Ammar whispered in his ear, "Brother, we'll take care of her once this is over."

The man jumped at the voice. He recovered himself, looking

Ammar up and down. "If you police would do your job, the streets would be empty of this blasphemy."

"I hear you. The Marketplace Inspector has jurisdiction here. I'll get hold of her afterward and make sure she's handed over to the religious courts."

"The religious courts!" The man scoffed, "You think those judges rule by God's Law? God curse them, and the chief judge himself! If they will not care for the souls of the people, then we will."

Ammar kept his voice cool, "I can see why you're frustrated, brother. In that case, for you, I'll put her into a cell in the walls of the Round City without so much as writing her name down. She'll be lost forever. No one will know." He gave a quick nod. "What she deserves."

Shocked at the admission, the man whispered conspiratorially, "It's a shame the Matbaq Prison is shut. Its deep holes were the right place for the likes of her."

"All I'm saying is, stand down. I have this."

The crowd was becoming impatient for her answer. Several more picked up the chant, "Tell him!"

The man considered Ammar for a moment, then relaxed his stance. Ammar put his hand on the man's shoulder and whispered, "Tell me, what do you have in your hand?"

He laughed, then whispered back, "My cock."

Ammar laughed with him, and the two turned to see what the Seer would say. She stood still, then leaned in to listen. Ammar thought he saw the air beside her ripple in the bare outline of a man leaning towards her to speak. Or was it an animal who looked like a man? His breath caught in his throat, and he felt the prick of sweat under his arms. Then it was gone. The crowd fell into silence.

"I'm sorry," she called out over the crowd. "I don't know. My vision must be lost for today. May God bless you all and restore the coin that you have shared with us a hundred times over!" The woman in the good wool wrap came up behind her, putting her hand on her elbow. The Seer climbed down off her perch. The two quickly made their way through the Market Gate.

The man pushed at Ammar. "She's getting away! What are you doing standing here?"

"See that tall black fellow. He's mine. He'll have her in a moment."

The man saw Tein move in after the girl and nodded to Ammar. The crowd was beginning to disperse, a few people standing nearby turned to him, crowding in. "Well, then, what did you have?"

He fished around under his robe. Then his hand emerged, holding a reed pen. He held it up. "A pen!" He shouted so everyone could hear, "The girl could not guess a pen! Don't let these fools trick you! They are nothing but agents of Satan!"

Ammar clapped the man on the back and went to find Tein. He was waiting just inside the gate, holding the Seer in one hand and her associate in the other. Ammar said, "It's alright, you can let her go. They aren't going to make a move on her." Ammar turned to the assistant, saying, "Not now, anyway. You should be careful."

The Seer spat on the ground at his feet. "Speak to me directly! Do you think because I have no eyes, I have no mind?"

Ammar snorted. "Fine. Those men are dangerous. I don't know what they're planning."

"Why don't you do something about them?" She demanded.

"I can only 'do something' if they've committed a grave crime. If I get the word from above, I can pick them up and throw them in jail without so much as a hearing. But I can do the same to you if someone who doesn't like you has the power to command me. So watch yourself."

Tein sighed. Whoever got Barbahari's men released from jail would also make sure a crackdown against the men would never come.

The Seer gave Ammar a dismissive nod of her head. Her assistant pulled at her to leave, but Ammar asked the Seer before they could go, "Why didn't you know what he had in his hand?"

"My re'ya told me he had his flabby piece of meat in his tiny hand! But he also told me that if I said so, I'd be dead now." She stuck her chin out at him. "I didn't need my re'ya to tell me, though. Men like that always have their cocks in their hands. I knew the moment he asked." Her assistant pulled at her again, and they walked away. The Seer called back to them over her shoulder as they moved deeper into the market, "So don't worry about me, Police."

As they disappeared, Tein turned to Ammar, laughing. "See!"

Putting his hand on Tein's arm, Ammar said, "Tein. She was right. The man told me so himself."

"Well, I doubt he told you it was a flabby piece of meat in a tiny hand!" He raised his eyebrows. "She's an expert at reading people, Ammar. I can't believe you are falling for this."

Ammar ignored him. "Look, Barbahari's men are up to something. It's not our job to police public morality, but Ibn Marwan needs to pass this information on. I'll tell him later. Right now, we have to go get that curse writer."

Tein couldn't see a way out of it. His only hope was that the talisman makers and curse writers wouldn't turn on each other. If they did find her, he hoped she'd confirm that the talisman was not meant to kill.

They went back through the Market Gate to the farthest end of the square outside where the talisman makers, curse writers, and soothsayers sat. Only a couple of women were huddled together in front of a small fire in a brazier. The little cutpurse with the ratty turban was standing nearby, trying to get some of the heat. A warning must have gone out to scatter. There was no Turkmen woman anywhere.

Ammar cursed under his breath.

As they approached, one of the women pulled up her niqab. "What do you want, Police? Here to harass us like those animals with their turbans wound like Hanbalis but their mouths filled with filth?"

Tein watched the boy. He moved in even closer to listen. Tein realized that his scrap of turban was twisted under his chin. Was this boy playing at being one of Barbahari's men? Or were they using him as a spy? He yelled, "You back off, this is police business."

The boy bent down and picked up a rock and threw it at him. Tein caught the rock in his hands and pretended to throw it back at him. The boy turned on his heels and ran as fast as he could into the market.

Ammar bowed his head. "Auntie, we apologize. Have these men been around much?"

She pulled her wrap more closely around her. "They came the other day and dragged off Abu as-Sari, the old Jew, and beat him savagely for throwing the sticks."

"Did anyone tell the Marketplace Inspector?"

"What would he do?" The women looked at him as if he were stupid.

"He could have told us. Assaults are our jurisdiction. I'll look into it."

"We'll see if you do or do not." One of them scoffed.

Tein asked, "If everyone else has run off because of those men, why are you still here?"

"To take their business!" The woman who showed them her face exclaimed, "God is generous! That old witch Tansholpan's gone!"

"Tansholpan?" Ammar asked, "Is that the Turkmen woman here who writes talismans?"

She looked him up and down. "Ya Rabb, may she be in deep shit!"

Tein gave up on the hope the women wouldn't turn on each other.

Ammar laughed. "Why?"

"All the people line up behind her. They say her curses are very powerful." She wagged her finger at him, "But it's gossip."

"Why do people say that? What does she do?"

"Nothing." The woman tipped her chin. "She writes out talismans and wraps them up in leather like the rest of us."

"There must be something," Ammar pressed.

"Sometimes, she brings out that jooza of hers to impress the customers." She leaned over to her friend and asked, "What does she call that thing?" The other woman shook her head. She turned back to Ammar, "She plays it upright in her lap, rubbing its strings with a bow. She goes mad, swinging about. It's nothing but a show. But don't you know, people fall for it."

Tein looked at Ammar. It was just as the imam's wife described.

"Do you know where she lives?" Ammar asked.

She smiled at the other woman, nudging her. "Subhanallah, she *is* in trouble!"

Tein answered, "We're not sure."

"If she's in trouble, I'll tell you. Otherwise, you can give me some coin for the information."

Ammar answered, "She's in trouble."

"Good. She lives in the neighbourhood behind Crow's Square." The woman tipped her head at Tein. "He'll know where it is," then cackled at her joke, nudging her friend again who looked up at Tein, her eyes wild with fear.

Tein bit his tongue, then noticed movement again. He turned to see that the boy had snuck back. He threw another rock at Tein and ran off across the square away from the market.

Ammar said to Tein, "Let's go. It's not far."

9

The sun-dried brick houses leaned on each other for support, each wall holding up the wall of another. If one were to fall, eaten away by rains because just one person was too lazy to keep up with the constant daubing of mud and stuffing of grasses into the weak spots, they would all go. The fog from the Tigris and canals had burnt off, but each house Tein had gone into seemed colder and damper than the last. Tein leaned against a wall in the sun, taking the weight off his bad leg. He took a deep breath in and let it out slowly. His chest was tight. He stood up and moved to the next doorway. "Assalamu alaykum. Baghdad Police."

Before he said, "Police," he had heard movement inside. Now, nothing.

"You're not in any trouble. We're looking for a witness to a murder."

Nothing.

"We're asking for your own safety."

Nothing.

He couldn't walk away, or every house in the neighbourhood would know that they did not have to answer. "I'm coming in." He ducked through the low doorway. The room was dark. There were no windows. The only light came through the door and gaps in the mud-daubed reed roof.

An old Christian man stood before Tein, shielding his wife. She had pulled her yellow wrap around her and over her head so Tein couldn't see her face. The old man's back was bent to one side from work and age. His knobby shoulder joints stuck out from his thin yellow qamis and robe tied up with knotted rope. But he held his own for his woman, defiantly silent. Tein took a step back to show the man he wasn't going to hurt them, although there was barely space for the three of them in the room. There was nothing but one reed mat laid out and a bedroll neatly folded in the corner. Their cooking pot and water jug sat beside it, and a small bag of food hung from a peg on the wall.

"I'm looking for an older Turkmen woman who writes talismans. She has information about the murder of a religious scholar."

Nothing.

His chest tightened again.

It was so quiet, he could hear Ammar saying around a corner, "Have you seen the Turkmen woman who writes curses?"

When he and Ammar had entered the cluster of small houses and asked the first questions, all conversation stopped. From house to house, the word spread, and they were shut out. This wasn't how it usually went. Every week they went door to door looking for witnesses, asking questions, confirming accounts. They'd been ignored. They'd been told to fuck off. They'd had answers whispered to them where the neighbours couldn't see. But most often, anger and resentment would spill out into the street, one party accusing another, declaring to all that they had been wronged and the wrongdoer stood before them and before God. But today? It was silence.

Tein's throat was becoming as tight as his chest. He forced the words out, "We know she lives here."

Again, nothing.

He gave up. He stepped back through the doorway and left without saying anything. He stood in the middle of the alleyway. He took deep breaths, one after another until his throat and chest loosened again.

Steeling himself, he approached the next house, but his chest tightened again. He breathed through it until he could say through the doorway, "Assalamu alaykum. Baghdad Police. You are not in any trouble. We are looking for a witness to a murder. I'm coming in."

A woman in a tattered wrap cowered in the back corner of the room. Her trembling child was between her knees, a delicate-limbed boy with his arms wrapped around his mother's waist. Her thin arms were around her boy as if Tein had come to snatch him away.

He saw the boy and his mother as if he were watching them from the outskirts of the graveyards where his mother preached, where he circled the crowd, looking for anyone who might go too far in their zeal, or fall into fear of her, and hurt them.

For a split second, his mind reeled, and the woman's face transformed into his mother's. She was no longer a cowering stranger, but wore the gleaming face of his mother as she fell into ecstasy. The shaking boy with his shaved head became Zaytuna. Her face was buried in their mother's lap, her long black hair spread out, longer than he remembered, into tendrils entangled in the rough reed mat and crawling through to the dirt floor. They were too far away for him to reach. He could hear people gathering behind him. They streamed around him, straight through the door of the tiny room, falling one by one at his mother's feet. They trampled Zaytuna's hair to get to her. He could hear Zaytuna whimpering as they tried to pull her out of her mother's lap to get even closer. Then their mother let go of Zaytuna. She stretched her arms out to catch them all up in her glorious outpouring of love and deliver them to God herself. Tein tried to lift his arms to grab the men in front of him and pull them back to get at Zaytuna, but his right arm was stuck at his side.

He looked down at his arm to see why it would not move and saw that his hand held his dagger, freed from its sheath at his waist. He looked back up. The room was empty. His mother and Zaytuna were gone. The woman was crying, begging him to not hurt her and her whimpering child.

What have I done?

He put his dagger back into its sheath. He wanted to reach down and rub the child's head to break the fear, but he knew it would be taken as a threat. Men had patted his head like that when he was a boy, sizing him up, seeing if he'd present a problem.

Tein was suffocating. He left the dark room for the light of the narrow lane, hearing the boy crying behind him.

Ammar was there, leaning against the wall across from him. When he saw Tein's face, he pushed off the wall and took hold of his arm. "What happened in there?"

Shaking off Ammar's hand, Tein nearly pushed him back against the wall. He wanted nothing more than to walk away from him, from this, and be done with all of it.

"Okay, okay." Ammar took a step back, hands up.

Tein pulled himself together well enough to say, "No one is talking."

"This is new."

"What do we do?" He looked down the lane for a way out.

Raising his voice so people in the neighbourhood could hear him, Ammar said, "We'll have to come back with the watchmen and beat the information out of them."

Tein closed his eyes, a wave of nausea washing through him. He knew that it was an empty threat, but the neighbourhood didn't. Not that Ammar had not hit men with the broad side of his cherished Yemeni sword, or threatened them with its edge when needed. Not that he himself hadn't beaten men down or held them hanging by their throats to get what he wanted from them when less force, more carefully placed, would have been enough. The thought of it made him want to throttle himself. *What have I become?* He turned on himself, answering his own question, *Become? You've been brutal all your life.* Bile rose into the back of his throat. He swallowed it down.

Ammar asked, "The Square?"

They walked in silence through several tight alleyways, winding back to the small main square where shopkeepers had set out small stands of fresh vegetables, grains, and beans. There was a tavern masquerading as a gathering spot for old men to sit and talk while drinking watered-down juices out of clay cups. Tein looked at the tavern and wanted nothing more than to keep walking to it and sit down to drink the rest of the day.

Ammar stopped in the middle of the square so they could not be overheard. "Tansholpan's curses must be potent."

Tein eyed the tavern. "They're definitely afraid to give her up."

"We should drag that curse writer that's got it in for her over here to show us."

"Aren't we done here?" Tein sounded desperate.

"I still have to interview the men in the butcher's case."

"And me?"

Ammar looked worried. "We still have to have her."

He said what he should, "I'll keep looking."

"You don't need me?"

"Go."

Tein started feeling better out in the open now that Ammar was gone. He shook off what he'd seen in the woman's house, saying to himself, *You barely slept last night. You aren't going to end up in the madhouse. You need sleep. And a drink. First, find the woman. Let her prove that the talisman couldn't have killed the imam, in a language these people understand.*

He eyed the alleyways leading to neighbourhoods they had not yet questioned. But each time he meant to step toward one of them, his chest tightened. He was stuck in the centre of the square. It felt as if the square itself was closing in on him. Everyone was looking at him. A large, black policeman in the centre of everything. He could taste their fear and spat on the ground to get it out. Twinkling lights crowded the edges of his vision, and his head began to buzz. He wanted to pull the turban off of his head and rip his knife belt off of his body and throw it at the people staring at him. He had to get out of there. He strode out of the square to the main road, pushing past anyone in his way, nearly knocking them down, as if they were trying to keep him from drawing breath itself.

On the main road, he pulled aside a woman with reeds in a

bundle on her back. "Canal! Where's the water?" She shook in fear and stepped aside for him, pointing to his left. He thought he could see water there. The light was brighter. There had to be a canal. The road to the canal started to open up, but as it did, more people crushed onto it. He rushed past them, shouting, "Police, get out of my way." He pushed a man aside. The man turned to hit him, then seeing his black turban moved to make space. Tein heard the man spit in his wake. Finally, he could see the canal, the light reflecting off the water forced him to raise his hand to shield his eyes.

Tein tried not to knock over the men and boys carrying goods as he ran down the path. He pushed past them on the landing, where the round reed-boats and skiffs were being loaded and unloaded, to where the landing gave way to tall reeds. Forcing his way through the muck and reeds, he grasped at them, pulling some aside, kicking others down, scraping his feet even through his thick sandal straps. The reeds were hard as wood so late in the year and sharp as knives when cut. He frantically tried to pull one of them from its bed, then pushed it away. The reeds opened up ahead of him onto a patch of tall grasses waving softly in the breeze. A man was sitting among them.

Hundreds of birds flew out of the grass before him, breaking left and right into the sky, stunning him into stillness. He held his hand up to shield his eyes from the sun and watched them circle to the man. They tried to settle around him, but the man waved his arms, shooing them away. Then he stood, towering over the grasses, and faced him. "Tein, my son, you've come to visit me."

Tein stepped back, grasping a long reed behind him to steady himself, the way a child holds the finger of his father. He was crying. "Uncle Nuri."

Nuri held his arms out to him. "Come, come." The muck of the reed bed gave way to soft earth. Tein walked gently through the grasses, keenly aware that he was crushing them with every step. He fell to his knees before his uncle, the pain from his thigh shooting through his hip, the moist earth soaking through his sirwal. Nuri kneeled with him and took Tein in his arms. Tein shuddered, and

Nuri shuddered with him. Sorrow flowed through them like a wave. Then Nuri took a deep breath, and Tein breathed with him until calm washed through him with every exhale. Finally, Tein let go of his uncle and sat back in the grasses. He wiped his face with the heel of his palm.

"I know about the enslaved girl," Nuri said.

Tein was undone. "Does everyone talk?"

"Yes." He added, "You cannot save her."

"There is no one else but me."

Nuri frowned. "God is her Protector."

"Uncle Nuri, let's not do this."

"Do what?" Nuri's voice took on an edge.

"Uncle, please."

"Say it."

"Her master raped her. Where was God?"

"With her."

"And God was with her rapist, too." It was a statement, not a question. He was used to this kind of talk from them, his mother, the aunts and uncles, and Zaytuna. At least Saliha didn't bother with it. Nuri knew how he was, that he couldn't stand it. Why was he doing this to him?

"You saw what became of him."

"Uncle Nuri. I don't want to show you any disrespect."

Nuri tucked his head back, "How could you disrespect me? God jealously guards those in His care. He punishes those who harm His beloveds whether you believe it or not. He also pushes away those who try to elbow in, thinking they can take His place. Who are you that you think you can save anyone? You are doomed to failure in this protection business. You are his servant, nothing more."

With the word, "doomed," Tein felt as though a hand had reached into his chest and held his heart, freezing him and spreading numbing fear throughout his body. He held perfectly still. If he made the wrong move, he was sure it would crush his heart between its fingers.

"You will play your part in bringing her to God's end."

Tein said through the gripping fear, "I can save her."

"Could you save your mother?"

The fingers loosened from around his heart, and warmth slowly spread back through his body. He found his voice, "I did, at times."

"Not when you wanted to most."

"No." His chest tightened again.

"You couldn't have, even if you had been there."

He insisted, "I might have."

"Only if God had wanted it."

"Please, Uncle. I don't want to argue with you. I love you."

Nuri laughed and pulled at Tein's sleeve, saying, "There's no argument here."

The laugh flowed through Tein, pulling him back to his Uncle's embrace. Tein lay down and stared at the clouds driven forward by a wind so high they could not feel it. The grasses around them bent this way and that from a swirling breeze off of the canal.

Nuri lay down beside him and recited a line of poetry,

> *In my love of You*
> *I have kept frequenting a place,*
> *which bewilders those hearts*
> *that settle there.*

Tein listened but didn't know what he was supposed to understand. Nuri was a father to him, but Tein knew he was not a good son. Nuri had taught him to wrestle his temper down when he was just a boy. Nuri taught him that a man's strength was not in his anger but in his generosity. *Look at me*, he thought, *I've failed him, and he has never failed me.*

Nuri broke through his thoughts, "I watched you as a child. You observed the crowd swirling around your mother like a master. You could feel them moving. You knew their every movement. You knew where trouble was rising and you moved toward it. I watched you disperse trouble. I know what you've had to do."

"I failed her."

"Life or death meant nothing to your mother, only God. She held herself back around you and Zaytuna. She only drew away from you to be alone with God with no worry."

The implication hurt. "We were her worry."

"Yes." Nuri explained, "She told me that she begged God to take her." He looked up, remembering, "She told me that she begged, 'Oh Lover of the obedient, how much longer will You keep our cheeks in the dirt? Awaken us!' But God gave you two to her instead."

"I thought it couldn't get worse." Tein laughed bitterly.

"Listen. You had a purpose in holding your mother here. God's purpose. You protected her. Just not how you think." He got up on one elbow and looked at him. "Stop imagining that you know what it means to protect. Examine yourself and see what your purpose is in every moment."

"My purpose was to let her die on time."

"You did what you should. You left Baghdad when you should. Zaytuna needed to learn to walk on her own and you became a brother to the empire. You became a husband and a father, if only for a time. You fought rightly for us."

What pride could he take in being a ghazi, if he left his sister behind? If he could not protect his wife and child? What did being a frontier fighter do but put brutal form to the anger he carried with him every day? What nobility was there in it if all he'd done in the end was become police? So he had become an accomplished killer and an oppressor of the people. *Noted.*

Nuri touched Tein's arm. "What is ithar?"

"Are we in school, Uncle?"

"Yes."

Tein said impatiently, "To think of others' needs before your own."

"You know it all, then."

Tein felt it as the dismissal it was, and panic rose up and bound his chest. He reached out for Nuri in desperation, holding Nuri's thin arm in his large hand.

Nuri looked into Tein's eyes. "A man is not the owner of anything in this world. The man who fashions himself one is a coward. He steals the rights of God for himself and wields God's names brutally to control what he believes is his. What is most men's jealous protection other than this? No one is more jealous than God! When this sort of man thinks of others' needs, it is only to serve his own."

Tein's hand went slack, letting go of Nuri's arm. "Is this what you think of me?"

"I think that you have sacrificed yourself for others your whole life. But you believe you know best what you should have done then and what you should do now. That makes you someone who thinks he owns a bit of this world, or should, and tries to control it."

"So everything I've done, I've done for myself."

"As a boy, you wanted to save your mother and sister for yourself. You are no different now."

Tein looked at him and said, "I have been brutal."

"You have."

"How do I stop?" Tein sat up.

"You will stop as you give up owning this and owning that. You will protect when you stop believing that you are the divine Protector."

Tein looked down, unable to face him.

Nuri pushed his shoulder, ending the conversation. "Tein, listen to me. There's a green grocer. A man with a ridiculous turban in Balkhi Square, just beyond the Thorn Bridge. Have you ever seen this man?"

Confused, Tein looked up. "What?"

"Find him, and you'll find your talisman maker."

"How? I don't understand."

"I know everyone in Baghdad." Nuri smiled. "I don't sit in that house like your uncle, Junayd, talking about God in words nobody understands anymore." He smiled more broadly, slapping his chest. "I'm a man of the streets."

Tein knew he should laugh, that his uncle was trying to get him to laugh, but he couldn't.

"Go there."

Tein nodded.

"Remember what I said about ithar."

Tein stood. "I don't know how to do what you say."

Nuri stayed where he was in the grasses. "We'll see."

Tein bent down to grasp Nuri's hand to kiss it, but his uncle pulled it away and shooed him off. Tein made his way back through the grasses he'd walked on so gingerly before. They looked trampled as though cattle had been driven through them. He felt sick. He reached the reeds and heard hundreds of wings beating behind him. He turned to look back at Nuri, still sitting in the clearing, as the birds settled in the grasses around him.

He picked through the reeds and made his way up the hill and back to the square. A watchman was leaning against a wall eating an apple. Tein called out to him. The watchman straightened himself, took two more quick bites out of the apple, then put it in his pocket. They met in the middle of the square.

Tein said, "Go to the office of Grave Crimes in the Basra Gate and tell Ammar ibn at-Tabbani to meet Tein in Balkhi Square, by the Thorn Bridge, immediately."

10

Tein and Ammar stood in Balkhi Square. Small shops were jammed into every available bit of space. Barefoot boys strained as they pulled small carts with goods for delivery. Poor women draped in faded wraps stood in groups chatting or in deep negotiations with sellers of carrots and onions. A barefoot man in short sirwal and a moth-eaten woolen wrap thrown around his shoulders sat beside a careful pile of dung patties, hawking, "Fire! Dung! Fire!"

They had walked around the square twice and still had not seen a green grocer by Nuri's description.

Ammar asked, "You said this was a trustworthy lead?"

"Yes."

Tein's eye was on the tavern on the far side of the square. A tall man with a black turban pulled his head back quickly inside to avoid being seen. It was a watchman sneaking a drink on duty. He thought, *I wish I were with you, brother*.

Ammar tapped Tein on the arm and pointed to one of the produce stalls. There he was, emerging from the back of his shop. The grocer waved the woman who had been tending it through the door and shut it behind her. He was a middle-aged man, slim as a post, but average in every other way except that he was wearing a comically large green and blue turban. Worse, he wore it around a conical green quilted cap, like a judge.

Ammar laughed. "Fits the description."

"Yes, he does."

Ammar strode over to the shop, hand on the hilt of his sword. Tein hurried behind him. The grocer did not have a second to think or run.

"Baghdad Police. We're looking for a Turkmen curse writer. You aren't in any trouble if you help us find her."

The grocer lifted both hands in submission. He backed up slowly between the nearly empty boxes holding his produce, a few withered-looking carrots, leeks, onions, and garlic, yelling, "I don't know where that horror of a woman is! If I knew I would hand her over to you myself! She drove my wife out of my arms and back to her family with her curses!"

Ammar followed him in, crowding him against the door to the backroom. "You must know something. Tell us and we can handle her for you. You'll not be bothered by her again."

The man lowered his voice, glancing at the shop on his left, "I told you, I don't know where she is. She only held off destroying my business because I agreed to let my woman go." Then loudly, "I don't know where she is!"

Tein leaned over the stacked boxes. "Who is it over there that you want to hear your protests?"

The man's face drained of colour, and his eyes opened wide, he ticked his head to the left without saying anything. Ammar looked back at Tein who nodded and stepped out of the shop. Ammar stayed with the grocer while Tein scanned the square to read the situation. The grain seller to the grocer's left looked like he was ignoring them, but was observing their movements well enough. He was leaning against a barrel, using the tip of a small dagger to clean his nails. The narrow sleeves of his short robe were rolled up and his knife belt kept his robe close to his body. Nothing to get in the way of a fight. Tein could see by his stance and the natural, yet controlled way he held the knife that he knew how to use it. He was protecting someone within.

Tein stepped back into the green grocer's shop. The door at the back cracked open. A woman's arm came out and slapped at the grocer's arm, trying to get a hold of his sleeve to pull him into the back room. Ammar took hold of his other arm. "What was this about your wife being driven off?"

The man whispered, "This is my second wife. Now my only wife, thanks to that sorceress."

"Ah." Ammar addressed the woman behind the door, "Let him go, we're not going to bother him. In fact, I'd like to buy some carrots for my own wife, who, as it happens, has not left me."

The woman pulled her hand back and shut the door. The grocer side-stepped past Ammar to one of the stacked boxes. "How many would you like? I can give you a good price in thanks to your service."

"I've changed my mind. I've changed my mind about having a wife, too." Ammar said in a clear voice as he left the shop, "You let us know if you hear anything. Tell any watchmen. Tell him to take the news to Grave Crimes by the Basra Gate." Tein and Ammar stood at the shop's edge in the square. Tein knew Ammar would have seen the grain seller's knife. They approached his stall, understanding their roles without having to say a word. Ammar stopped where he could fall back with one step and pull his sword from its scabbard. His hand was not on the hilt, but it could be in the barest of a second. Tein held back. He could move in any direction to apprehend the man if he decided to push past one of his barrels into the square or take on Ammar. He hoped there was no laneway behind the shop, but that was unlikely in this neighbourhood. More likely, all he had back there was one room with no windows and light that he used to store goods or sleep if he had nothing else.

Ammar asked the grain seller, "How's business?"

The man stood up, relaxed still, his arms beside him, but had turned the knife around in his hand, pointing behind him so he could stab down or slice across in tight quarters.

"The way you're holding that knife," Ammar tipped his chin at it, "you look to be a fellow ghazi. Take a look at us and ask yourself if you can win this fight. Ask if she'd want you to die for her. Put the knife down and bring her out."

The door to the back of the shop opened, and there she was. She was calm but looked exhausted. Her craggy face sagged, pulling her mouth down into a deep frown. She said to the man, "No one will be harmed on my account."

He put the knife down on the barrel behind him and held his hands up so they could see. He bowed his head. "Forgive me, sister."

She wore the red and black coat with the lapels, like the imam's wife had described but was much lighter-skinned. What had the imam's wife said? She was as dark as a "withered date." This Turkmen woman was burnished by the sun and wind, that's all. *Curse these people.* She was missing her cap; her hair was greasy at the roots and tied in long thin braids, each one knotted off with colourful wool. Some had come undone, and straggles of oily grey hair lay against her dirty coat. She looked like she had slept in the back last night with nothing between her and the dirt floor.

"Nothing to forgive." She said, "I should have crossed the bridge like Yulduz told me."

Tein blurted out, "Yulduz?"

"Yes. She told me about you. A black man as big as Solomon's Gates coming to get me. She told me to curse you for it."

Ammar looked between the two of them.

"You are Tansholpan."

"Should I curse you?"

Tein shrugged but could see Ammar stiffen out of the corner of his eye.

She asked, "Aren't you afraid of me?"

"Sorry, no."

"Yulduz said you were godless." Tansholpan added, saying almost as an afterthought, "May God bring a spark of faith to your heart and may it set fire to longing for Him."

"If my mother could not light that fire, I doubt your prayers will."

Ammar interrupted, "Enough, let's go." He waved her forward, saying to Tein, "Take her."

She pulled back. "No one touches me."

Ammar asked, "You won't run?"

"I'll come. Are you bringing me to the girl?"

"First, we have to question you, then yes."

Tansholpan nodded. "Fine."

They started toward the main road out of the square, one on either side of her.

Ammar stopped, then spoke over her to Tein, "Go get that watchman out of the tavern and straighten him out. I want his name."

Tein raised his eyebrows, mocking, "You'll walk her back alone?"

"Catch up. No drinking."

Tein didn't bother objecting. It'd only be admitting he wanted it.

Tein watched them go, then crossed to the tavern. The old men sat on stools, cups before them, eyeing him with wine-soaked eyes. He called out into the shop, "Watchman, come out. You've been seen."

He stood in the doorway, drunk. Tein waved him forward. "Come on, it's a long walk back to the Round City, you'll have time to sober up."

The watchman slurred, "My office is on Qayyari road."

"But my boss wants you to come with me. He's going to have you drawn down."

The man grabbed the doorway to hold himself up as he leaned back to get the insult from his throat to spit at Tein, "Zanji! Come with you! Drawn down?" He grasped at the black turban half-cocked on his head and threw at it Tein. "Take your black turban. I'm done."

Tein let the turban hit him without reaching for it or flinching. It hit the ground without Tein so much as looking at it. But it hit its mark, a wave of exhaustion washed through him. "Don't go back to your office, then. They'll have news of you."

"I'll go for the wages owed me."

One of the old men tugged the watchman down. "Sit down and shut up."

Tein replied to the old man, "Not likely."

He left the watchman in the tavern, making his way out of the square, returning through the small streets and alleyways as quickly as he could without betraying his limp. Not far from the Fruit Seller's Gate, he saw the Turkmen woman's bright red robe and bare head in the crowd. She was as tall as an average man, and stood well over Ammar. He wasn't touching her, and she wasn't looking to get away. He caught up behind them, close enough to see that Ammar was walking with a strange gait, pulling to the left away from her then correcting back. It was slight, but it was there. Ammar was afraid.

Tein fell in beside Tansholpan. She did not acknowledge him but kept walking straight ahead. Ammar nodded at him. Tein wanted to mock him for being afraid of her. He was putting these women's lives at risk because he saw them as unworthy of justice. And him, who was he to Ammar? When would Ammar decide that he was not worthy, that he was too African, too unbelieving? Too lost?

Ammar suddenly stopped and looked behind him, searching in the crowd.

Tein asked, "What is it?"

"I heard somebody calling out to me. The same thing I heard before."

"What?"

Ammar turned around twice, searching, and didn't answer.

"What?"

Looking hard at Tansholpan, Ammar pushed ahead. "Nothing."

As they were partway up the bridge leading into the Basra Gate, the wind whipped around and pulled at Tansholpan's robe, loosening her sash and blowing her long grey braids every which way. She clutched at her robe so it would not blow open and raised her hand to her hair. Tein watched as Ammar nearly fell off the wide bridge as if her gesture were a ritual calling of demons. Tansholpan herself almost stumbled back from the wind. Tein put his hand behind her, without touching her, in case she needed help. Ammar looked at him, for just a moment, wild-eyed with fear, then it passed. Tein had seen that fear on the battlefield. They'd all had it. But for something real before them. Men with battle-axes and swords screaming forward against them, not an old woman with empty threats.

Tansholpan regained her balance and considered Ammar. "Afraid of me? You should be. Why do you think no one in that neighbourhood would give me up?" She spat on the ground in front of him. "No one but that pig of a grocer who can't keep his hands off the women in the neighbourhood."

Ammar ignored her and walked ahead of them at a fast pace, leaving Tein to bring her in. Ammar was sitting in the office by the time they came through the door. The old woman didn't wait to be told what to do, she found a spot she liked and sat down. It was an awkward position to Ammar; he'd have to move from where he was to question her. She picked a few of the pillows off from the low couch and propped them behind her, leaning back into them and making herself comfortable. She said to Ammar, "I could use some water."

Tein poured the water for her.

She addressed Ammar, "I didn't ask him, I asked you."

"You are not in charge here."

Tein handed her the cup of water and watched Ammar try to sit so he could face her rather than get up and move on her account.

Ammar finally asked, "Why was the grocer willing to turn you in?"

"Uff, that piece of filth. If the girls in the neighbourhood only listened to their mothers, they'd have kept a wide circle around him. He knew how to charm them. That's not his second wife in that store, that's his seventh. Why has no man in the neighbourhood killed him?" She turned to Tein, "You answer me that!"

Tein shrugged.

"One after another, he agreed to marry the girls to save the families from the shame. One after another, they left him, divorced like his mother's backside to him. They were ruined for a good boy, but at least free of him." Tansholpan said proudly, "It was me who got each one of them out of there."

"With curses?" Tein asked.

"Not everything is done with curses. No, by speaking to the girls and talking their families into taking them back. But that last one, her family didn't want her. They were getting their vegetables for free from him in payment. Them? Them, I threatened with a curse if they wouldn't take her."

Ammar asked, "Why didn't you curse the grocer?"

"I did. Can't you see how unhappy he is? And who buys from him but passersby? What did he have out front but rotten onions to sell?"

Tein sat down. He could see why old Yulduz liked her. Zaytuna would like her, too. He was looking straight at her as he thought, *And Saliha...*

She raised an eyebrow to Tein. "It won't be long."

Tein gave her a look, not understanding.

Ammar asked, "What won't be long?"

She smiled at Ammar, gesturing to Tein. "He knows."

Tein held his hands up. "She's trying to play us."

Tansholpan shot back, "You're the one playing yourself, not believing in God."

"She got you there." Ammar laughed.

Tein gave Ammar a tired look. "She collects information on people and uses it on them. She knows a lot about me."

"From Yulduz?" Ammar asked, "The one you mentioned before?"

"My sister's neighbour. It seems Yulduz tipped off Tansholpan that we were coming for her."

Ammar's look made it clear he was not pleased.

"Saliha talked about what happened at the hospital," Tein explained.

Ammar held up his hand. "Fine."

But Tein couldn't let it drop. "Saliha didn't know that Yulduz and Tansholpan knew each other. It was a hard day for her. You know women. They talk to feel better."

"I said it's fine."

Tansholpan looked between them. "Can we get on with this?"

Ammar faced her. "You wrote the talisman that killed Imam Hashim al-Qatafi."

Sticking her hand out to make her point, she said, "Yes. *But* she didn't want to kill him. She wanted me to shrivel his penis."

"So why did you write a talisman to kill him?"

Tein cut in, "Do you intervene on behalf of all the women in the city?"

Tansholpan shot back at him, "What are you doing to protect them!"

Ammar gave Tein a look for interrupting, then said to Tansholpan, "You didn't answer me."

"I don't have to answer you," she said. "I did it. She didn't. Let her go."

Tein waved, his palm up. "That's that, then. Mu'mina didn't do it."

Ammar turned to Tein, "We need Ben Hadad to take down her confession." Tein stood up to go get the scribe, but Ammar insisted, "No, I'll do it. I've got to speak to Ibn Marwan about this."

No, you're scared to be alone in the room with her. Tein sat back down.

Ammar walked out, leaving the door open. The two of them sat in silence, watching as streams of people passed by the arcaded offices.

Tansholpan let out a deep breath and settled back into the couch again. "The girl didn't kill him. I made a talisman for her freedom. I knew what was best for her, even if she could not see it herself. These stupid girls never do!" She nodded firmly with pride, "God answers my prayers."

Tein stood up and crossed the room to her. "I know she didn't do it, you ignorant woman. You can't kill a man with a talisman!" She didn't cringe from him, but sat up straight, the look on her face daring him to hit her. He saw what he'd done mirrored in her defiance and retreated to the other side of the room. "I hope what you said is enough to stop this. But I don't know. She could still be in danger. I need time. I can find out who killed him."

"You'll do your part."

"Stop trying to play me." He wanted to grab her but forced his hands to stay loose by his side.

Ammar walked in with Ben Hadad beside him, saying to Tein, "I need to talk to you outside."

The scribe came in with paper, a pen, and an inkwell case and sat behind Ammar's desk. Tein heard him say as they walked out, "What is your full name?"

"Only Tansholpan."

Once out the door, Tein burst out in frustration, "She told me that she didn't write a curse to kill him at all. I don't know what she's doing."

"You're right that she's playing with you." Ammar looked inside. Tein followed his gaze. She was speaking, her attention focused on the scribe. "She knows how to get under people's skin."

They stood in silence as the scribe did his work. Tein looked back at her again. She was staring at them this time. The scribe had finished.

He met them at the door. "I have her confession."

"That was fast."

"She didn't have much to say." He handed Tein a second document, the jail intake.

"Thanks." Ammar nodded to Ben Hadad.

The scribe bowed his head and walked past them, down the arcade to Ibn Marwan's office.

"Take her to the cells, Tein. Put her in with the girl."

"Why won't Mu'mina be freed? Tansholpan admitted Mu'mina is innocent."

Ammar deflected, "Her situation will be addressed by the police chief."

Turning back into the office in frustration, he saw that Tansholpan was already standing. "Are you taking me to the girl?"

Tein jerked his head toward the door, and she fell in behind him. He was too angry to walk beside her, and he knew she wasn't going to run. Tein stopped to wait for her before Solomon's Gates. He stood next to a wide bricked archway tall enough for a horseman to ride through, stave up. When she reached him, they walked through it together.

The road split ahead of them, to the left were a series of other archways leading to walled-off neighbourhoods nestled between the encircling walls of the city. In the old days, the whole city of Baghdad was here within the Round City. The wealthy, the courtiers, the grand administrators, great military families had their homes in these neighbourhoods, even the poor and the markets were within the walls. These days some families remained, mainly military people, but most had been turned into garrisons. The great families, including the caliphs themselves, had long moved onto estates built up around the old Round City and across the Tigris, the grand homes and palaces lining its banks.

They took the road on the right. It had an easy angle so that horses could walk up from the yards and stables below. The garrisons and stables were ahead, the jail around the corner, built into the walls below the arcade. Tein shivered at the locked iron gate as the chill and damp coming from the cells hit him. He yelled for the guard. A large man emerged from the jail halls. Taller and broader than Tein, he wore a leather cuirass big enough for a bull. He had a ring of keys on one side of his belt and a sheathed dagger on the other. He took the keys off the hook on his belt, unlocked the gate, and pulled it open. Tein addressed him, "She's to be held with the girl I brought down yesterday."

"That one's been throwing up," the guard replied, not moving.

Tein pushed past him. "Come on, let's go."

The guard held him back with an arm. "Paperwork." Tein thrust at him the intake that Ben Hadad had given him. The guard took it from him and set it into a shelf along with a pile of others without looking at it, then walked them through the passageway past cells holding men. Some of the men were seated, others sleeping on pallets wrapped in blankets. One stood up, shedding his blanket to the floor, and walked casually to the bars. "She'd be a dry fuck, but I'll take her all the same. Put her in here for a moment, won't you?"

Tein lunged at the bars, thrusting his hand inside to grab hold of the man, but the inmate stepped back out of reach as casually as he had come forward and laughed. "Not today, then?"

The guard shook his head at Tein. "If you want to waste your muscle, I've got some cells that need mucking out."

"Get us to the women's hall."

Tein gestured for Tansholpan to walk ahead of him, making sure she was in the centre of the passage so no one could grab her.

They turned a corner into a passageway that was a solid wall on one side and cells on the other. They walked by two empty cells. The third held a pale woman with long, greasy red hair. She was sitting on a pallet and had pulled her thin bedroll around her for an extra layer against the cold and damp of the weeping walls. Tein confronted the guard, saying through his teeth, "I told you to get more blankets yesterday."

The guard stood toe to toe with him as not many men could. "I put in for them. They'll come when they come. If you are so soft on these women, get them yourself. I won't stop you from handing them out."

Tansholpan hissed at Tein, "The girl!"

Tein stood back. The guard led them past another cell in which three women were held together, huddling against the cold, then just beyond them, Mu'mina. She was retching into the latrine sluice in the corner of the cell. The guard took his keyring out too slowly for Tein's liking. Tein barked, "Hurry up," at which the guard slowed his movements, but finally got the door unlocked. Tansholpan pushed past him into the cell.

The guard stood back. "Never seen one eager to be locked up!"

Tein went in behind her. Tansholpan kneeled beside Mu'mina and held her forehead with one hand and put a hand on her back with the other. The girl retched one more time, bringing up nothing but bile, and gasped, breathing into the space between heaves. She retched one more time, then stopped.

Tansholpan looked at Tein. "Water."

The guard leaned against the bars and pointed to one corner. Tein wanted to punch him, but he got the bucket for her instead. Tansholpan unwound the sash at her waist and soaked the end of it in the water, then used it to wipe the girl's mouth. She spoke to her quietly. Mu'mina nodded, took some water in her hand, and rinsed her mouth.

Tein moved back near the door and looked away to give Mu'mina some privacy but saw the guard was staring right at them. He pointed outside the cell. "Come on, let's go." They stood outside while Tansholpan and Mu'mina spoke quietly. After a few moments, Tansholpan got up and came over to him.

"Does she need a doctor?" Tein asked.

Tansholpan looked up at him. "More like a midwife, but I expect she'll be fine and doesn't need one. It's only the normal sickness that comes with pregnancy."

Tein shot his head back, his eyes wide.

"Yes. Make sure she's getting decent food."

She returned to kneel beside Mu'mina again, and said to her, loudly enough that Tein could hear, "Don't be afraid. This man here is going to get you free. And from that baby in you, if we can get it born alive, you'll be a slave no more."

---

11

*Z*aytuna checked Layla's writing tablet to make sure she'd washed it. She tucked the tablet behind her box, putting the pen and ink beside it. She shook her head. *That girl, she's here too much. She has Maryam to care for her. It's good she wants to learn to read and write. Since Salman won't teach her hadith, walla, if she wants to, I'll make Mustafa do it.*

She stuck her head out through the curtain to check the sky. There was some time yet before sundown prayer. Still, she hurried, wanting to get to Uncle Abu al-Qasim's home early for the sama. No, she corrected herself, *Shaykh Abu al-Qasim's home.* She pulled on her clean qamis and sirwal over her everyday ones for extra warmth. She got her good wrap out of the box where she kept her things, saw the tablet again, and muttered to herself, "I'll speak to Mustafa tonight about her. But that girl is mistaken if she thinks I'm going to be some kind of mother to her."

She poured herself a cup of water from Mustafa's jug. "Bismillah." Despite her hurry, she crouched to drink it, like the Prophet, in three sips, willing herself to feel Muhammad's presence in doing as she did. She closed her eyes for a moment and breathed out, "Alhamdulillah." She stood and pulled her good wrap around her, draping it over her head wrap. The shape of her mother's colourful beads, threaded through her one long matted strand of hair, stuck out through the fabric. She touched them as she prayed, "Lord, help me on this path. I need You," and stepped into the courtyard.

Saliha came out. "Off to your Uncle's?"

"Yes." She took Saliha's hand. "Won't you come with me? Today is the sama. You don't need to take part. You can sit back and just listen to the music and the recitation."

"I need to sleep." Saliha squeezed her hand. "See you in the morning, inshallah. And Zaytuna?"

"Yes?"

"Pray for me. Your fool of a friend."

"Inshallah." Zaytuna let go of her hand and left, ducking through the passageway and into the alley wondering if it would be faster to go through the square or the lanes surrounding it. She thought of Salman sitting in front of his tavern with his smug smile and having to stop and greet him. She muttered, "God protect me from that man," and went around the back way.

As she arrived at Junayd's home, the door had just opened for three men. She hurried to follow them in so she wouldn't have to knock for the door to be opened for her as well. She slipped past the young man holding the door. "Assalamu alaykum, Ziri."

He bowed his head. "Waalaykum assalam wa rahmatullahi wa barakatuhu, Zaytuna. I was told to tell you that the shaykh Abu al-Qasim wants to speak with you."

She froze for a moment. *Why does he want to see me?* It had to be her impatience with YingYue yesterday morning. Or maybe he wanted to commend her for struggling with it successfully? *No, it can't be good.* She held her voice steady, "Is he downstairs?"

"Yes, he is seeing people now."

She peeked around under the stairs in the reception hall, as she always did, and was happy to see a young seeker tucked in underneath deep in contemplation as Junayd and others had done themselves early on the path. Zaytuna had played there as a child, mimicking their movements and voices until one of the seekers came to take her place. She wondered if she had the right to sit in meditation there now. The main hall was already filling with people greeting each other and catching up on news as the always did. She grumbled to herself at the noise that they were making, thinking it unfitting on the night of such a ceremony, and wove through them out to the courtyard where the remembrance ceremony would take place.

Woven reed mats covered with sheepskins were laid out along the walls and extended into the courtyard itself, open to the sky, leaving an empty space at its centre. A young man was lighting the lanterns hanging from the archways and those nestled in niches in the wall. When night came, the flames would flicker through the cut metal lanterns sending elaborate patterns moving along the walls. To her, it was as if the light itself became a body moving in ecstasy along with those swaying as they chanted from their places seated on the mats and those who rose to dance and turn as the ritual overcame them.

Dawud was readying the drums for the night, correcting their tone in the kitchen by the fire. She was eager for the sama to begin and pull her away from the voices in her head that nagged her all day. The music and poetry opened a door onto a part of her that knew some peace with God and invited her to sit with it for a little while. Everything was easier for her in the days after each gathering. There was a way to bring bread to the broken beggar children in the street without causing a scene or cursing the man that ran them for money. She didn't feel abandoned by Saliha. Mustafa's face became a light to her. Tein could not irritate her. Salman's greetings could be returned without insulting him. Then it would fade, and her dark view of the world would find its way back to her.

Shaykh Abu al-Qasim was busy speaking with people. She gestured to Abu Muhammad al-Juwayri, Junayd's closest companion and the assumed inheritor of the community upon Junayd's death, to let him know she was here. He nodded to her, then she went to sit with the women gathered near the kitchen. She looked for Uncle Nuri. *Or should I call him "Shaykh" now too?* He and a few of the other older uncles—who had been in this community since before they used the word "Sufi" to describe their all-encompassing love of God —usually sat near the old women, long on the path themselves. The old friends of God, men and women alike, would chat together and distract the children who were playing and making noise but who would, eventually, fall asleep on the sheepskins to the sound of the drums. Mustafa was there, sitting with the men, but talking with Auntie Rahiba just on the edge of the women's section. He didn't notice her. Zaytuna was pulled toward him, her stomach fluttering. Then the image of Mustafa as a donkey on a rope that Tein had thrown in her face hit her. Scolding herself, *Let him go, woman,* she sat as far away from the men as she could.

She kneeled before the old women, giving each of them a greeting, kissing the hands of those nearest to her. As she went to kiss the hand of Auntie Hakima, instead of pulling her hand away, as was the custom, she let Zaytuna kiss it. Then there was Mustafa's voice behind her, "Assalamu alaykum, my mothers!"

Auntie Hakima gave her a sharp look before hailing him in return. Zaytuna was confused and twisted around awkwardly on her haunches to find that Mustafa was standing right behind her. He kneeled down to face her.

"Walaykum assalam," she said. "You weren't here for the last sama."

His eyes searched hers. "I've missed you."

She didn't answer, not wanting to pick up the rope around his neck, and looked down, realizing too late that her face was burning from being so close to him.

"I have news. Ibn Shahin has hired me permanently to tutor his children. I am to come everyday now. The children like me, thank God, and he is pleased with what they are learning."

She looked up, smiling, her eyes pricking with tears. Her face was still hot, but she didn't care. This was what he had been working for. A reliable job like this would give him greater freedom to study the sayings of the Prophet. If he saved, it would allow him to travel to memorize and write down hadith of the masters in other cities. He might have the chance to enter into the networked ranks of scholars someday, or maybe be sought out as a master himself. "Mashallah, Mustafa. So no more throwing pots for you?"

"No," he said, restraining a grin. "But I spoke to Master Jalaluddin. He told me I can go there to make the jugs and cooking pots for the community whenever I like."

"May God bless Imam Abu Abdurrahman al-Azdi. Obtaining that ijaza certificate to transmit the hadith of the Golden Chain has made all the difference."

"Amin, he was generous to me. I cannot thank him, or God, enough for it."

Nudging him, she teased him, "Come on, give me your chain of transmission for the hadiths of the Golden Chain...what is it?" She looked toward the sky. "Hmmm, Mustafa al-Jarrari, the Potter, the son of Zaytuna, a housecleaner, who heard it from Abu Abdurrahman al-Azdi, who heard it from Abu Ali al-Yamani, who heard it from Imam Malik, who heard it from an-Nafi, who heard it from Ibn Umar, who heard it from the Prophet himself!"

As she recited the chain, he smiled sheepishly and looked down as if his scholar's turban were heavy on his head. She knew the gesture well and that he was close to weeping in gratitude.

Zaytuna looked away to give him a moment and to check if Shaykh Abu al-Qasim was ready to see her. Looking back at Mustafa, she suddenly worried about what his new position would mean. It would bring him into a world of people far from her. Her heart clenched at the thought of him traveling. Mustafa would be gone for months, years when it got to that. She feared, too, that even though Ibn Shahin was a Sufi like them, Mustafa would change. He had already bought all new clothes. Now he would be keeping company with people who would never have spoken to him before. People who would never accept her and he would forget about her.

But he would not forget about YingYue. She felt sick. YingYue would fit in those circles perfectly. *She'll make him a good wife.* Zaytuna closed her eyes and heard the nagging voice within her say, *God took your mother. Your brother left your side. Saliha has moved on. Now Mustafa is gone.* A hole opened within her, and she feared she would fall into it. Zaytuna remembered the words of the old woman in the cemetery that she must step away from the pain that binds her and pulled herself away from the hole's edge. It was all she could manage to do. She opened her eyes, now filled with tears to find that YingYue was standing before her.

"Assalamu alaykum, Shaykh Abu al-Qasim will see you."

Zaytuna glanced at Mustafa. His head was down, but she could see he was blushing. She stepped back towards the hole within her, and sorrow turned into anger at its edge. As she stood up, Zaytuna sucked her teeth at him, *My God, Mustafa, have some shame.*

She followed YingYue and found her spot before her shaykh on the sheepskin. Abu Muhammad al-Juwayri sat beside him, as usual. She greeted them both, "Assalamu alaykum," then took Junayd's hand to kiss. He pulled it away before she could and put his hand on her head instead.

"Wa alaykum assalam. I'll be brief. I am putting YingYue in charge of the women of the community. Just as the men must come to Abu Muhammad first, you should go to her first with your questions, then to your Auntie Hakima, then to me, if you need."

Zaytuna had not expected this, and she had no defences in place. She spoke back to him, hearing her words as if someone else were saying them, "YingYue? How old is she? I have been in this community longer than she's been alive. And why her? I should see Auntie Hakima, instead. She teaches the women and even some of the men."

He held her eyes. "Do you know what Moses said when he approached God's throne, and he saw another man sitting there?"

"No," she said, sinking down. A story about God's education of one of the prophets was never a good sign.

"Moses, may God grant him blessings and peace, saw a man sitting beside the throne of God and demanded to know, 'Thanks to what is this man sitting there!' God answered his question, 'He is there thanks to not envying anyone on account of the favours God has bestowed on them'."

The slap of the lesson hit her as surely as if God Himself had reached out and hauled her around as He had done to Moses. Involuntarily, she slapped her own hand, saying, "I am sorry, God forgive me."

Junayd leaned forward and touched the hand that had slapped the other. "Not like that." With his touch, she felt the rush of those oceanic waters flow from him to her, surround her, and her disgust with herself subsided, but she was still stuck.

She was stuck in-between the sinking shame at her failure to keep up with the most basic instructions he had given her starting out on the path, on the one hand, and rising jealousy that he had compared YingYue to a man sitting beside the Throne of God, on the other. The two pulled on her so that she thought her arms would come right out of their joints. She wanted to scream. She wanted to explain. She did not know what would come out of her mouth, repentance or resentment. Inside herself, she twisted around sharply to loosen their grip, pulling first the hand of resentment free, then the hand of repentance. Zaytuna nearly fell back as she released herself, bursting into tears and moaning in pain before her shaykh and Abu Muhammad.

Through her tears, she could see Abu Muhammad looking at her with bare-faced concern, then to Shaykh Abu al-Qasim. Junayd signaled him to stop her. She gasped. *What have I done?* Abu Muhammad got up quickly and knelt beside her. "Zaytuna, all is well. Be quiet and wipe your tears."

Junayd said gently, "Zaytuna. I told you it would be more difficult. Everything that has always been wrong will be clearer to you now. You will be no worse than you were, but it will feel worse. Better you are pained by what you see here than in the next world. Sufis die before we die, so that on That Day when your sight will pierce your soul, you will not be hurt by what you see."

She wiped her eyes with the heel of her palms, like a child.

"My daughter." With those words, she felt his love wash through her, enveloping her, and holding her to him as if she were wrapped in a sling against her mother's breast. As his love ebbed, she was utterly calm and wept again, but this time soft, grateful tears. She sat up straight, looking at her dear uncle and shaykh, and threw the love she felt toward him with all her heart. He smiled, knowing, and nodded to her that she should go.

Zaytuna moved to kiss his hand goodbye, but he pulled it away. She got up and looked behind her. Several people were waiting to see him. They looked at her strangely, but she didn't care. Mustafa was still sitting with the old women, watching her. She reached out to him with the love she felt from sitting with Junayd, the love expanding beyond her. He caught it, bending back just slightly from its force, and smiled broadly. Somehow, even though he had not moved, Mustafa was restraining himself from holding both arms out to her. She wanted to throw herself at his feet and tell him, *I don't know how, but I can marry you. I will marry you.* Then the old pain came back, reminding her that she could not do what would be asked of her in marriage. *He is a brother to you only.* Crossing the courtyard, she sat near him again, but far enough away that the love she was feeling would not be taken for something else.

Mustafa did not speak immediately and she was grateful for it. They watched people coming and going, finding their places to sit for the sama. Finally, he asked, "How are you?"

"The same. I'm alone much of the time. Tein is busy with Ammar. Saliha is busy with her training." She said, "Alhamdulillah," without any bitterness or, as she did in her worst moments, sarcasm.

But he replied as if she had, "If God has given you this trial of being alone, then maybe it's for a reason. Perhaps you should speak to Uncle Abu al-Qasim about it or Auntie Hakima?"

Zaytuna scowled at this unasked-for advice. "Thank you, Shaykh Mustafa." But as she said it, she was reminded that she would not be going to her uncle or auntie anymore, but rather to YingYue for guidance. Whatever peace Junayd had settled on her fled. She couldn't help but look across the courtyard at YingYue. The girl was in the reception hall helping an older woman walk to the their side of the courtyard.

Mustafa followed her eyes. "You know her father left his paper company behind in Taraz to find her a shaykh. She had to leave her mother and brothers behind. They sacrificed a lot to be here."

"Yes." Zaytuna shifted uncomfortably. "She and I talked for a long time yesterday."

"Really?" His tone changed. He was suddenly eager. "Did she tell you how Abu Muhammad had seen her in a dream? He knew that she was coming. Then they got a letter from Uncle Abu Bakr..."

Zaytuna felt sick and cut him off, "Mustafa, please. Stop talking about her. It's enough. I may not be able to marry you, but that doesn't mean this is not hard on me. Especially now, she is to be one of my teachers."

His eyes widened just slightly in surprise, then he said softly, "I'm sorry."

They sat in silence a few moments longer. When Mustafa spoke again, it was a question Zaytuna knew was meant as a peace-offering. "What happened with the murder of that poor woman they found." He swallowed audibly, "The one who was eaten by dogs in the field? God have mercy on her soul."

"Oh! I was able to help them identify her." Zaytuna faced him eagerly. "They never found her head. But they had one of her hands. It was hennaed."

He paled at the description.

Zaytuna ignored his state, becoming more excited as she explained, "This is interesting! Once they found out who she was, it was not long before they found who had killed her." She sat up on her knees. "It was her neighbour. Her neighbour thought the woman had sold herself for sex to her husband, so she killed her. But the wife couldn't find a way to get rid of her, so she hired a butcher's apprentice to cut her up and carry her to the field for the dogs to eat."

Mustafa looked sickened. "Jealousy in women's hands has no good end."

Her mood turned. "I see, only you men have the wisdom and strength to transform petty human jealousies into protecting care worthy of God's own?"

"Fine Zaytuna," he sighed. "Women can jealously guard those in their care as well." He looked away. "But why would the apprentice agree to do such a thing? Where is his fear of God?"

"Because he is poor, Mustafa. Tein said he was in debt from gambling at a nahariyya. Now you have such lofty employment, you don't remember what it is like to be without anything? He carried the garbage from the butcher shop out to the field for the dogs. I imagine he thought, 'Why not this too?'"

They easily fell back into their old ways. "Zaytuna, you just said he gambled at a nahariyya. Obviously, he was not a good man." He shook his head. "He deserves what he gets."

"That's a dangerous prayer!" Zaytuna tucked her head back in a gesture of pious censure. "May God protect you from a prayer like that! Imagine, coming before God to get what you deserve!"

He was wide-eyed with the realization and corrected himself, "God, protect me and teach this man where he has erred so he can repent of his actions before he meets you on the Last Day."

"Oh, you have become a scholar now! You cannot even say, 'God forgive him'."

His shoulders slumped. "Zaytuna, my God, please don't let me become one of them."

Realizing she was under the watchful eyes of the old women nearby, especially Auntie Hakima, she did not lean in, but coaxed him back to her with a whispered, "Won't I always tell you?"

"Yes."

"You didn't ask how they found her."

"Zaytuna, I don't want to know."

She ignored him, "Tein asked the henna artists if they'd ever seen work like this before. It had an odd design, the moon with the face of a woman within it."

"My God," he gasped. "Did he carry the hand to the henna artists?"

Zaytuna laughed at him. "No, they had someone do a drawing of it."

"Of course," he shook his head. "Had no one reported her missing?"

"She was a prostitute who worked on her own."

"The poor woman, may she be made whole again, and may God forgive her for her sins."

"Her sins, Mustafa?"

"She was a prostitute, Zaytuna."

"And how did she end up there?"

"Women have choices. She could have remained with her family. She could have married for protection."

"You know a lot about women, do you?"

Mustafa fell silent.

"So pious. You know what Tein is investigating now? The murder of one of you scholars by his slave. Women have choices. She chose to kill him. You can imagine why."

Mustafa turned to her. "What? Who was killed? Do you know the name?"

"al-Qatafi, I think."

"Imam Hashim al-Qatafi?"

Zaytuna nodded. "May his grave be narrow."

His eyes widened. "Look at you! You just criticized me...," then sighed, "I know why she killed him."

"Tein told me, but you, how?"

"Burhan, a fellow hadith scholar," Mustafa shook his head, "sent by God to test my patience and my control over my anger."

She couldn't help but laugh; her anger towards him passed as quickly as it had risen up in her. "He must be awful to test your patience, I have been training you in keeping patient since you were a little boy."

"Zaytuna, this is serious."

She turned on him, "You don't think I know murder is serious?"

Ignoring her, he said, "He was brutal to her. I don't want to say. Burhan told me that she complained of the situation to a scholar, Abu Mubarak Sherwan Ibn as-Salah al-Kurdi. Ibn Salah is a good man. He brought the case before the judge in Karkh to stop the harm being done her. He even argued for her release. Burhan's father was the judge." He huffed. "With such a son, you can only imagine the father. He ruled against the woman and returned her to the imam."

"On what grounds!"

"That one cannot," he looked around to make sure no one heard them, "rape a woman one has sexual rights over. He advised her on how to keep her prayer from interfering with his needs."

She whispered, "Mu'mina was right to kill him." Then she paused, "Tein thinks she's innocent. What she admitted to wasn't murder. But I don't know, Mustafa, she could have done it still. We just don't know how."

Mustafa agreed, "If she did, she had good cause. God forgive her." He looked around. "I don't know how I did not hear of his funeral prayer, but I'm glad I missed it. I would have had a hard time praying for him. God help me, it's going to be bad enough I'll have to go to the house to pay my respects." He looked up to the heavens, saying, "God forgive me."

She leaned in and said, "It's alright. This is a terrible thing."

"Have they arrested her?" He asked.

"Yes."

"Tein must have this information, then. It must be taken into account when she goes before the chief of police to be judged."

"I could tell Tein, but it is better if you speak to him directly. You heard the whole story. Give him everyone's names."

"Yes, I will." He paused, "Zaytuna, don't take this the wrong way, but more than the girl's life is at stake. The reputation of the scholarly community as well. If we do not hold our own accountable, who will trust us? There was some outcry when Abu Burhan sided with Imam Hashim in the case she brought against him."

"Take it the wrong way? You must hold corrupt scholars to account!"

He leaned towards her. "Burhan told me that they ruined the reputation of Ibn Salah's son, the man who brought her case against Imam Hashim. I think Burhan meant to threaten me with the news."

He sat up straight. "I will not be bowed, Zaytuna. She must get the fairest of trials."

"Good!" She smiled warmly at him.

He sighed in relief. "I will go to see Tein in the morning. May God protect the girl and forgive her for what she was driven to do."

Satisfied with this prayer, Zaytuna said, "Amin." Dawud was giving the call to prayer; young men began laying out reed mats and sheepskins in preparation for it.

He looked in the direction of the young men, agitated. "I'm upset. I don't know how I can sit here for the sama. I'll pray, then maybe I'll go. I don't know."

Seeing his agitation, she realized how undone she herself had become since she arrived. She had fallen into spasms of resentment in front of her shaykh. Then shame. Then he pulled her back to love to rescue her. Then she just as quickly fell back into resentment again. Then anger at Mustafa. She gasped, "My God," as she looked at herself. Forgetting the words of warning that Junayd had just said to her, she despaired. *Why don't you just leave? Uncle is being kind, no more. He's put you in YingYue's hands because he won't be bothered with you.* She wanted to throw up, and tasted bile in the back of her throat. She muttered under her breath, "You are nothing."

YingYue across the courtyard. She had been watching her and Mustafa deep in conversation the whole time. The girl looked like she was going to cry. Zaytuna's gut warmed. She failed to repress a smile, wanting to spit the bile she'd been tasting in YingYue's direction. Keeping an eye on the girl, she leaned close to Mustafa, whispering in his ear, "You'll do better if you stay." He nodded, leaning into her whisper, and Zaytuna watched YingYue's misery with pleasure.

Suddenly she felt a sharp pain in her chest. She pressed her hand against her heart, looking down, feeling inexplicably as if she had been shot with an arrow. Looking up in a panic, she demanded of herself, *What were you thinking? How could you be so cruel?* She stood up in a rush, nearly losing her balance in the shame of it, and took a few steps towards where the women were lining up to pray. There was a clear path to the reception hall and wanted to leave. What was the point in praying with such a filthy soul?

Someone placed a hand on her shoulder and she was rooted to the spot. The hand lifted, and just as suddenly she could move again. She turned to see Auntie Hakima. Zaytuna looked down into the old woman's grey eyes and was gripped with fear.

Auntie Hakima said, "You'll pray. Go, then, if you think you are so extraordinary as to be beyond God's reach, but you are obligated to pray no matter what state you are in."

Zaytuna nodded. Auntie Hakima had known everything. The conversation with Mustafa. The pleasure she took in YingYue's suffering. How she had despaired. The shame was smothering. She struggled to breathe evenly as she followed the old woman dutifully to take a place in the last rows behind the men. When the prayer was finished, after giving her greetings to the angels on either side of her, but before Abu Muhammad had recited the supplication for them all, she rose and slipped out the front door into the darkening street.

THE THIRD DAY

12

M ustafa woke long before the dawn prayer. He slept fitfully throughout the night, fearful that he would miss Tein at the police offices. It would be a long walk to the Round City. He'd have to be ready to explain himself to the Night Watchmen. If he were stopped, he would simply tell them the truth. He was going to pray the dawn prayer at al-Mansur's mosque before consulting with police investigators on an important matter. *They should believe me.* He placed his scholar's turban on his head. Yet the thought of what he was about to do stopped him in place and weakened him at the knees. It was bad enough that he was going to help bring to light evidence that would challenge powerful men, but the scholars and the police had no love between them. More often than not, the police were the ones inflicting the political will of the caliph and his courtiers against them. Either the elite scholars or the police could ruin him before he had a reputation to be ruined. He put his hand against the wall of his room to steady himself.

As he stared at his bedroll, unmade in his haste to leave, his eyes were drawn to the small blanket hanging on his wall, made by his mother when he was still in her belly. It was like a patched Sufi cloak for a child but embroidered around every seam with vines and leaves.

It hung low on the wall so he could see it easily when seated or lying on his side. He thought for a moment that he would sit down and look at it for a while to reorient himself. His mother, also named Zaytuna, was a strong woman if there ever was one. He missed her. *May God protect her secret.* He remained standing.

And what would his love say? His own Zaytuna would not think twice about her reputation in the pursuit of justice. *But what reputation does she have to lose?* He sighed, *My own Zaytuna.* She wasn't his own anymore, maybe she never was. The loss of it hit him and made him want to sit again. He thought of her last night, urging him on to hold these men to account, and the girl, guilty or not, sitting in that prison. What could the Abu Burhans of this world do to him? Ruin his reputation as they did Ibn Salah's son? They would have to lie to do it, but who would believe it? So he would be driven out of the circles of hadith and go back to being a potter. Zaytuna would be proud of him. He snuffed out his oil lamp, opened the door to his room onto the small courtyard he shared with four other families and walked out into the dark alleyway ahead.

Pulling his quilted robe close, he tightened the sash around his waist against the morning cold. He hurried along, keeping his eyes to the side roads around him. His coin purse was under his arm, slung across his body against his skin, under layers of clothes, where no thief in a hurry would be able to get it. There was a night watchman ahead of him with a torch casting eerie moving light and shadow onto the streets that was almost worse than the darkness itself. The watchman turned around and walked toward him. As the torchlight reached him, the man gave him a hard look. Mustafa greeted him, his voice catching. The watchman said nothing in return and Mustafa rushed past. A person here and there walked like him, pushing ahead, saying nothing.

The smell of baking bread hit him from the marketplace road and he realized how hungry he was. He scolded himself for not bringing some dates. It would be some time yet before the bread would be ready. He looked down the marketplace road toward the bakeries within. He thought of the wheat and barley loaves in every shape, some thin as paper, others round and thick, and still others pulled oblong with sharp twists at the corners. The bakers stacked them, one on top of the other, in great bins or on wide shelves, sometimes reaching as high as the ceiling of the shop. His stomach grumbled at not getting what it wanted. A watchman emerged from the market and yelled at him, "You! What are you doing!" Only then did he realize he'd stopped at the smell of the bread and was looking into the marketplace like some kind of fool.

He couldn't think to answer and walked as quickly as he could without running toward the Basra Gate High Road. He looked behind him, the watchman's torch was getting further behind. Mustafa slowed down and took a deep breath and saw the High Road opening up before him. Come sunrise, the wide thoroughfare would be thick with people walking or riding. Donkeys would part the crowds, pulling delivery carts or the wares of hawkers who sold door-to-door. Wealthy men would ride on horseback, their women in litters. Dung collectors with their carts were never far behind. But at this hour the road was nearly empty. He could see just one man ahead, pulling his cart himself, strapped in where the donkey should be. There were two guards on horseback in the distance, their staves raised high, riding toward the fortified city.

As he passed the road leading to the Sharqiyya Mosque, he heard the call to the night prayer coming down its wide avenue. At the rate he was walking, Mustafa hoped he would be early. He needed time to sit in peace in al-Mansur's mosque before going to the police offices.

Finally he could see the Gate House. It was lit by great torches moving in the early morning breeze, their flames casting moving shadows onto the road ahead of him. Several men were standing along its bridge. Their arms were crossed and they were stomping their feet to stay warm while they waited for the guards to finish pulling the gates open for the day. He reached the bottom of the bridge and stopped. The acrid smell of the torches hit him and he was suddenly cold and trembling. He heard himself say aloud in a voice unlike him, "What is this? Are you afraid? Move. Now." Nodding to himself, he stepped forward.

The guards were lashing open the great doors of the Gate House as he reached the top of the bridge. He called out, "Good morning!" and they grumbled their own greetings in return. Smiling grimly at them, he thought, *I'd rather not be here either, my brothers.* Then he heard the call to prayer coming from the great mosque at the centre of the Round City and took it as a slap, muttering, "God forgive me."

In the dead of the morning, the call traveled further than it would in the din of the day. A repeater stood high in the Gate House sending the call out to nearby neighbourhoods. The mosques in those neighbourhoods would pick up that call, sending it on in turn to neighbourhoods further out, until the whole city resounded in the quiet of morning with these voices, some mellifluous, like angels singing, and others grating, like the sound of jagged metal dragging on rocks. "Hurry to the prayer! Hurry to salvation!" He heard the words as if they were coming from a voice within him and replied aloud, "Here I am God."

People were coming up behind him as he stepped out of the Gate House onto the bridge crossing the first of the ramparts protecting the City. There were more than a dozen men behind him now, quickening their step in response to the call. The four Gates of the city would be open now. Men from neighbourhoods close to the city, and those who lived within its walls, would be making their way through the four main roads to al-Mansur's mosque at its centre.

Mustafa hoped he'd have time first to collect himself before praying. His mother had watched over him as he did his ritual ablutions when he was little and learning to pray, making sure his ears were clean and the dirt was out from under his nails. Then she'd tug his clothes straight before letting him stand on the prayer rug. If he fidgeted during the prayer, she'd slap him on the back of his head afterward he finished, once knocking his cap off his head, scolding, "Do you know where you were, boy? You were standing before the Throne of God!"

Passing the smaller arched gates leading to the neighbourhoods nestled within the City walls, he saw a good number of men were coming out onto the torch lit road. Mustafa rubbed the back of his head as he looked on them with approval. Here at least were men who understood that prayer, and prayer in congregation, is better than sleep.

He slowed as he walked past the police offices, wondering which was Grave Crimes. He felt sick. *Go pray. Go pray.*

Finally, he passed the last gates before the gardens and to the green-domed mosque of al-Mansur at its centre. Men encircled the fountains outside the mosque, performing their ablutions. They cupped the flowing water to wash their hands, head, neck, arms, and bare feet, even in this cold. He stood waiting his turn. He finally found a spot among them, but had to stand sideways to get a hand into the bracing water. A man laughed with the first shock of it, saying to the one beside him, "The cold is early this year. There'll be ice gathering before long." Mustafa looked harshly at them for speaking while doing their ablutions. He said, "Alhamdulillah," loud enough that they could hear the scolding for what it was. But he kept his eyes down, not wanting to face them after it, but at least there was no more chat.

He finished and gave up his space to another man, then found a spot in the ever-growing prayer lines in the main hall. Mustafa tugged his robe straight, and asked God to accept him and his prayer. He raised his hands and said, "Allahu akbar," opening his two cycles of prayer in greeting to the mosque, but he couldn't focus. With every movement he worried about getting involved in this case, then scolded himself for his fear of doing what was right. Afterwards, he sat back and recited God's name, Allah, to himself, over and over, to centre himself. He exhaled slowly, "Aaaaa," slowly, then inhaled, "llaaaaahhh." The pain in his gut eased.

He looked around him, falling into admiration of the mosque, lit so exquisitely from oil lamps hanging from every archway. The building expanded over the years, mirroring the growth of the city itself. People came to the city of Baghdad from every quarter of the empire and the great mosque could not hold them all. There were grand mosques elsewhere in the city, but this one at the centre of the empire was the sign of its greatness. The caliphs' palace had been here once, alongside the mosque, until they moved across the Tigris to fortified estates on the east side of the city. The abandoned palace had, little by little, been properly given over to the needs of the people. No matter what the caliphs did, no matter how they played politics with the scholars' lives, the religion and this place belonged to the believers.

There were two great courtyards amidst the rows of archways. Over fifty carved teak columns held up its high roof, each column topped by glorious capitals. Where the yellow-brick walls were not covered by gypsum, there were tiles painted with the richest blue. Its ornately carved minbar on which the imam stood to give the Friday sermon, could be matched by none in the world. Nor could its tiled mihrab, indicating the direction of Mecca, and its maqsura, guarding the caliph so that he could pray out of view from the people be compared to any other. And where was there another mosque with a water clock keeping time for the prayers and the people?

The call came to stand in prayer. Men filled the mosque from column to column. No women. He knew Zaytuna would have something to say about that. *But*, he answered her imagined objection, *it would be inadvisable for them to venture out in the dark to pray at the mosque. Why doesn't she consider these practical matters before becoming incensed?* He tugged at his robe again and prepared himself to stand before God, but all he could think about was the task ahead of him. He apologized to his mother as much as to God as he moved through the cycles of prayer.

Afterwards, he walked with the throngs of men in a hurry to get out of the mosque. He held his new robe close against himself to protect it from catching on the metal of scabbards he saw on men here and there. A man who had left the mosque ahead of him, went into one of the police offices.

A guard stood before the first door. The guard's robe was stained and too thin for the cold of the morning; he was obviously wearing every bit of clothes he had in layers and only had a scrap of black cloth on his head for a turban. Mustafa felt the warmth of his own robe and the firmness of the well-wound cloth of his scholar's turban on his head. He said a prayer for the man, then greeted him, "Assalamu alaykum, I'm here to see Ammar at-Tabbani of the Grave Crimes Section."

The guard looked at his turban and didn't even ask his name. "Walaykum assalam, Imam. He's the one who walked in just ahead of you. That office down there. Four doors." The guard paused, "Hold on, I'll walk you there." The guard sounded embarrassed, "I would have been at the prayer, too, but I can't leave my post. I'll make it up later." He paused again, then asked, "Imam, do you think it is a sin?"

Mustafa bought some time by repeating his question, "Missing the prayer because you have to be at your post? They will not excuse you?"

The guard said, "No, I have asked. They will not permit me."

He was unused to this despite it happening to him more and more. He'd counselled in his own neighbourhood, but he knew those people, and they knew him. They most often came to the right answer together. But now that he could afford the clothes that made him look the part, he often found himself in situations like this with nothing to say or, he feared, the wrong thing.

In his distress over the morning and surprise at the question, he could not remember how Imam Ahmad ibn Hanbal would respond. It was not an excusable illness, but it was not out of laziness, and it was not his choice. Grasping, he said, he hoped, in a tone of voice that conveyed assurance, "The Prophet, alayhi salam, said, 'Works are with their intentions'." He thought for a second, then added, "You only need to look into your heart to know."

The man stopped before the door and faced Mustafa. "My heart?"

Mustafa wished he had not said the second part. The man just wanted simple guidance. He wasn't a scholar of the law, but these questions, they were answered by hadith scholars in the past. He was barely a hadith scholar himself. But these kinds of questions were answered by the aunts and uncles in the Sufi community. *One does not need to be a legal scholar to share the wisdom of the Prophet with the people on matters such as these. It is not as if this is a marriage contract or a detailed point on ritual law.* He stopped himself. *Perhaps it is a detailed point on ritual law?*

He didn't know what to say, then thought of his Uncle Abu al-Qasim. He was a legal scholar himself, but he would say these questions were not about the law, they were about people's relationship with God and the people needed to be put at ease and pushed gently to do better, to become better human beings. Mustafa spoke again, more confidently now, "The Prophet said, 'Consult your heart'. That which is right puts your soul at ease and makes the heart tranquil. Wrongdoing is when your soul wavers and your breast is uneasy, even if people have repeatedly given a legal opinion in favour of it."

"Oh," the guard said, his head down, "Then I am sinning. My heart is not easy."

Mustafa closed his eyes for a moment in frustration. *Why is this so hard?* He took a breath. "I meant that the Prophet, alayhi salam, wanted us to cultivate a beautiful character within us so that we can rely on our heart's compass rather than having to go to scholars for every little thing."

"May God reward you," the guard nodded. But by the look in his eyes and how he sounded, Mustafa knew it wasn't the answer he wanted.

Mustafa gave up. "You did not sin, but you must ask again if you can be relieved to pray."

The man smiled then, relief washing the worry from his face, and opened the door for him, indicating for Mustafa to fall back so that he could be introduced. Mustafa saw Tein sitting on the couch on the far side, leaning over, rubbing his eyes awake. The guard said, "Excuse me, Imam, I forgot to ask your name?"

"Mustafa ibn Zaytuna," he paused, he wasn't sure if he should say 'al-Jarrari' anymore since he was no longer a potter. Then he felt the loss of who he was for who he was becoming and consciously took the name for himself, saying with pride, "al-Jarrari."

The guard looked at Mustafa oddly, the way some people did when they heard him using his mother's nasab, 'son of Zaytuna', and left it out when he introduced him, "Ghazi Ammar, Imam Mustafa al-Jarrari is here to see you."

Tein looked up at hearing his name, stood and came forward quickly. "Is anything wrong? Why are you here?"

Mustafa stepped forward past the guard, nodding to him in thanks, then addressed Tein, "No. Nothing! Alhamdulillah. I have information for you."

Tein nodded with relief and said to Ammar, "This is Mustafa."

"How have we never met?" Ammar stepped forward. "I heard stories about you late at night when we were camped along the frontier."

Tein went to the far side of the room and indicated to Mustafa to sit on the main couch where he had been sitting a few moments earlier.

"Information?" Tein prompted.

Mustafa nodded, and brought himself to the task at hand. "The girl you are holding for the death of Imam Hashim. Do you know what her life was like with him?"

"Yes," Tein said. "She told us. She was his slave and he used her…"

Mustafa interrupted, somewhat harshly, "It was more than you suspect."

Tein leaned forward.

"I know she was his slave and should expect," Mustafa stammered, "expect him to have intercourse with her as he liked. But this was different. She's a pious girl. She prayed for hours on end. Even when he had called her to bed, she would not go but remained in prayer. Any decent man would respect her piety and leave her alone." Mustafa grew hot. "Walla, he should have been grateful for the blessings such a slave would bring to his household!" He stopped to collect himself before going on. "My apologies, I find this man so abhorrent. He is a stain on the scholarly community."

Ammar himself sat forward. "What happened?"

"The imam took her from the prayer rug. He took her while she was in prostration." Mustafa looked at Ammar, who he could see wondered how he had this information. "He admitted all this in court."

"Wait, this went to religious court?"

"Yes." Mustafa continued, "His treatment of her was so bestial that one day when she was in the marketplace she stopped a legal scholar and complained to him about it, begging him to bring a complaint to court on her behalf. The man, may God reward him for his good character, is Abu Mubarak Sherwan Ibn as-Salah al-Kurdi. He filed a complaint claiming physical harm and prevention from worship."

Tein drew in a sharp breath. Mustafa turned to him, saw the worry on his face, and said, "You see why I had to come."

Tein nodded.

"What else?" Ammar asked.

"Imam Hashim admitted it all as his right established in law. Ibn Salah countered that the harm was not permitted. He also argued that due to her great piety and the harm already done to her, that Imam Hashim should release her."

"And the judgment?"

"The judge was not sympathetic. He was a friend of Imam Hashim."

"Was this in the district of Karkh?"

"Yes."

Ammar stood up. "So Qadi Abu Burhan's court." He turned to Tein, "You haven't had to deal with him yet. He's the religious court judge for the district of Karkh. If there's a case involving family disputes or contracts, Ibn Marwan sends the people involved to handle that part of the case there. You know exactly how he's going to rule every time." He turned to Mustafa, "Didn't Ibn Salah know about him? Why would be bring the case before him?"

"I don't know."

"Mustafa," Tein asked, "what happened in court?"

"Abu Burhan agreed that it was Imam Hashim's right. His opinion was that while injunctions to release pious slaves were well-meaning," Mustafa paused, looking out the open door, his eyes unfocused on what was beyond it. "*Well-meaning*. He described God's call for us to release slaves about whom we know any good *well-meaning*." He shook his head and turned back to Ammar, "He ruled that these 'pious injunctions' are not legally binding. In other words, Imam Hashim did not have to sell the girl."

"Was this case held in public?" Tein interjected.

"Oh yes." Mustafa said, "I understand, there was a great deal of criticism leveled at both Imam Hashim and Qadi Abu Burhan."

Tein turned to Ammar, "There must be people who wanted to see him punished. And what about his wife? Have we even considered that she would want him dead for humiliating her in public? Or frame Mu'mina for the humiliation?"

Ammar ignored him. "What about the harm to the girl?"

"Oh there!" Mustafa exclaimed. "He instructed her to pray her obligatory prayers on time, and to ask Imam Hashim's permission before praying supplemental prayers, so he could use her for his needs without interrupting her in the future," he explained bitterly.

Ammar looked pained. "She certainly had just cause to kill him."

"So did others!" Tein interrupted.

Mustafa replied to Ammar, "I understand that religious scholars are divided on whether or not a slave is to be executed for murder, but the police chief should know that she killed him in self-defence. That should only be the blood price."

"You don't understand." Ammar leaned in. "The police chief is under no obligation to take anything you religious scholars say about the law into account. So he'll decide what he wants to do with her. And what you think of as 'self-defence' will only read to him as motive. What you've said makes it more likely that the police chief will accept her confession as intentional murder and she'd be executed."

"Oh." Mustafa's head sank.

"Right now, the case is going to him as an unclear confession of intentional murder or a confession of unintentional murder. The chief will decide which. I've seen people go free. I've seen the blood price ordered. But he could also execute, even on unintentional murder. I wasn't here when this happened, but..."

Tein interrupted, "Even on an unintentional killing?"

"Listen." Ammar said, "A man was guiding another man who was blind and not watching where he was going. The blind man stepped on a sleeping beggar, wounding him and the wound ultimately killed him. The police chief was going to let them both off with a blood-price, but someone who wanted the blind man dead whispered in his ear. He let the guide off and not only convicted, but executed the blind man for murder."

"Someone whispered in his ear!"

Ammar took a harsh tone, "Tein, you don't like Ibn Marwan, but this is why he only sends clear-cut cases to the chief. Every ruling is the chief's discretion." Ammar turned back to Mustafa, "I have to ask you, why do you care?"

"Because of what was done to her." Mustafa looked to Tein, afraid he would disapprove, but said it anyway, "Because of who did it to her. How can the people trust the scholars of this community if we do not hold a beast in our midst to account? Everything depends on the righteousness of our character." He paused. "Abu Burhan's son, Burhan, threatened to destroy my reputation if I stood up on matters such as this. These animals must not be the bearers of our faith."

"I agree with you there," said Ammar.

Tein asked Mustafa, "If it comes out that you helped Mu'mina? What then?"

He answered with a confidence he did not feel, "It is in God's hands. I must do what is right." Then the resolution came to him. It was the only way to help her and to bring Abu Burhan to account, he said, "Her case must be adjudicated in a religious court!"

"The crime happened in Karkh," Ammar scoffed. "That's Abu Burhan's jurisdiction. I would imagine he'd look forward to seeing the girl punished if your account of the trial is correct."

"I mean another court," Mustafa shook his head. "Abu Burhan's treatment of her in the first place must be exposed as well!"

Tein sat up.

Ammar said, "I'd not be sorry to see one of you elite pieces of shit brought low in one of their own courts."

Mustafa's face burned at the insult.

"He doesn't mean the likes of you, Mustafa." Tein pleaded with Ammar, "Come on, this man is my brother."

Ammar did not reply.

Mustafa put a hand to his face, embarrassed that his offence showed so easily, but felt he must defend himself. "I assure you..."

"Mustafa." Tein stopped him.

He nodded, taking the correction. "Please, Ghazi Ammar. Please send the case to a different religious court. It is the only way to see these scholars punished."

"That's not how it works." Ammar laughed at him. "We don't transfer cases to the religious courts. The police only arrest the political cases of heresy and deliver the defendant to the chief judge's office at the Mazalim High Court. Like I said before, if a case has non-criminal elements, we advise people to seek arbitration or petition the lesser religious courts themselves on those matters. We don't bring cases to them. It'll have to be petitioned by an outsider."

Mustafa felt embarrassed again; he should have known.

"And if you can get the case to religious court, be prepared. You think they won't use all their connections against you?" Ammar looked Mustafa up and down. "I'm not sure you have the stomach for that."

At this further insult, Mustafa stood, crossed the room to Ammar, and looked down on him with his hands tight at his side. "I will go speak to Ibn Salah today on this matter."

Tein stood and put his arm around him. Mustafa acknowledged it and gratefully took a step back.

"If it gets moved to a religious court," Tein said to Ammar, "that would at least give us time to prove she's innocent. We can start by stopping at the hospital to speak to the doctor about poisons on our way to Baratha today. You told them we'd be coming for it. It won't take much time."

Ammar put his hands on his knees and stood, saying to Mustafa,

"Fine, see if you can get the case moved." Then to Tein, "Since it's on the way to my parents, I'll do this one thing for you. If that corpse washer friend of your sister's is there, I can ask her a few questions. You'll see how this adds up against the girl, Tein. The rest is on your head." Ammar pointed his finger at Tein, making sure he understood. "I'm doing this for your sake, on the honour of our friendship. The girl is guilty enough to be prosecuted one way or another and I'll prove it to you."

Mustafa stood suddenly in his relief and turned to Tein who looked angry at Ammar, but grasped Mustafa's arm, nodding all the same. Tein said, "We have what we need to keep investigating."

13

The hospital guard was no better than a boy with a decent scrap of turban on his head and a beard just filling in. He stood wide-legged and eyes sharp as if he were waiting for a riot to come over the Hospital Bridge. Ammar gestured to Tein as they walked up. "Look at this one. Ready for anything." The guard caught sight of them and looked afraid. Ammar was in his leather cuirass, that anyone could see had been well-used in battle and that he had placed his hand with intent on the hilt of his sword. Tein rolled his eyes at Ammar's posturing and tried to look friendly as they approached; but he saw the boy had begun to shake visibly, his face draining of colour.

Ammar said loudly enough for the boy to hear, "I wonder what this one has been up to?"

Assuring him as they approached, Tein followed up, "Don't worry, we're not here for you. We're here to see Doctor Judah ibn Isa, please get someone to tell him that the police from the Grave Crimes Section are here."

The boy ran off inside the hospital, leaving the door unguarded.

"What was that?" Tein asked as they entered, heading for the courtyard.

"What was what? Look Tein, let's make this fast. I don't want us to be late to take my mother to the mosque and you don't want to miss your best meal of the week."

The breeze picked up speed in the arched vestibule, sending cold air through the central courtyard. Tein shivered and crossed his arms. The doctor didn't come immediately, so Tein settled himself against the wall in the sun, looking down the long courtyard, wondering if Saliha was there.

The guard didn't return. Instead, a young Jewish doctor dressed in a blue robe, matching turban, and zunnar belt returned. "Doctor Judah is with a patient and cannot meet with you immediately. He's asked me to get the pharmacist to come and speak with you."

He gestured to them to sit on one of the benches surrounding the fountain and the lemon and bitter orange trees. Tein remained standing in the sun, but Ammar sat on the bench in the shade. He looked at Tein like he was a fool. "You'll catch a chill going in and out of the sun like that."

Tein ignored him and kept an eye on the back of the hospital. An older black man came out of the back, walking directly to them. Was this the pharmacist? The man was tall and slim, with a red turban matching his red patterned, quilted robe over deep brown wool qamis and sirwal. He wore expensive boots and his belt was made of finely tooled matching brown leather. As he approached, he rolled down the narrow sleeves of his robe. Tein admired how he walked slowly and with purpose and unconsciously tugged at his own robe.

"Assalamu alaykum, I am Firdaws ibn Ali ibn Sahl at-Tabari, the pharmacist."

"Waalaykum as-salam, Ammar at-Tabbani, and this is my colleague Tein ibn al-Ashiqa as-Sawda."

The man nodded in Tein's direction, smiling. "The famed ecstatic was your mother?"

"Yes." Tein's heart skipped that a man such as this knew her.

"I was a young man when I saw her preach. I have never forgotten." His eyes narrowed slightly as he looked at Tein. "I remember now, there was a boy circling the crowd, watching out. I was impressed with the focus of his observation. That was you. Fitting that you came to be police given your experience in observation and inclination to protect. I walked by that graveyard many times, hoping to see her again, but I never did. How is she? I would be honoured to visit her if she would permit it."

Tein lowered his eyes. "May God have mercy on her soul. She died many years ago."

"May God protect her secret."

Ammar added, looking between the two of them, "Amin."

Ibn Ali nodded. "Doctor Judah explained the situation to me. I wish I'd had a chance to see the body before he was taken out. The doctor's account was sufficiently detailed to give an opinion, but no more. You would like to know if the man could have died from poisoning or as the side effect of some substance he may have been exposed to?"

"Yes." Ammar answered.

"Several substances could have produced such symptoms, including greater sensitivity to bruising. I am inclined to believe the man was beaten, given the eye injury, and exclude that as a symptom from my assessment. Doctor Judah tells me that there was no burning around his mouth or excess salivation, although," he closed his eyes in obvious frustration, "he neglected to check the anus for burning as a suppository might have been used. I understand neither was there vomiting." He said firmly, "Given the facts to hand, I would suggest belladonna as the primary agent, although other substances may have been involved. It is readily available from a pharmacist or herbalist in the marketplace or could be found growing wild for that matter."

Tein stood straight, his shoulder back, and his legs apart, and tipped his head with respect to Ibn Ali as he asked, "How easy would it be to give him belladonna without him knowing? Or could he have been given it in error?"

"A simple matter. Ten to twenty of the dried or fresh berries, or two to three of the leaves, ground into spiced food would pass unnoticed."

Ammar asked, "And how quickly would it work."

"Immediately. I would suggest that your culprit was with him right before he died."

Tein looked at Ammar. That would mean it came from his home. It could have been Mu'mina, but it also could have been anyone.

"Is it used for anything else?" Ammar asked, "Is there any reason they would have had it at home, and he took it in error?"

"In very small doses it is used for nausea, vomiting, and other digestive ailments, as well as some respiratory difficulties. A poultice can be used on the skin to relieve localized pain. It is also employed with other herbs for seizures, sometimes for sleep, although there are other, better choices. If anyone in his home suffered from one of these ailments, they might have had it readily available. His wife may have used it in drop form to dilate her pupils, although why she would do that rather than using kohl for the same seductive effect, I would not know."

Tein said to Ibn Ali, as a way of saying to Ammar, "Then anyone in his home that morning could have given him the poison. It is only for us to look for motives."

"I understand that the accused enslaved girl used a talisman from a Turkmen curse writer. Belladonna is used in some ritual ceremonies meant to induce visions. I am not familiar with the use among Turkmen shamans. It is possible that the curse writer gave the enslaved girl the poison herself."

Tein gritted his teeth, wishing he had not said anything.

Ammar turned to Tein, "See, it still falls back to her."

An objection was nearly out of Tein's mouth when Judah came out of a nearby ward, wiping his hands dry on a cloth. He snuck a quick look at Tein and addressed Ammar, "Good morning. Has Ibn Ali explained everything?"

Ammar nodded. "Yes, thank you, we have..."

"I brought Ibn Ali up to speed," Judah interrupted. "He agrees with me that barring the involvement of an ifrit, we suspect he was most likely exposed to a poison that caused hallucinations, difficulty breathing, chest pain, and sensitivity to bruising."

Tein glanced at Ibn Ali, but the man's face was passive as if his rank had not just been belittled and his findings mischaracterized.

"Of course, it is up to you to find out if it was accidental or purposeful and, if purposeful, who would have given it to him."

"There is one other thing you can do for me, Doctor Judah," Ammar replied. "Is the woman who helped with the imam's wife that night here? The corpse washer? I'd like to ask her a few questions."

Tein shot a look toward the back of the hospital looking for Saliha.

Ibn Ali stepped in, "I must return to the pharmacy. I will look for her and send her out. She came in this morning."

Tein put his hand on his heart and bowed his head to Ibn Ali. "Thank you, sir."

Ibn Ali bowed his head to all three men and left.

Judah thrust his thumbs in his zunnar belt, and began to add, "I've had some other thoughts..." when Saliha emerged.

Tein noticed her first, and the other two men turned to follow his gaze. Judah fell silent. Her work wrap was wound on her waist like an apron. Its long end draped over her head and around her upper body, covering her, but also uncovering her, showing the perfect balance of her curves and leaving her beautiful face, with its broad smile and laughing eyes, for all to see. Her gaze rested on Tein for just a moment too long then turned resolutely to focus on Ammar.

Tein could see that Saliha was enjoying the attention, and he smiled at her pleasure in it. There was not a twinge of jealousy in him as Ammar and Judah watched how she walked, swaying her hips, and he was relieved. If there was no jealousy, there was no wanting her for himself. But he could not help but notice that Judah's face flashed lust, then anger, until finally settling into an expression more fitting a man who was not her husband. Tein became concerned for her sake. *Look at her, keeping her eyes on Ammar alone. She hasn't looked at the good doctor once. She'll drive that pittance of a man out of his mind, and then she'll feel the wrong end of it. Maybe I should just drag him into the street and get it over with. Make sure he knows he doesn't have a hand over her.*

"Assalamu alaykum, Ghazi Ammar, How can I help?"

Ammar bowed his head with his hand over his heart. "I have a few questions about the night that Imam Hashim died. Can you tell us what his wife said and did?"

"There are things a woman sees that men do not." Tein interjected, taking a step towards her and cutting Judah off, who was, then, forced to step to the side out of Tein's way.

Ammar looked at Tein, eyebrows raised.

Saliha tipped her head in recognition to Tein, but answered Ammar, "Hanan was out of her mind with grief. She firmly believed that their slave had killed her husband with a talisman."

"Hanan's grief was sincere?"

Saliha gasped, "Oh, you suspect her!"

"We suspect everyone until we have enough information."

Tein's anger flashed. He had to wrestle himself back from reminding Ammar with the back of his hand exactly how he had failed this principle, putting Mu'mina's life at risk. His anger escaped him as a suppressed grunt. If Ammar heard it, he didn't show it. Saliha did, and looked at him questioningly.

She turned back to Ammar, "At one point, she had mistakenly pushed against her husband's chest to lift herself up and was horrified that she might have hurt him."

Tein interjected, "That doesn't necessarily mean she didn't want him dead. It could have been guilt over having killed him."

"Perhaps." Saliha shrugged one shoulder suggestively.

"How did she feel about Mu'mina?" Tein asked.

Saliha held Tein's gaze, again, just moments too long. "She hated her."

Ammar asked, "Why? What had the girl done?"

Saliha's eyes hardened, and the warmth of her face dropped away as she turned to answer Ammar. "Nothing. When a woman hates another woman like that, it's the man between them who's done something."

"Noted." Ammar conceded.

Tein inclined his head to Saliha. "Mu'mina suffered under both of them."

"Yes. I can imagine." She looked at Tein again, her features softening.

Judah broke in, "Do you remember anything else?"

Tein glanced at Judah and shook his head at the doctor's pathetic effort to get Saliha to look at him. *Don't work so hard, little man. Who she chooses will be her choice, not ours.* He looked back at Saliha. She was watching him. *Ours.* He had thought, *Ours.* So he did want her for himself. The tremor of the realization moved through his muscles, sinews and bones. Suddenly, wanting her enveloped him, holding his heart and tugging at every cell in his body. She had not looked away. Her face was still, yet shimmering. She saw what he was feeling and he was not ashamed. He threw his shoulders back and opened his whole body to her. He heard her stifle a gasp.

Ammar coughed, breaking the moment. "That's enough. Thank you. We've got what we need." He slapped Tein on the back and tugged his sleeve, forcing Tein to look at him.

Judah stepped forward to break the tension between Tein and Saliha.

Tein did not reply but shifted in his stance away from her. Saliha drew her wrap across her face and cast her eyes downward.

Tein didn't see that Judah had stepped forward again, making a move against him until Ammar had already stepped in front and around Tein, taking a firm grip on both of Judah's shoulders. Tein held back a laugh. Ammar was trying to bring Judah back to where he was, in the hospital, and away from the street where Judah no doubt wanted to drag him to beat the life out of him.

Tein nodded to Saliha and started to back away to give Judah space to calm down, when Saliha said, "Ghazi Ammar, just one thing. When her brother-in-law came in…" She paused, winking at Tein. "A woman notices these things." Then continued to Ammar, "He seemed closer to her than he should be. He did not seem concerned for his brother at all. His attention was entirely focused on her."

"Do you remember anything he said?"

"No. Just how he was with her."

Ammar nodded, one hand still gripping Judah's shoulder. "Thank you. You have been very helpful."

Saliha bowed her head to the men and returned to the back of the hospital. Tein tipped his chin to Ammar, indicating he was going outside. He left without acknowledging Judah and walked through the courtyard, past the young guard, and into the street where he found a spot against a wall in the sun and took a deep breath. He looked up and down the road to see if there were a tavern nearby, out of habit, but also wanting a drink. He wasn't sorry he didn't see one.

He pushed off the wall when he saw Ammar came out.

Ammar grunted, then pointed his finger at him. "If we have to interview her again, you're not coming."

Tein shrugged, then made his point, "Mu'mina would have admitted to giving him poison. You know it. She wasn't ashamed of having killed him with the talisman. She had motive, and she had opportunity. But she didn't do it. Why don't you think more about the brother-in-law?"

"I will give you that it complicates things. But you also heard what the pharmacist said about Turkmens using belladonna for trances." He looked irritated. "I'll interview the family again tomorrow. Alone. I don't want you there with the way you are about this girl. You're free to follow up on the poisons." Ammar looked Tein in the eye. "I'll give you the space you need to follow up this lead. I'll deal with the butcher and whatever else comes up. You just better hope Mustafa can get this case delayed."

"You sound like you doubt her confession now."

"I don't, Tein. I think she did it. I would have killed him too, if I were her. I want you to be sure as well so you can walk away from this when she's executed."

Tein smiled in response, nodding in agreement.

Ammar pulled back. "Is there something wrong with you?"

"I'm going to prove you wrong. If it was poison, then the imam had it the morning he died. It had to come from someone in his house. If he died from the beating he got from gambling debts, I'll find that, too. You promise that you'll question the family about the poison?"

"Didn't I just say that?"

Ammar's heart sank at his friend's confidence. *This could end you.* He was always on the edge of losing his way, turning up drunk or not turning up at all. He'd never come back to himself from her execution if he couldn't see that she was guilty. She wanted the imam dead. She had the means and opportunity to do it, and the curse writer helped. He thought of the scars running across her face and shivered. If Sayyida Fatima were truly by her side, she'd not be in this situation. He looked up at the location of the sun in the sky and said, "Let's go, or we'll be late to take my mother to the mosque."

They crossed the Hospital Bridge in the direction of Baratha. The army encampment was ahead of them in the field just before the Ushnan Bridge. Defensive troops had been stationed there so long that the tents and outdoor cookhouses and latrines had been replaced little by little with permanent barracks. Men were sitting along its walls, resting in the sun, drinking from skins. Boys ran back and forth doing errands.

Tein had told Ammar he was a boy like that, filling skins with water and wine for the men after his mother died. They would throw him a chink of coin and call him "little ghazi." One showed him how to wield a sword. Tein laughed with pride when he described how he could lift it above his head with only one hand, and he was barely eleven years old, dreaming of nothing other than heading out to the frontier. Ammar looked over at Tein. He was still that boy, wanting to be a hero. *My good friend, you are too good. God protect you from yourself.*

Steam and smoke swirled out of the cookhouses, and the smell of grilled meat reached them as they passed. Tein's stomach growled loud enough for them both to hear. Ammar laughed. "Hold on. You'll be at my mother's table after the prayer."

"At least with you Shia, there's no Friday prayer until a leader from the Prophet's family rules the Muslims once more. No boring sermon to withstand."

"Can we not open that up? I have to listen to my parents fight about whether or not we've even got a living Imam. Keep your mouth shut when we get there."

"I swear," Tein raised his hand in a solemn oath, ignoring Ammar, "But I would bear up under a Friday prayer and the worst sermon for a taste of your mother's roasted goat and bread pudding. I would listen closely to that sermon just to smell that meat sizzling in the tannur and know its fat is dripping onto the pudding."

Ammar couldn't help himself and laughed. "You are going to hell, friend. Does your sister's friend know you don't believe in God?"

Tein shrugged. "Probably, those two have no secrets."

"It never bothered Ayzit?"

Tein turned to look at him. "She was barely Muslim herself. She only ever talked about spirits to me."

Ammar asked, "But..."

"The head man of her town said the shahada for all of them when the Muslims arrived. 'Pay the poll tax or join up'. You know how it goes. So he joined them all up. Smart man, he saved them a lot of money." He laughed. "She said they only found out they were Muslim when someone came to teach them to pray."

"But I saw Ayzit pray."

"She knew how to keep the other women in our camp happy. Why do you think she was so eager to marry a man like me, one who would not force her to believe in a god she had no feeling for?"

Ammar shook his head. "I never thought about what happened to people after our troops secured the towns."

"You didn't think," Tein voice turned cold. "Did you think they sent preachers to the vanquished to recite the Qur'an and tell stories about the Prophet, and everyone was so moved that they converted on the spot?"

Ammar felt ashamed, but he didn't understand why. How could he have known? Why was Tein being so harsh with him about it? He changed the subject. "There's the Ushnan Bridge."

"I can almost taste your mother's judhaba."

Ammar joked, hoping Tein's mood had passed. "You only love my mother for her food."

"No, not just that." Tein jibed, "I love your mother mostly because every time we see her, she has a new girl ready for you to marry. There is no better entertainment than your discomfort with her efforts."

Ammar didn't laugh. He knew Tein, and he wasn't trying to be funny. Ammar pushed back at him, knowing how much he hated being called "Bilal," as if all black men could be reduced to the Prophet's companion. "You don't mind her calling you 'Bilal' instead of Tein?"

"Ha! Not your mother. She can call me whatever she likes. Be kind to her, Ammar," resentment crept into his voice, "Your mother is alive. And your mother is good to you."

The reproach felt like a slap, but he said, "Alhamdulillah."

They crossed the bridge, leaving Karkh and entering the suburb of Baratha. They left the main road, winding their way past the larger homes, some grand with two stories, large courtyards within, and no shared walls, through the alleyways with narrow passageways leading to smaller homes, shared by several families, and on out to the edge of the city. If Ammar's mother could not live near Imam Musa al-Kadhim's grave, then she would live in imagined sight of the plain of Karbala. She forced his father to build their home here. Ammar had often found her outside the walls of their home, looking out into the far distance, wailing, "Ya Husayn!" He would join her, and they would weep together over the slaughter of Muhammad's family. His grandson Husayn, so tragically betrayed, robbing the Muslims of his family's noble rule to this day.

Ammar pushed open the gate onto his family's courtyard. The breeze picked up swirls of dust from the dry ground making small mounds of dirt against the bricks that lined the vegetable garden. Gourd vines were still growing on trellises nearly breaking under the weight of the fruit. Ammar's mother had already pulled up and braided the onions and the garlic. She hung them up alongside the dried herbs in the storage room next to the stable, other vegetables would be stored in a cool spot dug underneath it or pickled in large jars lining its shelves. His brother had surely been by to tend to the goats. God knows his father hadn't. Ammar had spent his childhood driving the goats into the plains beyond and watching masses of soldiers marching out across the great road that connected Baghdad to Kufa wishing for a way out.

Ammar opened the new door to the family house. It was tightly fitted into the brick, and he took pride in the sturdy feel of it. He touched the plaster jammed into the cracks in the planks and smiled to himself. The workman he'd hired had done a good job.

Tein put his hand on the wood as they walked through. "Was your father happy with you at last?"

"He didn't try to hit me, so I think that is a 'Yes'."

"I do not smell meat roasting."

Ammar looked back at him. "She'll have something in the pot. Stop it."

His mother ran toward them from the back of the house. "Ammar, Habibi! And my Bilal, your black face is as beautiful as ever. Your eyes shine like the light of the moon on a dark night! Mashallah! How is your sister? She never comes to visit me."

"She's busy with work, Auntie. I hardly see her myself."

"Shameful not to see her brother, but even more shameful that she doesn't visit me. You two without a mother and me without a daughter." She put her hand on Ammar's cheek. "This son, will he ever give me a daughter-in-law to love as my own and to help me around the house?"

Ammar looked toward the back of the room where his father was lounging on a low couch, ignoring them. He looked down at his mother's pleading face, and softened, saying, "Inshallah."

"Inshallah. He always says 'God willing,'" she slapped his cheek lightly. "We know you do not mean if God wills, you mean if you will. God forgive you, you'll put your mother in her grave without grandchildren."

"Mother, you have grandchildren. My brother has given you four.

And I know that Tahirah comes and helps you around the house just as Muhsin comes and takes care of your goats along with his own. They live just next door."

"Muhsin was just here, alhamdulillah. But Muhsin and Tahirah's children are not your children, habibi. Not yours. Do not let your mother die unhappy."

"Auntie," Tein said, "you must know of someone for him."

Ammar shot a look at Tein.

He was busy trying to squirm out of his mother's grasp when his father called across the room, "Get money from this son!"

Not even a salam from the old man. Ammar went to his father, took his hand, and kissed it. "Assalamu alaykum, Father."

His father faced him when he spoke, but the words were yelled across the room to his mother, "Give your mother the money for the khums; I'm not paying tax to these people who say they speak to an Imam we can't see."

"Do not say such things!" His mother screamed, nearly in tears.

"You are above my command now that Lady Fatima speaks to you!"

Ammar looked toward Tein and jerked his head to indicate to take his mother outside. Tein spoke to her quietly. She pulled her wrap off the peg on the wall and wound it around herself, ready to go to the mosque. Tein opened the door for her, and the two of them went outside to wait.

Ammar looked back at his father. The few greasy straggling hairs left on the sides of his head curled back behind his ears. The old man's robe had fallen open, and his fat belly pressed at his qamis. Ammar thought he could smell alcohol on him. His father slurred slightly, "Be a good son and give your mother the money."

"Will you come to the mosque today with us, Father?"

He pointed to his foot, no more swollen than it ever had been, and said, "This old foot. I can't do much with it anymore. You go on."

Ammar bowed to him and left, shutting the front door firmly behind him. Tein and his mother were waiting at the gate to the street. At the sound of the door closing, his mother stepped forward to face Ammar, pleading, "Habibi, you cannot do it!"

"I'll give you the money for the khums, mother, don't worry."

"No. The girl." She looked up at Tein, leaning on his arm, and asked, "Her name?"

Tein bent down to her. "Mu'mina."

Now Ammar understood Tein's mood. It was too much. Tein would get that meal in him, then he'd hear about this the whole way back to Baghdad. *Using my mother against me! Ya Rabb!*

Holding his hands up to his mother to placate her. "Mother you don't..."

"No, habibi," she interrupted. "Thank God, I understand now. I had a dream." She reached out taking both of his hands. "More than a dream. I woke in the night and walked out beyond the house to look to Karbala. Light was shining from it, rising from the plain to the heavens. Sayyida Fatima walked out of the light." She squeezed his hands tightly. "She walked out of the light, but her clothes were light itself, her face was light itself. She spoke to me, and her words were light. She said, 'Do not let any harm come to my daughter. She was enslaved. She lost her mother. I have taken her as my own. She belongs to me'."

Ammar was perfectly still. His mother's eyes were glistening with tears and joy, a kind of joy that he had never seen in her before. Then he heard a voice behind him, "Ya Ammar! I have glad tidings of paradise for you!" He spun around, but there was no one behind him. The door was shut. His brother's house was closed against the cold. Ammar shook off his mother's hands and ran around the side of the house. There was no one there.

His mother called out to him, "My son! My son!"

Tein was behind him before he knew it. "Ammar!"

Ammar looked at him wildly, grabbing him. "The voice."

"What?"

"The voice I've been hearing behind me. I heard it again."

"What's it saying, man!"

His mother reached them, taking hold of Ammar again. "What is it?"

"I've been hearing a voice, calling to me, 'Ya Ammar! I have glad tidings of paradise for you!'"

"My son! Don't you recognize that as what the angels said to Hurr before he left Yazid's army to side with Husayn defending the Prophet's family at Karbala? The promise of paradise! The promise of paradise! He was martyred in Husayn's cause!"

He stared at her wide-eyed, unable to speak.

"This is a call to you to be Hurr. Like Hurr, you must leave your own army to join Husayn. Like Hurr, you must put your hands out to Husayn and beg for forgiveness. Join the fight for justice, my son! There's time for you and time for Mu'mina. Do not be late!"

His head started buzzing, he began to feel dizzy. He wanted to put his hand over her mouth, make her stop speaking.

Her voice dropped. "Sayyida Fatima spoke of you to me. I didn't know that she meant you when she asked that this girl be protected." She looked back to Tein, tears in her eyes. "I didn't know until my Bilal explained." She squeezed Ammar's arm again. "Lady Fatima begs you to save her!"

Tein pulled back and whistled on the inhalation.

He turned his back on them both and searched the horizon for Karbala. *What have I done?* Flashes of his fear of the girl rose up within him. He tried to turn away from it. The fear came round to face him. She was a black dog with a scarred face, baring its teeth and crouched before him ready to attack. *What have I done?* He strained his eyes looking for Sayyida Fatima. Falling to the ground, he begged for forgiveness. He begged her to show him the girl as she saw her, but the scarred face of the snarling dog remained before him. Ammar looked up at his mother, choking on his shame. He was still afraid, but he forced himself to declare, "No harm will come to her."

He expected Tein to be triumphant, throwing his guilt in his face. He would deserve as much, but instead, his friend seemed hopeful. Ammar stood, leaving the dust of the earth on his knees and hands, and said to him, "We will do this. We will find a way. I will go see the widow and brother-in-law today. You must investigate the poisons. This is all that matters."

Looking out toward Karbala once more, Ammar said, "I'll hold my hands out for forgiveness, like Hurr, to Ibn Marwan."

He faced Tein, but the hope in his friend's eyes was gone, replaced by profound sadness as if he would weep.

Ammar touched him. "Tein. I promise, I will fight for her."

Tein shook his head at him, as if Ammar did not understand.

His mother nodded to the two of them in gratitude. She stepped between the two men giving them an arm each as they walked through the gate and on to the mosque.

14

M ustafa was just making his way into the courtyard when he heard Yulduz, "Will that woman ever learn to keep out of everyone's business?" He thought, *What has Zaytuna done now?* Marta and Yulduz were sitting against the wall, legs out. They were right up next to each other, sharing Marta's honey-yellow wool shawl around their shoulders. Marta had a pile of leeks beside her and was carving off slices of the white ends with a paring knife; the bits dropped into a basket in her lap. Yulduz was sorting beans and so intent on her work and complaining about Zaytuna that she did not see him come in. Mustafa called out his greetings and bowed his head to them, hand over his heart. "Assalamu alaykum."

Marta replied for the two of them, elbowing Yulduz to take note.

Yulduz looked up, pointed to Zaytuna's room. "She's in there, muttering away at God."

He looked at her in shock. *God protect me from these women.*

Marta returned to her conversation with Yulduz. "Atournia doesn't mean any harm. She just likes to help, and well..."

Mustafa closed his eyes for a moment and rebuked himself. *They were not speaking about Zaytuna.* God forgive me.

Rhythmic breathing was coming from within Zaytuna's room, one breath in, one breath out, for every syllable, "La illaha illallah, la illaha illallah, la illaha illallah," over and over again. He stood still listening for a moment then coughed to let her know he was outside. The breathing continued.

He said, "Assalamu alaykum," through the curtain, careful not to look inside. Focusing his eyes on the curtain's threadbare weave and shredded edges, Mustafa sighed inwardly at Zaytuna's pious frugality. She should let one of us get her better things.

"La illaha illa'llah, La illaha illa'llah, La illaha illa'llah."

He coughed again and said a little louder, "Assalamu alaykum."

Her breathing slowed. She heard him. He dropped to one side of the door, squatting down beside it to give Zaytuna enough time to pull herself back into this world and its cares.

Umm Farhad yelled from within her room across from him, "You rascal!"

Farhad tumbled out of his mother's room with a long piece of floral cloth dragging behind him in the dirt and ran with it out through the passageway. Marta raised her eyebrows and tipped her chin to Yulduz in disapproval.

"Her good headwrap! Marta, she's ruined that boy. The poor woman who has to marry him."

Marta muttered in assent.

Umm Farhad stumbled out of the room, bareheaded, hastily pulling a wrap around herself, and ran out after him.

Mustafa shook his head at Umm Farhad. Thank God, the families in the house he shared had men at the head of each, keeping things under control. *It was hard for a woman without a man, but still*, he thought, *Umm Farhad could do better. God knows, my mother did.*

Zaytuna pulled the curtain aside and poked her head out. She was still on her knees from prayer. They were face to face, only inches from each other. Her eyes were soft. Her skin was bright. The lines that usually drew across her forehead and around her mouth from worry and anger were gone. She said his name, "Mustafa," and the sound was timbered with care, not the harsh tones he often got from her when she was upset about things and taking it out on him because he was nearest to her, and, he knew, because he was safe.

He said softly, "I'm sorry to interrupt."

Casting her eyes down, she blushed. "Mustafa, you can never be an interruption."

"I wanted to let you know that I saw Tein and Ammar this morning."

Her head shot up, her eyes narrowed, and a wrinkle of worry returned to her forehead. He realized that she had, while remembering God, forgotten about the case.

"Yes! Ya Rabb! What happened?" She ducked her head back into the room, careful to close the curtain completely, and said, "I'll be out in a moment." She came out with a second wrap around her, saying, "That's better now. Let me give you some water."

"Alhamdulillah, I've just come from the baths and could use it."

"You should have been drinking while there," she scolded, as she handed him the cup filled with water.

He took it from her, careful not to touch her hand. "I did, but it was not your water, Zaytuna, and not from our jug and cup."

She sat down next to him and took a deep breath. "Before you tell me. I want to say that I've been terrible."

"What have you done?" He said with concern.

"I've wronged you. I've wrong YingYue. I've wronged myself."

Mustafa became suddenly afraid she'd spoken to YingYue about him. His temper flared. "Tell me what you've said, Zaytuna."

"No! Nothing!" She pulled back from him. "*In me*, Mustafa, *in my mind*, I've wronged you in my mind. I'm sorry."

This was so typical of her moods, always recriminating herself for real and imagined sins, to the end of putting herself first. But he reassured her all the same, "God is The Forgiving."

She sighed, "Inshallah."

"Zaytuna, the girl..."

She reached to put her hand on his arm, then pulled it back. "I want to say first, Mustafa, whatever the news, alhamdulillah. There is a purpose in this, a plan, an organization to it that we cannot see. We have our footing, we just need to trust it."

She was right. Mustafa closed his eyes and took her reminder to trust God. God's verses of consolation came to mind. He took a deep breath and recited, his voice was thick with feeling.

> *Did We not expand your breast?*
> *And lift your burden from you?*
> *The burden that weighed down your back?*
> *And raised you in esteem?*
> *Surely with hardship comes ease.*
> *Surely with hardship comes ease.*
> *So when you are empty, keep working.*
> *And let your Lord be your longing.*

When he finished, she completed his recitation with the seal, "God Almighty speaks the truth."

He took a breath then said, "The news is not good, but we have an avenue open to us."

"Tell me."

"Tein doesn't believe that Mu'mina did it at all. Ammar thinks she did, but he is willing to concede it may have been unintentional. That may only be a concession to Tein, though. Her case is being sent to the police chief to decide."

"I don't understand. What is the avenue?"

Yulduz interrupted, "What's that! How is Tansholpan? What about her?"

Mustafa answered her. "We don't know yet, Auntie."

"And why not!"

Zaytuna shot back at her, "Auntie, my brother, the one you doubt so much, is out there right now trying to prove Mu'mina innocent so she and Tansholpan can go free!"

Marta put her hand on Yulduz's arm, but Yulduz spat the words at Zaytuna, "If he wanted to protect her then he shouldn't've arrested her in the first place." She shook off Marta's hand and pushed her old body off the ground to stand, letting her sorted beans fall to the ground. She yelled at the two of them, choking back tears, "He better get'er free!" Then turned away from them, escaping into her room. Marta got up, gave them an apologetic look, and followed her.

Zaytuna felt sick. She said to Mustafa, "We've only been thinking about Mu'mina."

"Thinking about Mu'mina is thinking about Tansholpan. If she is exonerated, then Tansholpan will go free, too."

She nodded hopefully. "What avenue have you found?"

"I am to find Ibn Salah. I mentioned that he is the one who presented her complaint against the imam in court. He may be able to get her case moved to a religious court, outside of Karkh. I have to go to the mosque where he teaches. Zaytuna, I want you to come with me. I know we can't be together in the mosque, but I'd feel better knowing you were there. It's a long walk across the river, so we would have to leave soon, but I can explain everything on the way, and if we find him, we can think it all through together on the way back."

Zaytuna held herself back from leaning into him. *Is this what it is to love someone? Or is this just who we are? Are we only childhood friends who know each other better than anyone else could?* She closed her eyes. "Yes."

"Are you ready?"

"I just need a moment." She ducked back into her room and pulled her good clothes over her worn ones for warmth and grabbed her slipper-shoes instead of her sandals. Once in her hand she saw the soles were wearing thin. The sickening shame that she was no good rose back up and took hold of her, pushing out the quiet acceptance she'd built up word by word during her remembrance of God this morning. She was torn between wanting to be with him and needing to be alone, to hide herself away. "Go," she said to herself, and slipped her bony feet into the shoes, pushed the curtain aside, and joined him.

By the time they reached the pontoon bridge spanning the Tigris between Karkh and Rusafa, they had exhausted all talk of the case and had fallen into companionable silence. The Tigris sparkled in the sun, cold and bright. The usual smell of fish was lost in the breeze. Round wicker boats and skiffs crowded the waters, carrying goods and people up and down the river and through the canals. She could, just faintly, hear music and laughter coming from the balconies off the multi-story homes of the wealthy built on the river.

They waited their turn to step out onto the bridge, catching their balance as the bridge swayed with the force of the current and the shifting weight of what must have been more than a hundred people walking in two lines in opposite directions, some balancing goods on their backs or heads. Once on the bridge, she slowed to look up at the homes along the water. Men and women leaned on balconies, chatting, and looking out at the river scene. One couple stood too close to one another, half-concealed by fluttering, sheer curtains, and she saw herself and Mustafa, fleetingly, in their places.

She heard a man's voice behind her, "Tch Tch! Get moving, woman!"

She shook herself back into awareness and prepared to give the man a piece of her mind, but Mustafa was tugging on her wrap, saying, "Keep walking."

Once on the other side, they could see the Rusafa Mosque in the distance. As they approached, she admired the mosque's arched facade, heavily-tiled in blues and greens. Where there was no tile, intricate calligraphy and vegetal designs had been carved into the stucco. There was money here, not just in the estates of the wealthy lining the river, but also in the high-walled neighbourhoods beyond. She could barely breathe from the beauty of it, then instantly felt as though she had betrayed her own Shuniziyya Mosque, more humbly decorated and acting in service to the people of her poor neighbourhood.

Mustafa broke their silence. "There's time yet before the call to prayer."

The expansive prayer hall felt nearly empty except for small groups of people here and there in study circles and those who came early to rest or have time for contemplation.

She asked, "Should I stay with you?"

Mustafa was worried. "I think it's better if I speak to him alone. I don't know him or what he thinks about women in the mosque. I'll tell you everything afterwards."

Even though she nodded, he saw her colour rise at the suggestion. She bent over and picked up her slippers and strode to the rear of the mosque without a word. He called after her, "Meet you here after the prayer?"

There was no answer, just her back to him. Mustafa wanted to run after her and pull her to him. He wanted to apologize for caring what any of these people think. He wanted her by his side when he approached Ibn Salah. He took a step in her direction, then caught himself and stopped. He corrected his wants. *Yes, I want her with me. But I don't want her to talk. And she would not be able to keep quiet. It's for the best and I'll apologize later. She needs to understand what this world is like. I certainly can't change it.* He sighed aloud in frustration, "Zaytuna," then looked around to see if anyone had heard him. A man was behind him taking off his slippers but did not look up.

Near a pillar, a group of students sat around a blind Qur'an recitation teacher. They recited clearly, yet softly in unison; then each one individually, as he gently corrected their pronunciation, their voices were, to him, like bird song. A couple of men in scholar's turbans stood not far off.

He kept an eye on Zaytuna as he found a place to pray. It looked like she was heading to the rear wall. What made him think he should marry her? *Love is not enough.*

How much easier things would be if he were to marry YingYue. She had gentle manners. They would keep each other on the Sufi path, and she would be a fine wife of a scholar. He would never worry about how she would act in situations like this. He blushed, thinking of her. Her skin was soft and pink like the palest rose. *She is so beautiful.*

Yet Zaytuna. Stopping for a moment, he watched her pray her two cycles of prayer in greeting to the mosque. He saw himself following her around in awe when they were children. She noticed wrongs where he saw nothing. When Zaytuna was no more than ten years old, not long after her mother died, they were running in a busy square when she pulled him to a stop. She pointed at an old woman sitting outside a shop, her granddaughter beside her. The old woman had the girl by the hand and was pinching and twisting the bit of fleshy skin between the girl's thumb and forefinger, smiling, while the girl held her face still from long practice bearing up under pain.

Zaytuna walked right up to the old woman. He braced himself for the cursing Zaytuna would give her. But when her foot landed firmly before the old woman, without pausing or warning, she pulled her hand back and slapped her across the face. The old woman shrieked and let go of the girl in shock, then quickly recovered. Without moving from her spot, she hit Zaytuna so hard with the flat of her hand that Zaytuna was knocked down and smacked her head on the ground. It all happened so fast that by the time he reached Zaytuna, she was already sitting up on her elbows, getting an earful from the shopkeeper while passersby stepped around her, cursing her for being in their way. The old woman was sitting again as she was, her granddaughter beside her, twisting the flesh on the girl's palm. But now the girl was in tears. He would always love Zaytuna for wanting the world to be better. But she was still that little girl who didn't understand how the world worked.

He turned away from her, facing the front of the mosque to perform his own greeting prayer, but couldn't relax into the movements and keep his mind on God. Every muscle was tight with the frustration of her and worry about approaching Ibn Salah. He greeted the angels on either side of him to close the prayer, his tone towards them a little harsh. He muttered, "God forgive me," then got up and crossed the mosque to the two men talking by the pillar. The older of the two wore a grand turban in deep blue, wrapped in the manner of the Hanafi school of law. He was draped in an elegant woolen robe and wrap over that. The fabric was pure white and shot through with blue thread. There was nothing humble about his dress. Mustafa thought he'd not be out of place with the Abu Burhans of this world, but he put his hand over his heart and bowed his head, saying with all the graciousness he could muster, "Assalamu alaykum, blessed Friday prayer."

They replied, "Blessed Friday prayer."

"I was wondering if you could direct me to Abu Mubarak Sherwan Ibn as-Salah al-Kurdi, I understand he teaches here?"

They looked at him, obviously noticing his turban tied in the manner of the Hanbalis. The elder of the two took a moment, then replied, "He is not teaching today, but he is over there, sitting near the library door, as he regularly does on Fridays, if anyone needs to ask him a legal question."

The younger one looked to the elder for direction. He nodded to the young scholar, who said to Mustafa, "I'll bring you to him."

The young man walked him to the library side of the mosque in silence then bowed his head to Mustafa, hand over his heart, and left him standing before Ibn Salah. The scholar he had been seeking was instructing a young man sitting beside him. Ibn Salah nodded at Mustafa, indicating he should sit, then returned to the conversation before him.

Mustafa did as he indicated, and observed the man upon whom so much would rely. Ibn Salah's back was straight, but not arrogantly so. He leaned in to speak to a young man before him, his face animated with apparent interest. His turban was neither too large nor too small, making no statement about his greatness nor his humility. He wore a quilted robe of tightly woven cotton, and a simple brown woolen wrap draped over one shoulder. He held himself with unmistakable dignity. Mustafa imagined himself in Ibn Salah's place, students surrounding him at the mosque, and listened.

Ibn Salah's voice was kind, but scolding, "I do not diminish the opinions of our great scholars, for many times I am consulted on a problem and were it not for what I had memorized of their statements I would not know where to place my foot. That said, we cannot simply rely on earlier scholars' legal opinions. Do you think that they could foresee every problem that would come to pass in this life? New situations will always arise. Even if you were to lead behind you a donkey-cart filled with all the books of all the fatwas of all the scholars everywhere you go, it is still possible that there would be no answer to a novel problem brought before you." He sat back and slapped his knee lightly. "For this reason, we must endeavour to determine new rulings. Now, occasionally, we may find an analogous ruling from which we can determine the right way forward in this new matter." Ibn Salah leaned in again, excited. "But other times, there is not even that! It is only our knowledge of the methods our fore-scholars used to determine their own rulings that guide us. In that, we infer the right way forward and produce new rulings on which those who come after us may be able to rely."

The young man nodded at Ibn Salah's every word, but he could see that he found it shocking.

He felt more than a little sympathy with the young man. He was obviously in no position to argue these points at this stage in his education, but the young man's conscience was correct. Ruling by analogy was dangerous enough. The soul could imagine it sees all kinds of analogous situations to rule for its own benefit! Even worse was not giving primacy of place to our pious forebears, those wise men who followed the Prophet, and determining rulings based on nothing other than 'method' alone! God protect us from evil things. There is no telling where this might lead. The young man got up to leave, clearly dissatisfied. Mustafa sorely wanted to pull him aside and tell him to come and sit with the Hanbalis. He would find himself in a safer home than this one.

Ibn Salah interrupted his thoughts, "I see you follow the Hanbali school, what do you think of what I've said?"

Mustafa blushed, feeling caught out. He did not have the requisite knowledge to dispute with him. He must not agree, but he must not engage! He found his answer, "I would respectfully disagree," and bowed his head, his hand over his heart, "But I am not here to discuss the merits of our different methods of drawing God's intent from the Qur'an and the Sunna of our beloved Prophet, God bless him and grant him peace."

Ibn Salah's face lit up with interest. "No?"

"Do you remember the case of Imam Hisham al-Qatafi's slave?"

He frowned. "Yes, Mu'mina, how could I forget? Imam Hashim died recently, it seems as a result of the hardship he placed on the poor girl. May God forgive him."

Mustafa said it, but did not feel it, "Amin."

"And rumour has it that she had a curse put on him. It was understandable. But, I am sorry, do you mind me asking what do you have to do with all this?"

"A childhood friend is an investigator with Grave Crimes and felt that you may be of some help."

"Why did he not speak to me himself?"

Mustafa stumbled, unsure of how to describe himself, "I am involved in the investigation as, as a consultant."

Ibn Salah nodded. "What can I do?"

"The case is not as straightforward as it seems. The girl confessed, but it may be that she did not intend to kill him. Although, one of the investigators, my friend, does not believe she killed him at all."

"And her confession?"

"As you heard, she bought a curse. But the curse was, uh, to reduce the imam's sexual desire, not to kill him. The curse may have unleashed an ifrit who did the job. This confession, and an amendment citing that the killing may not have been intentional, was sent forward to the police chief."

"When does the case go before him?"

"As soon as it reaches its turn on the docket. It could be tomorrow or the day after."

"Unintentional murder would typically be punishable by payment of blood money, but the police chief is not bound to follow religious law in his rulings."

Mustafa tried to interrupt, "It's..."

Ibn Salah ignored him, looking out across the expanse of the mosque. "The family would no doubt demand her execution and he would allow it." He turned back to Mustafa, "They are an influential family, there is no reason that their slave would be shown mercy in this case. It is most likely to go against her."

Mustafa let out in a rush what he had been trying to say, "That is why I am here. There is, perhaps, another way."

Ibn Salah leaned in. "Tell me."

"It is possible that he was killed by poison, intentional or accidental. Anyone could have done it. It could even have been from a beating. We don't know."

Ibn Salah sat back, confused. "Then why was her case moved on to the police chief's court so quickly?"

Mustafa chose his words carefully, "Her confession was submitted before they reflected on the other possibilities."

"And where is Mu'mina now?"

"She is being held under suspicion, along with the woman who wrote the talisman."

"Ya Rabb, you know what will most likely happen? The police chief will put aside her case and leave her and the talisman maker in jail indefinitely. He would not release her on the basis of doubt, as a religious court might, unless the political circumstances warrant it."

Mustafa said, "You see the problem."

"Yes. God help these poor women; many people have been lost forever in those cells."

"We thought it might be possible to petition to have her case moved from the police chief's court to a religious court for examination. It would delay the consideration of the evidence, giving the police more time to investigate."

"This crime happened in Karkh. Abu Burhan should hear it. Is this what you want?"

"That is why I am here to speak to you. We had hoped you could help us get the case moved to a different court. Perhaps the court here in Rusafa."

"A petitioner would have to bring a case against her to Qadi Ibn al-Zayzafuni's court. It cannot simply be transferred. I am surprised the police sergeant is not aware of this."

"My sense is that the investigators' sergeant would prefer the two women be convicted quickly, or, as you mentioned, sit in jail, as they have other cases before them. Thus they are proceeding with his permission, but without his guidance, which," he nodded to Ibn Salah, "is why they asked me to query you on the matter."

"Because I had petitioned the court against Imam Hashim on Mu'mina's behalf previously."

"Yes. The investigators hoped you might once again."

"You don't understand, someone has to petition the judge to hear the evidence against her, not on her behalf." Ibn Salah continued, "You must find someone to bring a case against her. You could ask the family, I suppose, but why would they do that when they are more likely to see her executed in the police chief's court?"

Mustafa replied, finally understanding, "God help us, who?"

Ibn Salah replied, "Ask yourself who would like to see her get a fairer hearing than she would get at the police court, then approach that person. I can, perhaps, query some colleagues. But you must do the same."

"Yes, I will," he said with relief.

"Good." Ibn Salah hesitated, then said, "I can see that this case matters to you, more than simply consulting for the police. Do you mind if I ask why?"

Mustafa replied carefully, "I first heard about the case you brought on her behalf from Burhan, Qadi Abu Burhan's son. At the time, I objected to Imam Hashim's behaviour and the ruling itself, which so unaccountably favoured him. And which did not," he paused, "properly consider the nature of the harm being done to her."

Ibn Salah sat back. "Ah, so you feel for the girl."

"No!" He scrambled, embarrassed by the suggestion. "I mean, rather, I feel for the injustice done to her. But it is greater than that. It is that the injustice was done at the hand of fellow scholars." His voice rose, "How can the people trust us to interpret God's intent for them if we act not out of love of God and the Prophet but out of a desire to preserve our own rights over others at the expense of the most vulnerable!"

Ibn Salah raised his eyebrows. "It is true that there are scholars who do not like their power challenged and will strike back. I assume you are aware of their retribution against me through my son."

"Yes, and Burhan threatened me similarly if I were to object publicly to his father's rulings."

"I will not take this case as a matter of retribution on my part," Ibn Salah said carefully. "I will do it so that justice is served, no matter the harm that comes to my family and me. God turns every injustice into justice." He paused. "Alhamdulillah, my son quit gambling as a result of his shame and is apprenticing as a papermaker."

Mustafa's eyes widened at the wonder of it. "Alhamdulillah." Then, asked, "Do you think that Qadi Ibn al-Zayzafuni would take the case if petitioned?"

Ibn Salah considered it for a moment. "I believe that he would see the wisdom in taking the case to demonstrate that we hold our own to account. Moreover, I have heard him complain that the police judge capital cases, those in which the crime and God's punishment is mentioned in the Qur'an, rather than the religious courts. I imagine he may not want to miss the opportunity to demonstrate that the religious courts are more capable of evaluating the evidence and judge fairly, in keeping with the established principles of God's law." He paused. "I will speak to him."

The call to prayer finally came, and they both stood. They waited until the call was completed, each repeating its lines under their breath. Mustafa feeling the words, "Come to salvation," expanding his chest in gratitude for God bringing him to this man. They walked together toward the front of the mosque to sit and wait for the sermon to begin.

After the prayer was finished and everyone was standing to leave, Ibn Salah put his hand on Mustafa's shoulder and asked, "Would you join my family for our Friday meal?"

Mustafa lit up. "Yes!" Then stopped short, realizing Zaytuna was with him. "But I am here with my friend, not the investigator I mentioned. His sister."

"His sister? Are you to be married?"

Mustafa tried to explain, "No. It is not like that. They both are like cousins to me. Family. We grew up side-by-side."

Ibn Salah replied, "Of course, she is welcome. My mother, wife, and sister will be glad for her company."

Mustafa involuntarily looked towards the rear of the mosque and saw Zaytuna standing there, not at all sure how she'd feel about the change in plans.

15

———

The mosque was filling fast. Women lined up in front of her. She looked around the women and over their heads but could not see Mustafa anymore. Leaning against the back wall of the mosque, the cold tiles sent a scolding chill through her. She slid down the wall and sat, pulling her wrap over her head. *What have you done, woman?* She'd pushed Mustafa away from her and traded the love of an uncle for the guidance of a shaykh. YingYue was at the head of both losses. YingYue was blocking everything she wanted. YingYue had her mother's love of God, Mustafa's attention, the approval of her shaykh, and, now, control over her. She wept quietly, but all the weeping did was remind her of how beautiful YingYue had been when her eyes welled over with tears. She wiped her face with her sleeve and said under her breath, "You are nothing but ugly, bony, and tall."

The imam stepped partway up the stairs of the minbar so that everyone could see him. But all the way at the back of the mosque, she could barely hear. They had one repeater toward the rear of the men's section, but they needed another to amplify his voice to where the women were seated. She put her hand to her forehead as she strained to hear. Here was one more miserable thing. Bits of the prayer for the Prophet and his companions reached her. She heard parts of verses from the Qur'an that she recognized well-enough to reconstruct for herself. But she became more and more frustrated with every word that she could not make out. Then came snippets of the required extravagant praise of the caliph. She snorted. The woman next to her gave her a scolding look. Zaytuna returned the glare. But then the praise seemed to go on and on. *My God, is the whole of the sermon in praise of al-Muktafi? Salla Allahu alayhi wa salam ala Muhammad! We praise this man as if he were the Prophet himself! As if he cared about the likes of us!* She heard the imam say, "The character of the Commander of the Faithful is that of a majestic lion, a crashing wave, a bewitching moon, and a glorious Spring." She snorted again. This time the woman in front of her turned around, gesturing, palm down, for her to be quiet. Zaytuna gave the woman a hard look for her trouble. She wanted to yell across the mosque at the imam, at the lot of them, "May God make your mothers regret you!"

No sooner had she realized that she'd cursed them that she regretted it, begging God's forgiveness and praying for them all, *and* their mothers. She forced herself to remember God to try to calm herself. She breathed rhythmically, one breath in, one breath out, for every syllable, saying within herself, La illaha illallah, la illaha illallah, la illaha illallah. She tried to lose herself in it, but the comforting waters of God's love stayed just out of reach. She called them, extending her remembrance out to their edges, but they pulled away from her. Her chest felt tight. She feared she would begin to cry again. A woman to her right touched her arm. She looked up, everyone had stood, and she had not noticed. Zaytuna sniffed and wiped her eyes again and stood for the Friday prayer.

Afterward, she remained behind, her back against the cold tiles, waiting for enough women to go so that she would not be crowded as she left. Looking for Mustafa, she at last saw him walk out with Ibn Salah. She filed out behind the women and saw the two men standing outside waiting for her. Now she could see Ibn Salah up close, she was taken back, he wasn't what she expected. His clothes were simple. Very fine, but simple. He had a gentle bearing. Anyone seeing him would know him for his importance and admire him for his humility. This is how Mustafa will be before long. She felt sick. *There is no room for me in that world.* As she got closer, she could hear Ibn Salah's voice. It was clear and kind, yet carried the energy of his interest. She slowed down to listen. "I was asked when she might return to prayer after delivering the stillborn child by cesarean. The wound by which it was delivered was still seeping. I ruled that the case was analogous to postpartum bleeding in a typical birth. Because the fluid was no longer red, she must return to her prayer. So how would you Hanbalis answer such a query?"

Mustafa's shoulders tensed. He was unsure of himself. She hurried forward. "Mustafa!"

He turned around, and she saw the worry on his face fall away, grateful for her interruption.

"Ibn Salah, I would like to introduce you to my cousin. Zaytuna bint al-Ashiqa as-Sawda ash-Shuniziyya."

Ibn Salah's eyes widen slightly at her mother's unusual name. He placed his hand over his heart, bowing his head, saying, "Good to meet you." He continued, "I have invited Imam Mustafa here to my home for lunch, and we would be grateful if you would join us."

Her back stiffened. She was stuck for words. She and Mustafa were meant to walk home together and talk. She could not go to this man's home and sit with his women. Her best clothes were not good enough for anything other than being their washerwoman. She looked at Mustafa, trying to convey her discomfort, but he simply smiled and nodded to her. She didn't reply, which they took as assent, and began walking along the mosque road, deeper into Rusafa and further away from the bridge that would bring them back to Karkh.

Ibn Salah addressed her, "I found the sermon edifying."

Her lips were tight. What could she say? That she had barely been able to hear it and what she had heard inspired her to curse the imam, indeed them all, before she stopped trying to listen entirely?

Mustafa must have sensed her mood, he broke in, "Zaytuna is aware of the case we were discussing. She has, on occasion, been able to help the police in their investigations. It would be helpful to me if you included her in our discussion."

Ibn Salah's eyebrows raised. "Truly?"

She wanted to spit the word back at him, but she kept her mouth shut for Mustafa's sake.

"Well, then," Ibn Salah said, "I would like to clarify a point from our earlier conversation."

"Yes?"

"I believe I might have left you with the impression that I was unhappy with the outcome of Imam Hashim's hearing. I was not. I was concerned that Qadi Abu Burhan's relationship with Imam Hashim would overshadow the case unfairly. If so, I would have appealed it to the Mazalim High Court for examination by the chief judge. Despite the judge's obvious preference for the defendant, Imam Hashim, the ruling was not unfair in and of itself."

Zaytuna was confused.

Mustafa said, "I thought you were angered by the result."

"No. I was angered by the threat that scholars should not have to face charges brought by the vulnerable against them, and their retribution on my family for doing just that."

"But..." Mustafa said.

"Let me explain, I petitioned the court to address the harm being done to her. Ideally, a pious young woman such as that should be freed. Slavery is not ideal for such people, except in cases where the family who cares for them values their worship and helps them preserve it."

Zaytuna's mind was screaming, *'Such people'! So, then, there are people who do and do not deserve to be enslaved!*

Mustafa was focused on Ibn Salah. "But you said that if she killed the imam, it would be understandable."

Ibn Salah explained, "Yes, I did. For the behaviour she had to endure previously."

Zaytuna's eyes were on the ground, and her mind was racing. *Previously? As if the harm had ended!* Her voice rang in her ears. She looked up. Both men were staring at her, Ibn Salah concerned and Mustafa horrified. She realized she had spoken her protest aloud, not to herself. She straightened her back and would not be ashamed.

"Fine, then," and went on, demanding, "Don't you think he still took her as he liked?"

"Ah," Ibn Salah said, bowing his head and taking a reasonable tone, "I grasp the misunderstanding. His taking her as he liked was not the source of the harm. The source of the harm was the interruption of her obligatory worship. Qadi Abu Burhan's ruling solved the problem. The harm done to her was now in her own control. If she did her prayers on time, then her obligations to God would not be interrupted when he chose to be with her."

Zaytuna's face grew hotter with his every word, "But she did not want to have sex with him!"

He spoke slowly, "A woman's 'wanting' or 'not wanting' is no arbiter of what is best for her once she is married or enslaved and thus is not a matter of legal redress. It is harm that we must address, and harm was addressed in this case."

She looked at Mustafa, but he did not say anything. His face was hard and his eyes were on the road ahead of them. She replied to Ibn Salah just as slowly, "No. The harm is in her not wanting."

Ibn Salah stopped walking, and Zaytuna turned to face him. Mustafa carried on a few steps, then turned back. She took one look at his blanched face and knew all was lost. He was not going to support her.

"Fascinating," Ibn Salah said. "Your position is that even when a man has sexual rights over a woman, her want should be the determiner of whether or not they engage in sex; otherwise, there is harm, or, would you even argue, rape?"

She didn't mean to, but she heard herself screeching, "Yes! And that is exactly what she said! He raped her," then added with sarcastic venom, "even after the 'legal harm' was addressed."

He took a step back from the force of her words, his brows knitted in worry. He looked at Mustafa to intervene. Mustafa only looked between the two of them in shock. She kept her hands flat by her side to keep from slapping them both.

Ibn Salah turned to Mustafa and said, "Perhaps today is not a good day for lunch, your cousin is quite upset. We can meet in the morning to discuss these matters."

Mustafa turned and looked at Zaytuna. She could see he was no longer confused nor shocked. Colour had returned to his face and he was furious with her. She took a step back. He had never once in his life looked at her with such censure. They had disagreed. They had fought. But never had she seen this look. She exclaimed, "God protect me!"

Mustafa answered Ibn Salah, but had his eyes on Zaytuna, "My cousin feels things deeply. She speaks from her heart. I apologize to you for the tenor of this conversation." He turned to Ibn Salah, "I assure you all will be well, or I would send her home without me. Most important, the enslaved girl's case must be addressed. I beg of you, if it would not inconvenience your family, that we go on."

Ibn Salah bowed to Mustafa, never looking at Zaytuna, and said, "Then please come ahead, we are just there on the right."

The two men walked on while she stood still, wanting to run screaming in the other direction. But she found her feet following them, walking behind them, until she was through the door to his home. A servant, *or is she a slave*, she thought bitterly, guided her into a room off of the central courtyard in which three women sat on couches around a low table, while two boys played with wooden horsemen on the floor beside them.

The servant spoke to the eldest woman quietly. She looked Zaytuna up and down, then smiled and graciously called her over to sit with them, "My dear, my dear! What a blessing from God, come and sit."

Zaytuna walked to the table, hardly knowing how she moved. She only came to herself as she sank into the thick couch and felt the softness of the silk covering the cushion under her hand. The women smelled of jasmine and vanilla and wore richly embroidered, quilted gowns, their hair uncovered. She did not compare the roughness of her clothes and head wrap, but instead straightened her back. Her mother was a greater woman, a queen who sat beside God's throne, a finer woman in her rough woolen shifts and wraps, than these women sewn up in gold thread and skin so pale they looked like they never left the house.

She could only just hear the men talking in the courtyard through the thick curtain that covered the arched doorway. As much as she hated Ibn Salah, she was furious all over again because she was barred from hearing the facts of the case alongside Mustafa. She wondered if he would share them with her, or if she was no longer "sensible" enough to warrant inclusion in their debates about women's lives.

The elder woman had been speaking to her and she realized she'd not heard the introductions and did not know their names. She tried to focus on what the woman was saying, "My son says you are the cousin of his guest? Are you married?"

"No, not married. He isn't my natural cousin; we were raised together."

"Ah," his mother said.

Zaytuna watched her search for an acceptable definition for their relationship given that they were out in the street together without a chaperone. Then his mother found it. "You are milk-siblings, alhamdulillah."

She sorely wanted to tell her that she and Mustafa had not, in fact, nursed from each other's mothers to make them as good as blood-siblings, just to see her reaction. Instead, she nodded in assent.

Ibn Salah's sons complained from their place on the carpet that they were hungry. Their mother shushed them, then returned to look at Zaytuna, eyes wide, like a lamb to slaughter.

Ibn Salah's sister raised her hand to a servant, waiting across the room, then said, "You were at Friday prayers? We never go."

"What would you do in the mosque my daughter other than expose yourself to men who are not in a position to marry you?"

"You would have me expose myself to men in a position to marry me?" His sister stifled a laugh.

Her mother slapped her hand lightly. "You know that is not what I meant."

Leaning in toward her mother, she assured her, "Of course not."

Ibn Salah's wife quipped, "No one is in a position to marry her."

The women laughed at this comment, leaving Zaytuna at a loss.

His sister explained, "I am all the scandal, I will not marry. They complain that all I do is write poetry and ignore men who are chosen for my benefit."

Zaytuna looked at her, amazed. A woman like her. But why? She seemed so happy and secure in herself. What had Zaytuna done but push away a good man she'd known her whole life into the arms of another woman because she was in too much cursed pain to accept him? If she had the easy confidence of this woman, maybe things would be different. Her anger turned to exhaustion and she felt like she might cry. She set her jaw and opened her eyes. *I will not cry.*

The servant came in with a pitcher, basin, and a towel for them to wash their hands before the meal. The girl was a well-fed Arab from the countryside, dressed in clothes far better than her own. Her wrap was around her waist like an apron, and her headscarf tied behind her head, allowing a straggly braid of reddish-brown hair to hang down her back. The wrap and scarf were in matching material, a beautiful block-printed repeating design of large red flowers, so many petals you could fall into them, like twenty roses become one rose. The girl placed the basin before Zaytuna first. Zaytuna flinched, then held out her hands over the basin. The girl poured a thin stream of warm water from the long-nosed pitcher over them. She rubbed her fingers together and then around her palms. She didn't know how women like this washed their hands in front of others, at a table like this, but she refused to be ashamed. If it was wrong, so be it. The servant put the pitcher back and offered her the towel to dry her hands. She took it from her, drying them completely and handed it back. The servant placed the basin before Ibn Salah's mother, who, Zaytuna, was relieved to see, washed her hands in the way she had herself.

Ibn Salah's wife asked, "Are you married?"

Zaytuna allowed the pain of the situation to show on her face, a look as if a terrible secret had been wrenched from her, and said, "God in His wisdom has made me barren, no man will have me because of it. Walhamdulillah, my cousin," nodding to the old woman, "my 'milk-brother', Mustafa has taken pity on me and cares for me now that my own mother and father are long passed, may God have mercy on their souls."

Ibn Salah's mother and wife gasped. His wife tried to reach across the table to her to comfort her. But his sister only looked at her, one eyebrow raised with a critical smile, as she washed her hands. Zaytuna nearly yelled aloud at God, *Protect me from these women!*

Ibn Salah's wife spoke, her voice strangely cheerful, given Zaytuna's revelation, "God's wisdom is gracious. I never see my Abu Mubarak, he is so busy with work. You are better off as you are."

The women sat in awkward silence as the servant retreated to bring in the food. Zaytuna could hear Mustafa's voice in the next room and became angry at that again, too.

Mustafa watched in awe as servant bore a large platter for the men heaped with lamb shank stewed with gourd and apricots and large rounds of white flour bread. Ibn Salah tore off a piece of bread and put it before Mustafa, then picked up the shank before him and placed it closest to Mustafa in the communal dish and said, "Please, bismillah, eat."

Mustafa replied, "Thank you, bismillah ar-rahman ar-rahim," and tore off a piece of the bread, dipping it into the stew. Mustafa, so distracted by the case they had been discussing, placed it unthinkingly in his mouth. The moment he tasted it, he sat up and turned and looked at Ibn Salah with a look of wonder on his face, at the depth of flavour, the delicacy of the spices.

Ibn Salah smiled and gestured again to take another bite, and he took his first. They ate in silence. Mustafa was grateful. He did not know how he could talk and eat this food at the same time. It would be a sin to deny the beauty of the meal and a sin to enjoy it while speaking of Mu'mina's case. Mustafa ate more than he intended, more even than he could manage, and finally said, "Alhamdulillah."

Ibn Salah laughed lightly. "I won't insist you eat more, you seem sated."

Mustafa looked at him guiltily. "God forgive me, I have lost touch with the Prophet's example of only filling one's stomach one-third with food. May it be a compliment to your home."

"Our cook has a golden hand. But the Prophet, God bless him, peace upon him and his family and companions, ate heartily when there was gourd in his stew." Ibn Salah winked at Mustafa. "Since today we ate gourd, there is a sunna for your indulgence."

Mustafa laughed uncomfortably, knowing that Zaytuna would disagree.

Ibn Salah reprised their conversation, "Is there any chance she is not guilty?"

"My old friend, Tein, insists that she is innocent. He argues that it is unlikely that she killed him, and certainly not in the way she believes. Her confession is based on her own misunderstanding, but she will not hear otherwise! She will not retract her confession beyond saying that it was involuntary. My understanding is that she wants to be held responsible for it in this life rather than pay for it in the next."

"Her fear of God is commendable, but she must not be allowed to confess to a crime she did not commit. You must understand that I cannot speak for her as her representative if she is present to address the plaintiff's accusation of murder herself. If she affirms her written confession orally, she will be found guilty and sentenced." He took a moment to think. "But there may be a way. I could put myself forward as her representative, despite her presence in the court, by claiming that she is not intellectually capable of speaking to her confession." He nodded in satisfaction at his solution. "She is a woman, a slave, and black, it will not be difficult."

Mustafa was stuck in-between the horror of the comment, made so easily and implicating the capacities of those who were family to him, and the hope that using such a ruse presented. He was never so glad that Zaytuna was not with him.

Ibn Salah continued, "Barring exculpatory evidence, I can dispute her confession and introduce doubt. We must hope that evidence pointing in other directions will come to light."

"But surely it should be enough that there is insufficient evidence to determine her guilt?"

Ibn Salah said, "There are many 'ifs'. If her confession is set aside. If Ibn al-Zayzafuni is willing to hear the case. And if your friend is permitted to give evidence as an expert to the unreliability of her confession and other possible means of murder. He must be investigated for his trustworthiness first, though. He may not be approved."

Mustafa became afraid. One look at Tein's drinking habits and he would be denied. "No, it would not be my friend. It would be his superior, Ammar at-Tabbani. Ammar is an honourable man. He is a ghazi; there should be no trouble there."

Ibn Salah picked a piece of lint from his wrap. "That will hold weight, but the police are not considered reliable overall."

Mustafa surely saw the reason in that, most were thugs. But not Ammar, and not Tein, despite his weaknesses.

"I believe Ibn al-Zayzafuni will be willing to entertain these doubts in his court. He and I have discussed his longing for the days under the Umayyads when judges were as King Solomon in his court, asking questions of those presenting evidence to get to the truth of the matter. He has railed that a judge's acumen is limited to simply weighing the evidence before him rather than determining the truth for himself." Ibn Salah frowned. "Privately, and do not share this, he has called the present system no better than a judicial marketplace, litigants coming and going before him so quickly that he can see as many as fifty cases a day."

"And the fate of the curse writer?"

"That is another issue."

Mustafa said, worried, "I don't know if they have the talisman or not. Will they need it?"

"If the judge is so inclined, he could have the talisman maker investigated for a new trial of heresy even if Mu'mina is let go. She would have no way to defend herself without the evidence of the talisman herself. God knows there is nothing wrong with written prayers of protection, but we don't know that is what she wrote." Ibn

Salah pivoted, his eyes alight with new interest, "My son is working for a Chinese man, new to Baghdad. He is producing prayers of protection to hang on the wall using the technique of block printing."

"A Chinese man?" *Could it be YingYue's father?*

A servant came in and placed a tray of small pastries before them. He had only ever seen them in shops. Gazelle horns. Almonds ground with white sugar and butter, then baked in a thin pastry shell. So out of reach had they been to him until now, he had not realized that he had craved them. He looked at the pastries and realized he could now afford them and smiled.

Ibn Salah lifted the tray to him. Mustafa took one. The crust flaked away with his first bite. He savoured its delicate filling, sighing with pleasure.

Ibn Salah smiled. "My cook is from the Maghreb. She makes these for me, although they can be found in the shops. I'll have some of these wrapped for you to take home with you."

Mustafa smiled at the thought of it and asked, "The man your son works for, what is his name?"

"Ahmad at-Tarazi. Do you know him?"

"Yes! I do." He stopped short of mentioning YingYue or Junayd's community. He wasn't sure what this man would think.

Ibn Salah talked over him, "It is the most extraordinary thing, he wants to produce a block printed Qur'an. Could you imagine? The work of carving the blocks would be painstaking. If he did accomplish this task, anyone who wished could have a Qur'an in their home." Ibn Salah shook his head at the wonder of it.

Mustafa sat up in pride, for knowing him personally, and his daughter.

Ibn Salah said, "After lunch today, I will visit Qadi Ibn al-Zayzafuni and ask him for a letter to bring to the police chief to indicate that he is willing to have the case moved to his court should a petitioner be willing to do so." He inclined his head to Mustafa. "You must find the petitioner."

Mustafa nodded, biting into a second gazelle horn.

Indicating the meal had ended, Ibn Salah said, "With your

permission, I will begin preparing for my visit to Qadi Ibn al-Zayzafuni." He indicated to the servant that Mustafa was ready to leave. They stood, and Ibn Salah directed Mustafa to the reception hall. The servant held open the heavy curtain that separated them, and Zaytuna emerged.

Mustafa knew that face and she was angry. Ibn Salah didn't seem to notice and chatted about the garden as he walked the two of them to the gate, but Mustafa could not hear a word of it for the worry of what Zaytuna would say. Ibn Salah turned behind him, waiting for the servant to come and open the gate. Two female servants rushed out with packages in their hands, one small, which he hoped were the pastries, the other so large that the girl was holding it like a child against her chest. One handed him the small package, and the other handed the large package to Zaytuna. He looked at Zaytuna, questioning, but she looked even more angry, as if such a thing were possible.

Mustafa bowed his head to Ibn Salah. "Thank you, we will speak tomorrow?"

"Yes." He said, bowing in return.

The gate shut behind them and out it came.

"Why did you bring me here? Was I supposed to investigate the crime while I was in there with the women and the squirming children? Did they have some information?"

He defended himself, "This was unexpected!"

"And why wouldn't you answer him about the harm before!"

He looked down, realizing in his worry that he had gripped the pastries too tightly and crushed them. *Look what she made me do!* Mustafa's voice betrayed his frustration with her, "He has a point."

She glared at him.

"Zaytuna, let me ask you this. What is it that you oppose? Do you oppose that he took her while she prayed? Or do you oppose that she must have sex with him at all?" He turned to her, finding a new voice within himself, "Do you oppose that men should have slaves as wives?"

"My God, Mustafa, she was no wife to him!"

"But how different was her situation as a slave to that of a wife? Both must come to their master when he desires."

Zaytuna spat on the ground. "And you wonder why I will not marry!"

The accusation hit its mark. The resentment he felt for her endless comparisons of him to the Prophet, to whom he could never measure up, spilled out of him, "And the Prophet, did he not have slaves for his sexual use? Did his wives not come to him as his slaves did?"

"All of them chose to be with him. They chose! By God! He withdrew from Asma bint an-Numan when she refused him!"

Her face was mottled red. He thought she would begin bleating at any moment. For the first time in his life, he did not fear it, but stood firm in the face of her fury. He responded calmly, "And this makes you think they objected to his right over them?"

"They came to him willingly!"

"And what about his slaves? Rayhana? Mariya?"

She threw her hand out. "There you have it! Rayhana rejected him when she was made a gift to him. If he asked Rayhana what she wanted, you think he did not ask Mariya, too? He asked them all! He respected them!"

Mustafa smiled coolly. "No, he took Rayhana without asking."

Zaytuna visibly shook with anger. "You know there is more than one hadith about the Prophet and Rayhana! Some say he kept her as a slave despite her wish to be left alone. Others say she rejected him, so he freed her, and she left to return to her people. Still others say that when she rejected him, he freed her, and they married later at her choosing! *She is not here to tell us what she chose*, but look at what *you choose* to tell about her!" She jabbed the air with her finger. "That choice is about you, not about the Prophet's guidance for us." Her voice rose, "So don't you dare say you speak for him!" She looked at him harshly. "Mother told me to never marry a man unless he would be Muhammad to my Rayhana. 'Only marry', she said, 'if you are free to refuse'." She looked him up and down. "I was right to reject you."

Mustafa lost control and threw all he had at her, "You say you love the Prophet, but if you loved him, you would love everything that he has done and all that he has shown us. Have you forgotten that he said, 'None of you will have faith until he loves me, Muhammad, more than his father, his children, and all of humanity?' That includes more than your opinion about how the world should be, Zaytuna!"

She turned on him, "And didn't he also say, 'None of you has faith until he wants for his brother what he wants for himself?'"

"What are you getting at?"

Her voice turned cold, "So then what you want is to be owned by a man who shoves his cock in you whenever he likes, just not when you are praying!"

"Zaytuna!"

"My point made."

His voice was tight, but clear, "This is what God willed for men and women. You will answer to God for not accepting His will."

She shook her head at him. "I cannot believe you could become a puppet of these scholars."

Mustafa became defensive, "Ibn Salah is a good man."

"How could he be a good man if he has a wife who is incapable of doing anything other than have babies? She sits there all day long with his mother and his sister. His wife says he is so busy that she rarely sees him. Does he not want to talk to his wife? What kind of man is that? What kind of love is that?"

"You don't know what their life is like! Perhaps he is grateful to have a woman who is not always pushing at him and arguing with him, but someone with whom he can be distracted at the end of his day!"

She looked at him as if he were lost forever. "What would your mother say if she heard you?"

Mustafa reflexively rubbed the back of his head as she turned and walked away, placing the package they had handed her in front of the first beggar she saw, leaving him to walk back to Tutha alone. He stopped and watched as the old beggar woman unwrapped the package, revealing folds of richly embroidered wool and silk.

16

The imam's widow screeched at Ammar, "Why is that girl still alive!"

Ammar sat on one of the family's luxurious couches and watched Isam closely, keeping in mind Saliha's observation that he felt more for his sister-in-law than he should. He could see that Isam wanted to comfort her, but that he held back. If there was no love there, he'd be freer to comfort her without worry that he would betray his true feelings. Saliha was right.

"It's only been three days, we must build our case, which is why..."

Hanan wasn't listening. "I told you she killed him!"

"Let's hear him." Isam tried to mollify her, "She'll be executed before long. God's justice is exacting."

She looked at Isam. "I told you, we must contact Qadi Abu Burhan, he can have this handled immediately." She threw her hand out from underneath her wrap, pointing at Ammar. "This man is incompetent!"

"I understand your frustration," Ammar replied coolly. "We are tying up a few loose ends right now. If I could just ask a few questions."

"And he comes to us on a Friday!" She looked him up and down. "'Ammar', that's a Shia name. For all we know, he spent his day cursing God's caliphs. He has no interest in protecting the rights of our family!"

"Hanan, they would not put him in charge of Grave Crimes if he could not be fair."

She shifted her body away from them, so that she was facing the far wall.

Isam sighed almost imperceptibly at this display. He inclined his head. "Please ask your questions."

Ammar nodded in thanks. "Did you find the talisman for us?"

Still facing the wall, Hanan said, "I found it and threw it into a public well, the ifrit will follow it and never find us again."

Ammar closed his eyes in frustration. "We needed the talisman for evidence." He turned to Isam, "Maybe the girl used a poison to kill him, rather than the talisman? Are there any poisons in the house that would have caused his symptoms?"

Hanan turned back to face Ammar, "His symptoms? He died!"

"What herbs do you keep in the house? Any medicines? Anything to kill rodents?"

She waved her hand in the direction of the room beyond them. "Ask the servants. How am I to know what is in this house? I am healthy. I take nothing. My beloved used pennyroyal for colds, but he hadn't been sick in years."

Isam looked at her quizzically, then answered Ammar himself, "I use a mixture of rue, dill seed, and belladonna to control my epilepsy. It reduces the incidence somewhat, but I cannot see how it could kill him. I take quite a bit of it," he spread out his arms, "and here I am."

"I'll need to speak to whoever would have access to your medicine."

Hanan shot back, "My servants did not do this. I have told you. It was the slave."

"Is there anything else?" Isam asked.

Isam's face told him there was something Hanan was holding back. Maybe he could prod it out of them. "This may be difficult. I'm sorry to be the one to tell you, but she may not be executed if convicted, or, if so, not immediately. As a slave, her punishment may be argued to be half that of a free person. She would be flogged, then sold if you do not want her."

Hanan's silk niqab nearly blew open from the force of her words, "*Want her*?"

"I assumed as much." Ammar answered, "The proceeds from the sale would belong to you, and the blood money would be paid out of the caliphal coffers. The master would be liable for the blood money paid out for their slave's transgression, but that obviously won't work in this case."

"My God, we don't want the money!" Isam exclaimed, "Send it all to the poor house."

"I'll let the administrator for the Chief of Police know your wishes. But there is another complication."

The two of them stared at Ammar in disbelief that there could be anything else.

"She is pregnant."

Hanan screamed and fell back across the couch, flinging her hand over her face.

"Anat Hiia!" Isam yelled, "Come!"

A servant ran into the room. Ammar recognized her name as Mandaean, but she wasn't wearing any distinguishing clothing marking her as a non-Muslim. It had been a long time since any caliph had enforced these laws, so people had become relaxed in their practice. He thought, *God protect us from any caliph who does.*

Anat Hiia called out behind her, "Bihrun!" She rushed to Hanan and lifted her up, patting her on the back, saying, "Here, here." There was an unmistakable look of disgust on her face.

Another servant came in quickly, a boy, he guessed her brother by the Mandaean name, carrying a cup of water. Anat Hiia took it from him and indicated to him to wait, then deftly lifted Hanan's niqab just enough so she could drink. "Small sips, Ma'am. Small sips. There you go."

Ammar kept an eye on Isam. He was distressed and watched Anat

Hiia care for her as if he wished he could do it himself. This man could have killed his brother to be closer to his brother's wife. But Hanan's reactions, and from what Saliha observed, he didn't think the feeling was reciprocated.

"Take her elsewhere to rest," Isam said to Anat Hiia.

Anat Hiia gestured to her brother. Both got on either side of Hanan and tried to help her stand. She moaned, her knees buckling slightly. Anat Hiia said gently, "Come now, let's get to the other room where you can rest."

The housekeeper ran in. The wiry old woman pushed past Ammar and checked Hanan's eyes, saying, "I'm back now, Ma'am. Look at you going and fainting when I step out for just a moment. I'll have something that will fix you right up." She patted her hand. "You can stand now, they have you."

Hanan nodded and stood, gripping the arms of Anat Hiia and Bihram tightly, and walked slowly, dropping, then recovering, every few steps.

Isam watched her go. When she was out of the room, he asked, "What will happen now that Mu'mina is pregnant?"

"If she is convicted, and the baby is born alive, there will be no punishment until after the child is weaned. The child is legitimately your brother's and will inherit from his father's estate. He will be your family. As I understand it, you will have rights over him at birth. You can take legal custody of him when he is weaned, or even as a newborn with an appeal to the court or a mediator."

Isam was aghast. "You must realize that she will not allow that child into this house."

"Yes, I can see that. Then you'll have to make arrangements."

Isam leaned in, his voice dropping, "Ghazi, you should know my brother was not a good man. Hanan deserved better. As it became clear that she could not have children, he forgot about her. Her own love for him became more desperate as he moved on. He saw women when he needed to, in addition to his slave, and was a gambler as well. There were tensions recently concerning payments to women and gambling debts. She does not know this. But you should know who he was, for your investigation, and that the child *will not* come here."

"We'll follow it up, thank you. But I must press you on the matter of poisons in the house. If the slave poisoned him, it is the surest way to secure a conviction."

"Why do you think it was poison?"

"The symptoms, the pain he had in his arm, the clamminess of his face, his difficulty breathing, even seeing a jinn. All of it could have been caused by the ingestion of belladonna or a combination of that herb and others."

"But he would have to have had ingested so much of it!"

"The pharmacist said it would not take much belladonna to produce these symptoms."

Isam said, "I do not know the ratio in my mixture. There cannot be much belladonna in it, then, if that is the case."

"Are your herbs are pre-mixed for you or do they do it here?"

"I do not know. I am also unaware of what other herbs are present in the house. You will need to speak to the housekeeper, Ta'sin. But I do not take them in tea. They are mixed with dates. I take them in filled pastries to mask the taste."

"I know this is delicate, but is there any chance he took the herbs himself? If what you say about his debts is true, perhaps he took his own life?"

Isam sat back and thought about it, then answered, "Hanan does not know, but I have supported this family from the beginning. I am unable to marry because of my epilepsy. I have supported my mother, my younger brother, Hashim, as he trained to be a scholar, and my younger sister until her marriage. I have continued to support Hashim and will continue to support Hanan now he is gone. The entirety of his income went to his pleasures. As far as I am aware, he never gambled beyond his income until a few months ago. I assured him I would pay this one time, but he never took the money from me."

"So, he had no need to kill himself?"

"Ghazi, I am certain. But not because of the money, but rather because he had no shame. Why would a man with no shame kill himself?"

It was a reasonable assumption, he had to admit it.

Isam spoke again, unprompted, "Hanan imagines my brother paid for all this." He waved his hand around the lavishly decorated room, with its couches covered in silk, heavy curtains, embroidered pillows, and low copper tables shining in the light of the oil lamps burning even during the day. "But she need never know the truth. Her stability is the most important thing. It is why I live here. She believes they lived with me because I cannot live alone due to my illness. But, of course, with servants, one is never alone. Rather, I live here to watch over her, not her over me. We grew up with her. She is our cousin." He inclined his head. "It is my pleasure to care for her."

Ammar nodded in acknowledgment of the sacrifice. Isam displayed all the resentment of a man unacknowledged for what he does for the woman he loves. More the reason to kill his brother. But why would he dismiss the idea of suicide? If he had killed him, what better way to lay the fault than on his own brother's despair? The police could keep the suicide quiet. No one need know. The case against the girl would be dismissed. It would be written up, shelved, and forgotten. He'd seen it done before in high profile cases.

"One last thing, sir. Do you import anything that might be considered a poison that the girl could have got a hold of?"

"Anything would be locked in my warehouse," Isam replied.

"May I interview your housekeeper?"

"Let me see how Hanan is doing." Isam stood. "Ta'sin might be able to leave her now."

Ammar watched him leave then stood himself, looking around the room and wondering how many hungry people in the poor neighbourhoods of Karkh could be fed if this upholstery were just a little less luxurious. The housekeeper came in before long, saying, "What can I do for you?"

He looked down at the small woman's hard face. He asked, "Is there any poison in the house?"

"We have poison for the rodents locked up in a box in a shed in the kitchen courtyard. Mr. Isam's medicine, and everything else we have that would be dangerous for children, is in a locked cabinet. The family don't want the little ones getting into anything when they come to visit." She looked beyond him, then confided, "But the eldest boy, he could use a hard slap now and again or a taste of that poison to teach him a lesson."

Ammar did not react, "Oh?"

"Spoilt. Every one of them. But not my business. I run this house tight; that's my only concern here, and no one gets into that cabinet."

"And who has the key?"

She slapped her side. Keys jangled. She had belted her wrap, and the keys were hanging from it on a metal ring.

"What do you do with the keys at night?"

"They're in my room with me. I've got a door, and I bolt it."

Ammar laughed bitterly. What female servant would not give to have a door with a bolt? He doubted that Mu'mina had been given one.

"Other than Anat Hiia, are there any other female servants here?"

"No."

"Anyone else?"

She put her hands on her hips. "Come now, you saw the boy. There's also a man who handles the private things for Mr. Isam and the imam."

"And where is he?"

"He is out getting Mr. Isam's horse from the neighbourhood stable."

"Does Anat Hiia sleep here?"

She said without flinching, understanding his question, "Anat Hiia is new, never met Imam Hashim. She's taken up the work that Mu'mina left behind."

"Where do you get Mr. Isam's herbs?"

"From the pharmacist in the near market, a doctor ordered the mixture, and the pharmacist makes it up." She looked him square in the face. "I give it exactly as prescribed."

"The Near Market?"

She laughed at him. "The 'near' market, the one nearest here."

He took note of her attitude and the place. "Which stall is his?"

"Our pharmacist is the one closest to the fresh flower stalls. A fat man, smells of garlic. Abdallah ibn Barik."

He nodded. "And how do you think Imam Hashim died?"

"I wouldn't know, sir."

She was a steady woman. He tried to push her off-balance just a bit to see what she would say. "Did you give something to him? Even by mistake?"

She squared her feet. "I'm not the sort to kill."

"Everyone is the sort to kill when pushed hard enough."

"Well," she said, "Then I've not been pushed hard enough."

"Not even to protect Mu'mina?"

Ta'sin cackled. "That crow got what she was bought for. I don't know what she thought she deserved. She had a very high attitude, that one. She cleaned well enough, but never at my command and only at her liking. I suppose that's why the imam favoured her. He liked some fight in a woman."

Wincing at her words, he stood. "That'll be enough."

Ta'sin rose. "I'll get Mr. Isam."

Ammar said to Isam when he returned, "I appreciate your patience. I've got everything I need for now."

Isam nodded and indicated that he would walk him out.

Partway out the gate door to the street, Ammar said to him, "Inshallah, this will be resolved soon."

"God willing," Isam replied, and shut the gate behind him.

THE FOURTH DAY

17

Tein prepared himself to make the same useless speech to yet another herbalist in the Great Market of Karkh. Everyone dodged his questions. Ammar had checked the market nearest to the imam's house after his interview with the family, but no one would admit to anything. The family's pharmacist admitted to creating the prescribed mixture, nothing else. Who would admit to selling anyone poison to kill a man?

At the next stall, a small copper-skinned man on a ladder was placing a jar back onto a sagging shelf. He was wearing an undyed wrap around his waist with a short qamis and wool shawl over it in the same natural colour and a brightly embroidered cap instead of a turban. The shelves were heaving with jars of every available item while dried up birds, bits of bone, beaks, hide, and fur hung in net bags from a thin rope strung from one wall to the other. Clay and brass pitchers were labelled in script he did not recognize. Tein put his hand on the thin strip of counter separating customer and shopkeeper and coughed to indicate he was there, then said, "Assalamu alaykum."

The man twisted around toward him, still on the ladder. He spoke with only a trace of an accent, "Wa alaykum assalam, what can I get for you?"

"I need some help tracking down a person who may have bought herbs here."

The man climbed down the ladder and stood on a raised platform of bricks that served to bring him to average height, and asked, nodding to Tein's black turban, "You are police?"

"Yes."

"This is not about my goods? The Marketplace Inspector's man has been by to check my weights and measures. Nothing is out of place here."

"You've done nothing wrong. And if we find the person we are looking for, you will still have done nothing wrong."

The man looked skeptical.

"Even if the person bought the herbs from you."

The man leaned on the counter with one hand. "You have no way to guarantee that. The Marketplace Inspector, the Police, you all do what you like. You are fair when fairness suits you. What's your word worth?"

Tein had heard versions of the same objection all day, that is when people were willing to object rather than simply play stupid. He was exhausted by the game. "Nothing. My word is nothing. But an enslaved girl was raped by her master. Someone killed him, and she's been arrested for it."

"Get a confession out of her and leave us alone."

"It's just that, I don't think she did it."

"Oh? Since when do the police care about solving crimes?"

Tein said, "I do."

The man smiled. "I've heard stories about fair ones. But usually, they involve the caliph, that bastard, dressing up in the clothes of the people, wandering the streets. He happens across some terrible crime and solves it through his incredible acumen." The man started laughing. "Have you heard these?"

"Yes."

The man kept laughing, far longer than he should have.

Tein waited.

He finally stopped, choking a bit on his words, "They pay the storytellers to ply us while we are simply trying to relax. We are forced to listen to this drivel about how his jealous eye is over all of us, making sure we keep on the straight and narrow. And so here you are, his representative. It's true. He cares." He started laughing again.

Tein waited until he was quiet. "I'm going to save the life of this girl."

"And why do you care?"

Tein considered him. Maybe telling him the truth was the only way, "She reminds me of my mother. She's a fiery thing, backs down from nothing."

"She's Zanji, black like you?"

Tein didn't bother to correct him that he was Nubian, "Yes."

"You stick together, I suppose. There's a group of you Zanjis that sit outside Baraqan's paper shop, another Zanji."

"You're from Sind. Do you all stick together?"

The man sucked his teeth. "We're all Sindi here, no matter where we're actually from."

"Just like we're all Zanji."

The man laughed again. "Well-played. And, yes, we stick together, too."

"Stick together or not, I don't believe she did it."

"A woman raped will kill."

Tein nodded. "True."

The man retreated from the counter and sat down on a bench along the far wall, putting his slippered feet up on a box facing Tein. He did not respond to the rudeness of the gesture. From his ill-mannered perch, the herbalist asked, "So what do you think happened?"

"I think someone else in the household poisoned him and blamed it on her."

"Why couldn't she have poisoned him?"

"She could have, I guess you'll tell me that. Has there been a Zanji girl with small scars, bumps across her nose and cheekbones, in here asking for belladonna?"

"No."

"Okay, has anyone come in here asking for it?"

He replied, "I'll need more than that."

"An Arab woman, in a black wrap and niqab."

The man laughed. "Really?"

"She might have been alone, or with a housekeeper, or maybe the housekeeper came alone." He repeated the description Ammar had given him, "Small Arab woman, older, wrinkled face, brown eyes."

He laughed again at the general description. "No."

"A tall man, wealthy, light-skinned Arab, thin nose, angular face."

"No."

There was no use. Tein slapped the counter. "Well, thanks for your help."

As Tein stepped away from the stall counter, his leg was struck hard from behind. He nearly buckled, catching himself with his good leg and turning. A boy was on the ground with his legs up in the air. Tein reached down without thinking and grabbed him, the boy's ratty short robe nearly coming off his back as Tein lifted him up with one hand. "You alright?" Keeping a grip on the boy, he looked down the lane for whoever was chasing him. One of the Marketplace Inspector's officers was running after him, out of breath.

The officer stopped before them, breathing hard, hands on his knees. "Thanks. I'll take him."

"What's he done?"

"He took a coin purse off a woman back there in the Fabric Seller's Market. Just sitting there counting her coins and he stole the purse right out of her lap."

Tein looked down at the boy. He was terrified, looking back and forth between the two men. He imagined that the child did not know which of them presented a worse fate, but he would soon. Tugging on the boy's arm, he said, "Not very smart of her to count her coins where someone could just grab them like that? Someone in need takes what they can get, right?"

The boy was wide-eyed and didn't speak.

The officer said, "Okay, I've got my breath now. Let me have him."

"I'm police, I'll have him."

"Come now, petty crime in the marketplace isn't yours."

Tein looked past the officer's shoulder and smiled. The officer tucked his head back and asked, as he turned, "What're you looking at?"

"Me, I think!" Saliha was suddenly standing right behind the officer, but her eyes were on Tein.

Still holding onto the boy's arm, Tein asked her, "What are you doing here?"

She held up a sack. "Getting lotus leaves and camphor for the hospital. What are *you* doing here?"

The officer interrupted, "I'm not only in charge of petty crime here, but I'm also in charge of what you two are doing. No lewd talk between men and women, so give me the boy and move on."

"What did the boy do?" Saliha asked.

Tein answered, "He stole some coins from a woman who was not minding her purse."

"In the Karkh Market?" She laughed, turning to the officer, "Shouldn't you fine the woman for being stupid?"

The officer yelled, "We are here to stop this sort of thing, so the woman does not have to watch her purse! Now give him to me."

The boy began pulling away from Tein with all he had. Tein tipped his chin toward him and raised his eyebrows at Saliha, hoping she grasped what he meant. He said to the officer, "No harm done. I was just having some fun with you. A little inter-agency rivalry," and held the boy out to him.

Just as he did, Saliha stumbled forward and fell down in faint, bumping into the marketplace officer. Tein let go of the boy to catch her but missed. The boy fell to his back as Tein knelt down beside her. The officer had to push past them to grab the boy, just catching him by the edge of his robe. The boy kicked the officer in the face with his filthy foot, his heel catching the officer's cheek and knocking his head back. The boy scrambled up and ran for his life. Tein watched him go, soon lost in the crowd.

Two Persian women in face veils rushed to Saliha, one yelling at Tein, "Get back, you! Get your hands off her!"

Tein stood up and checked on the officer. "You alright?"

The officer touched his face.

"No blood," Tein said.

The officer glared at him. "No thanks to you."

Tein stepped back while the officer stood. The women had propped Saliha up and were trying to make sure that she stayed properly covered. One had collected her bag so no one could run off with it.

Tein asked from a respectable distance, "Are you alright?"

Saliha was still moaning.

One of the women demanded, "Who are you to her?"

He tapped his turban and whispered menacingly, "Police."

The woman shut her mouth.

Tein called out to the herbalist he'd just been questioning, "Can you give us some water?"

The herbalist looked over his counter and shook his head, having seen the whole thing. "Get your own water. You're blocking the way to my shop."

One of the women yelled at him, "What is wrong with you Sindis! Can't you see the woman's fainted?"

The herbalist didn't move.

Brushing himself off, the marketplace officer said, "If you'd just given me the boy when I asked! What's your name? I'm going to report you to the Inspector. He'll speak to your boss."

Tein refused and laughed at him.

"How many black men of that size do you think they have working for the police in Karkh." The herbalist leaned on his counter. "Just describe him. He let that boy go, and I'll swear to it."

"The woman fainted, what was I to do?" Tein objected.

"I'm turning you in. And you be careful with that woman. We

have eyes everywhere." The officer turned on his heels and took off back to the Fabric Seller's Market.

Tein said to the two women helping Saliha, "I'll take her from here."

They wouldn't let go.

Pointing to his turban again, he said, "Police."

The women helped her stand and handed her over to him unwillingly. Tein took the bag from one of the women, and Saliha by the arm. As they went on their way, they looked back to make sure all was well. He said to Saliha, "Let me walk you back to the hospital with this."

She pulled her wrap over her face so only he could hear her, "Oh no, I'm heading back home. I'll take it to work tomorrow morning."

As they walked, he said, "You did good just then."

She smiled. "Why, thank you. And what were you up to?"

"Getting nowhere interviewing herbalists about members of the imam's household who might have poisoned him. The pharmacists answer immediately but are no help. No one is getting anything that wasn't prescribed."

"Household?"

"The poison would work immediately, so it had to be given to him at home."

Saliha tipped her head, "It could be Mu'mina, then?"

"But she'd admit to it. She wants to take the blame. So, no."

"Oh." She began, "Tein, if no one is telling you anything, maybe you should..."

Tein interrupted, "Ammar has already questioned everyone in the market by the imam's house. The rest of Karkh is up to me."

"You'll be here all week! No need to walk me home."

He winked at her. "I'll get back to the questioning soon enough."

They had not gone far when Tein's gaze fell on a man crossing the market lane into an alleyway. *Is that the pharmacist from the hospital?* He asked, "Do you mind if we make a small detour?"

Saliha pressed against his arm. "Not at all."

The narrow alleyway was lined with shops selling paper, ink and pens and was covered by sheets of woven reeds. Sunlight dotted the alleyway and walls of the shops. Ibn Ali turned in at the very end and sat down. As they got closer, Tein saw three black men, including the pharmacist, sitting on stools around a table, chatting.

Ibn Ali caught sight of him, stood smiling, and called him over.

Tein returned his greeting, but Saliha was tugging him in the opposite direction. She had pulled her wrap over her face so that only one eye was showing and had turned her face away from the men entirely. He realized suddenly that she couldn't be recognized with an unrelated man in public and keep her job.

"Please come and sit..." then seeing a woman was with him, Ibn Ali said, "I see you are busy. We won't hold you. But my friends and I often come here to chat. Please come by sometime."

He was torn for just a second, wanting to send Saliha back on her own and stay and chat, but he bowed his head to Ibn Ali, promising, "I will."

Saliha kept her head down until they were back on the market lane, when she said, "I wonder if he recognized this wrap. I wear it to the hospital every day."

"Don't worry." But Tein had no doubt that every man at the hospital knew her and would recognize her wrap, even if her face were covered. "If Ibn Ali says anything, you were with me on police business about the murder you witnessed at the hospital."

Saliha nodded, not sure that Shatha would understand, but what else could she do at this point? She was not going to miss this chance to be alone with him. They turned the corner onto the main thoroughfare in the market, falling into the rhythm of the crowd. Every step they took together sparked with tension.

She wondered if he was going to talk. He seemed to be considering what he should say, then came up with, "Is that a new wrap you are wearing? It's very pretty."

Saliha nearly burst out laughing with pleasure. The awkwardness of the question was delightful. She quipped, "Zaytuna's not very happy with it."

"What has your pretty wrap done to her?"

"It's a reminder to her that I have a new job without her."

"You know Zaytuna, quick to hold a grudge, long to let go of it."

She nudged him. "That's not very encouraging!"

"It'll be fine."

His arm brushed against her own through her wrap. She held herself still inwardly, wondering if it was by accident or if he had intended to touch her. They fell back into an awkward silence. She looked up at him and smiled. He looked down at her, his eyes lighting up with a small smile, so different from the dull haze of pain he typically carried.

Looking down the road again, he abruptly craned his head. He smiled more broadly, and called out, "Khalil, Khalil!"

She looked to where he was calling, stung that this broad smile had not been for her. There was a tall Arab, almost as tall as Tein and as solidly built and muscular, leaning against a wall with a thin miswak in his mouth. He wore his dark blue turban wound under his chin in such a way that it fell across his face, just slightly. As they drew closer, Tein leading her through the crowd to him, she saw that his brown eyes were lined with kohl, and his thick linen robe hung off him as if he would shed it in a moment. Recognizing Tein, the man smiled in return; his perfect small, white teeth shone, ready to bite. He pushed himself off the wall and stood, his shoulders back, his legs apart. She drew a sharp intake of breath. He did not have a sword, but there was a dagger on his waist strap under the short robe, its hilt worn from use. It was like Tein's, a knife meant for violence. Khalil came to them, unworried whether or not he was in anyone's way and people in the road parted for him. Saliha drew her wrap around her body more carefully, covering all but her eyes, and standing somewhat behind Tein, but did not look away.

Khalil tipped his chin at Tein, indicating his turban. "I heard you'd joined the police. Bad pay. Why didn't you come to work with me? You'd have a purse full of coin and wouldn't be wearing such a shabby coat!" He looked down. "And sandals in this cold."

Tein laughed at him. "You must have tapped some big debtors with talk like that, Ghazi. Last time I saw you, your clothes were not as fine, and you didn't make such a strong case." He slapped the man on the shoulder. "Had I known where it was going, I'd be with you now."

Looking past him and seeing Saliha, he said, "But you seem to be paid well enough for a woman like this."

Tein's smile collapsed and he took a step forward against Khalil, when Saliha came out from behind him, saying with sharpened eyes, "You couldn't afford me, brother. I choose my men, and I would not choose you."

Tein looked down at her in shock, but she could see that the shock was mixed with pleasure, and she smiled.

"Ah! A sharp-tongued one!" He slapped Tein. "Worth every fals."

"As it happens," Tein said, "I've been looking for you."

Khalil held up his hands. "Whatever it is, I did it!"

Laughing, Tein said, "I'm looking into the death of a man who may have had some debts that required persuasion for repayment."

Khalil raised his eyebrows, taking the miswak out of his mouth. "Imam Hashim? Word is out on him. Everyone agrees. It was a well-deserved death. God protect us all from what we deserve."

Saliha said under her breath, "Amin."

"What did you hear?" Tein asked.

"He was late with his payments. He wasn't one of mine. But if you are asking whether or not he was beaten to death, no matter how late a man is with his payments, beating him to death is not going to get the money back."

"It could have been a mistake," Tein offered, "a beating might have gone too far."

Khalil said, looking directly at Saliha, "True. More than one of us takes pleasure from our work."

Tein stiffened. Saliha touched him to let him know she was alright, but she didn't feel him relax.

Khalil frowned in thought. "But if the Amir wanted him dead..."

Tein relaxed his stance at the mention of the Amir. "Give me his real name."

"As if I know the name of the man who runs the best brothels and gambling houses in Baghdad."

Tein huffed, but did not press him, asking instead, "But why would the Amir kill a client like that?"

"If the imam offended him?" Khalil shrugged.

"A well-known religious scholar?"

"Ibn Rashid at-Taymi! You remember that? The Amir ordered it. A servant in the household was paid to smother him. You police said he died in his sleep."

"How do you know this?" Tein was defensive. "The family doctor reported it was a natural death."

"It's not a secret. It was meant to be a warning to others. You police are the last to know! Anyway, I heard an ifrit killed Imam Hashim."

"Maybe not."

Khalil looked down the street, scanning the people of the marketplace. "Whatever the case. He's well-dead. These scholars, such hypocrites. Do the people deserve them?"

Tein called him back to the conversation, "Imam Hashim. His debts. Where did he gamble?"

"You'll go there?" Khalil looked surprised.

Tein nodded. "I'll need to."

"The Pomegranate Nahariyya. It's in a dead-end square just after the last of the wool sellers and before the furniture makers. You can't miss it. You'll need to say to the guard that your mother raised you to be an honourable man."

"What?"

"It's the password. They'll know you're coming with a reference."

Tein laughed.

"I heard he had a regular woman there," Khalil added, looking at Saliha.

Saliha gestured as if she were flicking a piece of filth from her fingers. "These scholars, such hypocrites. I don't take their money."

Khalil smiled at her but asked Tein, "Where did you find this one?"

Tein looked at her. "Friend of my sister, actually."

"The sister who prays all night and refuses to eat?"

"And I pray with her," Saliha snapped. Then she turned slightly, tugging her wrap, so the curve of her ample bottom was outlined. "But I eat."

Khalil tipped his head to her in appreciation, then said to Tein, "Listen. I haven't heard that any of us killed him. I have to go, but I'll keep an ear out. Remember that I was good to you once if any trouble comes my way."

Tein touched his turban, and said, "I will."

Khalil then bowed his head to Saliha, offering her a wink and a hungry smile, and left them.

Once Khalil was out of earshot, Tein said, "You were convincing!"

"You should take me with you to the nahariyya! If you aren't getting anything from the marketplace, what makes you think you'll get anything out of a brothel?"

Tein turned serious, "It wouldn't be safe, Saliha. I can't do that."

She looked at him under her lashes, eyes wide. "But with you, how could I be in any danger?"

"No. That's final."

"Fine then, I've got work to do anyway. I cannot leave Shatha empty-handed, and," she lifted one shoulder to him, "maybe I'll run into Doctor Judah after work."

"That's not going to work with me."

She scolded, laughing lightly, "You are not immune to my charms."

Tein did not return her humour. "No, I am not, but I won't let you put yourself in danger."

"I can help."

"No."

"And if I don't come and I could have been of use, will you wonder if you did everything you could to prove that girl innocent?"

"Saliha, that's not fair."

"All the same, it's true."

He raised his eyebrows. "And not a moment ago you were worried about being seen with me and losing your job."

"I am wearing the wrap I come to work in everyday! Ibn Ali might have remembered. If I go with you, I'll wear my old wrap instead and my face will be covered. No one will recognize me."

He looked down the marketplace road at the lines of shops, then back at her. "Will you do exactly as I say?"

She replied quickly, "Yes, Ghazi, sir!"

He shook his head at her, exasperated. "Tomorrow morning?"

"I will go by the hospital first to let Shatha know I can't work. I'll make something up. Blame it on Zaytuna. One day of missed work, I won't be in any trouble."

"I'll meet you there?"

She looked concerned. "Better not."

"Where then?"

"There is a line of places that sell juice and snacks just before the Wool Seller's Market."

"Around duha time? I'll be coming from my place by the Basra Gate."

She nodded.

"Would you mind if I don't walk you home, after all? I need to head to another marketplace before it closes and keep interviewing the herbalists and pharmacists."

"Not at all." She smiled. Then just as she was about to leave, she said, "It might be the black turban causing the trouble getting people to talk. You need a disguise."

He reflexively touched his turban, then handed her the bag of lotus and camphor. "Good point."

"Head back to the Fabric Seller's Market, then. If you're lucky, you can snatch the purse of some unwary rich woman to pay for it!"

18

Ammar woke up angry from a dream. He stood alone on the plain of Karbala. He was too late. The surviving women and children of the Prophet's noble family had already been captured and driven from the field of battle by men glorying in death and victory. The heads of the martyrs had long been carried away on pikes or slung to the sides of camels in sacks that slapped against the animals' bellies with every rolling step. Ammar stared at the blood that had dripped from the pikes and camels' sides onto the hard desert ground. Each drop glittered with eternal light marking the path to Ibn Ziyad's court in Kufa. Tracking the trail of blood back from the horizon to where he was standing, he realized his feet were bare and he could feel the warm thickness of blood between his toes. White ash blew on a biting wind, first around his feet, then rose, swirling around him, binding him in place. He opened his mouth to scream. An atom's weight of ash alighted on his tongue, and he tasted the burnt remains of the women's tents.

He had twisted himself up in his blankets such that they had bound his ankles, leaving him uncovered on his bedroll, yet sweating despite the cold. Sitting up in the dark of night, he unwound the blankets, freeing his legs and feeling the soles of his feet for blood. Then he got up on his knees, pulled off his nightshirt and used it to rub the sweat off of him, then threw it to the corner of his room.

Standing, bare-chested, in only short sirwal, he went out into the shared courtyard. His neighbour Jamila was outside, tending a fire, for God knows what reason at this hour. But the light meant that she saw him, half-naked, walking to the barrel where they kept their shared store of water. She let out a small scream. Ammar snapped at her, "Go inside, woman, if the sight of a man scandalizes you."

Her drunk husband came lolling out of his room ready to fight, but stumbled, and fell back to sleep where his body had dropped not far from their door. Ammar ignored them and poured cup after cup of icy water over his head until his hair and beard were soaked through. He wiped his face down with one hand, pulling at the end of his beard, then shook the water from his hand and went back into his room.

Ammar leaned against the wall in the darkness, finally feeling the cold as the water dried on his body. He pulled off his soaked sirwal and felt along the wall for his sword, hanging in its scabbard by a belt. Putting it on, he felt the scabbard slap against his bare thigh. Ammar reached around and pulled out the sword, noiselessly, and held it up to God, his knees shaking under the weight of it, and he finally fell to the ground, closing his eyes. When he woke again, it was to the sound of the call to the dawn prayer, naked and cold, his sword unsheathed in his hand, and still angry.

He dressed angry. He ate a loaf of bread on his way to the police offices angry. He waited for Ibn Salah and Mustafa angry. He greeted them angry. And now he walked angry ahead of them out of the Khurasan Gate.

The police chief's Palace and offices on the Tigris were soon in view. They were late, and the lines would be long. People would be already crowding the secretaries' desks and waiting in hopes of being seen that day or the next, or maybe the day after that. They had to stand in line with everyone else. A dedicated administrator for the police would not play well. This police chief wanted to make it seem as if they served the people and not the caliph and his cronies, but it made going to these offices feel like an administrative swamp. More trouble for nothing but play-acting.

Ibn Salah and Mustafa chatted behind him, Ibn Salah holding court. Ammar knew the type. He'd only met the man this morning, but he talked like one of those scholars who cover an intellect and will as hard as stone with a gentle voice and carefully measured gestures of propriety. Mustafa was evidently stunned by it. Tein was going to have to wise him up.

Ibn Marwan was more than happy to have the case transferred to the religious court in Rusafa. It was an embarrassment, and he wanted it off his hands. He had the report written up in such a way that it carefully left out the details of Ammar's botched investigation so there'd be a clean transfer with no administrative recriminations. Ammar had burned when he saw it. His weak interrogation ending in a faulty confession sent up to the Chief of Police's court and his refusal to investigate thoroughly had set all this in motion. Hiding it didn't make him a man. He wanted to hear that voice again, the voice calling him to martyrdom with Husayn, "Ya Ammar! I have glad tidings of paradise for you!" But there was only silence and a dream that left him on the plain of Karbala too late for the battle.

He could half-hear Mustafa arguing some point. It didn't have anything to do with the case, he knew that much. They still needed someone to petition Ibn al-Zayzafuni's court, and Mustafa hadn't found one. His little friends weren't going to risk the possibility of future positions teaching children in grand homes by petitioning the court on behalf of the family of a controversial dead Imam.

The outer gate of the Palace was open, three guards standing along either side. The gates were as high as the walls, too tall for any man to scale, and held open from dawn until dusk every day to give the impression that the police chief was available to an audience at any time. The guards stood still, looking ahead. He wanted to yell at them, *Keep your eyes open! You're the first line of defence, you fools!* But what could six of them do anyway if the people decided to riot? Better for them to step aside and let the people make their demands by ripping the Palace down. *Curse the enemies of the Prophet's family! Every bit of the caliphate and its justice was a lie!* Ammar called out with all his heart, *Sayyidi Husayn! I am your servant! I will fight in your cause!*

He felt a hand on his shoulder. He stepped forward and pivoted, his sword clearing its scabbard before he saw Ibn Salah's face tight with terror.

"Ghazi, Ghazi, please!" Ibn Salah stepped back, his hands up.

Mustafa yelled, scrambling back away from Ammar, "Ghazi!"

Ammar pulled himself back and stood firm, his heart pounding in his chest. He turned his wrist and raised the hilt of his sword, returning it smoothly into his fleece-lined scabbard. He put up his hands, but conceded nothing, "Don't touch a ghazi from behind."

Ibn Salah recovered himself and put his hand over his heart, bowing his head. "You have my apologies, Ghazi."

Mustafa stood still. Ammar could see he was still afraid.

Let them be afraid.

He walked straight through the gardens and its pomegranate trees, picked clean of its fruit, and the long pools of water fed by the Tigris. There had been multi-coloured fish in the pools once, but the poor would come when the gates were open and catch them with nets to cook for their dinner. Now the pools were empty, their surfaces like glass in the cold sun of morning.

They reached the palace gates, here there were more guards at least, six by each side of the door. The men were better armed with short staves, useful for fighting and controlling crowds.

As they walked through the doors, two wealthy men rushed past them to get ahead in line. Ammar wanted to stick his foot out to trip one of the men. Others came in at a resigned pace, knowing they'd be there all day. The vast room was carpeted, there must have been a hundred great rugs laid out end-to-end, in every colour and pattern, all thickly woven. Low couches lined the walls broken only by guards standing at attention at regular intervals. The secretary's desk was at the far end of the room, raised on a carpeted pallet, and a snaking line of people were already there waiting.

Ibn Salah said with some irritation, "We'll be here all day."

"This moves quickly," Ammar said. "We're just registering our names and cases here. He'll refer us to the secretary in the police chief's office who can get us a hearing."

"Don't they have a different process for the police?" Mustafa asked.

"No."

Ammar got in line right behind the man he wanted to trip. The fool smelled liked he had doused himself in rose water and Ammar wanted to slap his excessively wrapped turban off of his head. He noticed the edging on the man's outer robe and laughed aloud. His taraz was the height of vanity; the banding of calligraphy said his full name, over and over and over again. But this ass could not afford to have it embroidered, it was merely inked. The fool turned around, looking him up and down. Ammar goaded, "You should check with your taraz-man, it seems he's written your name in one spot here on the back as 'Abu Abdallah Ahmad ibn Muhammad ibn Ghalib al-Bahil' rather than al-Bahili. But perhaps he saw you were nothing better than a she-camel on the loose and made the change accordingly?"

The man opened his mouth to object, but he saw the black turban, sword, and Ammar's demeanour, and settled for a huff.

Ibn Salah asked over his shoulder, "Is this necessary?"

Ammar didn't answer. He watched the fool ahead move bit by bit as they snaked forward until at last they were standing before the secretary themselves. "I am Ghazi Ammar at-Tabbani from Grave Crimes for Karkh. Ibn Marwan has sent me with a request to have a case moved from the police chief's court to the religious court in Rusafa."

The secretary said, "The request, please?"

He handed over the document. The secretary read it, rolled it back up, and returned it to him. "First, I need all your names." The man wrote down their names, their purpose, and made a mark on the document, then pointed toward an arched doorway leading into another great room. "Proceed directly to the administrator through there. He will take this further."

As they moved on to the next room, people grumbled at them for advancing without a wait, they who had already waited so long. A small, barrel-chested man, who looked like a butcher just short of his leather apron, saw them coming and thundered, "The police and two scholars! Look how they put each other ahead!" He yelled at the secretary, "These police won't do a cursed thing for me! I'm here to complain about it to the Chief, but the way you treat them tells me I won't be seen or heard fairly in this court."

One of the guards nearby said, "You, quiet!"

The butcher turned to the man next to him. "See?"

Ammar looked back at the secretary, who had stood up and gestured to the guard to quiet the men down. He replied so all could hear, "Each of you will be seen in turn. If your case were urgent, you would be moved ahead as well."

The man grunted, "Lies," but sat back down.

Another man called out from the side, "My case is urgent, but I've been waiting three days, coming here each day, then walking clear across the city and back again just to wait again."

The secretary replied, "Get back in line and I will review it."

That was a mistake, thought Ammar. Sure enough, that man got up, but so did many others who filed their way to the back to get their cases reassessed, making the serpentine line before the secretary even longer.

Ammar gave the guard a wry look over the scene, who smiled and nodded sagely. "He's new."

The next room was smaller by half but still grand by any measure; it had the same carpets and low couches. People waited more patiently as they were that much closer to coming before the Chief himself. The administrator sat at another desk on a similar pallet covered with sheepskins.

As they joined the line, Ammar said to Ibn Salah and Mustafa, "You can go sit down."

When Ammar reached the front, he kneeled before the administrator's desk and handed over the letter. The man unrolled the document and examined it. Ammar broke in, "Ibn Marwan has sent me with his approval for a request to move a murder case to the court in Rusafa. The request to move is from the judge of Rusafa himself, Qadi Ibn al-Zayzafuni."

"You are from Grave Crimes. Ammar at-Tabbani, correct?"

Ammar nodded.

"Well, Ammar at-Tabbani, why don't you just tell me the reason, since you won't let me read this."

"The reason isn't in there." Ammar explained, "That's why I'm telling you. An enslaved girl is accused of killing her master, a scholar. It's politically charged. It needs to be handled by another religious scholar to demonstrate that the caliphate is handling the issue fairly. We do not have a petitioner yet, but will by the end of the day."

"Oh, the case of Imam Hashim? You are not the only one."

"What do you mean?" He looked back at Ibn Salah and Mustafa and waved them to come forward with urgency.

Once beside him, Ammar said, "Would you tell them what you just said?"

"Are all of you here now? I do not want to repeat myself. The judge for Karkh, Abu Burhan, has been here himself and spoken with the police chief directly. The case has been moved to his court. They have a petitioner. We haven't put the paperwork through yet, but it has been decided. You are too late."

Ibn Salah pulled a rolled-up document from his sleeve and handed it over. "With respect, we have here a letter from the judge of the court of Rusafa, Qadi Ibn al-Zayzafuni, who has approved that the case be brought to his court should a petitioner be found."

The administrator scanned the document. "I see that according to Qadi Ibn al-Zayzafuni, the objectivity of the judge of Karkh is compromised due to his relationship with the deceased. But," he offered, "one could argue that his familiarity with the case makes him the ideal adjudicator. In fact, I understand that is what he argued to the Chief this morning."

Ibn Salah said, "On the contrary, her case is inflammatory. I myself petitioned the court on her behalf on a matter of extreme cruelty perpetrated by Imam Hashim against her. Qadi Abu Burhan's ruling was in keeping with the law, but it was unpopular, to say the least. There were accusations of judicial impropriety and favouritism among the people and scholars alike. This case must be handled with the utmost care, or I fear the people and the community of scholars will find ground for complaint to the caliph."

"If this case is so sensitive, it should go to the chief judge in the Mazalim High Court."

Ammar looked at Ibn Salah for some sign of what this could mean for them, but his face was impassive.

Ibn Salah continued, "I do not think it should be taken that far. I would argue that it would raise difficulties of another sort. While we must be seen as taking this situation seriously, we should not make so much of it that it becomes a popular scandal on trial." He paused. "I ask you to consider the people's response if they knew a slave was on trial for killing her master, a scholar, who had sexually mistreated her."

The administrator nodded in understanding.

"Her case must be heard objectively, shown to be done so by scholars themselves. We must be seen as holding ourselves to account. Yet, it should not be so public as to become a show trial, as it would in the Mazalim High Court."

Mustafa was silent, his mouth drawn tight.

The administrator turned to Ammar, "And you?"

Ammar found his voice, "As his letter states, Ibn Marwan agrees it needs to be handled carefully, and specifically by Qadi Ibn al-Zayzafuni's court. Complicating matters, the case against her is not clear. We have a weak confession and no direct evidence."

The administrator seemed shocked. "Why has it come this far?"

Ammar owned up to it all, "It is my doing. Her confession was clear at first, so I refrained from pushing her in the interrogation and considering alternative suspects. I had her confession taken and submitted to Ibn Marwan's office. Ibn Marwan sent it to you based on my certainty. It was only when my colleague insisted that I question her further that the doubt came to light, but it was too late."

The administrator asked, "And what of the other woman," he read her name out, "Tan-shol-pan?"

"She is accused of providing the murder weapon, a talisman," Ammar replied. "Ibn Marwan is asking that both be tried together. Again, the caliph would not be happy for the police to be the cause of another riot in Baghdad." He lowered his voice, "That complaint from the caliph would find itself on the Chief's lap, and he would blame those beneath him to save his own neck."

The administrator blanched, but he recovered with a small laugh to break the tension, "Can you imagine how many slaves the caliph would have to free and how many convicts we would have to let loose from the prisons to quiet the people?"

Ibn Salah nodded. "Just so."

The administrator stood. "If you will excuse me, I will go speak to the police chief's assistant on this matter."

He got up, slipped his stockinged feet into leather slippers, tugged his quilted robe straight, and walked to an adjacent room, nodding to the guard as he passed.

Ammar looked at Ibn Salah whose face showed the strain of the conversation. Mustafa had turned to face the door. Ammar said, "Looking to run, Mustafa?"

"If only such a thing were possible," he sighed.

Ibn Salah nudged Ammar. The administrator was on his way back.

He gestured that they should follow him, saying quietly as they walked to the Chief's door. "This case will be finished in a moment." At the door he said, "Just wait until they leave, an officer of the court will present you before Chief al-Amrawayh."

Ammar had only seen the Chief once before, and at a distance. Al-Amrawayh had ordered a few hundred of the thousands of men he governed to be lined up in his palace courtyard for inspection. It was to be a display of the higher offices of the police, not the watchmen who patrolled Baghdad's streets day and night, the guards of the caliph's courts and administrators' palaces, the officers of the judicial courts and prisons, nor the men who policed the great roads outside the city. Al-Amrawayh had lined up under his eye the administrators of the various quarters of the city, the men who ran the offices that handled sensitive crimes, those who ran the spies and the men who worked undercover infiltrating criminal gangs or political and religious enemies, and them, the investigators of Grave Crimes.

Military life in the police was different from the frontier where it was men fighting as brothers, foot-soldier and officer alike deep in the fields of battle, all the men and their families living in the camps when they pressed beyond the towns, expanding the empire's borders, one bloody skirmish at a time. This here, in Baghdad, was another world, and he didn't like it.

They slipped into the Chief's office and stood along the back wall. The Chief sat on sheepskins on the carpeted floor with a simple backrest to lean against. He wore a black robe and woolen wrap without adornment and sat with his legs tucked beneath him. Ammar appreciated the performance of humility but the braziers on either side of him for warmth gave the Chief away. Ammar had heard the Chief was a rough man. He had argued so brutally with Caliph al-Mutamid's son, he caused the man to have a stroke. Yet here was the great Chief himself, using braziers so early in the cold months. This man, who had more power than any man should, could not manage an early autumn chill.

A couple of guards stood against one wall looking at Ammar, Mustafa and Ibn Salah. One whispered something to the other who then quietly exited the chamber.

Two men stood before the Chief, one looked like a merchant, the kind who sold paper or copper pots but doesn't make them.

The merchant said firmly, "I demand it."

The Chief leaned in. "I will not permit you to kill this man. I would be happy to see your daughter married to him instead."

"Never!"

"Yet the caliph's coffers will happily pay the dowry for her and offer a present to your family in celebration of the marriage."

"No," the merchant said, "I demand that the man be killed."

The man in question looked like no more than a boy, a pretty boy at that. He trembled before them.

The Chief called to a guard, "Fatih, bring me your sword."

Fatih started to pull his sword from the scabbard. "No, man! Give me the belt, the sword and the scabbard, too."

The boy cowered, putting his hands against the back of his neck.

Ammar thought, *He's going to give this man a sword to kill the boy!*

Mustafa grabbed Ammar's sleeve, horrified.

The guard gave the Chief his sword in his scabbard, the belt hanging off it. The Chief asked the merchant to come forward. The Chief held the scabbard and offered the hilt to him, saying, "Take the sword." The man pulled the sword out clumsily, letting it hang by his side.

Ammar braced himself to intervene, no matter the cost.

The Chief said, holding out the scabbard towards him with one hand. "Now put it back in." The merchant tried to return the sword to the scabbard but the Chief jerked it away just enough that the man missed it with the point of the sword. The Chief slapped his knee and said, "Come on, put it back in!"

The merchant tried, but the Chief moved the scabbard again so he could not return it. He became frustrated and demanded, "Why won't you let me do it?"

The Chief replied, "If your daughter did not want the man, he would not have been able to force her. If you want to kill him for what he did, then you must kill them both."

The man returned the sword to the scabbard and fell to his knees before the Chief, begging, "Let them marry."

The administrator came up next to Ammar and whispered sharply, "I didn't say to wait inside!" Ammar retreated from the room, pulling Ibn Salah and Mustafa along.

Mustafa whispered, "Will our intrusion go against us?"

"He breaks with God's law!" Ibn Salah grabbed Mustafa's arm.

Ammar cut in, "You didn't know that he rules as he likes?"

"Yes, yes, of course." Ibn Salah shook his head. "But I am shocked to see it. They are fornicators; lashing is called for, not execution or marriage!"

"How did he know what the daughter wanted?"

Ibn Salah looked annoyed by Mustafa's question, "We must get this case out of his court."

"I hope you're right about Ibn al-Zayzafuni," Mustafa said.

"There will at least be some principles by which her case is examined!"

The merchant and the young man left the court, neither looked satisfied.

An officer came out and called out their names into the waiting room.

Ammar raised his hand. "That's us."

The officer said, "Stand before the chief and do not speak."

The chief's secretary kneeled beside him, speaking to him quietly and pointing to documents before him in several places.

The chief handed the documents back to the secretary, then held his hands out in supplication. "May God bless these proceedings with His wisdom and may He be pleased with my decree humbly offered in His name, and with the permission of our caliph Abu Ahmad ibn Ali Muhammad al-Muktafi billah, may God protect him and his glorious rule. If I should decide wrongly, may it become known to me, and may I be held to account for my errors." He said, "Amin," into his hands, and as he lifted his head sighed, "Bismillah." He looked at the three men sitting before him, slapped his thighs with both hands, and said, looking at Ammar, "You are from Grave Crimes?"

Ammar's throat caught on the words, "I am, sir."

"Is it you who sent this case forward before it was fully investigated?"

Ammar nodded.

"Yes?"

"Yes, sir."

"I will be sending an account of my displeasure to Ibn Marwan. I will leave it to him to decide whether or not you are to maintain your position." He gestured to the documents. "You have shaken the foundation of our justice with your ineptitude. Now this case is being called to go before a court that is unfamiliar with adjudication of grave crimes. These religious scholars sit around all day in mosques debating theoretical murders that no man has ever committed and concocting legal resolutions that no one could administer in the world outside their legal fantasies." He raised his hand. "I face the people who have committed these crimes every day. I face their victims." He waved his hand in dismissal. "God guide these scholars, for they are ignorant."

Ammar held firm before the judgment against him.

The chief leaned in and looked in Ammar's eyes, saying slowly, "Any injustice done is yours to face before God on the Last Day."

He said in a clear voice, "Yes, sir."

The chief leaned back, let out a great exhalation of air, and slapped his thighs again. "Good. Despite the right of my court over the murder, I grasp the sensitivity of the situation as that fool Qadi Abu Burhan made his case this morning." He frowned. "Now, I see there are further complications of which he did not apprise me. I agree to let the case go from my jurisdiction on the condition it is seen in Qadi Ibn al-Zayzafuni's court. I understand you do not have a petitioner for the case?"

Ibn Salah spoke up, "That is so, sir."

"Qadi Abu Burhan's son was to bring the petition forward to his father's court on behalf of Imam Hashim's family. It seems only fitting that he should do the same in Qadi Ibn al-Zayzafuni's court. Of course, I cannot force him, but I will send a letter strongly suggesting it given his father's misrepresentation of the facts before me this morning."

"Thank you, sir," Ibn Salah answered.

He directed himself to Ammar, "My secretary will draw up the papers to transfer the prisoners from the police jail to Ibn al-Zayzafuni's cells."

Then he said to all three, "It's done, then. May the outcome be one that restores order to our city," then to Ammar, "and saves your sorry soul."

Mustafa replied, "Amin....sir."

Al-Amrawayh laughed. "The 'amins' are to God, young man." Ammar felt someone behind him and nearly jumped out of his skin. The chief waved his hand to the officer behind them. "Take them out. I have many cases before me today."

The three men followed the officer. Ammar's legs were numb and shaking. He walked as carefully as he could until they got through the door. The officer pointed to the administrator they had spoken to. "He has your papers. You'll need to wait for them."

Ammar leaned against the wall after they got out, shaking his feet to get the feeling back in them. Mustafa wandered out behind him and stood beside him on the wall, breathing deeply.

"You two are as wide-eyed and pale-skinned as houris," Ibn Salah mocked.

Tipping his chin to Ibn Salah, Ammar objected, "My legs fell asleep standing there."

"What do you think Ibn Marwan will do with you?"

"I'm his best man," Ammar said with an assurance that he did not feel.

Ibn Salah said, showing his temper, "That man is a danger to the faith. He has no right to adjudicate such cases over us who have spent our lives discerning God's legal intent. And his complaints of us! He knows better!"

Mustafa nodded.

A young man walked over with several rolled documents. "These are from the secretary."

They looked over the papers, everything was there. The letter to Ibn Marwan, the approval of the case to be transferred to Ibn al-Zayzafuni's court, and the transfer of the prisoners.

Ibn Salah raised his eyebrows. "He's making you take your dressing down to Ibn Marwan yourself?"

"It is a good sign that he trusts you to do so," Mustafa said weakly.

Ammar shook his head. "No. It's a test. If this document didn't make it to Ibn Marwan, you'd find out about it when they came to take my ignoble head."

THE FIFTH DAY

19

Tein looked down at the stool offered to him to sit at the tavern and shook his head. It was early yet, but they were serving. He decided against sitting in the tavern. *She shouldn't think I'm a drunk.* He looked down at the line of stalls nearby selling sliced fruit and unfermented juices. *She knows you're a drunk.* Making his way to the closest juice stall, he considered the only open stool. It was too short for him, sized for a woman or a child. He found a bit of wall and leaned against it, tired. He pulled himself off the wall so he wouldn't look tired to her. Then, he leaned back against it, trying to look casual, one shoulder against the wall, one knee slightly bent, looking down.

He got there early so she would not have to bear up under men's looks and jibes for simply standing still for too long in the marketplace. God forbid she'd have a cough; she'd be taken as a prostitute signaling her availability to passing men. What was he even thinking taking her with him to the nahariyya?

He reminded himself she was proud of doing as she likes, even at risk to her reputation. Tein didn't know what to do, caught between wanting to protect her and wanting her wildness. He looked at the men around him. What kind of man was he that he wanted this woman who would never accept a man's right over her? *Look what became of mother.* He wondered then what his mother would think of Saliha. *Impious Saliha. Mother would say something incomprehensible to her about God, taunt her openly, and love her fire.*

He pushed himself off the wall again and smoothed his robe, tugging it down where it had pulled out a bit around the leather waist strap for his dagger. His hand went up to adjust the blue and green turban he'd bought so he wouldn't look like police, as Saliha had suggested.

"There you are!"

He swung around at her voice behind him and ended up pushing his turban out of place. He stared at her. She was in a shabby wrap pulled a little too tightly around the curves of her body and tugged just so over her face so that nothing showed but one beautiful, heavily kohled, eye. She coughed lightly and said, "Do you like my disguise?"

His face became hot. Suddenly, heat was all over him. Turban forgotten, he tugged at his robe, looked behind him for the too small stool and sat down hard on it, legs wide, knees almost up near his ears, but at least hiding what she'd done to him. He looked up. Her eye was wide, then crinkled with a smile. She knew. She laughed, pleased with herself. It somehow made him feel more the man for her pride. *How did she do that?*

She started to reach for his turban to straighten it. He bent his head toward her to meet her touch, but it only made it worse for him, as if that were possible. When she finished, he lifted his head to meet her eye. She winked. "I like your disguise as well." Then she let the wrap fall away, showing herself to him. She was smiling, her teeth parted, and he thought he could hear her exhale. She waited before speaking, long enough that the hum of the marketplace fell away into the hum of his body. Then she broke the spell. Her eyes crinkled. She ticked her chin in the direction of his lap, and asked, "How long do you think we're going to need to wait?"

He laughed from deep within himself, letting loose a rumbling roar that made everyone around them look over. Saliha looked as people turned around to see what was going on. She bent over him, laughing again, saying, "Shhhh!"

The boy who served for the stall came over. He looked nervous.

Saliha raised her eyebrows. "Yes?"

"My boss asked if you would leave."

Saliha gave Tein a questioning look. He stood, his smile still uncontained, and loosened his robe around him. She leaned toward him, saying conspiratorially, "Our disguises are working."

She pulled her wrap back to cover her face and they made their way through the marketplace, drawing stares now and again, and a *tsk* from a good woman here and there.

Tein saw the wool sellers up ahead. He looked at her. "According to Khalil, it's down here."

They turned at the last of the stalls, packed floor to ceiling with loose tufts of wool, the sellers haggling with weavers, felters, and those looking to stuff their couches. The walls of the alleyway narrowed, then it curved and they couldn't see beyond it. Tein had to turn sideways at one point. It opened up beyond the curve exposing single-story walls rising to three stories on his right and two on his left.

He flattened his hand against the wall and looked up. It was built with fired brick. Wooden beams stuck out of it at regular intervals to support the upper floors and the roof. There would be no weak reed and plaster second floors that you had to walk on gingerly or fall through. *A lot of money was coming in and out of this place.*

The alleyway curved again, blocking the view of what came ahead. He turned back to make sure Saliha was alright, then looked up. A boy was watching them over the roof of the three-story building, and then turned his head back and called something out. Tein couldn't hear it, but he knew they'd been announced.

Tein was ready as he came around the curve. His hand was not on the hilt of his knife, but it could be in a moment if he needed it. A small courtyard opened up before him with two-story rooms around to the left and a three-story complex surrounding the rest of the courtyard.

The three-story buildings were constructed like the great homes on the Tigris. Balconies overlooked the courtyard with gauzy curtains blowing in the breeze. Someone unseen was plucking at a stringed instrument. Three young boys were running around playing khatra in the courtyard. One had a whip made out of rags in his hand and was trying to beat the other two, while they tried to tackle him before he could.

A wiry young man stepped out in front of them blocking their way into the square. His dagger hung off his belt and his hand was on its hilt. "Assalamu alaykum, what can we do for you?"

"Waalaykum assalam. My woman and I would like a room."

"There's lodging that'll rent you a room elsewhere, we don't do that here."

"A friend told me you do."

"Your friend was wrong."

A few women came out onto the balconies. Their long hair was hanging loose and they had wool blankets thrown over their shoulders, grasped tightly around them. The women looked like the disturbance of their arrival had awakened them. Even sleepy with kohl smeared eyes and wrapped in blankets, they were still beautiful. He looked away quickly, ashamed before Saliha. He took Saliha's hand, saying to the young guard, "He said to tell you my mother raised me to be an honourable man."

The young guard nodded. "Why didn't you say so?" He stepped aside and pointed toward the door at the end of the square. "Rooms for rent by the hour are through there. If you want to use the bathhouse, that's extra." He grabbed the arm of a boy running past, hauling him up. The boy had thick brown curls down his back, like a girl, and no turban. The guard said, "Go get Afif." The boy looked at Tein and ran off into the nearest doorway.

"We could use something to drink first."

"Go in that door over there." He pointed to one of the two story buildings.

Tein kept hold of Saliha's hand. He looked at her for any sign she was afraid. She was looking back at the guard quizzically, then turned to Tein with bright eyes. She squeezed his hand in answer.

The door to the tavern was just a bit too low for him and he ducked his head as he went through. The room was empty except for a series of low couches around its edges and two large octagonal tables set in front of them where the three long couches met in the corners. Nothing was on the walls.

There was a doorway leading to another room. He could smell something cooking from within. He stuck his head inside. "Assalamu alaykum." No one was there. It was a kitchen set up to feed a large number of people, with three hearths for great pots on iron stands, but only one fire was lit simmering a stew. Small windows were cut into the wall to circulate air around the fires. There was another door at the far end of the kitchen.

He looked back at Saliha. "Wait here, but yell if there is a problem." He walked through the kitchen and looked out the back; there was a small courtyard with two doors leading off it and a two-story wall abutting a small garden on the other side.

Tein called out again, louder this time, "Assalamu alaykum!"

"Waalaykum assalam! Give me a minute."

A barrel-chested older man came through the door. Deeply-tanned and craggy-faced, he looked and walked like a man from the Steppes who had lived his life on horseback. He had a long cloth wrapped around his waist. He smiled at Tein while shooing him back through the kitchen into the tavern. "I'm Hushang. Please, have a seat! Are you hungry? A drink?"

He sat down next to Saliha on the couch. "We would like a drink, but I wondered what games you had on."

"As you can see, no one is here yet."

Tein faltered at his blunder. "When does that begin?"

"After the sunset prayers. They file straight from the mosque to our doors. But I've got nabidh, small beer, and date and grape wine. We've also got wormwood wine if you want something stronger. It's a house specialty." He gestured to the kitchen. "I've also some stew on hand if you haven't eaten this morning. The broth will be thin still, but it might do."

Tein turned to Saliha and asked, "Are you hungry?"

She nodded.

"Two bowls of whatever that is you are cooking and a nabidh for me." He looked at Saliha and took a chance. "Nabidh? Small beer?"

She drew her hand out of his and slapped his arm with the back of it, winking. "What kind of woman do you think I am?" She turned to Hushang, "Water is fine."

Tein laughed but wondered if he should change his order.

Hushang nodded and disappeared into the back.

Tein got up from where Saliha had chosen to sit and moved to the couch at the farthest corner of the room. She followed, questioning why with her hand, but he shook his head and patted the seat beside him. She looked irritated by the direction, but she did as he said.

He leaned over and whispered, "From here we see out to the courtyard through the window and the door leading to the back of the house. No one can come in and surprise us."

She nodded, eager to learn. He regretted bringing her here. He didn't need her as a prop. He could have come later in the day to gamble. *Be honest, man. You only let her come so you could be alone with her.* He said, "I shouldn't have brought you here. Let's go. I'll come back later by myself."

She looked out the window at the boys who'd gone back to their game. "Don't be silly."

"You don't know what the risks are."

She looked him in the eye. "I'm not leaving."

He put his hands down on the couch and pushed himself up so they could go. He felt her hand on his. Her face was hard. She said, not bothering to whisper, "Sit down."

He stood instead.

She sighed but did not move.

Hushang walked in with a tray with two bowls of stew, fresh bread, and two small pitchers and glasses. Tein sat back down. The man placed the tray on the table before them. "Eat it with health." He poured out Saliha's water, then Tein's nabidh.

Saliha replied, "And God give you health. Won't you sit with us?"

The man looked at Tein for direction. Tein nodded, and he sat down on the couch across from them. "Go ahead, taste it."

Tein took the nabidh and downed it in one gulp without thinking. He looked at Saliha out of the corner of his eye; she didn't seem to have noticed. The lightly fermented juice didn't even begin to soften the edges in his mind, even on an empty stomach. Hushang started to get up to pour him another glass, but Tein gestured to him to remain seated and poured it himself. Despite wanting to drink it, he left it sitting in front of him.

He picked up a piece a bread and dipped it into the stew. Fat glistened on top, but the broth did seem thin. Saliha did the same. She held her wrap out before her face to shield them from seeing her as she ate. He took a bit of the bread and meat. The stew was watery, without salt, and was overpowered by too much lemon. He bit into a piece of gristle and moved it around in his mouth until he could swallow it down. He didn't dare look towards Saliha. Then he heard her moan with pleasure.

"Subhanallah," she said, "you have a golden hand! This is better than my mother's. May God have mercy on her soul. I am glad she is not alive to know that someone could make laymunia better than she!"

Hushang grinned and leaned back against the couch, "Even as it is?"

Tein put another bite in his mouth, mumbling, "It's delicious."

Saliha broke in, "An old client of mine, Imam Hashim, God have mercy on his soul, told me about this place. I insisted to my man here that he bring me."

Hushang laughed. "God have mercy on his soul? Must be a different Imam Hashim than visited us! Who would say the obligatory words over that man's body! I hear he died an ugly death."

Tein said, "What was the problem?"

He shrugged, as if what he had to say was only the half of it, "We had to beat him for our coin."

Saliha said, batting her eyelashes, "I always got my coin out of him."

The man looked outside at the children playing in the courtyard. "You are one of the lucky ones then." He turned back to her, "And he never liked my cooking, either. I always had to run a boy out to get cookies stuffed with dates and nuts for him and those rolled-up sandwiches baked with caul, egg, and ground meat." He sounded irritated, thrusting his hand out, "And only the ones from that one shop that adds nard to the meat. The man thought he had rights to the caliph's kitchens." Hushang got up and went into the kitchen.

Tein reached out and squeezed Saliha's hand.

Hushang came back out with a small pitcher and a glass for himself and sat back down. He poured himself a full glass of wine. He took a long pull on it, drinking half. He raised the glass to Tein. "Sure you won't have something stronger."

Tein wanted it, but he shook his head.

Saliha said, "I can't even begin to guess who gave the imam those broken ribs and black eyes."

Hushang took another pull on his wine. "We did. Several times."

She giggled. "I had to be gentle, don't you know!"

The old man raised his eyebrows and looked at Tein. "You let her talk like this around you?"

"No one tells this woman what to say," Tein looked at her, worried, "not if they want her company."

Hushang finished his wine and poured himself another. "She must be a woman of great skill. Does she sing?" He turned to Saliha, "What instrument do you play? Can you turn a fine line of poetry?"

Tein picked up his glass and drank, worried about how she'd answer.

"I am a turner of bodies," she said, raising one eyebrow.

At that, Tein nearly spat out his drink and coughed to cover up his laughter.

Hushang merely smiled and brought his hand to his chin. "Perhaps you would consider us your home?"

She nodded graciously in acknowledgement of the offer. "Thank you, but I could not compete with the women you have here."

Hushang opened his mouth to reply but Tein interrupted, "You said the imam's death was ugly?"

Hushang looked at Tein. "Well-deserved," and said no more. Hushang drank another half-glass of wine in two long sips. He should be at least a little drunk, but he seemed sober to Tein. He knows how to hold it. Let's see if he can hold his tongue.

"Because he wouldn't pay his debts?"

Hushang sat forward, putting his glass down awkwardly on the tray edge, then readjusting it. "Much more than that." He looked outside again at the young boys in the courtyard.

Tein followed his gaze. "What about these children?"

"I shouldn't speak."

Tein felt him itching to talk and wondered how he'd ever kept a job in a place like this. He prodded the man, "Is one of those children his?"

Saliha leaned forward, hand on her chin. "Oh, tell."

Hushang gave in, relaxing into the wine, "The mother of one of them died. She was his favourite." His voice caught in his throat, "God have mercy on her soul." He turned to them, "She was stupid, this girl, Farzaneh. She told many men the boy was theirs just to get more money out of them."

"Did they give it?"

"Some did. That's why she did it. It worked. But not all men want to hear this news. They don't want some boy showing up at their doorstep letting their family know what they've been up to. She was warned off it by the other women here, but she didn't listen."

Saliha asked, "This Farzaneh, did she threaten Imam Hashim?"

He frowned and took a small sip of wine. "Yes, and he had her cursed for it. The curse brought on a tumour in her womb. It grew to be as big as a baby and killed her. The doctors couldn't do a thing. We only just buried her."

Tein felt Saliha move suddenly next to him, then she said, "May God make her whole in Paradise."

The man and Tein said together, "Amin."

"Did you report it to the police?" Saliha asked.

"One of the girls here did. They did nothing." He sighed. "Chandi went every week to demand they act on it. The morning we took her to be washed, Chandi went one last time to accuse him of murdering her. Nothing."

Tein became angry. *So we are willing to chase down and charge an enslaved girl and a talisman writer for murder by curse, but somehow I've heard nothing about a scholar doing the same? Ammar better not know about it.* He looked at Saliha, his anger showing on his face, and shook his head.

She looked away from him quickly and asked Hushang, "Who did she tell? I have a contact in the police." She winked. "A friend. I could ask."

"I don't know, you can speak to her if you like. She'll be upstairs."

"Word is, Imam Hashim died from a curse. Fitting death, I suppose."

Hushang answered her, "God bless the one who did it. When I heard, I thought Farzaneh's brother had killed him."

"Her brother?" Tein asked.

"He came every Friday for prayers and a meal afterwards."

Tein asked, "If she had family, why..."

Hushang went to take another sip of wine, then put the glass down instead. "She liked the work. She was a tough one. She'd go with him on Friday and take the meal. She loved her brother, but she wasn't going to leave this world."

Saliha tipped her head to Tein. "We're not all lost girls you know, waiting to be rescued."

The man nodded and glanced out the window.

"Her brother," Tein asked, "what's his..."

Hushang stood suddenly. "Chandi!" He said to Saliha, "She's just outside. Let me get her for you, maybe you can take her to your man in the Police." He rushed out the door.

Tein stood just as quickly after him, knocking the table hard and spilling what was left of the stew. "If she's been to Grave Crimes, she might recognize me. This ends now. I have to get you out of here."

Saliha grabbed his arm from where she was seated. "No, Tein. Do you want to give up on Mu'mina for my sake? Chandi won't recognize me! Only men brought us Farzaneh's body to wash." Her eyes widened with insistence. "I knew I recognized the guard. He was one of them! Thank God, my face was covered when I came in."

"What? I don't understand."

"Tein, I washed her for burial. I washed Farzaneh's body."

They looked out the window. Hushang was speaking to a beautiful, copper-skinned woman in a warm, but coarsely woven men's gown. He gestured toward the tavern. Tein stepped out of view so she couldn't see him.

She stood and made her way to the door. "The one who carried the woman from the hospital can't see my face, but she will recognize you."

Tein tried to pull her back. "Maybe there is a way out back for me. You go out the front. If they ask, say I changed my mind."

Shaking his hand off, she insisted, "No. Wait here." And she walked out the door to the courtyard before he could stop her.

———————

20

I t was nearly dark by the time Tansholpan and Mu'mina were marched by guards out of the Round City, across the boat bridge into Rusafa, and to a cell in Qadi Ibn al-Zayzafuni's home meant for those awaiting trial in his court. Tein had told them not to worry, but the guards taunted them that the judge's cell would be worse than the one they'd left. "You'll be begging to be executed after one night in that sewer!" After crossing the bridge, they turned onto the river road and stopped before a three-story mansion on the river. The guard laughed as he knocked on the gate. "You'll be knee-deep in river water and have to sleep standing up!"

The judge's guard opened the gate to the house and took control of them from the police guards. He pushed the two around the side of the house and up a stairwell. Tansholpan thought, *We'll not be in water after all.* They came out into a long hallway. The guard stepped ahead of them, unlocked a heavy arched double-door and pushed Tansholpan and Mu'mina into the room that would be their cell. Tansholpan let out a small cry and looked to the girl. Her eyes were wide. This was no prison; this was a guest room fit for the caliph himself. The only difference to her was that the door could only be bolted shut on the outside. *So this is how the wealthy waited for their day in court.*

A magnificent oil lamp stood on the floor. The copper had been shaped into a Solomon's Seal three hands wide. Wicks lay across the gutters in each of its six points. Not just that. Seven copper lanterns hung from the beams in the roof and swayed with the breeze coming from the balcony, pin pricks of light scattered throughout the room.

Why her? Why Mu'mina? Rooms like this were not for the likes of them. The guard, too, was surprised. "Who are you two to be getting this?" He looked them up and down. "They should take you both to the stables to scrub you down." He tipped his head to a door on the farther side. "They shouldn't even let you bathe in there. God knows they'll have to burn all of it after you've gone from the vermin you've brought with you from the prison."

The young guard's accent made him out to be from the countryside, where she didn't know. Her Arabic was not good enough for that, but it wasn't a Baghdadi accent. His shoulders and arms were bulky like he'd grown up lifting sheep and goats. His muscles strained under the black robe of his uniform.

He walked over to the bed where clothes had been laid out. These were fabrics Tansholpan had never touched in her life. She'd only seen clothes like this up close when the wealthy women came themselves to ask for curses that they could not entrust to their slaves or servants. The guard was none too happy about the clothes, either. He lifted a long rectangular red scarf that floated away from his rough hand. It was silk patterned with flying birds with glorious wingspans. The guard pushed the scarf at her. "Cover your hair old woman! Just because no man can put a kid goat in you doesn't mean you should be letting your hair hang the way it does." He turned on her, "What are your men like that they don't know how to keep you in line?"

In the yellow light of the oil lamps, he had the face of a child. Soft, feminine, and innocent. No, it was like a woman who had never lived. His wide brown eyes had large black irises like the houri girls of Paradise. *Should I tell him,* she thought, *that he is, with all his muscles and ugly manhood, no better than one of the young creatures meant to be a virgin fucked over and over and over again into eternity?*

They waited along the wall for him to leave. Mu'mina had her hands flat against it as if she thought she could spring away in flight if he came near. She did not have to worry. Tansholpan knew how to kill a man like that. Turkmen girls grew up learning to wrestle just as the boys did. Each one a warrior, an archer, a spear-holder. It wasn't all weaving and animal husbandry, for God's sake. She could, especially now in her old age when she would be underestimated, move around behind a man, even when he'd laid hands on her already, and catch his throat in the crook of her arm and press it shut for good. But she kept her back to the wall, too. Let him think he was their master. *No need for you to prove yourself on us, boy.*

He finally left the room after looking them over, as if to say that he had decided not to rape them. He wouldn't do that. *Not this one*, she thought. *He loves his purity.* But the threat of rape, that was delicious to him.

She heard the bolt slide into place and tried to take Mu'mina's hand, but the girl pulled it away with a jerk.

Tansholpan walked ahead of her, past a tray heaped with every sort of fruit, cheese, and bread, all beyond her imagination, to the room where they would wash. Mu'mina followed her. The scent of jasmine so filled the room that she caught its scent before they even entered. She took a deep breath, savouring it. A long, oblong tub made of hammered copper sat in the middle, each dimple in the copper catching the light of the lanterns. There were only four small lanterns but that was better. No need to see how filthy they were. A thick carpet was covering the whole floor. She supposed the wealthy didn't worry about such fine things getting wet.

There were no servants to help them, but the tub had been filled already. She touched the water. It was hot, the kind of water that got all the pain out of your bones. The first would get a clean bath. She walked around it. There was a tap at one end to empty the tub's water to a sluice that went out the wall facing the Tigris. A copper kettle too big to be carried by one person sat on a beautifully wrought brazier, water simmering over hot coals.

Light flickered beyond and she realized there was a third room. She left Mu'mina beside the tub and went in. She laughed. "A latrine!" There was a hole in the floor and pots of water next to it for washing and squares of old cloth in a pile on a small table. She looked out the small window. It was too dark, but she could smell that the dung collector needed to come by and clean out the catchment below. *So this is how it's done in the big houses?* She turned to the girl, "I was in the baths two days ago, you get in. I'll use this kettle here to wash up when you are done." She pointed to towels folded on a bench along and squares of soap and a loofah and left the rooms.

Two glorious beds had been laid out for them on either side. Beds. Not bedrolls. Not mattresses filled with straw, either. She lifted back the linens and felt it. It was feather with something firmer within. She sat on it. It had to be feather surrounding wool. And the food laid out for them? There were soft and hard cheeses, nuts and fruit, dried and fresh, laid out on a low tray in the centre of the room. There were soft, moist dates speckled with fennel seed. Pomegranates were cracked open to reveal the red jewels within. Apples had been sliced and rubbed with vinegar so they would not brown. There were dried melons and grapes, a mountain of grapes. The tray was as wide as her arms could stretch, and it shone like silver. Its edges were inlaid with bone and red and orange gemstones. She laughed with pleasure when she saw the bread. There were loaves made from white flour, still warm from the oven and not even burnt around the edges. Next to them was a bowl of quince jam flavoured with saffron and sugar.

A large bowl and pitcher was set out for washing hands on its own tray near the food. She kneeled before it. The rug gave beneath her, soft on her old knees. She poured water into the bowl, and the scent of citron hit her, tingling her nose. She rubbed her hands together in the water until they were clean enough, and wiped them dry on the hand towel folded beside it, then set about the food.

She folded her long sleeves back so she could dig in freely. There was no need to wait for Mu'mina. She said aloud to herself, "I've never had white flour bread, let me have that first." Then she reached across for the jar, "And jam." She'd only ever had the scent of saffron at the marketplace. Her friend, Fatiha, teased her that only a curse meant to kill the caliph could be bartered for a few of its delicate stems. She tore off a piece of bread, revealing shiny white gaps where the leavening had made it rise like nothing she'd ever seen. She pulled at a bite of it with the sturdy teeth on the right side of her mouth and chewed. It was soft and sour, substantial and good.

She took her wooden spoon out of her robe pocket and laid it beside the delicately hammered spoon next to the jam pot. She laughed lightly, saying to the old thing, "We've come far, you and me. From tents on the plains to this palace on the Tigris. I think you deserve to go into that pot of jam, don't you?" She dipped the thick edged spoon into the jam pot, filling its bowl, and then stuck the whole thing in her mouth. Tansholpan savoured the depth and warmth of the saffron's golden subtlety, the brightness of the quince holding it like a jewel. She swallowed and laughed again. She laughed so loudly that her gut began to jiggle, then she began to cackle, cough, and cry from the pleasure of it all. She called out to Mu'mina, "Get out here before I eat all this jam!"

Mu'mina came out not long after, wound in a towel so wide and long that it dragged behind her, looking all the rich lady except her shorn head. *No, not a lady*, Tansholpan thought. The golden light caught her high cheekbones with those extraordinary scars lining them to draw the eye just so, the elegant shape of her skull exposed, lifting her as if she were a glorious black bird from another world, unknown even to Tansholpan herself. The words burst out of her, "You come from royalty! You are nothing if not a queen! Bilqis, the Queen of Sheba, before she was under the thumb of King Solomon!"

Mu'mina looked at her harshly. Tansholpan wrinkled her brow, not understanding. *It was a lovely thing to say! What woman wouldn't want to be compared to Bilqis?* She shook it off and pushed herself up away from the food. She met the girl beside the bed, and they sorted through the clothes. Tansholpan took a large gown, a beautiful white muslin with soft and delicate embroidery on the edges, and a robe in red quilted silk to cover herself and went off to the bathroom to wash.

When she came back out, she noticed that Mu'mina had also chosen a muslin gown. The embroidered sleeves fell out delicately from the wide-sleeves of an outer robe, woolen and striped in different shades of green. She had wrapped her head in the red silk scarf that the guard had handled. She was kneeling before the food, reaching over the large tray to take a piece of dried melon.

"Take a small bite only, see how it goes down," Tansholpan warned her.

Mu'mina looked at her askance.

Tansholpan took up a small copper pitcher with a long-nose. "Have you had this?"

The girl nodded, then closed her eyes as she took a large bite out of the melon.

Tansholpan filled a glass with the dark, milky liquid speckled with poppy seeds and looked at it in the light. She sat down then took a sip, wincing at its sickening sweetness.

Mu'mina said, "It's awful," then indicated another pitcher on the tray. "There is plain water in that one."

"Thank you." Tansholpan raised her eyebrows.

Without looking at her, Mu'mina asked, "When you went into a trance, for the curse I got, using that instrument you played..."

"The kobyz."

"Were you born like you are? Did your people know?"

"Yes." Tansholpan tore off another piece of the white bread.

"What did your people do about you?"

She took a moment to think about how she should tell the story. Mu'mina should know that she understood what she was going through. She, too, had been stuck by forces beyond her control and had found a way out.

"I was small. My father was out with the men, hunting. I saw through the eyes of the deer he was after. I heard his footfall and saw my father raise the bow to me. I was gripped with fear and fled without thinking. My body, the deer's body, leapt and the arrow flew by. I turned and tried to tell him that I was his daughter. I heard myself bleating, screeching in the deer's voice. He raised his bow again and I ran into the woods. Then I woke up to myself. My mother bent over me. I was trembling, cold and hot all at once. I told her everything."

"And your father?" Mu'mina asked.

"He forced me to live in the old shaman woman's tent with her bones, claws, bits of fur, and drums. I hated it. Her food was not like my mother's. Her blankets smelled of the herbs and bones she boiled. I tried to escape three times but my father took me by the ear and dragged me back. So I learned the kobyz from the old woman, so she would think she taught me something. She did teach me. I learned how to leave my body whenever I liked. I would play the kobyz and go visit my mother. I smelled the meat and bulgur cooking. I saw that she missed me. So I snuck out of the tent one day and told my mother what I planned. She held me, sobbing, and told me not to do it. She said I must stay. I did it anyway. I pretended I had lost my gift so I could live with my mother again and learn to wrestle and fight and weave like the other girls. The old woman made me take the kobyz with me, but she let me go."

"So," Mu'mina said, "you thought you could do as you liked with such a powerful gift."

Tansholpan pulled her head back at the words, but more so the dismissive tone, objecting, "I was smart."

Mu'mina did not answer. Her silence a rebuke Tansholpan did not understand. *Why wouldn't this girl speak?* She pushed her, "Who shaved your head?"

Mu'mina glared at her. "Imam Hashim's wife thought it would stop him from coming to me." She turned back to the food. "If that would have worked, I would have shaved it myself."

"You sat still for it!"

Mu'mina looked at her as if she had lost her mind. "She had a razor in her hand."

Tansholpan raised her eyebrows, thinking she'd have done something.

Mu'mina grasped another piece of melon. "Why did you make a talisman to kill the imam?"

"I didn't write it to kill him." She explained, "I wrote it to free you. If that is how you were to be freed, then so be it."

Mu'mina's voice was cold, "I didn't ask you for that."

"Don't you want to be free!" Tansholpan's anger flared.

Mu'mina looked her in the eyes, unflinchingly. "If I wanted to have the blood of another human being on my hands, I would have killed him myself."

"I don't understand you." Tansholpan stood in frustration.

Mu'mina gripped the table. "You did what you wanted. I'm paying the price."

"But you will be freed!"

"You filthy, stupid dog." Mu'mina hissed, "At what cost to my soul?"

"You speak this way to me after all I've done for you!" Tansholpan began to shake as she looked down on the girl.

Mu'mina's voice rose with each word, "You put a man's death on me. Then you, you and all these people deny me the right to pay for it in this life by execution. You all have damned me in the next!"

"I've freed you!" Tansholpan shouted, "I can see it. *I* have the vision. *You* do not."

She turned her back to Mu'mina, took off her robe, got into the bed, and pulled the covers over her as she turned toward the wall to end this conversation. She fussed with the linen. *What a thing to accuse me of!* She turned over, unable to get comfortable in the soft bed, then turned back to the wall. She pulled the covers up over her head, grumbling. Then she smelled roses. The linens were scented with rose water. She took in the scent. Focusing on it soothed her. *That girl, she doesn't know what's right for her. She'll see. Then she'll wish she thanked me. It'll be too late, then, so God forgive her. She's not the first girl to give me a piece of her mind and regret it later.* She took a deep breath, then another. Observing her breath, she finally felt the softness of the feather bed hold her. She rolled onto her back and snuggled down into the covers. She wanted to feel every bit of this bed before she died. Who could deny her a few of the pleasures of this world before she traveled to the next? *I don't have much,* she thought, *but I'll take this.*

Tansholpan opened her eyes with a start, wondering that she'd slept at all. She had fallen asleep without realizing as she lay in bed trying to savour every moment, waiting for moonrise so she could see its light cast on the Tigris. Now it was morning and she had to face this ungrateful girl. She hoped a good night's sleep in such luxury brought some sense to her. *Of course,* Tansholpan reasoned, *she is angry over all that has happened to her. She needs someone to blame.* Tansholpan accepted the burden of it. *I will be that for her, then.* But she was still reluctant to turn and face her. There was a sharp knock at the door. She shot up and yelled, "Ho! You wait! We're not dressed!"

"Breakfast!" It was the young guard.

The tray that had been laid out for them overnight had been taken. How could she have slept so deeply that she had not heard anyone come in? Mu'mina scrambled to grab a wrap off the floor. She hastily covered her head and body, then nodded to Tansholpan, who was now standing with her robe on.

Tansholpan called out, "Come!" She wanted to cross the room to sit by Mu'mina when the guard entered, but the door was opening before she knew it. She could smell the goat stew before it was fully open. She glanced at the girl to see if the strong smell would make her sick, but Mu'mina was looking out the balcony window, ignoring him. She had to admit that she liked this girl's fire. *Not giving him an inch.*

The young guard carried a small tray with two bowls of steaming stew on them, keeping his eyes on it as if he were someone who couldn't balance the thing. *Absurd. Who hadn't grown up, boy or girl, carrying trays to guests? What is he up to?* The guard put the tray down hard in-between them, turning it so that one bowl faced Mu'mina, the other her. It clattered on the stand. Some of the stew splashed out of the bowls onto the spoons and a glass beside them. Angry with himself, he went back out and took a pitcher from someone she couldn't see. He returned to place it on the table, then left, shutting the door behind him.

She looked down at the stew then to Mu'mina. "How are you taking the smell of that?"

"I should have some bread first." The girl tucked her legs under the edge of the tray, pulled the cloth underneath it over her lap, then tore off a small piece of bread, eating it slowly.

Tansholpan was relieved she was speaking to her this morning. Her voice sounded even. Maybe she'd thought it through. Maybe she understood. She asked, "Are you feeling sick?"

"No, just taking care I don't." Mu'mina chewed another piece of bread, bigger this time, then a sip of water to wash it down. "I'm hungry." She examined the two bowls and said, "I want that fatty layer in your bowl."

Tansholpan wondered how she would stomach it but held her tongue. She took the bowl on her side of the tray and switched it with Mu'mina's, saying, "Eat it with health."

Mu'mina was ravenous. She took a large chunk of bread and soaked it in the thick sheen of hot fat on top of the stew, then put the entire thing in her mouth. Her cheek ballooned as she chewed and swallowed. Tansholpan dipped a small piece of bread into the broth. It was strongly spiced with cinnamon and clove. She laughed and said, "This feels like a taste of what waits for me in the next world!"

Mu'mina tore off a piece of meat and chewed, then asked, "Will they execute me if I'm pregnant?"

"They wait until the baby is weaned, but that won't happen." Tansholpan didn't know how to assure her. God had answered all her prayers. But she knew saying so would only anger this girl.

Tansholpan watched the girl wipe her bowl clean then got up to step out into the open air on the balcony and left the table. Mu'mina called out, "May I finish yours?"

She wanted to stop her, but didn't dare, answering, "Of course!"

Somewhere, not far away, even this early in the morning,

someone was playing music. A boy's voice lifted out over the breeze. From the balcony, she could just see the top of the green dome of al-Mansur's Mosque with the statue of a mounted horseman at its tip over the roofs the grand houses on the other side of the Tigris. The river was already filled with skiffs and round-reed boats making deliveries. The cries of the boatmen mixed with noise from the lines of people crossing the pontoon bridge. She heard Mu'mina come up behind her and turned to welcome her.

They leaned over the balcony together. She tried to start a conversation, but the girl didn't want to talk. Every question was met with sharp one-word answers or no answer at all. *What a prickly thing.* After a while, they became tired again and lay down for a nap. Tansholpan lay in the soft bed and watched the watery reflection of light as it moved on the ceiling. Not moonrise, she thought as she drifted off, but beautiful.

Tansholpan woke up suddenly to the sound of Mu'mina moaning and turning in her sleep. She got out of bed and went to the girl and shook her lightly. "You're having a bad dream."

Mu'mina turned towards her, her eyes wide open in terror, and grabbed Tansholpan's arm so hard that she yelled from the pain and tried to pry Mu'mina's hand away. The girl's other hand was pressed low on her belly. Mu'mina's mouth opened in a gasp, then she screamed. Tansholpan leaned back from the force of it, then put her hand on the girl's belly too.

Mu'mina was breathing heavily. "It's a knife. A knife is stabbing me."

She's losing the baby. Tansholpan got up and ran to the door, banging on it. "Open! We need a doctor! Bring a midwife!" She didn't hear anything immediately. Mu'mina was screaming. Why was there no one coming with all this noise! Finally, the door opened and the guard came in, upset. She expected him to hit her, to push her aside, but he said with the force of a prayer pulled out from deep in his gut, "God forgive me," and ran to the girl.

Tansholpan dropped to the floor, softly, entering into a trance state she did not recognize. She fell away from herself without her will.

When she came out of her trance, she found she had been laid out on her bed and the light had shifted again. The door was still wide open. A woman was bent over Mu'mina; she hoped it was a midwife and not just some woman from the household.

The guard stood half in the door, half out, obviously fearful for Mu'mina. He noticed her sit up and his face changed; lines drew down his mouth into a hideous mask of disgust. He hissed at her, reciting from the Qur'an,

> *I seek refuge from the Lord of Daybreak,*
> *from the evil of what He created,*
> *from the evil of darkness when it settles,*
> *from the evil of the blowers on knots,*
> *from the evil of the envier when he envies.*

It wasn't the first time those verses of protection had been whispered at her by someone who did not understand her gift. *Does he think I did this to the girl?* Shaking her head, she desperately insisted, "No! This was not me."

He walked toward her slowly, as if his body were floating outside of time. She didn't understand why she wasn't reacting. He took her by the neck, then she relaxed under his grip and felt herself falling unconscious. *Why are you not fighting?* Then her body jerked, violently gasping for air. He was no longer on top of her. She rolled to her side, coughing and pulling breaths deep within her.

The woman who had been tending to Mu'mina was pushing him with her whole body, yelling, "Stop!"

He shoved the woman to the floor and stood. Pulling his head back, he spat on Tansholpan from the back of his throat then retreated, shutting and bolting the door behind him. She began breathing slowly, in her own way, and the burning pain in her neck started to ease. The woman sat on the bed next to her, and reached out to touch Tansholpan's neck, but she brushed her hand away.

The woman said, "You were in a trance when I got here. You were saying things we couldn't understand. It looked like you were rubbing a bow across some invisible instrument. He thinks you consort with the jinn. He stood in the doorway, praying for her protection from you."

Tansholpan had trouble speaking but managed, "Are you a midwife?"

"Yes. I gave her what she needed. The pain's gone." The midwife looked at her seriously. "Did you do this?"

Tansholpan tried to get up, and objected as well as she could, croaking, "On the soul of my parents, no!"

"What happened?"

The extra layer of oil on the stew, she realized. "Food. Poisoned!"

"Why aren't you sick too, then?"

She sat up and pointed to the pitcher of water. The midwife got up and poured her a glass. Tansholpan sipped from it, then tried to speak. Her voice came out in croaks and whispers, "Maybe it was meant for me. The girl took my bowl, it had an extra layer of fat on it." Tansholpan looked over at Mu'mina, sleeping. "She wanted my bowl. A craving. I let her eat it. We need to tell someone."

"You can't tell that guard." The midwife pulled out a knife from her bag and placed it in Tansholpan's hand. "Keep this."

She took the knife and placed it on the table. "Will she lose the baby?"

"If the bleeding doesn't come in the next few days, the baby is safe. I gave her something to stop the cramping and rubbed a salve to close her cervix." She stood. "I'm going to go. I stalled because I did not want to leave until you were awake and could defend yourself."

"Can you do something for me?" Tansholpan pleaded, "I need you to tell a friend what's happened here. Her name is Yulduz."

21

S aliha strode out to the tavern courtyard, leaving Tein behind. The prostitute turned away from the tavern keeper and walked toward her. "Assalamu alaykum, Hushang says you can help me with the police, but..."

Saliha took her by the arm, saying to Hushang, "Don't let my friend in there get lonely, would you? I'll just be a moment," and tried to lead her away from the room where Tein sat. "Let's find a place to talk."

The woman pulled against Saliha, "I don't need any help; the man who killed her has been killed himself. God's justice is swift."

Hushang whispered something in the woman's ear, then said to Saliha, "This is Chandi." He gestured toward the three-story building, "Please, go and chat."

Chandi sighed, then turned to Saliha, "Maybe something can be done."

She took Saliha's hand as they walked toward the central door of the three-story building. As they entered, Saliha let her wrap fall so that her face could be seen. Another woman was there, lying one of the low couches hugging the walls, half-asleep, under a pile of moth-eaten blankets. Saliha thought bitterly of the men who came to take

Farzaneh's body. They had covered her in a blanket just like this to take her to the mosque for her funeral prayer, and she had thought it was the best they could do. They could have afforded more, something better, but they didn't think her worth it. And the living women here? What were they worth?

The half-asleep woman lay on her back, her bare arm thrown over her head, her fingers toying with strands of her long blond hair. Her unusual pale skin seemed transparent, blue veins traced up her arm and neck, whereas Chandi's skin shone like copper. Chandi's long nose was just a little too close to her full lips and pierced with a large filigreed gold stud giving her a kind of beauty that Saliha longed for herself. They were an extraordinary pair but what was this life for them if Farzaneh was treated without respect in death? The pale-skinned woman lifted her head and nodded in Saliha's direction, then let it drop back onto the pillow, her eyes half-closed. Chandi waved her hand, "Don't mind Agnes, she had a long night."

Agnes said in heavily accented Arabic, "We all had a long night."

The room was lavishly decorated. Saliha had never seen a place like this. She imagined this must be what it was like where the caliph's women live. The carpets were so thick she couldn't feel the texture of the reed mats laid out underneath them. Small octagonal tables with bone and precious stone inlay were set out here and there before luxurious couches. A set of copper pitchers were on a small bureau near a door that led to a room beyond. Lanterns with designs cut out of them hung from the ceiling. The only thing wrong was the smell of the place. For all its beauty, it wasn't clean. The smell of vanilla, sweat, and burnt, bitter herbs saturated the room. She said, "Maybe I should stop working on my own and join you all here?"

Chandi drew her to sit, then took a delicate glass from within the bureau and poured her some water, saying, "That is why Hushang made me bring you in here. He wants me to talk you into joining us. Look, this room is for the men. We don't live like this. We get them drunk and randy enough here that by the time they get to our rooms, they don't notice the pitted walls or the rough bed they fuck us on."

Saliha laughed in return but heard the resignation in Chandi's voice. "I'll stay my own boss, then. At least I get to choose my men," she winked, "and my mattress."

"Yet, Hushang tells me you chose Imam Hashim."

"It sounds like he was different with me."

Chandi sounded suspicious, "When did he even find the time for you?"

Saliha leaned in, realizing he must have been here most nights. "I was his midday meal."

Chandi handed Saliha the glass. "How much do you make? Maybe I'll leave myself."

"It's not what you think," Saliha scrambled, not knowing what to say. "All I have is the choice over who lies on my belly. I don't make much, and I don't have any protection."

"You think these men protect us if the customer has money and reputation? You think we didn't try to get Imam Hashim removed? Word came back that the Amir wouldn't allow it. Hushang helped how he could, but none of us has any power."

"Good old Hushang," Agnes said lazily.

"But we have a family here. That's something. I wouldn't give up my sisters." Chandi sat down by Saliha. "And the children have a safe place to grow up. For a while, at least." She looked out the window onto the courtyard. "If the children are blessed with ugly faces, the Amir gets the boys an apprenticeship and marries off the girls."

"And the pretty ones?"

Chandi pulled her head back. "You act like where the pretty ones end up is news to you."

Agnes laughed. "Who is this woman?"

Saliha asked quickly, "What happened to your friend?"

"Farzaneh."

"Yes, Farzaneh. Maybe I can help? One of my clients is in the police. I could say something."

"Imam Hashim is dead," Chandi said with angry satisfaction. "He's the one who killed her. We have retribution. I want to kiss the face of the girl who murdered him." She laughed suddenly. "And how fitting that he died by a curse!"

"God has a sense of humour," Agnes said.

Saliha replied, nodding, "I worship the God who laughs."

"You can tell your man that the police wouldn't help," Chandi said. "I saw her belly growing and I knew it wasn't a baby. We got a midwife in here who confirmed it was a tumour. She tried to tell us it's a sad fact of life, but we knew Farzaneh was cursed by Imam Hashim. Toward the end, I went as often as I could to get them to question the imam. They turned me away. I even went to the police on the morning they washed her. Nothing."

"May God have mercy on her soul," Saliha prayed.

Chandi looked disgusted, "He came the night she died. When he heard, he simply demanded another woman. I had to spend the night with that murderer's cock riding me while my friend lay dead in a room downstairs."

"My God," Saliha exclaimed. "How could they force you!"

Agnes laughed at her. "You *should* stay your own boss."

Saliha ignored her, asking Chandi, "How do you know he cursed her?"

"He admitted it! He told her he had an African slave who knew how to call the jinn. Farzaneh said he told her that the girl was jealous and would do anything to protect him." She leaned over. "He said she uttered the curse in her language as she counted out spells on the scars cut into her face."

"She what!"

"You didn't know that is what their scars are for?" Chandi looked shocked. "Imagine keeping a girl like that around!"

"If the slave killed Farzaneh to protect him, why would she kill him, too?"

Agnes lifted her head and looked at Chandi. "Is she stupid?"

Saliha realized what she'd missed, then said, "Of course, her jealousy destroyed both lovers." She paused. "It is only that Hushang said he thought it was her brother who killed him."

Chandi scoffed, "The brother's barely a man. He had an obligation to kill Imam Hashim. She even told me once that she prayed in front of him that the imam would be damned, and he chastised her for it." She said sarcastically, "Apparently, the scholars are the representatives of the Prophet and we must have a good opinion of them no matter what they do." Waving her hand dismissively, Chandi added, "Her brother didn't have what it takes to protect her. He only came here once a week to preach to her and leave."

"Maybe you could get blood money out of the family for her son?"

"Blood money? You are out of your mind!"

Saliha stammered, "But my friend could help."

"I appreciate you wanting to help, but there's money for the boy. She gave it to me. He'll get it. We're family." Chandi sighed again and looked out the window, tears coming to her eyes. She raised her sleeve to wipe them away, "I miss her."

"You'll raise her boy?"

"We all will. He can't go back to her family."

"But the money?"

Chandi said harshly, "It's something, but it's not enough to escape here."

Saliha suddenly realized the beautiful young boy out front was the child of the woman she had washed. He looked just like her. She froze for a moment in the despair of it, then found her voice, "He has her curls. Her beauty. He's going to end up here. For the men?"

"He'll be fine, Chandi," Agnes chimed in. "Stop worrying. One of the older boys is already teaching him how to sing, recite poetry, the rest." She raised herself up onto her elbow, "He'll be in demand."

She was about to reply to Agnes when she realized Chandi was giving her a skeptical look, "How do you know that boy out there looks like her?"

Saliha froze, then said, "Hushang. He told us."

Agnes sat up completely while Chandi leaned over casually to her, then at the last second reached out and grabbed Saliha's wrist, digging her fingernails in, "Maybe he did, but there's more to you." Chandi stood up in one movement jerking Saliha's arm with her. "All these questions!"

Saliha let her body go slack against the couch, pulling against

Chandi to yank her arm free, then tried to lift her feet high enough to kick her, but they were too close to each other. Saliha jammed her feet down, hoping to hit Chandi's foot. She found her mark. Chandi yelled, jerking her foot back and knocking over the small table and the glass with the water in it onto the floor. Agnes was up and had crossed the room, grabbing hold of Saliha's other arm. The two of them pulled her up to standing in one movement.

Chandi's grip loosened for a moment, and Saliha broke free of her. She swung her arm back, twisting it out of Chandi's grasp and tried to run for the door. She felt her wrap pull against her. One of the women had grabbed it and yanked her back. Saliha lost her footing and put her arms out behind her to break her fall, hitting the glass on the carpet, breaking it, and feeling a sharp pain on her palm and wrist as she landed. She raised her arm and saw she was bleeding, cut by the shattered water glass. The women stood over her.

"You, sit!" Chandi ordered.

Agnes objected, "No, bring her outside, she's bleeding all over the place. We'll have to clean this up."

Chandi grabbed her under one arm and Agnes by the other, forcing her up. As soon as she was at the door, she broke free of them and rushed into the courtyard, yelling, "Tein!"

The women were right behind her. Agnes yelled, "Grab her!"

The guard was running to her. His dagger was already pulled from his sheath when Tein burst out of the tavern and into the courtyard, Hushang right behind him.

Chandi stopped short at the sight of Tein. "Police! He's police!"

Tein charged into the gap between the guard and Saliha, pulling his own dagger, ready to cut the guard down if he took another step toward her. The guard turned towards Tein, but his knife was on the wrong side. Tein grabbed hold of the guard's short robe and pulled it down hard and to his left. The pull forced the guard to turn faster than his feet could follow. He lost his balance, pitching forward onto the ground. The guard quickly rolled onto his back to jump to his feet, but Tein stepped hard on his right hand, pinning the dagger to the ground, then dropped his knee into his stomach, while pointing his own dagger directly into the guard's throat.

Tein turned back to Saliha. She was sitting, Hushang beside her. The women were hovering nearby. Tein said calmly to her, "Are you alright?"

She nodded.

Tein saw that she had wound one end of her wrap around her hand and wrist and was holding it firmly.

Hushang took two steps toward Tein, both hands out gesturing for calm, "Please. What can we do for you?" He turned to the women, "What have you done to her? Get back now!" Then to Tein, again, "I'm sorry."

"Will this boy keep fighting if I let go of him?" Tein asked.

Hushang said to the young guard, "This man is going to let go of you. You go into my kitchen."

Tein turned back to the young man and then the stench hit him. He had fouled himself. Tein looked him in the eye, "I'm going to take my knee off of you. And then I'm taking your dagger. I'll give it back to you when I leave. Do you understand?"

The young guard nodded.

"You go and get yourself cleaned up. There's no shame. Every ghazi has a story about shitting himself on the battlefield."

Tein let go of him. The guard got himself up and hobbled toward the tavern, holding his loose sirwal up tight around him. Tein put the guard's dagger in his belt and went to Saliha, kneeling beside her. She was in pain, pale, but not too weak. She wouldn't faint. *Not yet, anyway.*

Chandi repeated, "He's police!"

Hushang shot back at her, "I heard you. Let me handle this."

Tein called back to Hushang, "Get her some winding cloth, we need to put more pressure on this."

Hushang indicated to Agnes to go get it for him. She walked slowly to the kitchen, and deliberately so, pulling her long hair up and winding it into a loose knot.

Tein yelled, "Run, woman!"

Agnes looked at him over her shoulder and walked just as slowly as she did before.

He looked up and around. Women and children were hanging over the balconies watching the scene, while the young boy with dark curls peeked out a door in the rear.

Agnes sauntered back with a rag. Hushang held up his hand indicating he'd hit her if she didn't hurry. She ignored him and spat on the ground before Saliha as she handed Tein the cloth.

"Let's get a better dressing on this," Tein said gently. He carefully pulled back the blood-soaked wrap and saw the cut. It was jagged and deep, across her wrist to the pad of her palm. She would not die of this if they could get to the hospital to get it clean and closed and if it did not fill with pus and fever later. But they had to leave soon. Tein tied the rag firmly around her wrist. He took her free hand and looked her in the eyes. She was afraid. "Hold it tight and up. It'll help stop the bleeding."

Her eyes were wide with fear.

"I saw a lot worse than this on the battlefield. You trust me, right?"

She nodded.

"Can you walk?"

She nodded again.

"Let me get you up."

As he helped her up, Hushang demanded, "What were you playing at? We pay you police good money, the Inspector's men too."

Tein put his arm around Saliha to steady her and started to walk out.

"Hold up." Hushang shook his head at himself, "I understand now. The questions. You think one of us killed Imam Hashim."

Chandi spat out, "Of course he's not here to investigate Farzaneh's death. No one cares about her!"

Saliha mumbled a response that only Tein could hear, "I do."

Tein held back for a moment, ashamed because he knew Chandi was right. He said, "I would have had investigated it had I known."

Then turned to Hushang, "Yes, we're here about Imam Hashim." He gestured with his head to Saliha, "We have to go."

Hushang walked alongside them, "You listen to me. Anyone here kills someone, we'd turn them in and be done with it. If he got beat too hard over his debts, if that's what killed him, we'd turn the man in. The Amir would make sure of it. We don't want any trouble."

Saliha was becoming more pale by the moment and she began to wobble. Tein said to Hushang with calm force, "I believe you. Now get out of the way, or I'll have to make you move."

Hushang stepped aside. "The boy's dagger?"

He pulled the guard's dagger from his belt and handed it to Hushang.

Saliha slumped against him with all her weight. He lifted her up and against him. She was nearly dead weight in his arms, but not heavy to him. Her head lay on his shoulder, and he could feel her breathing against his neck. He called back to Hushang, "Come here and fold her arm up so her wrist is up by my neck."

Hushang did as he said.

Tein felt the softness of her body against him, then pushed the thought away. He had no right. He had failed her. How could he have let her go with that woman on her own? How could he have brought her here at all?

He walked with her in his arms out of the courtyard, then through the twisted alley, until he was out past the wool stalls. People got out of their way, pulling others aside who did not see them coming. Others raised their hands in prayer for her. Every step of the way he looked for a donkey cart. Anything to get her to the hospital faster.

She murmured something he couldn't understand.

He said, "I'm taking you to the hospital. It's not far. I have you."

She buried her face in his neck. He could feel her breath through gap of his collar. *I did this to her. If she dies. If she dies...*

There was a donkey cart. The driver pulled the cart to a stop, waving him over. Tein laid Saliha inside it and walked beside her, holding her good hand. Her eyes were open, and she smiled at him wanly. He turned away. How could he look at her knowing what he'd done?

Finally, they reached the hospital bridge. As they neared the doors, he yelled out, "She's bleeding!" The guard ran inside. By the time he had lifted her out of the cart and carried her through the doors, a female orderly was there. She directed them to the women's surgery in the back beyond the courtyard. The orderly opened its door where a bench table stood in the centre. Tein gently laid her down. Her face brushed against his neck, and he felt her lips against it, pausing there, for just a moment, then whispered, "Not your fault."

The orderly took her wounded arm, inspected the bandage, then put it back down across her chest, saying to her, "A doctor has been called, he'll be here immediately." The orderly went to the far side of the room to prepare a pan of water. Tein watched her as she added something to it. He couldn't see, but it smelled antiseptic.

Saliha began to weep. "Oh Tein, Chandi was forced to have sex with Imam Hashim the night her friend died. While Farzaneh was dead below!"

He leaned over her, nodding, holding back his own tears. The idea of being without her crushed against him as if he would die of it. He nodded to her, not touching her, but wanting to hold her face in his hands, and whispered, "You were perfect."

She managed a smile, and sighed, as quiet tears streamed down her cheeks, the kohl lining her eyes smearing her face, "I was."

Then a man's voice, "Saliha!"

Tein stood and turned in one movement toward the door. Judah.

Judah faced Tein, his look damning him, "What are you doing here!"

"I brought her in." Tein stood firm.

The doctor was by her side in a moment and gently unwrapped the bandage. He bent over her to speak. Tein had to hold himself back from pushing him away. Judah said, "The bleeding has stopped. The skin is too thin to cauterize, though, so we'll sew it close. But first, we have to wash it clean."

The orderly pulled over a small table and placed a low basin of antiseptic water on it. Judah placed her wrist over it and bathed the wound.

He turned to Tein, "There's no need for you to be here. You are not her husband. I have her."

Tein did not move. Saliha reached out with her good arm to hold Tein with her, looking at Judah and shaking her head, "No."

He felt her small hand in his, wanting to grasp it tightly, but was afraid of hurting her more. He placed his other hand over it, wishing he could have shielded her from all of this.

Judah leaned toward her again, saying softly, "As you wish," then lifted his face to Tein, every muscle on his face drawn taut.

Tein wanted to let go of Saliha's hand and punch him square in the face as if all of this were Judah's fault, but he knew what he had done.

The doctor asked for the sutures and needle, and turned to Saliha again, coming down too close to her, "This will hurt, but then it will be over."

Saliha closed her eyes and gripped Tein's hand. He pressed her's more firmly against his own. She whimpered with every pull of the needle tugging the wound closed.

Judah tied off the suture, rinsing it again with fresh antiseptic water, and spread a salve over the stitches. Then the orderly handed him a long strip of clean muslin to wrap the wound. The orderly cut the end of the cloth, tied it closed, then laid her arm across her chest. Tein watched Saliha. She was quiet now and had closed her eyes.

Judah said to the orderly, "Please watch her for a moment." Then to Tein, "Ghazi, would you come outside?"

He placed Saliha's other hand gently down on her chest; she had fallen asleep from the exhaustion of it all, and he left the surgery.

Judah's back was to him when he got out the door. He turned around so dramatically that Tein almost laughed at him. *No better than an actor in a marketplace theatre act.* Tein shut the door and waited for the grand speech.

"How did this happen?" Judah demanded.

Tein wanted to answer, "Who is she to you that you can ask?"

Instead, he owned up to what he'd done, "She came on an interview with me. We were questioning some people about Imam Hashim's death. She fought with a woman there. I wasn't in the room. She was cut somehow."

Judah said, his voice dripping with disdain, "Somehow? How could you put her at such risk?"

"She wanted to come along. I let her."

"You let her?"

He took the blame. "I could have refused and I didn't."

Judah growled, "You should have."

Tein was suddenly struck by the sorrow he felt when he had been sitting with his Uncle Nuri by the canal. He heard within himself his uncle's words, "A man is not the owner of anything in this world. The man who fashions himself one is a coward." He asked himself, *Who is she that I 'should have' anything over her? But how do I protect her if I don't?*

When Tein did not answer, Judah said in a voice loud enough for Saliha to hear, "I would not have done this. I would never put her in harm's way. I would cherish her." He added in a strident tone, "I would give her a beautiful home. She would never need to leave it except with her servants trailing behind her. She would be protected and watched."

"You'll have to ask her if she wants that," Tein replied, exhausted.

Judah's rage finally broke through, "And the kohl! She has so much kohl on her eyes! By God! If she were mine, she wouldn't be speaking to the likes of you or any other man!"

Tein took a step back, tiring of him despite knowing Judah would mistake it for acquiescence.

Quieting slightly, Judah said, "If she were mine, she would not need to be a corpse washer. She would not want for anything."

"No man will ever own her. If you don't know that about her, then you don't know the woman you've had your eye on."

Judah took a step toward him, his hands ineffectively balled up as if he were going to be stupid enough to try to hit Tein. *The man had obviously never thrown a punch in his life. Let him try. Let him break his doctor's hands on me*. Then Judah's anger passed, his fingers relaxed, and he took a step back and then another until he was against the wall behind him.

Tein stepped forward until he was looming over Judah. "I'm going to marry her, if she'll have me. She'll be as free then as she is right now." He turned to open the door behind him and return to Saliha.

Judah pushed him from behind, almost causing Tein to misstep, and said, "You are no better than a goat or a dog who lets other men fuck his woman and who raises their children as his own."

Tein turned and took Judah with one hand by the throat, pushing him against the wall and lifting him up on his toes for just a moment. Then he let him go, leaving the good doctor gasping for breath and clutching his neck. Tein backed up until he was against the door, then turned and opened it. Saliha was sitting up on the bench, protecting her wounded arm across her chest, the orderly was helping her pull her blood-stained wrap around her and over her head. The kohl had been washed from her face. Tein helped her get to her feet.

Judah remained in the hallway, his back against the wall, humiliated. When they reached the door, she nodded to him, "Thank you for taking care of me." She gave Tein a look that told him to keep his mouth shut, then turned back to Judah, "I respect you Doctor Judah, and I hope you'll respect me and not share what has happened with Shatha or anyone else here. Please. It's my fault for creating this confusion between us." She lowered her head in a submissive gesture to him.

Having recovered himself, Judah put his hand over his heart and bowed to her, saying, "Of course. I do not need to speak of it."

There it was. Judah affirming he could say a word and ruin her. Tein wanted to choke him again, but this time leave him hanging by the throat until Judah feared him so much that he'd never think to harm her. He glanced at Saliha, who saw the rage on his face and shook her head. As hard as it was for him, Tein stepped back as she wished.

Judah bowed his head to her, his hand over his heart, saying, "No harm has been done, I am sure. Please take care of the wound, and see me again should it become hot, swollen, or red."

She nodded in thanks and turned to Tein, "Can you take me home?"

When they got far enough away, she said, "I want Yulduz to look this wound. She'll have the right poultice for it."

He nodded, and they walked on, he watching to see if she needed an arm to lean on, no matter what people might think, and she walking just fine on her own.

22

Layla held out the end of a length of cotton sheeting to Zaytuna. It was heavy, too big really for a girl of her age, but she was strong from being used to this sort of work. "Take it, Auntie Zaytuna."

"Listen to you nagging me! I've got it!"

Zaytuna took the heavier end of the length of sheeting and they twisted it again to get out the last drips of water, then stretched it over the line on the rooftop. Layla dug into the basket and pulled out a pair of sirwal and handed it to Zaytuna with two reed pins to make sure it didn't fly away.

The girl was good, she had to admit. She had the strength to slap and scrub the cloth on the washing sill and didn't pull the clothes out of the basket willy-nilly, letting the fabric catch on its rough ends. Zaytuna didn't see how she was able to do this and keep up with her work at Maryam's, but if she wanted to do it, well, she was glad for the help, and the company.

"Auntie Zaytuna?"

"What did the housekeeper downstairs want?"

"She needs an extra hand, I suggested Umm Farhad."

"For more laundry? Why not me?"

"Not laundry. But anyway, you're busy with me and Auntie Maryam."

"Auntie Zaytuna?"

"Yes?"

"Do you think it would be wrong of me? I mean, would it be insulting to Zayd's memory? I mean, well. There is a boy."

Zaytuna's voice turned hard, "Where did this come from? What do you want with boys?"

Layla said in her sing-song way, "He's nice."

"Nice for what?"

Layla laughed, but Zaytuna could hear the discomfort in it. She knew she'd hit her mark. "Stay away from boys."

"But..."

"And what does Auntie Maryam say?"

Layla took another pair of sirwal from the basket and squeezed the last drops of water from them. "I wouldn't tell her. She'd hit me."

"She *should* hit you." Zaytuna held out her hand for the sirwal and gave the girl a look she could not misunderstand.

Layla pouted, but did not object.

She held her hand out. "A pin." Zaytuna looked at Layla over the line as she pinned the sirwal up next to the other one. The girl looked like she was going to say something. *Don't say it girl. I don't want to hear it.*

Her little face was turning red from holding it in until she blurted it out, "He wants to marry me."

Zaytuna closed her eyes in frustration. *What am I supposed to do with this, God?* She dug in hard to make her point, "How long has Zayd been dead? And you said you loved him like you loved no other?"

Layla's face screwed up with embarrassment. "Why did I tell you!" She threw the wet qamis in her hands back into the basket and stalked off, looking down onto the neighbour's roof below.

Zaytuna watched the qamis fall to see how it landed. *It better not catch and fray. And here I thought she'd be a help to me.* She called after her, "Layla, I don't know why you told me that. Who do you think I am?"

"That's what Auntie Maryam said! She said I shouldn't be visiting you, that you'd be nothing but trouble for me!"

Zaytuna huffed out her nose at that old hen criticizing her and walked over to where Layla stood at the edge of the roof, saying as sharply as she meant it, "I'm trying to keep you out of trouble."

She was pouting again. "I thought you would understand."

"Understand? Have you menstruated yet?"

Layla didn't answer.

A girl about Layla's age was hanging clothes on the roof below. There was a lean-to attached to the vestibule stairwell leading down into the house with a thin bedroll folded up to one side of it. Zaytuna could make out a basket with some personal things nearby. She huffed again, *They don't even let that girl sleep indoors now the weather is turning cold.*

"What do you need a boy for?"

Layla was near tears. "I'm lonely."

Zaytuna took Layla's chin in her hand and looked into her face. "You have Auntie Maryam. You have a good place to live." She let go of her chin and looked at the girl on the other roof. "Who is this boy? He's a servant or a labourer? You won't live in Imam Ibrahim's house with him or where he works, either. The two of you will be holed up in a tiny room living on next to nothing, feeding some sick child, fighting with each other because you're hungry and the rain is coming in and he didn't repair the roof again."

She crossed her arms. "It's not like that."

"No? How is it?"

"He has a family. I would live with them."

"What do you think that's going to be like?"

"I could work washing clothes with you. He carries waste for a smith. His master says he'll teach him the trade if he does a good job and stays out of trouble."

"Will he wait until he is past his unpaid apprenticeship to marry you?"

"I don't know."

"Then ask him. If he won't wait, this is not about loving you. It's about sex; that'll put you pregnant and serving his parents like a maid. And you'll still be lifting wet clothes on this roof, but with a baby strapped to your back."

"How do you know they are like that?"

"Because his mother was treated the same and she's been waiting her whole life to be on the other side of it with someone serving her. She's owed it. If you grew up in a family, you'd know."

Layla turned her back to her, "You didn't grow up in a family."

Zaytuna winced at the remark, realizing only then what she'd said. She placed her hand on Layla's shoulder. "You're right. I didn't. That's how I know what you don't know. Neither one of us has family. We're alike that way." Without thinking of what she was doing she pulled Layla to her and held onto her. Layla threw her arms around Zaytuna's waist. Zaytuna looked down at her and let her arms go from around the girl, lifting them in the air, wondering how she'd got herself into this hug. She patted Layla on the back, "Enough of that."

Layla stepped back. "Why don't you marry Uncle Mustafa?"

"Because Mustafa is like every man."

"What does that mean?"

"Just wait until you are older. There is so much you don't know."

Layla started to cry again.

"Come and work with me when you can. You're a hard worker. And for my sake, test this boy. Bring him to us. We'll let Auntie Yulduz talk to him. If Auntie Yulduz says, 'Yes', we'll work out a proper engagement with him, starting with Auntie Maryam, then his family. Uncle Mustafa can write up the contract."

The girl nodded, sniffing, and reached to undo the edge of her wrap wound under her arms to wipe her nose.

"No you don't." Zaytuna forced a smile and grabbed her hand. "Are we going to have to go to the canal and wash your wrap again because you've got it all soaked in snot?"

Layla laughed. "No."

Zaytuna turned her around and pushed her. "Go over there and blow it into the corner. No one will know. There's a jug of water by the vestibule to rinse your face."

She looked over the edge of the roof to the other side and the girl was standing, staring up at them both, her face long and longing. Who was there for that girl, sleeping alone on the roof on her threadbare bed? She never knew loneliness like that, neither did Layla. She called out to the girl, "Assalamu alaykum!"

The girl just looked at her without answering, then turned to watch Layla who was walking back toward the line to keep hanging laundry. Zaytuna turned from the girl on the other roof, reluctantly, not sure if there was anything she could do. Maybe they could call on her next time. Maybe bring her a sweet. But she knew there wasn't anything. Feeling sick from it, she turned away and went back to finishing hanging the clothes with Layla. They'd need to move on to the next house soon.

Layla followed her to the next house, then came home with her. She didn't say another word about the boy. But the second they got around the passageway, she ran straight to Yulduz and Qambar, and it all came out.

Zaytuna looked into the water basin, it was nearly empty. She picked up the leather bucket to go to the fountain but saw Layla nearly in Yulduz's lap and followed her there. *Let's see what Yulduz has to say about this boy business.*

Yulduz took hold of the girl, saying, "Slow down, slow down." She tore off a piece of the loaf of barley bread next to her and pulled a piece of meat out of the pot. "Eat, then tell me what needs telling."

Layla didn't know whether to answer or put the food in her mouth and tried to do both, "A bthy..."

Yulduz reached forward and brushed Layla's nose with her fingers. "Chew, then swallow, then talk."

Layla nodded and chewed.

Zaytuna asked, "Where is Umm Farhad?"

"What do you want with her?"

"There may be work."

Yulduz smiled as if she had a secret. "I don't think she'll be needing that."

Qambar looked at her softly and shook his head, as if to warn her from saying anything.

"I think she's found a man." Yulduz said it as if Umm Farhad had been slinking around taverns and coughing to entice drunk men off their stools.

Qambar took her hand and kissed it. "Not like that, my love. Don't say it like that. A man to be father to her boy."

Zaytuna raised her eyebrows at that news. *Good for the boy.* "I'm going to get some water." She said to Layla, "Tell Yulduz everything and I want to know her answer." She got as far as the passageway, but had to jump out of the way as a large woman pushed through in a hurry, her wrap pulled in close so she wouldn't trip over its edge. "Who here is Yulduz?"

Layla scooted around to see while Yulduz waved the woman over to her. The woman crossed the short bit of courtyard, Zaytuna right behind her, the empty bucket still in hand. The woman spit the words all at once, "Tansholpan sent me. Someone poisoned the girl, but she thinks it was meant for her. She told me to tell you. I've treated the girl. She'll recover, but she may lose the baby. God protect them both."

Yulduz sat up, mouth open.

"Baby!" Zaytuna exclaimed, dropping the bucket.

The woman looked at Zaytuna, "The girl is pregnant. The poison might still do its work. I got there in time. Truth be told, I don't know how much is due to me."

"And Tansholpan?" Yulduz demanded, "Is she poisoned?"

"She was in some sort of trance when I got there. Praying it looked like, but nothing like I've seen before. Something you Turkmen do? Maybe that is what saved the girl. God knows best."

Zaytuna asked intently, "Did Tansholpan eat the poison, too?"

"No, it was only in the food the girl ate."

"It could have been meant for Tansholpan, not Mu'mina at all."

The woman replied, "Do you not listen? I said that is what she thinks. And more the shame, Tansholpan would have withstood it better. She seems like a sturdy old thing. But I think the poison was for the girl."

Yulduz took Layla's hand. "God protect her!"

"Do the police know?" Zaytuna asked.

"I don't know. There was a guard and a female servant. They must have reported it."

"This morning!" Yulduz demanded, "How are you just telling us now?"

"By God, you think I sit around all day? I had women to tend to!"

"But they are in danger!"

"Woman, they are in Rusafa! I spent good money on a skiff down the river to even get here. You should both thank God that I came at all." The woman turned to leave. "Ungrateful!"

Zaytuna reached out to hold her back. "How do you know the food was not just bad?"

The woman looked her up and down. "I know my business. I know the effects of herbs that abort. I know them exactly. That is what that was. It was meant for the girl." She pushed past Zaytuna.

Zaytuna ran after her. "What did the guard look like?"

"Tall and strong, but with a face like a baby. God hold to the Fire whoever did this!" Then she left.

Zaytuna turned back to Yulduz and Layla and said, "They would have told the police in Rusafa, not Karkh. Tein has to know."

Yulduz snapped back, "You think he cares? He's trying to get them both killed! What am I to do? What would Tansholpan think I could do?"

Zaytuna spat out at her, "Tell Tein!" She wanted to stalk across the courtyard to slap Yulduz's comment out of her mouth and stormed out of the passageway into the alley to keep from doing it.

She leaned against the wall and forced herself to breathe, but her mind was still racing. *That hag, who is she to put his name in her mouth?* Then she reached out with her right hand and slapped her left, saying aloud, "Quiet!"

A boy running by stopped and looked at her. "You mad old bird! I didn't say anything!"

She nearly bit his head off, "Walla, not you!"

He got his back up, no one else was in the alleyway and he saw his chance. "Give me a fals, then, if you are going to be so mean. I haven't eaten in a week."

She turned her back to him and put her hands against the wall to keep from saying anything or reaching down for a stone to throw at him.

"Lady, you're ripe for the madhouse." He ran off.

She kept her face pressed against the mud brick wall, feeling the grit of it against her skin, trying to focus on the small grains sharp against her cheek to bring her some kind of calm. She muttered, "Maybe I am going mad."

She felt a hand barely touch her on the back. "Zay?"

She turned her head to the side and saw Mustafa beside her.

He raised his hand to brush the grit off her cheek with his thumb, but she pulled back putting some space between them. "What are you doing here?"

"You were saying something to yourself."

Zaytuna gritted her teeth. "I'm alright."

"What were you saying?"

"I was praying."

Mustafa said laughing, "Oh Zaytuna, really. Keep that to your room. People on the street will think you're a saint."

"How are you here, acting like nothing happened between us?"

Standing back from her, he casually leaned against the wall. "What do you want me to do, Zaytuna? We disagree. It's not the first time."

"That fight was not like any other, not to me."

Ignoring her, he asked, "How long have you been out here?"

"You should know," she said stiffly, "that someone tried to poison either Tansholpan or Mu'mina. But Mu'mina ate it and may yet lose her baby. She's pregnant."

He pushed himself off the wall, becoming the Mustafa she knew again, "God protect them! I've got to tell Tein or Ammar. Ibn Salah must know."

"The midwife said they were in Rusafa."

He looked down the alleyway, as if itching to leave. "They've moved the women. That's why I'm here. I came to tell you. Their case has been moved to the court in Rusafa. They are in a holding cell at Ibn al-Zayzafuni's home. I will find Tein and tell him tonight. Don't worry."

Zaytuna begrudged him a nod in thanks, then asked, "You're sure moving the case will be better?"

"I saw the police chief rule on an unrelated matter yesterday. He truly rules as he likes, anything could happen. We must go before a religious court."

"What will a religious judge do about her confession?"

"Ibn Salah believes he can get the judge to lay it aside. It's complicated. It would take a long time to explain."

"Excuse me! Do you think I can't understand it?"

"Zaytuna, your moods! Fine, I'll say this much. A religious judge can release her if sufficient doubts can be raised whereas the police chief would remand her back to prison until exculpatory evidence comes to light. If it never comes, she will never be released."

"So when is the trial?"

"Tomorrow. Burhan petitioned today and the court has notified us. We are as prepared as we can be. I am certain we must have missed something, but we will discuss our plan tonight again. Ibn Salah knows the judge well so he was able to secure us an investigator to determined whether or not Ammar can give expert evidence before the court. Alhamdulillah, he has been approved. He is a good man, there is no doubt, but we were worried all the same."

"What will happen at the trial?"

"So much depends on whether or not Ibn al-Zayzafuni will be willing to entertain the doubts about the case that Ibn Salah and Ammar will present. Ibn Salah believes he will, but then we are at the mercy of his personal judgment of the matter not the evidence. They are Hanafi, I suppose that makes them more comfortable with this kind of judicial independence. But I worry. I am just a hadith scholar. Honestly, Zaytuna, this is beyond me."

Zaytuna didn't respond, she was not yet ready to reassure him.

He sighed. "Let's go inside. I'll speak to Yulduz, then I'll go."

Yulduz, Layla, and Qambar were eating. Layla was chatting and waving her hands, telling a story. Clearly, Yulduz was still upset. But Qambar smiled kindly, patted Layla's hand, then popped a broth-soaked piece of bread in her mouth.

Layla turned around when she heard them come in, and called out, "Uncle Mustafa!"

She got up and ran to hug him, but he held her off playfully saying, "Layla, sweet one, you're a bit old for that now," and patted her on the shoulder.

She held her hand out to Zaytuna. "Come sit, Auntie Zaytuna. Auntie Yulduz is sorry." She turned to Yulduz and furrowed her brow comically so that Yulduz would laugh. "Aren't you Auntie?"

Yulduz raised an eyebrow. "If the girl says so, it must be true."

Holding Zaytuna's hand and pulling her to the pot to eat, Layla said, "I checked on you. You were resting on the wall, so I left you alone."

Zaytuna sat down next to her. "Yes, thank you for leaving me there."

"All I can do is pray for Tansholpan," Yulduz nearly moaned. "I don't know what she thought I could do."

Mustafa said, "I'll tell the police and the man representing her at trial."

Qambar put his arm around Yulduz. "There will be justice in the end, one way or another."

"Well, come you two and eat," said Yulduz.

"I cannot Auntie," said Mustafa. "I am only here to give you the news that the trial is tomorrow morning, after duha in the Rusafa Mosque. We are preparing and it is going better than we expected, alhamdulillah."

Prodding Mustafa, Zaytuna said, "Tell her what Tein is doing."

"Auntie, Tein is busy trying to prove Mu'mina and Tansholpan innocent."

Zaytuna appreciated Yulduz's effort to ask nicely, "Doing what?"

"He is investigating in the marketplace to find if anyone sold a poison that could have killed the imam."

Yulduz shook her head. "No one'll speak to him."

"They just want to know who bought it. No one will be in any trouble."

The old woman looked at him as if he were stupid. "Everyone'd know they tell the police their business. They'd never have another customer."

Mustafa sighed. "You have a...."

"Poison!" Zaytuna interrupted. "He must ask about the poison someone gave to Mu'mina to end her pregnancy! If the imam was poisoned, then whoever did this to her, must be the one who killed Imam Hashim."

"Not necessarily. But," he conceded, "it is a helpful observation all the same. Ammar said he believes that the imam's brother, Isam, is in love with the widow. He could have killed the imam and tried to end the pregnancy for her sake. The brother's medication is too weak to do the job, so he had to have purchased the poison somewhere in the city. I hope Tein can find out." Mustafa's face lit up as he realized, "If the judge knows about the attempt to abort, it would help us argue that there is doubt over her guilt. Yes! Even if Tein never finds out, her case might be dropped."

Qambar said again with certainty, "There will be justice."

There was movement in the passageway, and they all turned around. Tein was nearly carrying Saliha in, her face deathly pale and she was holding a bandaged arm across her chest.

Zaytuna got up and ran to her. "Saliha!"

"She's alright," Tein said. "We've been to the hospital." He looked at Saliha. "She fell on some broken glass. The doctor sewed it up."

"Yulduz," Saliha said weakly, "I want you to look at it."

Yulduz was already standing and Qambar behind her. "Let me see it."

Tein and Yulduz helped Saliha sit down. Yulduz kneeled beside her.

Zaytuna pulled Tein away. "What happened?"

"What I said."

"How is it that you're with her? You were meant to be investigating who could have sold them belladonna."

Layla stood behind Zaytuna, listening closely.

"It went further afield than that. I'll need to tell Ammar and Ibn Salah."

Mustafa stepped forward, "You can tell me. I will pass it on."

Zaytuna looked between the two, "You can also tell me!"

They both huffed in her direction at once.

Answering Mustafa, Tein ignored her, "I made no progress on the poisons, but I think we can rule out his death being due to a gambling debt or his use of prostitutes. That's something."

"I was just leaving to find you. Ammar is at Ibn Salah's home preparing for tomorrow. Maybe you should come with me?"

Mustafa walked to the passageway without saying goodbye to Zaytuna while Tein pushed past her to kneel before Saliha. She watched Mustafa's back as he disappeared. She held still or she would run after him say every single solitary thing that needed to be said and not stop. She felt something tugging on her, she looked down.

Layla said, "Auntie, don't worry. You and I will go ask about poisons tomorrow. They'll tell us what they would never tell him."

Zaytuna's fury at the men found its object in Layla. She said coldly and with precision, "No you will not. You are not going to help me do anything of the sort. You are going to go home to Maryam. You are not coming by tomorrow. In fact, do not come back at all."

Layla's face crumbled, tears coming, "Not even for my lesson?"

"No." Zaytuna stood up, pulling Layla's hand off of her wrap and watched Tein leave in turn to catch up with Mustafa without so much as a word to her. Layla ran past him, pushing Tein so she could get into the passageway first. He stepped back to give way and looked at Zaytuna, gesturing to ask what was wrong with the girl. Zaytuna raised a shoulder to him, shrugging, and turned around to check on Saliha herself.

Yulduz had unwrapped the bandage and was clucking at the wound, "I hate to say it, but the doctor's done a fine job." She looked at Saliha. "Leave it for today. I'll get what's needed for a poultice tomorrow." Yulduz rewrapped the wound and said to Qambar, "Get some dates, she needs some sweetness in her. And get a cup, I want her to drink this broth."

Zaytuna offered, "I have dates."

He waved her off. "No, we have some. You sit."

Zaytuna kneeled down. "What really happened, Saliha?"

Saliha smiled, but said weakly, "I helped Tein investigate at the nahariyya where Imam Hashim went."

Zaytuna tried not to overreact. "That wasn't safe, why would he?"

"I made him, Zay. Don't be angry."

Yulduz gave Zaytuna a hard look. "Can't this wait?"

Zaytuna nodded, but her mind was working. *What are these men thinking? What are the lives of women to them? First Mustafa admits he's just like the rest of those filthy scholars who think women are nothing but meat for their pleasure. Now Tein leads Saliha into danger. He used her, and now look what's happened.*

Saliha laughed lightly. "Oh Zaytuna, I can see your thoughts."

Zaytuna reached across and touched her good arm. "I'm sorry. I'm just worried about you."

"Zay, I found things out, things that helped. It was exciting." She held up her arm. "It's nothing. I'll be fine. Yulduz will make sure of it."

Yulduz puffed up at that and gave a brisk nod.

Despite everything, there was a glint in Saliha's eye. "Let me tell you what happened."

Zaytuna looked at Yulduz. "May she?"

Qambar came out with a cup and the dates, handed them to Yulduz, and left the women to each other.

"She can after she's had some broth," she answered, filling the cup.

Saliha took the cup and sipped from it gratefully while Zaytuna watched every sip, waiting for her to finish and speak.

Finally Saliha said, "The woman I was washing the day Imam Hashim died, she was a prostitute that Imam Hashim used regularly. Her sisters at the nahariyya believe that he killed her with a curse because she was asking for money to support her boy." She looked between the two women. "You can't tell anyone this. Please, Yulduz, not even Marta."

Yulduz nodded, but Zaytuna wasn't sure she'd be able to hold to it.

"She died of a tumour. It was as big as a baby." Saliha started to weep, "Poor woman."

Yulduz put her arm around her, tugging her gently into her arms. "God have mercy on her soul."

"Amin."

Saliha wiped her eyes. "The women there said the imam told them he had his slave curse her and afterwards she grew the tumour. They meant Mu'mina. They believe she performed the curse."

"What?"

"He had to be lying. He said she was jealous of him seeing women there."

Zaytuna raised her eyebrows. "She wouldn't be. Never."

Saliha nodded.

Yulduz took the empty cup from her and filled it again from the pot, "What else?"

Saliha said, "They hated him. All of them, but especially the one closest to the woman who died. Maybe she killed him, Zaytuna, but I don't know how she could. If it was poison, Tein said he would have had to eaten right before he died and he was at home."

"So then Tein's right, it can't be due to prostitutes or gambling." She took Saliha's good hand. "You eliminated two possibilities. That's so important. But most important, you are alright."

THE SIXTH DAY

23

Yulduz brushed her robe one more time and placed her cap on her head, "I'm ready for the court, now."

Qambar said, "You're sure you don't need me to come with you."

She used her thumb to point to Zaytuna, "This one is coming with me. You stay here with Saliha."

"I'm fine," Saliha objected. "I don't need anyone to watch over me."

"I agree with Yulduz for once. But you need to rest. Qambar will get whatever you need." Zaytuna gestured to the water basin. "I don't want you so much as touching that bucket over there."

Saliha smiled and pulled her wool wrap around her. "Alright, Aunties."

Yulduz took hold of Zaytuna's wrist. "*Yalla,* as you Arabs say."

Zaytuna winced at being called an Arab, but Yulduz pulled her through the passageway before she could snap at her. In one moment, they were out in the alley, walking as quickly as they could out of the neighbourhood. Through the morning fog, she could just see a young girl walking towards them.

Yulduz asked, "Is that...?"

Layla called out, "Aunties!"

"We don't have time for this, Zaytuna."

When she reached them, Zaytuna demanded, "What are you doing here?"

Layla said in a tone as if yesterday had not ever happened, "I told Auntie Maryam I wasn't coming to work today."

Zaytuna replied with a calm that belied her frustration, "Walk with us, or we'll be late."

The girl ran beside them. "I'm going to investigate the poisons. They won't tell Uncle Tein, but they'll tell me. I know how to ask. I can make something up. How would they know that I am actually working for the police?"

Zaytuna lost her patience, stopped, and grabbed her by the arm. "Ya Rabb! You are not working for the police!"

Yulduz had kept walking, then turned back when she realized they weren't beside her, "Come now! What is she saying?"

Pulling Layla ahead with her, Zaytuna answered, "The girl wants to investigate the poisons!"

"Let her!" Yulduz said, "She could find something. This little one is wily. She won't get hurt."

"The two of you!" Zaytuna exclaimed.

Yulduz said sharply, "Come!"

As Zaytuna caught up with Yulduz, Layla on her heels, she said to the girl, "And what did you tell Auntie Maryam to take the day off?"

"I said I had to help you today with laundry."

Zaytuna stopped. "You lied to her, again. You'll lose your place."

"What do I care?" Layla protested, "I'll come live with you."

"I thought you were going to marry a smith's helper."

Layla's face turned bright red. "I don't need him, I'll take care of myself!"

Zaytuna looked down at her. "In one night you go from loving this boy as if he is the whole of your life, to you not needing him. What happened?"

Layla avoided Zaytuna's eye. "I asked him if he would wait."

Zaytuna huffed. "He said, 'No'?"

She didn't answer.

"You better not be in any trouble with Auntie Maryam." She put her hands on her hips and looked around the neighbourhood. The shops were starting to open and people were coming out into the street. Yulduz was far ahead. "Go back to Auntie Maryam's, now." Zaytuna turned her back on the girl and left her standing in the road.

Layla yelled after her in a sing-song voice, "Whatever you say!" Then she stomped off making her way directly to the herbalists closest to where Imam Hashim lived. *They don't even know that I found out where he lived. Did Uncle Tein look here? He probably didn't even look here!*

It was early yet, but the stalls were open except for a few here and there. She stood in front of the first shop she saw, and placed her hands on the sill, her chin just sticking out over it. A wrinkled Jewish woman, wearing a honey-yellow and blue striped turban with sprigs of dried flowers sticking out of the folds stood up to greet her. The woman's eyes crinkled at seeing the little girl standing before her. "Assalamu alaykum, dear one, what can I do for you?"

"Walaykum assalam, Auntie, I hope you are well."

"Alhamdulillah, and are you well?"

"Alhamdulillah."

"What do you need?"

"Oh! Yes! Auntie, I am sorry. The family I work for need some medicine. They told me where to go but I forgot. I have to go ask from shop to shop where to find them!"

"My goodness, are they alright?"

She smiled, replying cheerfully, "Inshallah!"

"What is the medicine?"

Layla scrunched her face. "It is...it is...*Oh!* Auntie, I forgot!"

The old woman leaned over, smiling. "Well, what is the medicine for?"

Scratching her head, she said sorrowfully, "Auntie, I forgot that, too." She started to sniffle as if she were going to cry.

The old woman patted her on the head. "Now, daughter, no need for tears, we'll sort this all out. What can you remember?"

Layla looked up, hope in her eyes. "They were very strong herbs. I know belladonna was one."

"Does the lady of your house shake sometimes? She falls to the ground and cannot control herself?"

She didn't know, but thought she might as well agree, "Yes, she does."

"Belladonna is used for that sometimes, but in very small doses. I would never give belladonna to a woman without talking to her first. It can make her lose her baby if she is pregnant. Is she an old woman?"

Layla hedged, "Not young, not old."

"I would take care giving most treatments to a younger woman just to be careful, I think you'll need to go back and ask exactly what they were."

"Oh, but they'll be angry."

"But if you bring home the wrong thing, you could hurt her."

"Alright Auntie," her shoulders slumped, "but I think I am going to ask around a bit first."

"I understand sweet one, but I don't think anyone here will help unless they know exactly what it was, or," her eyes lit up, "who it is! Why didn't I think of the first? Tell me her name, I will have her written down in my book and I will know exactly what was prescribed."

Why hadn't she thought of that, they'd want a name! Layla scrambled for a response, then jumped up and down. "*Oh!* Auntie, I remember where to go now. Thank you! May God reward you!" She ran off without a look behind.

She couldn't go to the next herbal shop, or she might see her, so she ran past two and went to the third. A man wearing a quilted leather cap and a closely cropped beard bent over to her.

"Assalamu alaykum, what can I get for you?"

Layla grasped the sill of the counter with both hands. "Wa alaykum assalam, Uncle. The lady I work for ran out of her medicine. But I forgot what it was exactly and forgot who she said she bought it from. I know it was either belladonna or..."

The man patted her on the hand. "Sweet one, just give me her name. I will look her up in my book."

She had thought of an answer this time, "Madam Aisha."

"I'll need her full name to check. I have many Aishas on my list."

Then she suddenly realized giving just any name wouldn't help. She scolded herself, *Auntie Zaytuna wouldn't make this mistake!*

He watched her thinking and squinted his eyes. "You cannot remember the full name of the woman you work for?"

Layla realized she'd be caught out and said quickly, "Oh! No! I just remembered where she bought it!" She ran off again yelling behind her, "Thank you, Uncle!"

Layla ran until she found a tiny square, small enough to be covered by a roof of reed matting, letting in spots and slats of morning light to the ground. There was a tree at the centre and a hole had been cut for the trunk so that its branches reached out through the matting and above it to the sun. Layla noticed a curve in the trunk from two big roots reaching out. It was as if the roots made a chair that could hold a person, so she settled down into it to have a think.

She looked at her feet sticking out from her sirwal, dirty and rough from always walking barefoot. She didn't need the sandals that Auntie Maryam had bought her, but she liked them. They were still new, and she admired the straps and imagined her feet clean and pretty without the callouses that made them look like goat hooves.

Haftiar only wanted to marry her to take care of his mother. She was nothing more than a servant girl with hooves for feet. She had run to him last night and told him what Zaytuna had said. He just shrugged and said, "What's wrong with that? My mother needs help. It's her time to rest."

Layla didn't wait to hear any more. She fled into the street, her eyes stinging with tears. She ran through the marketplace and over the Thorn Bridge meaning to see Auntie Zaytuna, then turned back. She'd just say, "I told you so," so she went to Auntie Maryam instead. But she would not be happy, even when she heard the outcome. She would not tell her. Once through the gate, she went to the well to get water to wash her feet before going inside. The door was shut to the kitchen, but she knew Auntie Maryam was there. She commanded herself, *Don't tell her a thing!*

But as soon as Layla got inside and saw the old woman sitting in her spot by the fire, she spilled the whole story out in Maryam's arms. When Maryam had understood the gist of it, she stood, spilling Layla to the floor. Grabbing her by the arm, she pulled Layla up to her feet again. Maryam swung and swung again with her free hand, hitting her hard on her backside and when Layla tucked in so Maryam couldn't reach it, Maryam slapped her on the back of the head. All the while saying, "After all that trouble you made with Zayd! After all that and you are still after boys! What have you done? There better not be a baby in all this! Lord! What did I tell you, girl! What did I tell you!"

That night, Layla did not cry. Not one bit. She had a headache, her arm was bruised, and she was going to have to sleep on her side, but she vowed she'd leave there the next day and go live with Auntie Zaytuna. She was mean, but that's because she didn't see that she could help. Auntie Zaytuna would want her after she found out who bought the poison. Layla packed up her things, including her new sandals, wrapping it all up in scrap fabric and hid it by the well.

She left the next morning, making sure her things were still hidden by the well so she could sneak back and get them later. Now Layla sat in the crook-chair of the tree and took stock. Auntie Maryam did not want her. Haftiar only wanted her to clean up after his mother and cook him food. Now, Auntie Zaytuna wouldn't want her once she knew she couldn't solve the mystery.

What good was she to anyone? She looked at her dirty hooves and gave the question some thought. She was good for helping with the laundry, cleaning the house, and cooking, and, later, taking care of other people's children. *Time to grow up.* There would be no more "putting on airs," like Maryam scolded her whenever she covered her face like the rich girls. She stood up from her spot in the tree, dusted herself off, and rearranged her wrap. She didn't care if anyone saw her. She wound her wrap under her arms, like a working woman, throwing the long end loosely over her head and caught in one arm, her face uncovered, and walked the longest possible way back to Imam Ibrahim's house to apologize to Auntie Maryam.

After she got through the gate, she saw that her things were no longer stuffed beside the well. Her gut tightened. *There'll be another beating for that.* She opened the kitchen door carefully. Maryam was there, in her spot by the stove, stirring the dinner pot.

The old woman said, matter-of-factly. "I put your things back in your room." She looked her up and down, then said, "Go wash up and get on a clean wrap, then come back down here."

Layla did as she was told, but tried to think of a lie that Maryam would believe about where she'd been all morning. Then she shook her head at herself. *No more lies.* She had stopped being *such* a child. After she got back downstairs to the kitchen, she said with all the strength she had left, "I went out this morning to investigate poisons." She picked up a large, unwashed copper pot that had been soaking and carried it to kitchen door to scour it by the well.

Maryam looked at her sideways. "Poison?"

Layla was careful how she answered. Maryam didn't ask the question very nicely. She knew that voice. It was supposed to be patient, but it was not. Layla crouched beside the pot, half in and half out of the kitchen door. Soaking all night hadn't got all the burnt food from the tinned bottom. It was her fault for not being there yesterday to take turns stirring the pot, and now she had to rub and rub at it with a salt, flour, and vinegar paste. Her fingers slipped off the leather square and the salt scraped her fingers, stinging where she had little cuts here and there.

"Well?"

Her head was nearly in the pot. "It's a long story."

Maryam said, "I have time."

Layla tried to say it carefully, but once she got started it all tumbled out of her, ending with, "The police, Uncle Tein, could not get any information about who might have poisoned the man because no one trusts the police and so I knew I could ask because everyone trusts a servant girl and no one would think that I was working for the police." She stopped for a breath, then got to the part where she had no better luck than Tein and didn't know what to say.

Maryam started, "And did..."

Layla interrupted, "I'll tell Auntie Zaytuna what I found out tomorrow. I can't tell you. If I did that, it would..." She tried to think of the right word. She learned a lot of smart words from Auntie Zaytuna. "It would *devastate* the investigation."

"And Zaytuna works for the police now?"

"Uncle Tein is in the police and she helps him."

"Who told you to do this?"

"Auntie Zaytuna."

There was a long pause. This was not good. Layla breathed deeply waiting for a scolding and continued to scrub.

Maryam said, trying to sound kind, "I know you're fond of that woman like she were family to you, but she's put you at risk. Family does not do that. If you had asked the wrong person the right question, you could have been killed to cover up the murder. Did she think of that?" Maryam's voice started to rise, "Did she consider that maybe the person who made the herbs to poison the imam was a part of the crime?"

Here we go, thought Layla. She rubbed harder, waiting for a slap. She had nearly got the burnt-on food out of the bottom.

But Maryam's voice had lowered when she spoke again, such that Layla had to sit up and pay attention to hear her. The old woman was sitting again on her stool by the fire. Food simmering in the pot nearby, other small dishes meant for the imam's lunch set out here and there. Maryam crossed her arms, as if to ward off a chill and said her piece, "Layla, my sweet, that woman does not think of what is best for you. I want you to be safe. When the time is right, I will ask the imam to help find you an appropriate husband." She sighed. "It's good you are learning to read and write. That's a useful skill, especially for keeping house if you want to rise above the hard work you do now."

Maryam got up from her stool and walked over to the door, leaning against its frame. "I'll speak to the imam about getting you a tutor here in the house. No need for you to go back to Zaytuna. If you are going to stay here under this roof, my daughter, then you'll have to follow my rules. You can still go out to do your errands, but just there and back. No talking to boys. No visiting Zaytuna." She held her arm out to embrace her. "I'd like to put you here under my wing where I can keep an eye on you."

Instead of getting up to be held, Layla stuck her head back in the pot. There was nothing left to scrub. She had even got the black soot out from when the fire had smouldered the outside. She put the pot on its side and rinsed it out until she could see it was perfectly clean. She turned it upside down to drain, then stood to get a clean linen rag to dry it so there would be no spots on the copper. Maryam liked it so the copper pots shone. She'd sit at night, after all was clean and put aside to rest, with a cup of apple-ginger juice and survey her kingdom. She said how she liked to see the warm light of the lantern dance off of those pots. Maryam was still standing in the doorway and Layla had to go sideways to get past her. She heard Maryam sigh above her as she squeezed past.

Layla took a neatly folded linen rag from the pantry and turned to go back and dry the pot, but Maryam was now blocking her way.

She felt herself start to cry. The tears were coming, but they weren't making a mess, at least. She wasn't going to blubber or have a hard time breathing. Her chest was tight, but she had the breath to say what she needed to say. "I know what I am. And no one is coming for me. No boy will ever love me for more than how I can serve his mother. There's nothing for me but a kitchen or a clothesline. But I look at Auntie Zaytuna and I look at you. And at least she's got something else other than this. Maybe I can have something else, too."

Maryam reached out and took her hand. "My daughter. I've got so much. I've got my friends. Don't I go and visit my friends? Don't they come here? I had my husband and he loved me with all his soul. And I've got the satisfaction of this work. More than that, I love all you children as if you were my own. You are my baby. This is a good life and a house with plenty." She shook her head and her own tears came. "Is this all because I beat you? Oh girl, if so, I wish I never had." She took Layla in her arms and held her.

Layla fell into the softness of her ample body, knowing she was loved by this good woman. But she pulled back from her, saying, "It wasn't the beating, Auntie Maryam."

Maryam lifted an edge from the workaday wrap around her waist and dabbed at Layla's tears, the rough material scratching, but in a reassuring way. Maryam said, "So you'll tuck in here under my wing?"

"No, Auntie. I can't. But can I visit you? Will you always be my Auntie Maryam?"

Maryam pulled her to her again, so hard Layla felt like she wanted to push away, but she heard her say, "Take your time to think about it. You don't know what you are doing."

"Can I stay here until I know?"

"My baby, always. You stay with me," she paused, "If you decide to go, wait until you find a good place. Then you come and see me as often as you like." Maryam pushed her back, putting both hands on her shoulders, looking at her like she meant business. "You'll be in trouble with me if you don't visit me, and Lord knows you don't want that."

Layla started to cry again, "No, Auntie, I don't want that."

24

Z aytuna had been listening to Yulduz breathing heavily since well before crossing the pontoon bridge. They'd walked at a pace the old woman was not used to; being a good hand at cutting reeds was not the same as walking as fast as you could for nearly two hours. As they entered through the mosque doors, Zaytuna pointed to her left. "There'll be pitchers of water by the wall just over there. I saw it when I was here for Friday prayers." Yulduz nodded, grabbed her sandals, and headed to them.

The courtroom was set up straight ahead on the far side of the mosque, exactly where Ibn Salah had been sitting on Friday, situated between the women and men's sections so there'd be a place for all of them to sit and listen. Zaytuna saw Mustafa and Ibn Salah seated near the growing line of people who had come to file a petition to have their case heard.

Yulduz was crouched beside the pitchers, and said to Zaytuna as she approached, "They'll need someone to refill this after me."

She out her hand for a cup. Squatting, she drank it down in three gulps, then returned the cup over the top of the pitcher. She checked the others. "These are full, don't worry."

Yulduz stood, her knees obviously bothering her, and began to walk directly to the women's side of the courtroom. Zaytuna caught up to her and tugged her sleeve, "We need to pray first."

Pulling her sleeve back with a jerk, Yulduz snapped, "It's not time for prayer!"

"Two cycles in greeting to the mosque?"

"You do as you like. I'm waiting over there," she said, pointing to the courtroom.

Zaytuna sucked her teeth without thinking, then found a spot to pray. She raised her hands to her ears, saying, "Allahu akbar," and lowered them, placing her hands, right hand over left, across her stomach, her elbows out, and sighed again, this time to focus herself. She let the words, 'Allahu akbar,' sit in her heart until she felt the force of them say to her, *'God is greater' than anything in this world, no harm, no joy is greater than God*. Then, she prayed, *God, guide me, let me know what I've done wrong*. She began to recite the opening chapter of the Qur'an to herself, and at the verse, *Guide us on the straight path*, it came to her that she had been guided, but that she would not accept it. The guidance was always before her, the most obvious thing, but she looked away. Her heart tightened from the shame of it as she recited,

> *...not the path of those who have demanded Your wrath,*
> *not the path of those who have gone astray.*
> *Amin.*

Then, she felt a verse come to her and she recited it under her breath,

> *You cannot guide the unseeing from their error.*

Then two other verses flowed into her heart. She heard herself whisper,

> *They are like those who pay for error with guidance,*
> *so that they gain nothing,*

so that they were not rightly guided.
They are like one who has kindled a fire,
and when it illuminated all that was around them,
God takes their light,
abandoning them to their darkness and unseeing.

She was petrified by the horror of it and not able to bow in prayer. The "tsk" she let out so easily at Yulduz rang in her ears, reverberating until Layla's tender face was before her, and each cruel word she had said to the girl shook her to her core. Every bit of what she'd done in the past five days since entering onto the Sufi path came rushing to her. She had been judgmental, jealous, cruel, short-tempered, resentful, and high-minded with small pieties. Zaytuna forced herself to face each moment as it showed itself to her. Losing herself in her careful accounting, she forgot that she was standing in prayer, and said aloud, "I did this. I did this. I did this," as each cold wave of memory slapped her and soaked through her every cell. Then, Mustafa's face came to mind and she turned away from it to God. *How could I have been wrong? How can the rape of women be right? The rest is me. I am mean. I am cruel. I must see this. I must. But that, no. I refuse to believe it. I refuse to believe it of You!*

A bell rang in her ears. The force of it made her raise her hands to the side of her head as if it would shatter from the vibration. Then the waves of sound slowed, and between each, words rose and fell, and she heard Junayd's voice cutting through. *The Lion, Ali, refused to kill in anger. If he had slain the man who had spit in his face that day on the battlefield, it would have been to satisfy his own soul, not the rights of justice. Fight or do not fight, but only with wisdom.*

She fell to the ground and a rush of freezing cold ocean water came up behind her and knocked her under its wave, trapping her beneath the surface. The mosque was gone. Just her arms and legs flailing, her wrap floating around her through the shafts of watery light. The world beneath the water shimmered and moved. Through the light she saw Junayd, her uncle, her shaykh, sitting in his regular spot on the sheepskins. She called out to him, but the water made her voice thick and slow. She called out again. Nothing. Then she took the water in her hands and pleaded as much as prayed, *Bismillah, In the name of God the Merciful, the Compassionate. Wash my sin from me. Wash my jealousy from me. Wash my resentment from me. Wash my cruelty from me. Wash away the dirt of this world that obscures my eyes, my ears, my hands, my feet, and my heart from knowing You.* She performed the full ablution with the water that surrounded her, rubbing her hands, her face, her body, her hair, her feet, and ended with, *Alhamdulillah.* The water dissolved around her and Junayd stood before her, holding his hand out. She did not grasp his hand but said instead, "Can you forgive me? Will you still guide me?"

He smiled. "My daughter, my companion, come with me."

She took his hand. "How can I make things right?"

"You will fail." He said, "Keep getting up. Keep examining your soul. Address the wrongs."

He let go of her hand and she was again in the mosque, standing in prayer, and heard herself say the words, "Allahu akbar." Her body prayed, as though it were someone else's. She said the required words as though it were another's voice speaking through her. She stood for the second cycle, and heard the voice recite the opening chapter of the Qur'an. Then her own voice returned to her, and she whimpered as if she were a wounded animal, saying, *amin.* And verses from the Qur'an came to her again,

> *By the morning hours,*
> *by the night when it is still,*
> *your Lord has not abandoned you,*
> *and does not hate you.*

> *What is after will be better*
> *than what came before.*
> *To you, your Lord will be giving.*
> *You will be content.*

Did he not find you orphaned
and give you shelter?
Find you lost
and guide you?
Find you in hunger
and provide for you?

As for the orphan,
do not oppress him.
And one who asks,
do not turn him away.
And the grace of your Lord,
proclaim.

She bowed, in tears, stood, prostrated, and quietly wept onto the reed mat beneath her. These were the words that God had revealed to Muhammad after he had thought himself abandoned. She sat back and said aloud, "God forgive me," with the voice of a seeker forgiven. She prostrated again, proclaiming silently, *Glory to God Most High.* She came up from her final prostration, turned her head to the right and the left to give the angels her greeting and gratitude, closed her prayer, and looked up at the courtroom in the distance. She held Mu'mina and Tansholpan in her heart out to God, and placed them in His care.

She found Yulduz easily. There were not too many women sitting on their side of the courtroom and approved of the spot. Yulduz had put them to the side of the courtroom so they could see everyone as they faced the judge. They watched as men were lined up before a clerk who sat, legs tucked underneath him, behind a small desk taking their names down. Two women got to the front and gave the clerk their names in a whisper. He handed them small slips of paper in return.

Yulduz asked, "What's that for?"

"He calls them by number so their names aren't said aloud in court."

She looked across to the men. Mustafa was looking straight at her, his face drawn and hard. *What has become of us?* She turned away from him to collect herself, facing the mosque door, and saw Ammar just coming in.

Zaytuna stood to meet him, coming at him so briskly that he backed up surprised, saying, "What is this?"

"Ammar, how is Mu'mina? Has she lost her child?"

"She made it through the night. It looks good."

"Do you know who poisoned her?"

"It had to be the guard or the servant, neither reported it to the judge's house staff. We have someone looking to arrest the guard. He didn't show up at work. The servant is already in custody but won't talk."

"Was it meant for Tansholpan or Mu'mina? Do you know?"

"We don't know until servant talks. But Mustafa passed on what the midwife said about it being meant for the girl despite what Tansholpan thought."

"I was thinking..."

Ammar closed his eyes. "Zaytuna, I need you to..."

"Why would the guard put the poisoned food in front of Tansholpan, if Mu'mina was meant to eat it?"

His eyes widened. "Right. Why? Maybe he wanted to protect Mu'mina? Maybe he was afraid of Tansholpan and wanted to kill her? I trust the midwife's judgment on this." He shook his head with the realization of it. "Who else would do this but Imam Hashim's family? They had to bribe someone. So the guard takes the money, but doesn't follow through? I don't know, but here is the thing! No one had a reason to poison that girl but them. That means they cursed-well know how to poison and were lying to me. I should have pressed the housekeeper harder." He looked across the mosque, "I have to go tell Ibn Salah." Ammar left her, got a few steps away, then turned around, putting his hand over his heart, and said, "Thank you."

She mouthed to him, "Go!"

More women were seated when she returned, but Yulduz had her hand planted in a spot next to her so no one would take it. She picked her way through the women, women like them in their best worn clothing. No upper-class woman would be found here testifying, let alone observing. Only a few looked concerned about the proceedings, maybe waiting themselves on a case. Most were there for the entertainment. They chatted eagerly amongst themselves, waiting for a show to begin.

Carpets had been laid out. The clerk's desk was placed closest to the people waiting. There was another desk behind him, perhaps for a scribe. A few sheepskins had been laid out where the judge would sit. A small desk for papers was beside it. There was no pallet raising him above the people, not even a backrest. Perhaps he would be fair, after all.

Tein was not sitting with the men. She hoped he was out investigating the case. Maybe he would find something in time. Ibn Salah, Ammar, and Mustafa were talking, their heads close together.

There was a sharp knock on the door, a guard opened it. The chamberlain emerged. He wore a large brown turban that balanced a long and luxuriantly oiled dark-brown beard. His quilted robe was a striking pattern of blue dots on a white background and cinched around a trim waist by a dark brown leather belt, and the brown of his sirwal and stocking feet. His back was straight. He looked beyond the crowd before him to the far end of the mosque and announced in a clear voice, "In the name of God, the Merciful and the Compassionate. Qadi Abu Abd ar-Rahman Yahya Ibn al-Zayzafuni al-Khurasani will now hear your cases."

The guard opened the door again. Qadi Ibn al-Zayzafuni emerged and walked to his spot on the sheepskin. She knew it was him immediately by his tall judge's cap, a quilted leather cone in black leather, with a turban wrapped around it. The judge dressed simply, making his chamberlain seem extravagant by comparison. His robes, sirwal, and hooded cloak were made of finely woven, undyed wool with the simplest banding. His beard was nearly all grey, shot through with red, which made his fair skin look even more pale. As he sat down, his robes pooled around him. Looking out at the room, avoiding the women's gaze, she felt tenderness wash out to them and she knew Mu'mina and Tansholpan would be in good hands.

Qadi Ibn al-Zayzafuni said, "May God guide me toward what is right. I will stand before Him on the Last Day and will give an account of my ruling in each case that comes before me. May God prevent me from disobeying His commands in each of my judgments this day and every other day. Amin."

The property clerk handed the chamberlain the names of those who were to be called. He looked over the list, then said, "Abu Umar Burhan ibn Abi Burhan Ibrahim ibn Awad ibn Salim al-Bayduni."

Burhan stood before the clerk. Zaytuna thought, *So this was him. So much ugliness from someone with such a plain face.* Behind him sat an older man. He must be Abu Burhan. The son obviously took his looks from his father. Here was the unremarkable man who caused Mu'mina so much harm. They both wore plain robes, deeply patterned but in subdued browns, blues, and yellows, with wraps of dark brown wool. Zaytuna grunted. What seemed sincere in the dress of Ibn al-Zayzafuni was a mere performance in these men. If Qadi Abu Burhan had only forced Imam Hashim to release her, none of this would have happened. She didn't know how the imam died, but it all seemed to centre around the injustice done to this girl.

The chamberlain asked, "Please identify yourself and state your case."

Burhan said, "Abu Umar Burhan ibn Abi Burhan Ibrahim ibn Awad ibn Salim al-Bayduni. I live on Abu at-Tuyur Street, in the district of Karkh, and attend the Sharqiyya mosque for Friday prayers."

Qadi Ibn al-Zayzafuni, nodded. "Please state your case."

Burhan said in a clear and confident voice, so all could hear, "I accuse the slave, Mu'mina, of killing her master, Imam Hashim Ibn Ahmad al-Qatifi, by means of a curse, and the curse writer Tansholpan, of supplying the slave with the curse that killed him."

The judge said, "Although we have the expectation that all who speak in this court will tell the truth, this is a capital crime. Thus I will take the step of reminding all those who will speak before me today to take care with their words. Should anyone lie in their presentation of the case, it will be a grave matter before this court and God. If I am made aware that she is convicted on false evidence, you will be liable for the same punishment as the accused. But God is The Aware, the All-Knowing, thus even if you are not found out in this world you may find that the sirat, the bridge to Paradise, to be a razor's edge and from that edge you will fall into the torments of hell."

Burhan visibly shuddered, then paused and looked back at his father. Zaytuna watched Abu Burhan closely. He looked as if he wanted to slap his son into speaking.

Zaytuna looked back quickly to Ibn al-Zayzafuni to see if he saw it as well, but nothing showed on his face. The judge replied, "You must consider the weight of what you are about to say. If you have doubts about this case, you must say so."

Burhan spoke, choosing each word as if he were discovering it before him, "I bring this case to you for your adjudication. I believe that the petition is sound. But God knows best. May the truth come to light and justice be done for Imam Hashim and those accused in this life and the next."

Zaytuna was shocked at the measure of his reply. A quick look at Mustafa confirmed the same. His fear of God was unexpected. How can someone act in this world as if God sees nothing and then in a moment like this suddenly become aware of God's encompassing knowledge and justice? *My God*, she thought, *these men are charged with protecting the legacy of the Prophet!*

The guard went back through the door and brought out Tansholpan and Mu'mina. Yulduz started at the sight of them and squeezed Zaytuna's arm. Tansholpan looked over at them, nodding. She seemed calm, resigned even, which worried Zaytuna. Tansholpan had her arm around Mu'mina to help her walk. The girl's face was drawn. She looked weak, still recovering from the poison, but with a spark of anger in her eyes. The guard brought them to stand before the women watching the court and within view of the judge. The guard allowed Mu'mina to sit but Tansholpan had to remain standing. The guard stood beside them both, blocking the view of some of the women behind them, who grumbled and moved, pressing against those next to them, in order to see.

Qadi Ibn al-Zayzafuni said to all those before him, "It is rare that a murder case comes before the religious courts, let alone a case in which an esteemed colleague is the victim. It was first submitted to the Chief of Police's court by the Grave Crimes section of the Baghdad Police. Due to the complicated nature of the case, it was agreed that our court would be a more appropriate place to hear the evidence. Lest you think that this case was brought here because we would like to see the accused found guilty without a proper hearing, I will correct you. The petition to move this matter to our court was based on the troubling behaviour of the deceased scholar with regard to the accused. It is imperative that you, the people, understand that we are watchful over our own.

The people in the court shifted. Some tittered with pleasure, others with frustration probably realizing that their case would not be seen today. Yulduz squeezed Zaytuna's arm again. "Good man."

"May God protect me and guide me, your judge is between Paradise and Hell on this matter, indeed on all that come before me." He said something in a whisper to himself, then, "May the case be presented."

The property clerk spoke, "I have in my possession Abu Umar Burhan ibn Abi Burhan's petition to the court, the scribal records of police interviews with relevant parties, including both of the accused, as well as confessions to the murder by the accused named 'Mu'mina'."

At the word "confessions," a number of people in the crowd gasped.

The chamberlain looked to the judge who seemed concerned at their reaction but did not address it. He nodded to the clerk to continue.

"I also have in my possession the court records of a petition, subsequently resolved, which was brought by the accused, Mu'mina, against Imam Hashim al-Qatifi, in the court of Abu Burhan Ibrahim ibn Awad ibn Salim al-Bayduni at the Sharqiyya Mosque."

The judge said, "We will hear first from the petitioner of today's case."

The chamberlain asked, "Would Abu Umar Burhan ibn Abi Burhan please come forward and attest to the petition before the court?"

The property clerk handed Burhan the petition. He confirmed, "Yes, this is the petition I submitted to this court."

The clerk nodded to him, Burhan went back to his place, and the clerk handed the petition to the judge.

The judge spoke, "Abu Umar Burhan ibn Abi Burhan, please present your evidence in accordance with your petition."

"I am petitioning on behalf of the family of Imam Hashim that Mu'mina, the slave of Imam Hashim, and now the property of his inheritors, killed him by use of a talisman. The talisman was purchased from the curse writer Tansholpan. I petition the court that Tansholpan should be held to account in this case as providing the instrument of his death. I would also petition the court that Tansholpan be questioned on the matter of heresy, as a writer of curses, rather than prayers, and transferred for examination before the chief judge in the Mazalim High Court."

Zaytuna looked at Tansholpan, but instead saw the guard watching over them turn around to nod at someone in the back of the court. Zaytuna followed his gaze and watched as the man he nodded to got up and left the mosque. She looked for Mustafa or Ammar, willing them to see her, so she could point it out to them, but it was over in a moment. God willing, it was nothing. She couldn't get up and go over to the men's side now court was in session.

Burhan continued, "In the documents supporting my petition, you will find the account of Imam Hashim's wife, not present to preserve her modesty. She has testified before two witnesses, in the court today, to speak to the veracity of the account before you and the accompanying police reports, that her husband informed her that Mu'mina had tied a talisman around his neck, telling him that it would make him more virile. Earlier that day, his wife had witnessed, by God's will and abiding justice, Mu'mina purchasing that very same talisman from the curse writer Tansholpan outside the Fruit Seller's Gate.

"Imam Hashim's wife suspected that the talisman was a curse rather than a prayer for his good health and pleaded with him to remove it. He refused. Not long after he began wearing the talisman, bruises began appearing on his body. More seriously, she discovered he had broken a rib and one of his eyes had been blackened. When she questioned him about the bruises and broken rib, he denied that he had been beaten by any man."

The crowd gasped, the women around them leaned into each other whispering. Zaytuna heard the word, "jinn," said by more than one.

Burhan had heard too, and looked back nodding to the crowd. Qadi Ibn al-Zayzafuni said to him, "Look to me. I am the judge of this matter here, not them." And to the crowd, "Have respect before this court."

The people quieted, but Zaytuna could feel their energy. They would not be able to sustain it.

Burhan said, "God forgive me." He waited a moment, then went on, "Imam Hashim told his wife that an ifrit was crushing his chest and had hold of his arm, causing him extraordinary pain and difficulty breathing." The crowd rose up again, but this time only in whispers. "She ripped the talisman from his throat, but it was too late. When the case was transferred to the police chief's court, his family was informed that the slave confessed to buying the talisman, tying it around his neck, and killing him by means of it. That is a summary of our case before you."

Ibn al-Zayzafuni said to the chamberlain, "Bring the two witnesses to the wife's account forward."

Two men got up and stood before the court.

"Do you testify to the accuracy of the account just given?"

Both nodded, each replying, "Yes."

"Do you have anything to add?"

Both answered, "No."

"Thank you."

The judge turned to the chamberlain, "I would like to hear how the defendant, Mu'mina, answers these charges."

The chamberlain said, "The defendant, Mu'mina will stand before the court."

The guard pulled Mu'mina to standing, but before she could, Ibn Salah got up and stood before the judge. "I must intervene."

The chamberlain instructed a guard to force him to sit, but Ibn al-Zayzafuni signaled to him to wait.

The judge said, "Identify yourself."

"Abu Mubarak Sherwan Ibn as-Salah al-Kurdi of Iyas al-Muzani Street. I attend the Rusafa mosque."

"Now speak."

"The defendant does not have the capacity to answer the charge."

Mu'mina called out, "How dare you!"

The judge put his hand up to stop her, "Quiet. I must hear him. I will also hear you."

She scowled, but said no more.

Turning to Ibn Salah, he asked, "On what grounds do you make this accusation?"

"As our expert will show, her behaviour throughout her interrogation has been irrational. Mu'mina confessed to the crime as stated by the plaintiff, but immediately afterward recanted it to a lesser crime of unintentional murder."

The crowd whispered and hushed each other. One man said audibly, "Recanted? How convenient!"

The chamberlain indicated to the guards standing along the edges of the crowd to handle it. One guard moved between the men until he found the one who spoke and lifted him by the arm. The man protested, "But I have a case here today!" The guard said nothing and walked the man out of the mosque, protesting all the way. The crowd watched him go and fell into silence. Zaytuna could hear Yulduz's ragged breathing beside her.

Ibn Salah continued, "Although the police presented her with evidence that she may not be guilty of any crime, she insists on it. Nothing can sway her. She is, as you can see, a slave of African heritage. It is said that the heat of the African climate affects their mental capacity, and that they pass this deficiency onto their children. I have no other insight on the matter."

The words shot through Zaytuna like an arrow on fire, she began to stand and open her mouth to object but Yulduz pulled her down and pinched her on the arm so hard that she yelped in pain. She looked at Mu'mina, wanting to reach out to her but couldn't see her face, only that the guard had his hand on her shoulder pressing her down. Zaytuna understood the risk of Mu'mina confessing again to the murder in court, but was there no other way? *Why demean her further? Why like this?* She wanted nothing more than to stand and walk across the court, knock the guard's hand from her shoulder, and slap the words out of Ibn Salah's mouth. She looked at Burhan. His face had turned red at the thought that she may not be heard and his father, Zaytuna took satisfaction in seeing, was wound up tight with fury. She thought, *Let him explode with temper and be dragged from the mosque!*

Ibn al-Zayzafuni considered his account, then said, "The defendant is present to speak to the plaintiff. She will speak before this court. I will determine her capacity." He turned to the chamberlain, "Bring her forward for my examination."

25

Zaytuna watched as the chamberlain indicated that the court guard should bring Mu'mina forward before the judge. The guard took her by the arm. She didn't move. Tansholpan leaned down to whisper in her ear, but Mu'mina gave her a harsh look. Mu'mina got up carefully, then pressed her free hand against her belly once she was standing. The crowd held still as he dragged her to stand between Ibn Salah and Burhan.

"I understand that you are weak." Ibn al-Zayzafuni said, "You may sit."

Ibn Salah took her arm, but she shook it off, glaring at him, and sank to the floor, exhausted by the effort.

"Please identify yourself before the court," the chamberlain said, then stepped back.

Mu'mina sat in silence. Her mouth pressed tight.

Qadi Ibn al-Zayzafuni turned to Ibn Salah, "Is this what you mean?"

He nodded. "She is stubborn to her own best interests. It is irrational."

The judge leaned forward. "If your interest is in confirming your guilt, now is your chance. Identify yourself."

She was shaking, looking at each of them with venom. "I am Mu'mina."

"Who owns you, where do they live, and what is their mosque?" The chamberlain prompted.

She spat back at him, "You know all this!"

The judge turned to Ibn Salah. "I see your point. Would you complete the identification?"

"She is Mu'mina, the property of Imam Hashim's inheritors, of Ajyad Road, and the Sharqiyya Mosque. May I take over, judge? You see she does not have the capacity to address the court."

"Not yet. I want to hear her first."

Zaytuna turned to see Isam standing, despite the efforts of those around him to pull him down. He bellowed at the judge, "How can the murderer of my brother speak in this court!"

A man yelled from behind him, "Sit down! We'll hear from her if she did it or not!"

The guards moved in, flanking Isam. But the judge called out, "Leave him, leave him. He grieves." Then he addressed Isam, "As much as it may distress you, it is exactly the work of this court to hear her account." The guards withdrew, but Isam remained standing. "Now sit. We are guided in our principles from His Just Word and the example of our Beloved Prophet, may God bless his family and companions. Have trust in these proceedings."

Isam sat slowly, wiping his face, his eyes still wild.

When all had quieted, Qadi Ibn al-Zayzafuni asked Mu'mina, "Are you Muslim?"

She continued to stare at him, her brown eyes narrowed, her chin lifted.

"You do not seem shy. Why are you not answering?"

Then, her face changed. She glanced toward the floor, tilting her head to one side, seemingly listening to an unseen voice. She nodded, but as if she did not want to acquiesce to it, then answered, "Yes. I am Muslim."

"Recite the shahada into the record and for all to hear."

She looked angered by the demand, but did it. "There is no god but God, and Muhammad is God's messenger, and blessings upon the Prophet's family, most especially his daughter, my mother, Fatima."

Qadi Ibn al-Zayzafuni's eyes widened at this unusual articulation of the testimony of faith and asked, "Would you explain what you said?"

"It was the Lady Fatima who brought me to Islam."

Zaytuna watched as the men leaned into each other, commenting, and heard the whispering of the women around her. The judge spoke before the guards could move, "I know this is of interest to the people here, as it is to me, but it has no bearing on this case." He turned to her, "Alhamdulillah. You understand that your words are said before God and that lying may benefit you in this world, but that you will answer to God for it in the next?"

"I have no reason to lie."

"Yet you recanted. So was your first confession a lie?"

"It was the truth when I said it."

"Explain."

"Imam Hashim raped me."

The men watching the court sat up at that and silently mouthed their objections that such a thing could be possible. Zaytuna felt the women around her turn into each other, pressing each other's hands, some with Mu'mina, others condemning her as their men did.

"I have the records of your first case. Let me be clear, he used you inappropriately, and I agree that he harmed you. He certainly did not act on the model of the Prophet Muhammad, God bless him and peace, but you were not raped. There can be no rape where there is a right to unfettered sexual access."

The men smiled. Their rights over their slaves and wives remained in safe hands. Zaytuna felt the anger of some of the women around her mix with her own and they moved, swaying, objecting with their bodies, yet silent.

Despite her exhaustion, Mu'mina's back was straight. "He *harmed* me and he kept *harming* me. The court did nothing to protect me." She looked Ibn Salah up and down with disgust. "So I got my own protection. I went to Tansholpan for a curse to shrink his penis so he had no more use of it."

At that, one woman called out, "Curse all of you men!" A guard waved to the woman to stand and follow him. The woman put her hand over her mouth, promising her silence, then begged to stay but to no avail. She stood up quietly, and the guard walked her across the mosque out to the main entrance.

Zaytuna looked at Mustafa. He seemed so alone, looking down, and was rubbing the back of his head.

"The police records show that Tansholpan has admitted to writing a curse for the purpose of killing him." The judge asked, "But you say otherwise?"

"By God, I asked her for a curse to unman him." She pointed at Tansholpan. "She took it on herself to write a curse to free me instead. She uses her powers without any concern for the people or God! It wasn't what I asked for, but I'm doomed all the same. Now here I am because an ifrit came to do the work she demanded and decided to torture and kill the imam."

What? Why had Tansholpan not done what she asked? Ya Rabb was that why all this had happened?

"Your admission is that you killed him unintentionally?"

"Yes," she said, as if he were stupid.

The judge leaned back and said to Ibn Salah, "I understand. You believe due to the harm she endured she is not guilty as it was a matter of self-defence. I disagree, the choice to buy the talisman was not made in a moment of passionate defence."

Ibn Salah opened his mouth to speak, but the judge held up his hand, saying to the court, "I will close the trial here with a judgment of unintentional murder."

Burhan spoke up, "There is no blood money that could pay for the loss of Imam Hashim. The family demands that it be a life for a life."

"With your permission, judge, I need to speak," Ibn Salah interjected.

Ignoring Burhan, the judge said to Ibn Salah, "If you will sit back you will find that I will consider the harm done to her in my sentencing."

"Forgive me," Ibn Salah said. "I was not referring to the harm done her when I spoke earlier. Rather her claim to have committed unintentional murder does not mean that she has, in fact, committed anything other than wishful thinking. The girl truly believes she has killed him, as you have heard." Ibn Salah inclined his head. "But it may be that an ifrit did not kill him. I mentioned that there is evidence that brings her claim into doubt."

The judge raised his eyebrows and sat forward. "I will hear it."

"May I bring our expert witness forward, Ghazi Ammar at-Tabbani, of Grave Crimes, to explain?"

"Yes. Let us get to the bottom of this."

Burhan looked back at his father who urged him on. He stepped forward, too closely to the judge, "This is highly unusual, with respect. My esteemed father, the Judge of Karkh, here in the court today, has taught me that it is not the work of the judge to investigate the truth of a case but only judge the evidence before him. You have accepted her confession and as you have just acknowledged, on that basis, she is guilty."

Qadi Ibn al-Zayfuna placed his hand on his heart and dipped his head to Abu Burhan, but said, "This case is unusual. Thus, I am willing to rest my decision to hear him out on the example of our Umayyad forefathers who had the Solomonic wisdom to come to their own judgment in difficult matters. I aspire to the same in cases requiring it."

The judge nodded to the chamberlain who read from his list, then called out, "Ghazi Ammar ibn Jundab ibn Suwayd ibn Saad at-Tabbani, approach the court and identify yourself."

Ammar stood and approached the judge, looking pale as he stated his full name, his address, using al-Mansur's Mosque as where he went for his Friday prayers rather than the Shia mosque near his parents' home. Zaytuna wondered at it, but let it go.

"Do you accept Mu'mina's amended confession?"

Ammar lifted his head, finding his voice, "I must admit before this court, and before God, that this trouble is my fault. When she gave her first confession, I accepted it without questioning her further. I brought her confession to my superior to be submitted to the chief of police's court. When my colleague pushed me to question her further, I conceded to satisfy him. It was only then that we realized her true intent. At that time, we received her amended confession and that was submitted to the chief's court as well."

The judge spoke gently to him, "I appreciate your desire to hold yourself to account, but that was not the answer to my question."

"Because the confession was submitted so quickly, we did not have time to fully investigate other possible reasons for his death, including natural causes."

"Have any of these causes been investigated in the meantime?"

"My colleague is not here at the trial because he is following up on these leads." Ammar spoke haltingly, yet clearly, "Had I done my job honourably and correctly, had I conducted myself according to the tenets of my position, I believe her case would not have reached the court at all."

Yulduz turned to Zaytuna with a look of disbelief mixed with hope.

The judge asked, perturbed, "You do not believe she is guilty?"

Ammar stated firmly, "There is no evidence against her."

The courtroom whispered, people looking at each other in disbelief.

Burhan tried to speak, but the judge shook his head at him.

"I don't understand."

"I should have said that there is no material evidence."

Burhan started, but said nothing.

Ammar looked at him and said pointedly, "All we have against her are assumptions that it was an ifrit based on her confession and Imam Hashim's account that he saw an ifrit on his chest."

Burhan blurted out, "That is damning evidence!"

Mu'mina exclaimed, "Yes!"

The judge growled at them both, "Silence!"

Burhan shrunk back and looked behind to his father.

Zaytuna thought Abu Burhan looked like he would wring Burhan's neck, not for speaking, but for not saying more.

Ammar turned back to the judge, "The doctor, whose interview you have in evidence, cannot determine the cause of death. In short, his symptoms, including witnessing an ifrit on his chest and death, could also have been from a widow spider bite, an illness, or even from poisoning."

The judge asked, "That is in the doctor's account? But he is not here to testify to it before me thus it can have no bearing on the trial."

Ibn Salah lowered his head and Ammar looked pained.

Zaytuna wanted to yell at him across the courtroom, *How did you miss this! Why is he not here!*

Then Ibn Salah raised his head, a look of having thought of a way through on his face, and answered the judge, "The doctor's opinion is a scribal account of a police interview by Ghazi Ammar; therefore, we would argue, he is the one to submit it as oral testimony rather than the doctor."

Qadi Ibn al-Zayzafuni looked at Mu'mina, then Ammar, clearly unhappy with this argument. "I will accept it. This is a day of exceptions. You are on weak ground here, so take care." He paused. "You will have to explain the bruises and broken bones, then. I am more inclined to accept it was the work of jinn as that accords with the girl's account. Her confession must take precedence. Moreover, the jinn have their own courts, their own laws, and their own forms of punishment. It is simply more likely that a jinn killed him."

Mu'mina nodded vigorously with the judge and gave Ammar a look as if she would kill him herself. Zaytuna thought, *I understand she wants to hold herself to account. By God, I do! But can't she see that she is begging for her own execution without actually knowing what she's done?*

Ammar bowed his head in understanding to the judge, but offered, "The doctor has explained that some bruising is possible, even a broken rib, from illness. But there is a more likely and more obvious reason. He was beaten by men. You have the account of my interview with his brother, also submitted to your court, that he was a chronic gambler who most recently was not able to pay his incurred debts. My colleague has confirmed this account with the gambling establishment."

At this, the crowd gasped and tittered. The guards pushed the men to be quiet and stood over the women, but there were too many of them.

Zaytuna shot a look at the brother-in-law, whose eyes shone with betrayal. Zaytuna thought, *Walla, he believed the police would protect him!* Then she realized what Ammar had said. Tein had ruled out that the imam was beaten to death for his debts. Beaten surely, but not to death. Ammar was cleverly pointing the judge away from the possibility of an ifrit. He was not lying, absolutely, but it felt like it to her. Her heart went out to him for taking this risk before the court for Mu'mina's sake.

The judge called out to the people, "Quiet! We cannot allow you to witness this trial if you continue to disturb our proceedings." Once the crowd had been silenced, he said, "His brother is here, but he has not been examined by my witness investigator. He cannot testify. Why have you come to my court so unprepared!"

Ibn Salah answered, "The brother was unlikely to agree to speak on the slave's behalf, and, again, I would argue it is unnecessary as Ghazi Ammar, acting as an expert witness, is orally attesting to his written interviews."

Qadi Ibn al-Zayzafuni sighed. "The brother's interest in the outcome should make no difference." He looked toward the imam's brother and shook his head, then said to Ammar, "Continue."

"The beatings coincided with his inability or refusal to pay his recent debts, thus reason suggests his injuries were due to his unpaid gambling debts rather than the involvement of an ifrit. Again, my colleague has received direct confirmation on this matter."

The judge objected, "This cannot be considered by the court without verification. You were not present to testify to the interview. Your colleague is not here. He has not been approved by our investigator as an expert witness." He looked to the chamberlain who nodded in agreement. "Neither are those he interviewed present to give oral testimony." Qadi Ibn al-Zayzafuni leaned forward, "You are on surer ground with the possibility of a bite, an illness, or a poison."

Zaytuna wondered what he could be up to, but then she realized once a thing was said, it could not be unheard. The judge might end up taking it into account without realizing it. Then she thought, *Did Ibn Salah coach him to do this?*

"Yes," Ammar replied, "any of the three you just mentioned could have produced the symptoms described, including hallucinations causing him to see an ifrit."

"But what is there to say that the girl did not poison him?" He looked at Ammar coldly, "No one has raised the point that the girl is pregnant with the imam's child. This is, in fact, the greatest motivation for killing him. At the birth of a child, live or still-born, she would be freed and the child would become his heir. She would not be the first slave to murder her master." He looked at Mu'mina. "And, if you have not noticed, the girl continues to object to attempts to exonerate her. I, myself, am not entirely convinced she is without her wits."

"Qadi, given the imam's various and constant habits there could be any number of people with equal motivation to kill him. As for the girl, what she believes she has done is of no concern. It is not for her to determine the facts of the case."

Zaytuna nodded at that, but thought, willing Ammar to hear her, *Now, the poison given to Mu'mina to abort her child, come on, say it! It implicates Imam Hashim's household!*

"My colleague has since interviewed all the herbalists and pharmacists in Karkh to see if Mu'mina, or anyone in the household, bought these herbs, but no one was willing to talk to him."

"That is not surprising. You police have only yourselves to blame for not being in the public's trust. I myself would be more skeptical of your testimony if you were not, in fact, arguing against your own interest."

"Nevertheless," Ammar continued, "if poison was used, it is possible that it came from Imam Hashim's house. The imam's brother shares a home with the imam and his wife. In fact, his brother uses a mixture to control his seizures that contains belladonna, the suspected poison."

This *was* a lie. Mustafa had told Zaytuna that the brother's medication was not strong enough to kill the imam. *God protect Ammar! He was building a case of doubt, just as Mustafa explained! They all planned this testimony together.*

The judge put his hands on his knees. "Then the slave still could have poisoned him."

Burhan looked pleased at this outcome and Zaytuna thought, *Now you are happy the judge is inquiring into the truth of the case!*

Then the judge said, "But so too, could the poisoning have been accidental."

Burhan's face fell.

"Yes," Ammar answered.

The judge added carefully, "Or perhaps he took his own life?"

"Yes."

The crowd was utterly silent at the horror of the suggestion. The imam's brother moved to stand again in protest, but was held down.

"Or anyone else within the home could have poisoned him."

"Correct. Given the speed with which belladonna works it is unlikely that someone outside the home could have done it. You have before you the account of my interview with his family indicating an alternative motive for his murder."

The judge said, "There is no need to mention that aloud in court."

The crowd quietly objected, while Yulduz gestured with her hand to Zaytuna, "What?"

"The brother loves the imam's wife," Zaytuna whispered.

Yulduz's eyes opened wide.

Zaytuna looked over at the brother who was staring defiantly at the court.

The judge crossed and uncrossed his arms. He looked out on the crowd, then at each person sitting before him, then finally at Tansholpan. Zaytuna saw his face. It was still, yet thoughtful. He showed no indication of what he was thinking. She held on, waiting for him to speak.

He addressed the court, "Imam Hashim seems to have had a troubling character. Not one befitting a man who has taken up the burden of the Word of God and the Prophet's legacy for the sake of the people. I can see that his slave may have been one of several with reason to harm him. She may have killed him. But then again, given the evidence before me, she may not have. I agree now that her confession is not conclusive. That is to say, there is sufficient doubt around her guilt to warrant the dismissal of this case."

Zaytuna put her arm around Yulduz and nodded to her. The old woman's eyes were filled with tears. The women around them sighed, leaning on each other, murmuring their gratitude to God.

The judge continued, "The case against Tansholpan is also to be dismissed from my court but transferred to the Mazalim High Court to be investigated on the grounds of heresy. She will be escorted from this court back to the prison in the Round City."

Yulduz put her hand over her mouth. They looked at Tansholpan, but her back was straight as before, unmoving, as if she had not heard what the judge had said.

"As for Imam Hashim's case, I will pray that if this was, in fact, a murder that the culprit will be brought to justice and the prosecutable evidence be brought to light. The slave will be returned to Imam Hashim's inheritors. They will care for her during her pregnancy and release her, and his heir, should the child be born alive."

Mu'mina turned sharply to look at Ibn Salah and said something Zaytuna could not hear.

Ibn Salah raised his hand. "Qadi, there is a complicating factor."

The judge turned to him. "Yes?"

"As you are aware, there was an attempt to abort the imam's child. We must consider that it came from within the household of the imam. It may not be safe for her to be with them."

Gasps erupted from the people. The judge closed his eyes in frustration and gestured to the chamberlain. The chamberlain raised his hand to the guards to leave the people where they were.

Once the mosque was quiet again, the judge said, "It was

explained to me that the poison was intended for Tansholpan. I understand this matter is under investigation by Grave Crimes in Rusafa."

"On the contrary," Ibn Salah said. "The midwife has given us an account that the herbs used were for the sole purpose of abortion. It seems the guard knew and tried to protect the girl by giving the poison to Tansholpan instead. Unfortunately, the girl ate it in any case."

A woman behind Zaytuna whispered, "On my mother's name, the wife tried to get rid of that baby after she killed her husband for putting it in the girl in the first place!"

"Where is this *noble* woman whose modesty keeps her from facing the truth in court?" Her friend replied.

The women around them all murmured in agreement, but Zaytuna thought, *Why turn on her? What has she been driven to do by these men?*

The judge addressed Mu'mina, "I must assume the claim of the midwife is true for your safety and the safety of the late Imam's child, although the court will confirm this matter. Thus, you will be protected until your pregnancy is resolved. You will return to my home, not a cell, and remain under the care of a trusted personal servant. If the child does not come to term, though, you will be sold at market and the proceeds will be given to the imam's inheritors."

Mu'mina pushed herself up off the ground and was standing over the judge before anyone could stop her. She screamed in the judge's face, "And me! And me! I am to burn in hell for not paying for his death with my life and live only to be raped again!" A guard rushed forward to grab her, but Ammar stood quickly and pulled her back as she screamed, "Execute me!"

"Stop now, girl." The judge raised his voice, "It is not for you to say what will be done with you."

Fighting Ammar's grasp, she glared at the judge, but Ammar had her firmly in hand. The judge turned to Ibn Salah and said harshly, "Control her!"

Ibn Salah spoke to her. Her eyes widened and she spat in his face.

He wiped the spit from his face with his sleeve and turned to the judge. "With your permission, Qadi, I offer to protect this slave during her pregnancy. But if she does not carry the child to term," he looked at Mu'mina, "I will buy her from Imam Hashim's inheritors. I would like to swear an oath, and have it written in the documents of these proceedings. By God, I will never use this slave for sex, nor will anyone in my household."

Without knowing what she was doing, Zaytuna started to push herself up to stand and tell all who could hear, *Release her! Why must you own her at all!* But Yulduz grabbed hold of her and kept her where she was, throwing her weight against her. Zaytuna struggled against her and looked across the court to Mustafa. She knew that face. *He had heard Mu'mina.* He believed her. His eyes were on fire. Not in anger, she knew, but with pride and love that she would dare to challenge the court for Mu'mina's sake, to speak out against the wrong done her. The man she knew her whole life was before her again. She fell back against Yulduz's arms and was silent.

Then the voice of a woman rose behind them, "I will purchase her now and release her now. She will become our mawla, a dependent of our family! She will be under our protection!"

They turned to look. *My God, Ibn Salah's sister!* Zaytuna grasped Yulduz's hand. A guard moved in to remove her, but the women crowded in around her, creating a barrier he could not pass.

Ibn Salah said to the judge, "It is my sister!"

Mu'mina looked back and forth between them in utter fury.

"Your sister is not permitted to speak in this court," the judge said. "But I see the benefit in selling her to your family. It is my right, based on the facts of the case, to enforce the sale of the slave to you. Should you choose to release her, that is your business. You may have use of my scribe to complete this sale immediately."

Burhan looked back at his father, but he had turned his face away from his son.

Ibn Salah's sister looked down at the women around her, holding her safely, and she recited in a voice that cut through every word and gesture, silencing the court.

As for the orphan
do not oppress him.
And one who asks,
do not turn him away.
And the grace of your Lord,
proclaim.

Zaytuna's heart widened and opened to embrace her at these words, these verses, that had only just come to her before when she was praying. *Subhanallah!*

At a nod from the judge, the chamberlain called out, "Guards, clear the court of this disturbance!"

The guards fanned out to surround the women, getting them up, then trying to herd them out the door, but the women would not move. The guards resorted to yanking them out, one by one, taking each to the main door of the mosque then going back to get another. In the confusion, Zaytuna scrambled forward on her hands and knees to Tansholpan, Yulduz right behind her. Tansholpan turned around. The guard standing beside Tansholpan took her roughly by the arm pulling her in the direction of the door leading out of the court. Her eyes fell on Yulduz. She called out to her, "Yulduz! Be good! I will see you in Paradise, my friend!"

26

The court guard brought Tansholpan to the door and pushed her through into the wide hallway beyond. The mosque library was on the right. Once the door to the mosque fell shut behind them, the guard grabbed her wrist, and bent her arm up behind her back with a jerk. She snapped at him in pain, "What are you doing? Where am I going to run to?"

"You aren't running anywhere. You're going to get yours for consorting with the jinn and cursing others."

She looked around in a rising panic. Now that the moment had come, she was not so accepting. The door to the library was open. A man was within, his head buried in a book, pen in hand, she yelled, "Help me!"

The man looked up from his book, saw her state and stood up in a rush, knocking over the desk before him, spilling ink on his robes. It all happened so slowly and she wondered at how time could move this way, until he was before her so quickly that she felt she had never seen him coming. He demanded of the guard, "What are you doing with this woman?"

The court guard said, "Don't listen to her. She's just trying to escape. I'm taking her back to the police holding cell."

"Go into the mosque!" Tansholpan yelled, "Find someone. He's going to kill me!"

"She's trying to trick you. That's what got her arrested in the first place."

The scholar looked at him, then raised his finger in the air. "Truly, do you have to handle her so?"

She pushed herself toward him despite the pain in her arm. "Help me!" She began to squirm, bending her body around to break his hold. He laughed at her attempt and twisted her arm up higher until she bent over and begged him, "Stop!"

He grunted from the effort of controlling her and told the man, "She just wants a chance to bolt and run. More of my men are outside. We'll get her where she is going safely."

"I'm going into the mosque to see about this, please wait here." The scholar left them, the mosque door shutting behind him.

The court guard loosened her arm but pulled her up and put a hand over her mouth with his other arm around her. She called after the scholar, her voice muffled, "Come back!"

She tried to loosen herself from him as best she could but the pain in her arm was too much. The guard dragged her out the door, hissing in her ear, "Just move." He continued to pull her down one alley and then another. *Where is he taking me?*

Around the next corner she saw him, the young guard, the boy from the countryside with the innocent face from the judge's cell, was waiting for them. A donkey was behind him, twitching its nose. The young guard gestured to the court guard, showing him he had a long length of rope. "Bring her hands around front, Parzan, so I can tie them!"

She tried to twist away as the court guard brought her arms around in front of her. There was no escape. As the young guard wound the rope around her wrists she knew the moment had come. She had seen this moment, months ago, when she had played the kobyz for a woman looking for a curse. The woman's husband had taken a second wife and she wanted the woman to lose her beauty. So Tansholpan played her kobyz and left her body, flying over Baghdad until she found the two together. She alighted in the room beside their bed and cupped her hands on his back, blowing a prayer into his heart that he lose his attachments to this world, find peace in God, divorce this woman kindly, and serve his first wife and children. She rubbed the prayer across his back saying, "Amin," then pushed away from him her arms out like wings, cupping the air.

As she flew back over Baghdad to tell the woman the curse was done, she saw a woman lying dead in the street, her wrists bound with rope, wearing the same red robe as her own. She drew closer, hovering over the body. It was herself! Pulling back in horror at the sight, she dropped from the sky, her arms wrapped around her, her knees pulled in. She tumbled down, uncontrolled, falling hard back into her body slumped over a cushion in her room, her kobyz beside her and the woman staring at her wide-eyed. She returned to her place knowing that she had seen her own death. She did not sleep that night. By morning she accepted it. But since then she had looked around every corner, asking if this was the day.

Parzan commanded, "Tightly, Naz. Make it so she can't move."

The young guard completed the binding and gave it a jerk to make sure the knot was tight. The rope abraded her skin, then cut into her. She leaned back, trying to break their grip and screamed. She felt an explosive impact on the side of her head, saw stars, then lost consciousness to nothing.

A sharp pain cut through her ear and stung her cheek like a thousand needles. She had fallen to her side, her head was thick and buzzing, her ears ringing. She half-opened her eyes, but she couldn't focus. Her eyes closed on her again and her head lolled to the ground. Then she remembered the two guards. She wanted to find a way to her hands and knees so that she could crawl away from them, but could not make her limbs do it. Hands grabbed her by the arms and pulled her in one jerking motion, throwing her backwards against the soft back of the donkey. She could feel it move behind her, the softness of its flesh give in here, the hard edge of its rib bones cut in there. The two guards grabbed her and tried to lift her up.

Naz complained, "God help us, she's heavy!"

They dropped her feet back to the ground, then took a firmer grip, turning her around and heaving her up and over the donkey so she was slumped over it. Her legs were out one side and her head and arms hung over the other. The donkey moved, her stomach pressed against its backbone, her head and arms swayed, and the buzzing and pain in her head overwhelmed her. She threw up, the vomit catching inside her nose, and dripping over her shut eyes and hair.

One of the guards laughed. "Look at this!"

Finally the donkey stopped. She heard a third man's voice, "Parzan, move her around to sitting!"

The guards pulled her off the donkey and held her standing, her back against it. Naz grabbed her chin, pressing hard against her cheek with the flat of his hand. It was rough against her skin. "Curse this!"

She managed to pull one eye open. A hand slapped against her other cheek, smearing it and the rest of her face with bits of something black. Her eye shut as the stink of fresh dung bit at her nose and she threw up again. The hand on her chin pulled away.

Naz said, "You bitch!" Warm vomit ran down her neck and onto her chest and she heard his voice again, laughing, "Slut of the jinn."

She forced her eyes open and tried to turn her head to see where she was but the sharp ringing and thick buzzing in her head only got worse with the movement. She looked down. A young boy was there. She knew him and came fully awake. *That stinking boy from the Fruit Seller's Gate.* The boy with his ratty scrap of turban and filthy robe tied up with rope who was always watching them. The boy who threw stones at them when no one was around to drive him off. *One of his stones finally hit its mark.* She pulled her head back and up to look at the men. The young guard pushed the flat of his hand against her face again, slapping more dung across her forehead and smeared it down across her eyes, nose, and chin. She drew a breath in shock and tiny bits of dung were sucked into her throat. She convulsed with coughing.

That man's voice again, irritated, "Come on, get her back on the donkey!"

She turned towards the voice. A young man in a white turban twisted under the chin like the Hanbalis with nothing but a few hairs for a beard, and a long sword tied at his waist, stood near the rear end of the donkey. He was joined by the ratty boy who walked over to him, both looking at Tansholpan with grim satisfaction. The two guards pushed and pulled at her until they got her up, straddling the donkey, facing backwards. A red-hennaed hand print was stained into the donkey's coat on both hinds. The animal's backbone cut into her. One guard was on either side, holding her in place, hands on her thighs, while the boy ran around to pick up the end of the rope tying her hands. It was so tight, she could not feel them anymore and her wrists were bleeding. The man in the white turban with only three beard hairs to his name seemed pleased. "It will all go easier on you if you just stay sitting upright."

She was finally able to look around without vomiting, but they were just in an alleyway she did not recognize. What good would it do to know where she was, anyway. The man in the white turban walked out of her sight, coming around the front. She felt the donkey move. He must have the reins. The sudden movement caused her to retch again.

She fell inside herself into prayer and called out to God. The world around her disappeared, the rope untied from her wrists, the filth on her gone, her legs free. She traveled over the city, following the curve of the Tigris, glittering below her. There was a house on the river's edge. She alighted on its balcony ledge, then made her way into the room.

There she was, in the judge's cell, lying on the floor in that luxurious room. Standing over herself, she watched as her body moved without her control, her eyes jerking in their sockets, and her mouth moving with unheard words. On the other side of the room the midwife cared for Mu'mina. She thought, *She's safe now*, then turned her attention back to herself and leaned in to hear what she was whispering. "My time for hers. My time for hers. My time for hers."

And then she understood that God had answered her prayer, as He answered all her prayers. Tansholpan had given her allotted days in this world for the girl's sake. Instead of the girl dying from poison, she, Tansholpan, would die. *Alhamdulillah.* Placing her hand on her body's forehead said, "Dear one, you'll be with God before long." The convulsing soothed and slowed and she fell into a deep sleep. Tansholpan pulled herself up out of the room, back into the world and onto the donkey.

The men had got her onto a main road, near enough a marketplace, so that there were plenty of people to jeer her as she was paraded in shame before them.

Naz called out, "Here is the Turkmen sorceress, Tansholpan! Guilty of killing a man with curses and consorting with jinn! Here is the Turkmen sorceress, Tansholpan! Guilty of killing a man with curses and consorting with jinn!"

A young man came out of a shop and watched her as the donkey passed. Without taking a moment to consider it, he stepped out of a sandal, bent over, took it in hand, and threw it at her as hard as he could. The sandal hit her on the chest, and she jerked back from it. Another sandal followed, this one just hitting her on the side of her head. She ducked away, tucking her head as low as she could, pulling at the rope holding her hands to raise them to protect herself, but could not. Sucking in a breath, she said aloud to herself, "Woman, go in peace!" She laid her hands down, despite her fear, and stopped fighting.

Looking down at the people yelling at her, she asked herself, *Which of you will it be?*

An old woman caught her eye, and shrunk back in fear. "God protect me from evil things! Don't you look at me!"

There was another voice behind her, "You black-faced whore of Satan! God banish you to hell!" Then she heard it more than felt it, a sharp crack, then nothing.

The court guard, Parzan, got to her first. She had fallen over the back of the donkey, blood was coming from scalp. Parzan tried to keep her from sliding off its back, yelling to the young guard, "Naz, help. She's knocked out!"

The young guard ran around, but she slid down to the ground in a slump, nearly under the donkey's back legs. Naz yelled to the man in the white turban, "Jahar, stop the donkey!"

The donkey jerked back suddenly, kicking a hind leg, its hoof coming down hard on her head, cracking it into pieces.

Parzan heard a scream behind him.

Naz yelled, "Run!"

But Parzan couldn't run. Everything slowed down and his ears were ringing. He turned to see Naz grab the boy by the neck of his robe and pull him away, Jahar in his white turban far ahead of them already. He pulled himself back to where he was and looked at the people. Some pushed back to get away against those who pushed in to get closer. He saw their mouths moving, yelling, but he couldn't hear it. Then another push, people moved to the side. There before him was a short man in a leather cuirass and a black turban, his sword drawn.

Parzan came to himself, hearing the din and cry so loudly he wanted to put his hands over his ears. People rushed past him to get away from the man with the sword. And all in one movement, he came to himself and pulled his own sword out while stepping over the body of the woman and slapping the hind of the donkey so that it would get out of the way of the fight.

He was taller and larger by half than the policeman standing before him, but he could see the man was skilled from his stance, the look on his face, the way he held his sword. But then the policeman made a mistake. In a single moment he looked down at the crumpled body of the woman on the road. Parzan lunged at him with a straight forward thrust. The policeman had no time to see his sword coming, yet somehow had lifted his own to deflect it to the side. The policeman took another step forward and before Parzan could pull his sword arm back and step out of his way, the policeman had slipped his arm over and around his elbow, hooking it. With his arm tightly trapped, the policeman braced his hand against Parzan's body and threw his weight on an angle against him. Parzan heard the sickening crack of his bone more than he felt it. Then the pain washed through him. His sword fell to the ground and he followed it down in a fetal position, cradling his arm and hearing his own guttural moans.

Ammar stood over the court guard, then called back to a watchman hurrying through the crowd to him, "Come here!" As the watchman leaned down to pull the court guard to his feet, Ammar said, "Take him to the cells for the Karkh Police and make sure they get a bonesetter in to see him."

Ammar turned his attention to Tansholpan, kneeling beside her. Her cap was gone. *Where's her cap? I need her cap!* People stood back in a circle, watching him warily. He begged, "Where's her cap?" Only then did he remember that he had dragged her to jail without it days ago. Turning back to her, he bent over her, and tugged at the sleeve of his robe, using the edge of it to wipe the dung from her face, but only smeared it.

Someone tapped him on the back, then he heard the words, "Sir, I have the cart for her." Ammar stood. Two more watchmen had arrived and stood on either side of her. They started to lift her, but her head fell back, her wound exposed, her face broken.

"Stop!"

They put her back down at his command. Ammar took his turban off his head, unravelling the long black cloth. "Help me. Put this under her head as I lift it and put the pieces back." The watchmen took the cloth from him. If the man felt disgust in the moment, he said nothing. Ammar only heard him whispering in shock, "Allahu akbar, Allahu akbar, Allahu akbar," with every exhalation. Ammar lifted her head gently with one hand, and found pieces of her skull with the fingers of the other. He cradled what was there, while the watchman pulled the unwound turban underneath and then up and around her head. The watchman was now openly weeping as they enclosed her wound and laid her head back down. Ammar nodded to them both. They lifted her again, this time with Ammar carrying her head and lay her down within the cart.

Ammar said, "Take her to the corpse washers at the Barmakid Hospital."

The men looked at him, questioning.

"I know how far it is. Take her there."

As the watchmen left with the cart, Ammar felt another tap on his arm. A young woman, her wrap edge clutched in her teeth, held a jug of water in one hand and a clean cloth in the other. "You need to wash your hands." He opened his hands and saw the blood and dirt, then kneeled and she kneeled with him. Holding his hands out as she poured the water over them, he rubbed them together. The water now stained with Tansholpan's blood ran onto the dirt of the road splashing the toes of his boots. Seeing it, he cried out within himself, *I was too late!* When the water ran clear, the young woman put the jug down and handed him the cloth. He dried his hands and gave it back to her. She pointed to his face and he reached up to touch it, finding it wet. "I'll need more water to wash the blood off."

She shook her head and looked down, blushing. "No, sir, you are weeping for the poor woman. God bless you."

"Do not bless me." He shook his head. "I just as good as killed her myself."

He stood, wiping his eyes with the sleeve of his shirt, but the tears kept coming. Walking slowly, bareheaded, he paraded himself in self-recrimination and shame back to court to find Zaytuna. All he could think was that the women who knew her should wash her. Every bit of this was because of his inaction, his refusal to investigate. His pace picked up faster and faster, until he broke out in a run, trying to pound the pain of it out of him.

He threw open the mosque door in the alleyway, stormed through the corridor, then the door to the mosque itself. Court has resumed, and a new case was being heard. Ibn al-Zayzafuni, his chamberlain and secretaries, everyone watching the proceedings turned around and looked at him, stunned into silence. He looked down and saw the blood stains on his cuirass and pushed past the guard, through the women's section. Women hissed at him, one slapped his leg as he ran past them toward the front of the mosque searching for Zaytuna, hoping she might still be there. Then he saw her, kneeling in prayer not far from the door. The old Turkmen woman she came with was nearby watching her. He fell to the floor.

Zaytuna stared at him, startled out of her prayer. "My God, is it Tein?"

The Turkmen woman drew close, "What is it?"

"Tansholpan has been killed. Killed in the street."

Zaytuna demanded, "What happened! Tell us."

"A man who had been in the library alerted us that the court guard was taking her away and it didn't look right to him. I checked the alley but they were gone. I found a few watchmen and we spread out to find them. By the time I got to her, I was too late. They shame-paraded her on a donkey. She fell from it and died."

Zaytuna's voice was cold. "The guard who did it?"

"He'll be in a police holding cell soon."

"Was there anyone else?"

"Yes. They got away."

He lifted his head and looked at Yulduz, avoiding Zaytuna's eyes. The old woman's arms were slack in her lap as she shuddered in tears.

Zaytuna said to him, "Look at me."

He did as he was told.

"Where did you take her?"

"She's going to the Barmakid Hospital. Can you go?"

"We'll go. You leave." She stood, then suddenly remembered she had been praying when he rushed up to her. She turned her head to the right and the left, closing her prayer, then looked down at him. He was still slumped at her feet. "Send a watchman quickly, by skiff if you have to, to bring Saliha there to meet us. She'll need someone to walk with her."

Zaytuna leaned down and pulled on Yulduz, "Come Auntie, Tansholpan is waiting for us."

Yulduz looked up at her but didn't move.

Zaytuna leaned down and wiped the old woman's face with the pad of her thumb on one side, and the back of her fingers on the other, "Come now."

Yulduz pushed herself off the ground and Zaytuna took her arm. They left without looking back at Ammar. She checked her pocket, finding only a chink of one fals. Not enough to get them in a skiff down the Tigris to the Isa Canal. They'd have to walk. Once in the street, she said to Yulduz, "It's a long walk to her."

Yulduz nodded, then said in a whispered hiss, "Damn him..."

Zaytuna cut her off, "Don't curse the man. He's in hell as it is."

Yulduz shook her head, "May he eat his hell for every meal."

They walked in silence. The city alive around them, but they saw none of it. Every building, every person, every animal and cart was nothing but sharp lines and hard contrasts to Zaytuna's eye. She winced at the sunlight. She recited the verses slowly with each breath, one word for each exhalation. When she finished, she began again,

> By the morning hours,
> by the night when it is still,
> your Lord has not abandoned you,
> and does not hate you.

> What is after will be better
> than what came before.
> To you, your Lord will be giving.
> You will be content.

Little by little, her heart began to calm and the world around her softened, the light no longer pricking at her eyes. She felt a sweet expansiveness settle within her, filling her limbs to each toe and through to her fingertips. She felt as if something were pushing her, lightly, carrying her along and if she would only lift her feet, she and Yulduz would fly. They stopped twice for Yulduz to rest. When the old woman's face would begin to crumble, she would curse Ammar under her breath. Zaytuna couldn't hear how he was to be damned, but if God were one to take instructions, Ammar would most surely become one of the people of the Fire. Zaytuna prayed for Yulduz's pain to be eased. Then, she prayed for God to forgive him.

They walked straight through the main entrance of the hospital and through to the courtyard. An orderly tried to stop them, but Zaytuna explained that they were going to wash a friend's body. He stepped aside and lifted his hands to pray for the woman's soul. They walked through the hallway with its long bench where the family would wait. No one was there. They opened the door.

Saliha, cradling her arm against her chest, stood next to the body. She turned to Shatha and said, "My friends are here. They'll help."

Tansholpan was covered head to toe in white muslin sheeting, a brown stain mottling the sheet where it covered her head. Zaytuna took firmer hold of Yulduz and let out a sigh, saying, "Allah."

Saliha gestured to Zaytuna to go to Shatha, then held her good hand out to Yulduz, "Come, Auntie, whisper the *shahada* in her ear. She can hear you."

Yulduz straightened her back and came closer. She squeezed Saliha's hand, then let it go. She turned to face her friend, bending down and whispering in her ear in a language Zaytuna couldn't understand. Yulduz lifted the cloth exposing her unbroken cheek and kissed it, then covered her again and stood.

"What did you say?"

Tears streamed down her ruddy cheeks, "I sang an old Turkmen song to her. We don't come from the same people but grew up singing the same songs. We would sing together sometimes. I wish Marta were here, we even taught them to her." She looked at Zaytuna, distraught, "How will Marta say goodbye?"

"Will you tell us what you sang to her, in Arabic, so we know, too, so we can say good-bye with one of your songs?"

Yulduz stood beside her friend, touching her arm lightly over the cloth, and sang,

> *I feel helpless I cannot reach you,*
> *separated, separated, separated.*
> *Worse than any pain,*
> *is the pain of separation.*

THE SEVENTH DAY

27

Zaytuna did what she did not want to do and walked to Imam Ibrahim's house to ask after Layla. She hoped Maryam had got some sense into the girl. But she hoped, too, that Layla wouldn't be angry with her. Hammering at the gate with the knocker, she steeled herself should Maryam open it instead of Layla. It opened a crack, then a bit wider, but not fully so. There she was, little Layla dressed like a proper working woman, her wrap wound under her arms, her hair tied up in a scarf at the nape of her neck, she noticed, a little like her own, and her face uncovered. Zaytuna wanted to remark on it, but held her tongue. She put a hand against the gate, leaning on it, and bent toward her, smiling. "I was hoping you would answer! Assalamu alaykum."

Layla laughed. "Oh Auntie Zaytuna, I can tell you feel sorry for being so mean to me! I forgive you!"

Zaytuna stood up straight, her eyes sharpening with defensiveness. She pulled exactly the wrong words out of her gut, *You forgive me?* They nearly made it out of her mouth, but she tightened her lips and her objection settled back down, lying in wait. She despaired. *Why is this so hard?* Closing her eyes, she took another breath, then replied, this time pulling the words from her heart, "I shouldn't have said one word of what I did to you. I was wrong."

Looking at her in all seriousness from behind the gate, Layla said, "You were only telling me the truth. Except for the part about me not coming back to learn to write. *That* was mean." She shrugged one shoulder. "I didn't believe it anyway."

Zaytuna nodded, feeling every bit of the sickening pain of having to admit it, "There are kind ways to tell the truth and I don't know them. I was mean, all of it was mean, not just when I said, 'No', to you."

The girl smiled, reached out and took her hand, shaking it lightly, then glanced behind her in the direction of the well and kitchen. "Can you wait outside here for me?" Then she said, "Oh..."

It was Maryam. "Who is it, girl? What's taking so long?"

She braced herself, while Layla looked at her in apology.

The old housekeeper swung the gate open wide. "It's you." She said the required words as if they were required, "It's been too long. Why haven't you come to visit?"

"I'm sorry, Auntie. Assalamu alaykum."

"Wa alaykum assalam. Come in, I have some of that apple and ginger juice you liked so much."

Zaytuna protested, as she should, hoping she wouldn't have to come in, "No, I couldn't possibly. I only came by to speak briefly with Layla. I don't want to bother you."

"It's no bother." She stood to the side. Zaytuna knew she had no choice and followed her past the fruit trees, long picked clean. Long lines of pomegranate skins were laying out on a bench to dry next to the wall leading to the kitchen entrance. Maryam opened its door. The room was warm from the cooking fire. Zaytuna saw eggs on to boil. A tray was laid out with breakfast for the imam and his daughter, Zaynab. Soft cheese, fresh bread made from fine white flour, apricot jam, and small bowls for those boiled eggs when they were done. The sight of the food hit her hard, her stomach growling. Maryam pointed to the same stool Zaytuna had sat on when she came here several months ago trying to find out the truth about Zayd's death. Layla stood in the doorway looking at her feet.

Maryam poured a bit of syrup out of a long-nosed copper pitcher into a glass, then water from another pitcher beside it. There had been such magic and sparkle as the light played off the glass when she held it the first time, months ago. She had tasted the sugar and ginger in the apple cider like it was a revelation from God. Maryam handed her a glass. It did not catch the light and she did not bother bringing it to her lips.

The old woman sat down in her place beside the stove. "I need to talk to you. I wondered how I would arrange that. God knows I have no time to come looking for you. Now God brings you to my doorstep." She gave Zaytuna an appraising look. "You've put on some weight. Drink that with health."

"And may God give you good health," Zaytuna replied, but without any heart in it, waiting for whatever was to come.

"This girl here wants to leave our home. I think she has in mind to work with you. I believe she thinks she'll live with you."

Zaytuna looked up sharply at Layla, who still had her eyes on the ground.

Maryam continued, "I want her to stay here. She could run a house someday. I'll teach her all she needs to know. And the imam will find her a suitable husband when the time comes." She looked hard at Zaytuna to press home the point. "She's safe here. I don't think you'll watch over her like I can. I can't imagine who'll she meet, the trouble she'll get into." She shot a look at Layla and said calmly, although the anger underneath was unmistakable, "You have her out doing police investigations, putting her life at risk."

Zaytuna started to defend herself, then shut her mouth. She closed her eyes and made herself admit it. She had encouraged the girl to do it, hadn't she? Then without warning, she was suddenly angry at Layla for telling Maryam. Her gut stirred with what she'd say to Layla once she had her alone.

"I can't stop her from leaving," Maryam went on, "but I want to know what you plan on doing with her. Her parents gave her over to work with the promise that she'd be cared for. They pushed her through the gate next door and never came back. There's no sending her back to them."

Layla would have to hear it. "I'm not planning on doing anything with her." After the words were out of her mouth, she suddenly felt sick. *My God, did I have to say it like that?* She dropped her head in silence.

"Is that all you have to say?" Maryam spoke to Layla, "Do you hear that is all she has to say?"

Zaytuna lifted her head, speaking softly now, "The women of my house have become very fond of her." Looking at Layla, she admitted to herself for the first time in saying it, "I've become fond of her, too." But as she said it she became afraid, as if in saying it she'd committed herself to the girl. Layla looked up and didn't smile. She seemed scared, too, but her fear looked more like she was afraid Zaytuna would take the words back. Zaytuna nodded to her to say they were true, then said to Maryam, "But being fond doesn't mean we can care for her like you do. Let me be clear, I don't think she should leave you."

Maryam threw her hand out, gesturing to Layla. "Hear that, girl?"

"There's no room of her own with us," Zaytuna continued. "No bed in our rooms. Maybe Yulduz and Qamar would take her in. We haven't discussed it. Yes, she's joined me washing clothes, and she's welcome to do that. I don't mind the company and I can get more work that way. But," she spoke directly to Layla, "This means you'll only earn enough to live rough like we do. You won't be sleeping on a comfortable bed or getting meals like you do here." She glanced at the tray, "There'll be no eggs and jam for breakfast. We've gone hungry at our house. It's Saliha who pays for the meat now. If she moves out, we'll be eating broth from a bone boiled too many times again."

Layla stood up. "I make my own choices."

"You do." Zaytuna nodded to her.

"Alright, then." Maryam stood. "I've heard enough. You've got no plans to care for her."

Zaytuna stood, placing her still-full glass on the tray with the imam's food while Layla went out to wait beside the well.

Maryam said to Zaytuna, "I can see now this is all in the girl's head. This one is going to have to burn her own hand to know the fire is hot. I can only pray it will heal quickly." She called out to Layla, forgoing any hint of propriety toward a guest, "Take her to the gate."

Zaytuna bowed her head, "Thank you, Auntie."

Layla walked ahead of her, not saying a word. When they reached the gate, she put her hand on the latch and turned to Zaytuna, her face mottled with anger and said half in fury, half in tears, "You don't scare me!"

"I should."

The tears overcame the anger and she pleaded, "Don't you want to know if I found out about the poison?"

Zaytuna's heart leapt at this, but she didn't know what to do. Encouraging the girl only made things worse. It put her in danger. It made her want to leave a woman who loves her and wants to care for her like her own child. For what? Her? A broken woman with a cruel streak? She forced herself to say, "No, I don't want to hear it."

Layla whimpered.

"The girl's case has been dismissed. We don't need any help."

"So you don't want to know who really did it!"

Zaytuna shut her eyes for a moment, then said, "Open the gate, Layla."

The girl did as she was told. As Zaytuna stepped out into the street, Layla blurted out behind her, "An herbalist said it had to be belladonna. She said it's easy to have too much of it. Just a little bit could kill a man. But she wouldn't give it to a woman because it might make her lose her baby." Layla started to cry, "That's all I found out. They wouldn't tell me anyone's name. No one else would talk to me. I'm not good for anything or anyone."

Zaytuna stopped, her arms slack by her side as she realized the import of what Layla had said. They had never asked the midwife what was in the concoction to force an abortion! She turned back to the girl. Her eyes were wide and she could barely get the words out,

"No, Layla. That's it! You got it!" She took Layla in her arms and hugged her, then let her go, "I must run!"

Zaytuna didn't hear Layla calling out behind her as she ran from the house. She barely saw the people in the street as she rushed past them. Then she stopped cold. Imam Hashim's house. Where is it? *For God's sake, woman, you're running without knowing where you are going!* She put her palms over her eyes. *Walla, I'm going to get this myself and bring it to Tein. Who mentioned where the imam lived? Was it at the trial? Think!* Then it came to her, Saliha had said that first day. Nahr Tabiq. Nahr Tabiq! The neighbourhood wasn't far. She went straight to the mosque. Someone there would know which house.

She reached it breathless and looked within. The scholars were sitting at the pillars. Young men, and the odd woman, sat in clumps around them, listening to the instruction or asking questions. She sighed, she couldn't just walk up to any pillar and interrupt them saying, "Does anyone know where Imam Hashim's house is?"

Looking up and down the road, she didn't see a man in a scholar's turban or a student looking like they'd wished they had one. A sturdy woman carrying a basket walked past her giving her a hard look. Zaytuna huffed and shook her head at the woman, thinking, *What could I have done to you?*

As if the woman could hear her, she doubled back to face Zaytuna, demanding, "What're you doing out in front of this mosque? There's scholars within and you're no student. Looking to flirt with one of those good men in there, are you? Did your mother teach you no shame?"

Zaytuna's eyes were wide at this entirely unsolicited and unwarranted interference in her affairs. She nearly shot back that mosques belong to the people and what she did was none of her cursed business, when she realized that God had brought her the exact person who would know where Imam Hashim lived! She forced a smile, "Alhamdulillah, Auntie, maybe you can help me. I am to interview for a job at the late Imam Hashim al-Qatifi's house, but I don't know where it is. I thought someone here at the mosque could direct me. Do you know?"

"May God rest his soul, the wrong to done that man!"

Zaytuna bit back a retort to that, nodding instead.

"And now we hear that little temptress has got off without so much as a warning. I was there last year in court when that slut brought the case against him. When will women learn to hide their shame? Bring down a good man, would she? Now she's been bought by some high-born woman who's set her free. Well, she shouldn't be too comfortable living under their roof." She nodded to herself in satisfaction. "God gives people a bit of rope in this life to hang themselves with in the next."

Zaytuna's fingers itched to slap her.

Her silence taken as agreement, the woman went on, "You'll be lucky to work there. His wife is a strong woman."

Coughing first to recover a neutral tone of voice, Zaytuna said, "You knew the imam well?"

She smiled, remembering. "God make his grave wide, he preached to us women especially. He'd come by the women's side of the mosque after prayers and give us lessons about our duty to our men." She nodded, "There were women in there who needed to hear that, let me tell you."

Zaytuna wasn't sure how much more of this she could take, "Do you know where they live?"

"Ajyad Road." The woman pointed, "You'll see a girl on the road ahead selling thorn bush and dung for fuel, turn left there, then right again." She looked her up and down. "You'll want the back entrance. Pass the houses and you'll find a way back and around, wide enough for a donkey and its cart. It's the third on the left. Green gate."

"You keep an eye on this neighbourhood!"

"If we good folk don't, who will?" She nodded firmly and began to walk away, saying as she left. "Watch out for that housekeeper."

Zaytuna asked, "What do you mean?"

The woman laughed. "You'll see."

Almost running in the direction the woman had indicated, she quickly found the girl selling fuel on the corner. A couple of turns and she was at the green gate, knocking.

A boy no more than seven or eight years old opened the gate. He looked like all the street boys but clean. His clothes were good, mended over, but still good. The housekeeper took care of him. She thought of Maryam and wished Layla would stay with her at Imam Ibrahim's. *I'm not going to mend that girl's clothes for her.* But the Layla in her mind stood up in front of her and insisted that she already mended her own clothes, thank you very much. Zaytuna huffed, relenting, and reassured herself that even if she did not, she'd learn quickly enough.

The boy said, "How can I help you, Auntie?"

"Assalamu alaykum, I'm here to see the housekeeper."

"I'll get her." The boy disappeared leaving the gate open. The back of the house was for the help, to be sure. She could see the latrine catchment around the corner of the far wall. But she couldn't smell anything. It must be regularly cleaned. The tannur oven was on the other side of courtyard, away from the house. She could see ripples of heat still coming off it. The bread would have been long baked. Now the smell of meat roasting with garlic, onions, and something pungent she couldn't place was thick in the cold morning air. Her stomach growled again. She pushed her fist in her gut to quiet it.

A large arbor was built over what she assumed was the kitchen door. Low couches strung with rope sat under it, but only one had a thin mattress laid out. The grape vines climbing the arbor were still green, only starting to yellow and brown, but the fruit had been harvested. Large and small flowerpots were set out. One was holding a large hibiscus that had not yet been cut back and covered to weather the cold. Neat rosemary shrubs grew against the walls. It would be a lovely spot in good weather. The housekeeper emerged from the kitchen door. She was short, wiry, and no nonsense.

Zaytuna realized in that moment she had not thought of a cover story to tease the truth out of her. What woman running any house would say anything against her employers? This garden, her life. Why would she threaten it? She thought, *I'll say I'm here about washing clothes. Then I'll work my way around to it.* But when the woman reached her, the truth came out instead, "Auntie, assalamu alaykum, I'm sorry to bother you. My brother is in the police investigating the death of Imam Hashim. I help them out now and again. His colleague came to speak to you all, but well," she paused, "When I heard what you'd had to say, I felt like there was more."

The woman looked her up and down and nodded sharply. She replied, "He was a fool, why would I answer him anyway? I work for the imam's brother-in-law, Mr. Isam. He pays me. He's a good man. I won't say a word against him. The other, well-dead." Squinting one eye at Zaytuna, she added, "May God grant him the justice he deserves."

Zaytuna nearly took a step back from the force of it. This was not a generalized curse for a man to be damned to hell out of anger or disgust, but much worse, a thoughtful prayer that God should not overlook one atom's weight of harm he's done when deciding his fate. "Where should we talk?"

The woman looked behind her and said, "Let me tell the boy to keep watch, I'll step outside here with you. God knows they've never once walked into my kitchen or out that back door, but I'm not taking any chances. Wait here. You just give me a moment and I'll tell you how he died."

At those last words, she wanted to grab the woman to make her stay, but she had already turned back to the house. Zaytuna stepped away from the door and put her hand on the arched frame of the gate, picking at the fresh paint with her nail until a bit of green came off. The kitchen door opened again and she stood up and away from the gate, flicking the paint to the ground. The housekeeper hurried to her and closed the gate partway behind them but didn't speak immediately.

Zaytuna couldn't stand it. "Who killed him?"

The woman laughed. "You'd think it'd have been that girl. Mu'mina had enough fight in her to do it. Imagine, bringing a court case against the man who owns you for doing what he owns you for!"

Zaytuna bit her tongue.

The woman went on, adding as if it were nothing, "It was his wife who did it."

Zaytuna stepped forward. "You think his wife killed him?"

She tipped her chin up. "I know it."

There it was. But the thrill of finally knowing sank into her gut and turned sour. If she'd only said it sooner, a woman would not be dead. She asked, "Why didn't you tell the police? A woman has been killed because they didn't know."

"Well, *I* didn't know it then!" The woman looked her up and down, "That policeman never came back to ask me!"

"When did you find out?"

"Only after the police said Mu'mina was pregnant."

"I'm sorry, of course you are right. Please tell me."

The woman nodded, accepting the apology, but still prickled. "I would have told if anyone came back. You're here now and now I'm telling."

"Yes, thank you."

"Madam Hanan used Mr. Isam's medicine for his epilepsy to kill him. She knew what it'd do. Mr. Isam had too much of it once. He used to have only rue with dill seed, but then the doctor added a bit of belladonna to the mix. He's more tired from it, but it's helped. That belladonna is dangerous, so the pharmacist told us to keep it locked up. A stupid girl we had living here years ago put too much into the date mix. I never let anyone but me touch the mix after that."

"What happened?"

"We make stuffed cookies for Mr. Isam. I fill them with ground nuts and dates with butter and a touch of camphor. It masks the taste. Herbalists will make them too, if you ask. We get our medicine from the pharmacist, so we make the cookies ourselves." She said with pride, "The whole family dotes on my stuffed cookies, so I make some for him with the medicine in them." She went on, "That one time he had too much medicine, Mr. Isam started seeing things. He saw his dead father before him. The old man was saying something awful to him by the way poor Mr. Isam was protesting. He turned bright red, and had a moment there with some trouble breathing, but he came back to us just fine."

The imam's brother lied to Ammar. He said his medication was too weak to cause the symptoms his brother suffered! Zaytuna asked too eagerly, "And so his wife fed the imam those same cookies?"

The woman's eyes sparkled at Zaytuna's tone. "The imam came home late that morning from a night of gambling and who knows what else. The sun was long up. She met him at the door and brought him up to their room. I brought them up some sage tea. He likes sage tea after a night out drinking. She told me not to come near but to leave the tea on the table by the door, so I did. Then the boy and I had to rush off to Mr. Isam's sister's house. But I saw him eating the cookies. She sat up with him, served him the tea herself, and sat with him while he ate them."

"But why would he eat them if he knew they were medicine?"

"Aren't you listening? I make these cookies for the whole family. They're a favourite. I make two batches of the same thing. I have presses to mould them. There is a different design for each. I know which is which." She insisted, "But I keep Mr. Isam's medicine and his cookies locked up in my kitchen. No one can get at them, but me. I'm the only one with a key. I told that to the policeman when he was here the first time."

"But then how..."

"I'm telling you, aren't I? After the police came and told her about the baby, she was so angry, I thought she'd die. Later I found her in my kitchen cabinet with my key in her hand. She demanded to know what we had that would make the girl lose her baby. She said she'd go down to the prison and feed it to her herself."

"What?" Zaytuna didn't know what to say first, object that she'd just said they never went into her kitchen, ask how the wife got a key, or confirm if the wife had poisoned Mu'mina. She decided, "Did she poison her?"

The housekeeper looked at Zaytuna as if she were stupid. "Of course not! What need would she have to do that when she could pay someone to do it for her?"

"Did she pay?"

"Who else would have done it to the girl?"

Zaytuna stared. "So how did she get your key?"

"I take them off my belt sometimes, don't I? How was I to know she'd seen me leave the keys aside? She's got no interest in how the house is run. She just wants it run right and I do it." The woman poked Zaytuna in the arm, "The point here is that Madam Hanan knew what the cookies would do, and she knew how to get at them."

Zaytuna said without meaning to, "If you'd only come forward..."

The housekeeper broke in, "I realized too late!" Her back was up again, "You don't want to know what I think."

Zaytuna put her hands out to assure her. "I do. Please."

She considered for a moment. "I don't think she meant to kill him. I think she meant to give him a scare. She just wanted him to see the ifrit that girl had brought on him and she thought the medicine would do it. Just like what happened to Mr. Isam. Then the imam'd take that talisman off. Then he'd sell the girl. Walla, Madame Hanan is jealous of that one. You think he'd have enough with the prostitutes he'd visit, but he always had time for that slave." She shook her head, "How could Madam Hanan know the ifrit would kill him?"

"And Mr. Isam, is he involved in this?"

The housekeeper stood up straight, "Never. He's a good man. He's a bit soft, but there's no harm in that, I suppose."

"How so?"

She laughed. "He loves Madam Hanan. They're cousins through the father's side. She was to be his by rights, he's the eldest brother after all. He grew up thinking she'd be his. But because of his epilepsy, her parents refused it, his own father too. So the parents agreed to marry her to the younger brother, Imam Hashim instead." She paused for effect, "Mr. Isam, he's never stopped loving her."

This woman didn't want to speak ill of Isam yet here she was obviously implicating him, as well as the imam's wife. She began to have a better sense of the warning she received about her. She was a woman who liked to stir a pot. Zaytuna no longer had any idea if any part of what she was saying was true. None of this made any sense to her. Why would she risk it? If any of what she said got back to the family, she'd be on the street. Zaytuna pressed, "Why are you telling all this now?"

The woman said plainly, "Because I feel like telling. There's nothing to be done now anyway. You can say all you like to that policeman; it won't come back to me. I heard Madam Hanan and Mr. Isam talking. That policeman is in hard trouble over the mess of the trial. They know important people." She nodded sharply, "Important people are going to have a word with his boss."

Zaytuna started with fear for Ammar, then shook it off. *Maybe this is what he deserves for what he's done. God knows His justice.*

The housekeeper went on, "At least now Mr. Isam has Madam Hanan to himself. Maybe they'll marry. They're old now. Who can stop them?"

Zaytuna was speechless.

The woman said, "Well, that's enough. I've said what I liked." She stepped back through the gate and shut it in Zaytuna's face without warning.

28

Zaytuna walked away from the house wondering if she should try to find Tein now and tell him what the housekeeper had said. But she didn't know where he was or what he was investigating today. The wife or brother-in-law had done it, or both of them. But the housekeeper was right, what did it matter? That woman would never pay for poisoning Mu'mina. And was there any need to see justice done for Imam Hashim? *I'm glad he's dead*, she thought. As the thought came up, she quickly tried to hide it from herself and God. Then the thought came back with force, defending itself, *Why can't we be glad the unjust are dead? Isn't that God's justice?* She answered her own question with a "Thank God," loud enough for all to hear as she walked away from Imam Hashim's house. God destroyed the man and freed the girl. Mu'mina was free, truly free at last. Then she remembered Tansholpan's death and her angry gratitude turned bitter. *Where was the justice in that? Surely, she set all this in motion. But what did God get out of her dying that way?* She felt cold water lapping at her toes. She ignored it. Her feelings suddenly turned against Ammar. *What about Ammar? Is he being held responsible?* Some part of her pointed to his crumpled form before her and Yulduz in the mosque. He *was* truly grieved. But she answered back to it that grief was not enough. She said, aloud, not caring who would hear, "God make him taste what he's done."

She walked in anger, her feet hitting the ground so hard, a slipper scuffed off a foot and flew ahead of her. "Allah!" She ran forward to get it, but an old woman had picked it up and held it in her hand. The woman was in a long and densely woven white wrap that had yellowed from long use. It was so thick it could not be tucked in on itself, so she had bound it to her waist with a rope. The wrap was so heavy over her head, and cut out the light so completely, it was as if she carried a nomad's tent with her. Colourful beads of different sizes and shapes were woven into the braided fringe along the wrap's edge and she seemed to be counting prayers on them with her fingers on one hand, while holding her slipper with the other. The woman's craggy face was as worn and yellowed as her wrap. Zaytuna held her hand out for the slipper, but she did not give it to her. Zaytuna shook her head, remembering her manners, and said, "Thank you, Auntie, May God find for you what you have lost."

"You have not lost your slipper, you have lost your footing on the path."

Zaytuna's eyes widened with shock, ice cold water seeping through her body, leaving her trembling.

The woman held out the slipper to her, "Should I give you your shoe and put you back on the path?"

She could not find her voice.

"No? Alright, then." The woman walked away from Zaytuna, her slipper still in her hand.

Zaytuna ran after her, her unshod foot feeling every grain and stone in the street. She fell in beside the woman, who kept walking and did not turn to acknowledge her. "Auntie, please."

"Please what?" The old woman said, walking and looking ahead.

"I don't know."

"No, you do not know. You remember that. Say it."

"What do I say?"

The woman stopped and turned on Zaytuna, the beads in her

fringe clicking against one another. "You fool. You do not know God's will, yet you judge. You do not know the heart of another, yet you judge. You do not know your own wrongdoing, yet you judge. You have condemned everyone in existence but yourself. Subhanallah! You sit on God's throne and see it all!"

Zaytuna's knees came out from underneath her and she fell hard to the ground. The woman's tanned and calloused bare feet, her fallen arches, her toes spread out on the dirt road. She threw the shoe down in front of her. "There is no blessing in this world other than intimacy with God and agreement with the way He chooses to dispose of His own affairs."

Zaytuna wrapped her arms around her to quell the shaking.

"Go see your Uncle Nuri. He is dying. Yet you sit here in the road rolling the dirt of this world around your tongue and calling it righteousness."

Zaytuna's head thrust up, saying, "Uncle Nuri!" Her slipper was lying in the road and the woman was gone. She looked frantically in every direction, she was nowhere to be seen. Shaking with fear, she pushed herself up off the ground slipping her foot out of her other slipper and taking them both up in her hands and ran straight to Tutha to Uncle Nuri's house.

By the time she made it across the Thorn Bridge and turned off onto the street where Uncle Nuri's family lived, she was long out of breath and walking as fast as she could. People were gathered outside. His house was small. It was his own, his family did not share it with anyone, but it was no larger than Zaytuna's. She began to panic. How could she get in? All these people waiting to see him. He would die and she would not see him. She ran down to the house.

Mustafa broke out of the crowd, stopping her.

"Mustafa! Is it true?"

"Everyone should go to Uncle Junayd's to wait on news."

"But I must see him!"

He held his hands out to calm her, but kept his distance. "I know. It's Juwayri. He told us not to strain the household. They are grieving, yet they'd have to serve us all. You must understand that. We have to leave."

"I will not go!"

His eyes welled with tears, his voice tired, "Are you the only one of us who loves him?"

"What happened?"

He looked suddenly afraid.

"Can't you tell me?"

He sighed. "Come, come to the house. Tein is here."

"Has he been inside?"

"Yes, but I don't know if he's seen Uncle. Come, let's find Tein."

He directed her to the wall near the passageway leading back to Uncle Nuri's home. "Let's sit here, we can watch for Tein." Mustafa sat and patted the ground next to him. Everyone she knew from the community was there, even Hilal stood waiting, not leaving despite Juwayri's instruction. She would not leave, either.

She put her hand over her heart to those who greeted her and slid down the wall next to Mustafa.

"Uncle fell into a state of loving God. You know how he is. Like your mother. You know how he loses himself, Zaytuna."

Her heart sank. Everything and everyone came to a halt around her. The air stopped moving. Sounds fell away. Mustafa's voice slipped into the distance.

"He ran into the freshly cut reed bed. His feet, Zaytuna. The reeds are sharp as knives." He began to cry, "You know. You know."

She didn't ask if a healer had come, if a doctor had been called, or if anyone was trying to save his life. This, she knew, was what he had prayed for months ago. And it was what she had, without wanting to, sealed with the word, "Amin." She tasted dirt in her mouth and wanted to grab the dirt from the road and throw it on her head. The old woman's words rang in her ears, "There is no blessing in this world other than intimacy with God and agreement with the way He chooses to dispose of His own affairs." She said aloud, "Amin." She threw her arms across her knees, put her head down, and sobbed, shuddering, saying, "Amin, amin, amin."

Mustafa said softly, "Zaytuna."

She took the end of her wrap and wiped her face with it before lifting her head. She looked up at Mustafa, smiling, her face mottled, holding the soaked end, and said, "Just like Layla."

Mustafa shook his head not understanding.

"It doesn't matter."

"Zaytuna, I'm sorry."

She strangely felt grounded, heavy, but free somehow. Tears came again and she said from somewhere within her she always did her best to ignore, "Don't be sorry. He is going to meet his Lover. This day is his wedding day. His death his wedding night."

He smiled through his tears. "Amin."

She suddenly realized that she had no urge to touch him and she felt nothing from him, unlike any other moment between them before. The braid of love that had bound them together since childhood had unravelled. She began to cry again for its loss. She wanted to pick up its ends and bind him to her once more, and say, *I love you.* But there was nothing for her hands to grasp.

"What I said to you at Ibn Salah's house, I'm sorry." He turned and looked away from her. "I heard Mu'mina say what he did to her. I could feel the slap of my mother's hand on the back of my head for not having listened before."

"That sounds like your mother."

"I forgot myself among those men."

She knew he realized it at the trial, but it was good to hear him say it. There was love and there was love. They would always have each other, just not in that way. She said softly, "You found yourself again." Zaytuna saw some movement out of the corner of her eye, hoping it was Tein coming out of the house but saw YingYue emerge with her father instead. She nudged Mustafa. "YingYue. Go to her."

At the mention of the girl's name, he blushed so deeply that Zaytuna desperately wanted to touch his cheek. *Sweet Mustafa.* She nudged him again. "Go."

He got up from beside her, bowed to her with his hand over his heart, and turned to meet YingYue and her father. YingYue saw him and smiled broadly, her cheeks bright and her eyes sparkling at the sight of him. Her father followed her gaze and his face turned hard at the sight of Mustafa.

She thought, *What could he have against our Mustafa?* Then she remembered YingYue saying that her father would never let her waste her love for God on a man. For the slightest moment she was satisfied. Then the thought tried to hide itself from her, but she snatched it by the ear and recited God's words,

> *No disaster befalls this earth, or you,*
> *without it being commanded by God,*
> *from long before it was brought into being.*
> *This is easy for God.*
> *So do not grieve over what slips through your fingers,*
> *nor gloat over what is in your grasp.*
> *God does not love those who delude themselves,*
> *and boast of what they imagine.*

The thought, chastened, sat down where she could keep an eye on it.

She looked back toward the passageway and saw Tein emerge from the knot of people crowding around it, a head taller than everyone else. She stood to meet him and he turned and looked at her. The knot of friends came undone as he made his way to her. He took her in his arms briefly, then pushed her away, still holding her hands. "They're telling us to leave."

"If we have to sleep in the street, we're staying."

Muhammad al-Juwayri, Junayd's closest companion, came out of the crowd toward them. She repeated to Tein, "We're staying."

Juwayri placed his hand over his heart, bowing his head. "Assalamu alaykum, your uncle would like to see you both upstairs. He has insisted that all his children come to him. One at a time, but he asked to see the two of you together. Come with me."

Tein felt relief and desperation wash through him as he grabbed

Zaytuna by the hand, pulling her behind him to follow Juwayri through the crowd. They came into the small courtyard. Despite Juwayri's efforts to get people to leave, the courtyard was filled with people. The aunties were there, sitting in one line along the wall. Nuri's daughter-in-law came out of a nearby door, looking at everyone. She looked exhausted, her eyes rimmed red from tears. A young woman from the community emerged from behind her, a tray of dates in her hands, and another woman behind her holding a tray of cups.

Tein wanted to clear everyone out for the family's sake, but also wanted to stay. And he knew none of these people could leave Nuri, no matter what Juwayri said. Juwayri pushed aside the curtain to a room. They ducked in after him and there he was.

Uncle Nuri was seated on his bedroll, but pale. His feet were bound with bloody bandages and were obviously swollen. The bedding underneath them was stained red and brown. Tein could smell the infection starting in and wondered how it could come so fast, especially in cold weather.

He wanted to find who was responsible. "No one has washed your feet?"

Juwayri shot him a look that told him to be quiet, but he didn't take orders from this man, this man who had joined Junayd's community long after Uncle Nuri had taken him, Zaytuna, and their mother into the fold to care for them as if they were family. He gave Juwayri a look that said his throat would be slit in a moment if he did not step back.

Seeing it, Nuri laughed, saying, "Go," to Juwayri who bowed and left. He said to Tein, "They've washed them. It's God's will." Tein started to object about God's will, but Nuri cut him off, teasing, "I'm dying, now is not the time to argue with me about God."

He realized he'd been holding tight onto Zaytuna's hand and let her go. She put her hand on his back and pushed him lightly. "Sit."

He fell to his knees beside Nuri. He heard Zaytuna sit nearby and turned to her. Tears were streaming down her face, but she was smiling, looking at their uncle in an odd way. He didn't recognize her.

He nearly asked her what was wrong with her when Nuri interrupted.

"She knows Whom I'm going to meet. She wishes it for herself, but she doesn't know it yet."

The words hit Tein such that he leaned back, wanting to grab his sister by her wrap and pull her around to face him, but his arms would not move. He still had his voice and demanded of her, "You want to die like this? You want to follow God into a reed bed and leave me stranded here in this life without any of you?"

She edged toward him, so that she was right beside him, thigh to thigh, put her arm around his back, and laid her head on his shoulder saying quietly, "I love you."

He did not shake her off as much as he wanted to shake them all off and stand and scream and ask what in this cursed world is wrong with the lot of them.

Nuri spoke, his words reaching around Tein and holding him in an embrace from which he could not break free, "Remember the day by the canal? Ithar? Nothing in this world belongs to you. None of it is under your control. Give, but give freely. Protect, but protect without recompense. Your conscience is your compass. It will be your guide."

Tein tried to speak again but could not move his tongue, a grunt escaping his lips. Zaytuna's arm pressed harder against him and he felt her fingers clutch at his robe. He heard her breathing, each breath trying to soothe him, but it only made him want to scream.

Nuri struggled and pushed himself up, leaning toward him. He demanded, "Look at me."

Tein shut his eyes. He heard himself moaning in pain. His eyes opened against his will. Nuri was looking at him as he had when he was a boy, telling him to wrestle his anger down, to pin it and make it submit to him.

"No one belongs to you." Then the tone of his voice shifted and changed in frequency such that Tein felt the room around him would somehow shatter from the force of it, "But all our love is yours." He felt Zaytuna trembling against him and he fell into himself and was gone.

He felt the floor hard underneath his hip. He felt the frayed edges of the woven reed mat pressing against his face. He felt Zaytuna's fingers brush his cheek. He heard her say, "Habibi, my brother." He opened his eyes.

Nuri had taken hold of his hand, his uncle's long fingers were cold and the tips had turned black. Tein slowly sat up. His turban had been knocked off his head when he fainted, but he didn't bother looking for it. Pulling his uncle's hand to his lips, he kissed his dying fingers, then raised Nuri's hand to his forehead.

"Come to me," Nuri said. Tein tried to lean over to him, his great body getting in his way, but he laid his head gently into Nuri's lap as if he were a boy. Nuri embraced him, laughing lightly. It sounded to him like the humming of bees and felt warm like the flow of honey or the light of the sun warming his bones. Nuri whispered in Tein's ear, "Goodbye, my son."

Tein lifted himself from his uncle's lap and realized that Zaytuna had not been able to embrace him. He moved back so she could find her way in, clumsily pushing against the mats on the floor. Zaytuna found her way through as he moved and held her uncle's face, looking him in the eyes. He heard her say, "All the gaps in my soul that you have filled."

Nuri took her hands into his own and kissed them, saying, "God is the one who filled them. God is The Eternal, The Caring. Turn to God," then let her go.

He said to Tein, winking, "Tell Juwayri, that administrator of all things Junayd, to bring Mustafa to me."

Tein burst out laughing, Zaytuna with him. The tension and hard grief fell from him. He began to softly weep again as they left the room, backing out, unwilling to leave the sight of him until they had no choice.

Juwayri was standing beside the door, just outside. He must have heard Nuri's request, and the jibe, but showed no sign of it. Zaytuna said, "He would like to see Mustafa, now."

Nuri's daughter-in-law, so exhausted by grief, was now sitting in-between the Aunties, swaying with them and held by their love as young women in the community tended to the guests.

Once outside, they looked for Mustafa but didn't see him.

Zaytuna saw Abdulghafur sitting against the wall opposite Nuri's house. His face was puffy from weeping. She squeezed Tein's hand and said to him, "Don't go. I have to tell you something. I'll walk with you wherever you are going. But give me a minute."

She went to Abdulghafur. "Sweet one, have you been in to see him?"

He sniffed and said, "No. Jurayri told me to go back to the kitchens. I'd be needed there. All these people'll need to eat." He looked at her, his soft face resolute. "But Hilal told me not to move."

She said, "Don't you worry. He's asking to see all his children. No one else is coming in. But you are one of Uncle's children as surely as I am."

Touching his knee to assure him, she stood up to find Hilal. He was in a crowd of men, talking. She caught his eye and gestured to Abdulghafur. He nodded and mouthed, "Don't worry," and pointed to Juwayri who was now out in the crowd looking for Mustafa. She did not see YingYue or her father, either. Zaytuna nodded to Hilal in thanks and went back to Tein, hoping that Mustafa would not miss his chance to say goodbye.

She put her arm in Tein's and they walked slowly together out of the neighbourhood. As they turned the corner, Mustafa, YingYue, and her father came up on them. They were holding sacks and a small tray from the market. They must have gone to get food for everyone. She felt a prick of jealousy that it had not been her, but YingYue, getting the food with Mustafa. She took hold of the part of herself that had pricked her and embraced it, saying softly, *Shhh little one. You are loved.* It quieted and found its place. *Alhamdulillah,* she thought, *Those three will have the blessing of bringing the food.*

Tein asked her, "Are you alright?"

She didn't know what he meant, saying goodbye to their uncle or seeing Mustafa with YingYue like that. She answered both questions, "Yes."

They walked in silence, arm in arm, and holding each other close, until they reached the Thorn Bridge. She pulled at him, letting him know she'd turn back there. "I went to question Imam Hashim's housekeeper today."

He was too exhausted by grief to object, saying only, "There's no more to be done. Ammar has to see Ibn Marwan today. He'll be getting the dressing down of his life. He deserves it, but they won't let this investigation carry on. They are done with it." He looked across the bridge, "There are other cases, too. Work we've let go."

"Let me tell you, so that you know for yourself."

He nodded.

"The housekeeper was strange, Tein. I've got no idea if anything she says is trustworthy. But maybe there is something in it. She implicated both Isam, the brother-in-law, and Hanan, the wife. I can't be sure what she was trying to do. She may have just been trying to spin me around. But she said that the day the imam died he had come home late in the morning from a night of gambling and drinking. She said she saw Hanan, his wife, feeding him the medicinal cookies that the imam's brother takes for his epilepsy. Not only do they have belladonna in them, but they have enough in them to cause the imam's symptoms."

He came awake. "Why would he eat them?"

"She made plain and medicinal versions of the same cookie. These particular cookies are a household favourite and the imam had to have them."

"But Ammar told me no one had access to the cabinet where the medicine was kept but the housekeeper."

"She admitted that she didn't always have her keys on her. She found Hanan in there after she found out Mu'mina was pregnant. She was looking for herbs to abort the baby."

"Ammar will need to know all of this."

"There's more. The housekeeper said that Isam had taken too much once and had the very same symptoms. His dead father spoke to him and nearly scared him to death. He was fine in the end, though. She believes Hanan only wanted to scare her husband, make him finally see the ifrit that she believed was tormenting him and rid himself of Mu'mina." She paused, "She thinks the wife killed him by mistake."

"How does this implicate Isam?"

"Isam loves Hanan, always has."

"Saliha saw that." He let out a long breath. "Well, all that makes sense. Why do you think she might be lying?"

"It's hard to explain. Maybe not lying, but not telling the truth, either. She's a woman who likes to make trouble."

"And the housekeeper is sure the cookies Hanan fed the imam were Isam's?"

"Uff!" She grabbed him, "Of course!" She wanted to slap herself for not realizing, "The housekeeper just assumed the cookies were Isam's! She only saw Hanan feeding him cookies from just inside the room. She couldn't have seen different patterns from there, only that there *were* patterns. She was just assuming." She huffed, "That's it. It's not that she lies. This woman likes to think the worst in people and make trouble. So she assumed they were the same cookies. But we just don't know." She paused, irritated by the realization, "We're back to where we started."

Tein barked a short laugh.

She pinched him, "Laughing at your sister?"

He took her hand, "I don't know how much Saliha told you about when we went to the nahariyya."

"A bit. Yulduz was taking care of her, then she went right to sleep."

"The man who runs the kitchen mentioned always having to have on hand a certain kind of cookie for him. It could have been them, Zay. The prostitute who fought with Saliha, she hated the imam enough to do it."

Zaytuna grew excited. "Saliha told me the prostitute was forced to have sex with him while her friend was lying dead below. Saliha washed the poor woman's friend, too. She said her tumour was like a child within her."

"More the harm. The prostitute, Chandi, she didn't believe the police or the Amir who runs the nahariyya would do anything about it. Her friend's death would go unavenged. She had reason to kill him." He looked down the road, shaking his head to dismiss the idea, "But she wasn't with him right before he died. The poison acts immediately. It had to come from the house. It's more likely that the housekeeper was right."

"But Tein, why couldn't Chandi have sent him home with the cookies?"

"She could have, I suppose. It was either Hanan or Chandi. I'll tell Ammar. He can question the family and I'll follow it up at the nahariyya."

She suddenly realized what this would mean to Chandi and that she hadn't cared what it would mean to the wife. As awful as the woman was, if his wife did it purposefully, she had every reason. *Walla, wouldn't justice be better served by letting it go?* She tried to put him off, "But the case was closed..."

He ignored her, interrupting, "I don't look forward to going back there after what happened to Saliha." He dropped his head, "I shouldn't have brought her."

"True, but there's no telling her anything."

He shook his head. "And Zay, she *was* good."

Zaytuna raised her eyebrows, "I don't doubt it. But Tein, the women..."

"I don't know what to do."

"What did Uncle say? Examine your conscience. Find your compass."

"Uncle Nuri told me that being a man is not owning anything or anyone."

She nodded gravely. "That's what he meant about acting for another's sake without wanting recompense. Ithar. If you believe that, then don't follow the case up with either woman. Let it go. He deserved it. His wife may not even have intended to do it. And God knows Chandi has been through enough."

"I feel for Chandi but if she killed him, as bad as he was, she planned it. It wasn't a crime of passion."

A swirling anger rose up in her. *How could he not see? How could she explain?* She felt Junayd's eyes on her. The image of Ali on the battlefield pushed through her anger until she retreated, finding her ground, a place within her where she could, at least, speak from what she knew, not her rage. She explained, "When a woman kills like this she is not just killing the man before her, but also every man who committed every horror before him. It's passionate self-defence against every man. We bear up under the thousands of horrors that have come before until we can't anymore. Planned or unplanned, these murders are the same."

He didn't say anything, but it hit him, because he knew. They had lived through too much by their mother's side and knew how deeply it had hurt him. He knew, too, from working in Grave Crimes. But then he said, "Not every woman kills."

"Tein, women's bodies are simmering pots heated by the fire of men's transgressions. Not every woman is as skilled a cook as Mother."

He raised his eyebrows, conceding, but said, "Her case won't go to Ibn Marwan. It's closed. I just want Ammar to know."

"Why?"

"He has to know that Mu'mina didn't do it. He did what was right in the end, but not because Mu'mina was deserving of justice."

She drew her head back. "I don't understand."

"I haven't had the chance to tell you. His mother told him about a dream she had of Fatima in which she instructed him to protect Mu'mina."

"Subhanallah! That's why he changed his mind?"

Tein said, "That's not the half of it."

"What?"

"He had been hearing a voice telling him to be like Hurr."

"Hurr?" She furrowed her brow. "The one who changed sides to support Husayn at Karbala?"

"Yes, him. Hurr went to Husayn with his hands out begging for forgiveness. Husayn put him into battle and he was martyred. So Ammar declared that he'd go to Ibn Marwan with his hands out and then go to battle for Mu'mina." His voice became thick with emotion, "He went to Ibn Marwan for forgiveness, not me. He should have been asking for *my* forgiveness. And to battle? He fought for Mu'mina for Fatima's sake, not her own."

She suddenly understood, remembering their late-night conversation the first day this began. "Tein, this isn't about Mu'mina. It's about what Ammar did to you when he denied her justice. He denied her because she is African and he feared her. But he didn't see you and she are the same. You'll be risking these women's lives to make him see you as you are, an African man, not the Arab he says you are in order to put himself at ease with your black skin."

He looked away from her.

"This is not ithar, Tein. You cannot act on anyone's behalf, if the action is to serve yourself, your own needs. I know he hurt you, but this is not the way. You'll be using their lives to teach Ammar a lesson, just as men have always used them."

"I just want him to know Mu'mina didn't do it."

"Proving her innocence doesn't prove she deserved justice. She deserves justice either way." She begged, "Please, Tein, don't."

He smiled. "Don't worry." But his smile did not reassure her.

"You will be no better than Ammar. You will have harmed a woman because you are giving in to your emotions."

He ignored her. "He'll have to go question Isam and Hanan. I'll see if I can go back to the nahariyya." He looked up at the sun, "The midday call to prayer is soon. There's plenty of day left."

"Tein, don't."

He took her in his arms. "You did good, my sister." He held her tight, "Zaytuna, Uncle Nuri won't make it through tonight. The funeral prayer will be tomorrow. Be ready."

She pulled back, searching his eyes, "How do you know?"

"Uncle's fingers, they were already blackened at the tips. It won't be long. I saw it on the frontier."

Only after he was long over the bridge and she was nearly home, did she realize she had forgotten to tell him to warn Ammar that it wouldn't just be Ibn Marwan calling him to account for what he'd done wrong. She felt some relief at that. If censure were coming from high places, then certainly there'd be no further investigation. Certainly nothing would happen to the wife, and Chandi would be safe. She shook her head. He feared Mu'mina and look at the harm he's done. *God forgive him.*

29

Ammar sat on the low couch against the back wall of the office. His cuirass and sword were beside him. His head was in his hands. Tein knew the posture, the particular slump in his shoulders. He had seen him like this after he'd killed a baby on the battlefield. A young Byzantine water carrier had a baby strapped to his back. The fighting burst out over the edge of the field and the water carrier got in the way. Ammar swung in the confusion and killed both him and the baby in one stroke. He said that he stood over them for only a moment then had to keep killing. Ammar nearly ran away from the camp that night. Tein kept him there. He stayed, but he was like this, slumped in pain, for a long time afterwards.

Part of Tein wanted to sit beside him and put off the conversation until he was on a more solid footing, but the other part told him that Ammar didn't deserve to wait to hear what he had to say. So Tein stood over him asking with all the pain he felt at his friend's betrayal, "Have you put out your Hurr-like hands begging for forgiveness from Ibn Marwan yet?"

Looking up, Ammar's eyes were pained. "I deserve that."

"I don't know that you understand why you deserve it."

His face contorted into an expression of painful confusion.

Tein continued, "Do you know why all this happened?"

Ammar straightened his back and looked up, straining to face Tein. "Because I betrayed my own principles. I didn't investigate her case. I didn't fight for the truth."

"Why?"

"Because I feared her."

"Why?"

"Jinn. I was afraid of the jinn."

"There's more to that. Why else did you fear her?"

Ammar didn't answer immediately.

Tein demanded, "Why?"

"I know what you want me to say. She's African." He furrowed his brow. "But everyone knows they worship the jinn like gods. I was just afraid of the jinn. I didn't know she was truly a believer, that she was under Sayyida Fatima's care."

Tein shook his head. "Am I African?"

Ammar nearly moaned, "Tein, where is all this going?"

"Am I African?"

"Your mother was noble. Your father was an Arab. Your culture is Arab. You are a Muslim. You are not African like that."

"So if you didn't know me. If you had no way to tell yourself that I was not African 'like that', I would deserve no more justice than you offered her?"

Ammar looked up at Tein with eyes full of pain. He managed, "I don't know."

Tein laughed bitterly. "At least you admit that much."

Ammar slumped over again, and put his head in his hands, breathing heavily. Then said, "I've wronged you." He looked up, tears in his eyes, holding out his hands, "I've wronged *you*, my friend. I wronged Mu'mina. I thought I already knew the extent of what I'd done. My God, Tein!"

"Don't grovel. I don't want it."

"Forgive me."

Tein felt a rush of sorrowful relief wash through him, so heavy it pushed him down. He knelt before his friend who still sat, hands out waiting to be bound for what he'd done. He took Ammar's hands in his own. "Look at my skin. Would Husayn or Ali put any of us beyond the reach of justice? If you would fight for me, fight for all of us."

Ammar straightened up. "I will. If I make it out of Ibn Marwan's alive, by God, I will."

Tein let go of his hands and looked him in the eye. "I'll be watching." He stood again and sighed, then took a seat beside Ammar.

Ammar wiped his eyes with his sleeve.

Tein asked, "When do you go before Ibn Marwan?"

"Now."

"Listen to me, I saw Zaytuna. She spoke to the imam's housekeeper. The woman insisted that Hanan paid to have Mu'mina poisoned to abort the baby."

"That confirms it. The poisoning case is with Grave Crimes in Rusafa. I'll bring what you've said to Ibn Marwan. They'll need to interview the housekeeper."

"There is more."

Ammar leaned forward, exhausted.

"The housekeeper insists, too, that Hanan had access to the poisons. She said Hanan took her key. The housekeeper said that she makes medicinal cookies for Isam and that she saw Hanan feeding them to him the morning he died."

Ammar sat up. "My God!"

"Wait. It may have been her. But there's also the possibility it was one of the prostitutes. The cook at the nahariyya told me that the imam demanded the same type of cookies be delivered to him there. There is one woman who hated him enough to kill him. She could have had poisoned cookies prepared for him and sent him home with them that morning. Those could have been the cookies that killed him."

"If I'd listened to you, we could have had this information long ago."

Tein broke in, "Stop it. I know there's nothing that can be done about it, the case is closed." He touched Ammar so he would look at him. "But we can go ask, still. We can make sure for ourselves if it was Hanan or the prostitute. I want you to know Mu'mina didn't do it."

Ammar stood, putting on his cuirass and strapping his sword around his waist. "Mu'mina didn't do it. I believe you. I'm going to tell Ibn Marwan. Maybe he'll agree to open the case."

Tein thought of his promise to Zaytuna and realized in the moment, now he had what he wanted from Ammar, that she was right. He felt sick with guilt for putting the women's lives at risk. *What have I done? How can I call myself a man?* He had used them, not protected them. *Ithar*, he said to himself, *ithar*. Then, to Ammar, "No, don't tell him."

"Why not?"

He scrambled. "There's been enough harm. What good can come of it?"

Ammar looked concerned. "Is this what you want?"

Tein stood. "Yes. But don't do it for me. Do it because it's right."

Ammar acquiesced and walked to the door. He stood half in and half out, his hand on the frame. He looked down the arcade. "My friend, I don't know what is right."

"Then it's what I want." Tein said, "Do it for me."

Ammar nodded. "I better go to face him now."

Tein stopped him. "What do you think is going to happen to you?"

"I don't know," he said and walked out the door.

Ammar told Tein he didn't know, but he knew the options. Maybe he'd lose his position. He'd get thrown back into the lowest rung of the military. He'd be mucking out stables. More likely, he'd be executed for it. He deserved death. Either way, he'd fight for Tein to take his place in Grave Crimes. But there was nothing he could do to protect his own family from the shame of it. His mother would grieve to the last. How could he be like Hurr when the sacrifice of his life for what he'd done would be nothing but a humiliation for them?

Every step to Ibn Marwan's office took more energy than the last. It was as if he were marching through mud. His head began spinning and he began to feel faint. He stopped. *Breathe.* He took several long and slow deep breaths. When he had steadied himself, he kept on, one step at a time.

Ammar stood in front of Nuruddin who was scratching away at the paper on the desk before him. He looked up briefly, acknowledging Ammar's presence but said nothing. Men sat on low benches along the wall waiting to see Ibn Marwan. Ammar finally knelt before Nuruddin. "Ibn Marwan has asked for me."

He looked at Ammar, one eyebrow raised. "Why are you asking me, then? Go in, like you always do." And he tipped his head toward the doorway leading between the two rooms, Ibn Marwan's office just beyond.

Ammar stood. He was surprised how he could feel everything. Where he had felt sluggish in the arcade, now every sight and sound was acute. He stood beside Ibn Marwan's door, hand on its frame, and looked in. He did not walk in as he usually did, hail him, and sit easily on his couch.

Ibn Marwan did not like him, but he was the best investigator of grave crimes in Baghdad. No one cleared cases as he did, and he treated this place like he owned it, demanding justice no matter the risk. He had stood resolutely in here one day when Ibn Marwan insisted on dismissing an investigation as unsolvable because the suspect was influential. He announced he would rather die than play politics with a case. Now look at him, all his pride in his righteousness shown to be nothing but lies.

Ibn Marwan lifted his head, saw him. "Stay standing, but you may approach."

Ammar took a few steps into the room but went no further.

"You should pray to your imams, or whatever you people do."

Ammar's chest tightened.

He eyed Ammar. "Don't you want to know why?"

Ammar stood stock still, but managed to say, "Yes."

"You've been forgiven. Imam Hashim's family complained of you, but it landed on the desk of one of the Banu al-Furat. One of yours. You Shia watch out for each other. So it never reached the vizier, al-JarJara'i. Although, I imagine he would have done as Abu al-Hasan advised." He looked at Ammar from under his eyebrows. "You are also lucky that word came to me directly and not through the police chief's office. To require the chief to think of you again? You would have been punished in a way you and your future children would have felt." He paused. "Then I find out, without you telling me, that you testified in defence of the slave. Would you like to go down to the cells and find another prisoner to defend in court?"

Ammar said, "Sir..."

Ibn Marwan held up a hand. "No, you wait. There is more. I am also visited by a representative of the Amir of the best gambling houses in Karkh. The Amir has complained. Why? Because he pays people more important than me to keep the police and the marketplace inspectors out of his business. Yet you send Tein into one of his establishments, with some woman, without my permission, to question them."

Ammar took it.

"I had to posture a bit to the Amir's man about the scholars. I said that, no matter the protection he enjoys, the scholars cannot be touched. The man graciously said he'd handle the trouble on his end."

Ammar stammered, thinking he was speaking in Tein's defence, "We have, uh, we have evidence gathered from that visit, that one of the prostitutes there may have killed the imam."

"You will be relieved to know, then, that we have her in custody." He looked at a paper on his desk, then lifted his head. "Chandi. She is already in the cells below."

"What?"

"As the man said, they would handle it on their end. So the Amir had her brought to us with the same man to explain. I didn't ask how they got it out of her, but she did not look in particularly good shape. She confessed to them that she got the poison from an herbalist she knew, some man from Sind, like her, apparently. He has also been arrested. She had poisoned cookies made and sent them home with the imam. He ate them and died. Case closed. I suppose we have Tein to thank for the resolution of the case, but at what cost?"

"But, sir, she may not have done it. There is also evidence that the imam's wife or brother-in-law could have poisoned him. And..."

Ibn Marwan held up his hand again to stop him. "They already complained of you to al-JarJara'i's office. You got out of it, but you want to get back into it? Do you want me to be executed by the vizier's command alongside you? The prostitute confessed. The herbalist will confess; we will make sure of that. I will not send it on to the chief, though. I'm not risking his attention on us. No, we'll leave them in the cells below and let them rot." He looked at Ammar so as to make his point perfectly clear, "You will not be involved."

Ammar forced himself to speak again, "Sir, we have a witness saying that the wife paid to have the slave poisoned, to abort her child."

Ibn Marwan slammed his hand down on the desk beside him. "Stop!"

Ammar shuddered as if he had been slapped with the broad side of a sword.

"I won't hear anything more about it. We're done."

Ammar began to feel sick to his stomach, churning, and dizzy. He put his eyes on the couch several steps from him and managed to put one foot ahead of the other. He sat down onto it and put his head between his knees.

Ibn Marwan mocked him, "I guess you thought you were a dead man. I don't want any more of your cock prancing among the hens around here. Don't think I didn't notice that Tein solved this case, not you. How do I know that hasn't been the case since he started working under you? I could get rid of you at any moment and be just as well off."

Ammar did not answer, he tried to focus his eyes on the pattern of the carpet between his feet. His head felt like it would explode and his turban was all that was holding it in.

"When you are ready to lift your head, tell me about the murder of the curse writer."

He forced himself to look up. He thought his head was going to split right open from the pain. He managed to say, "We have one of the men who did it in the cells, but I know who the others were."

Ibn Marwan replied, "Would you say you are among them?"

He winced. "Yes."

Ibn Marwan sat back. "Ammar, no one cares about the curse writer."

Ammar stared at him. "I care."

Ibn Marwan said, "I care about the reputation of this office."

"It was Barbahari's men who paraded her."

Ibn Marwan nodded. "Barbahari's men are a problem, but that's more complicated."

He wanted to get out of the room, but he knew he was meant to ask, "What do you want me to do?"

"Question the one in custody, get what you can out of him. Pass those notes on to me. It's not a matter for Grave Crimes."

"Don't pursue the other men?"

"Did you hear me? This is a problem of public control and challenging the state. Not our office. Now, get out."

Ammar stood, wobbling only slightly, and made it through the door, then past Nuruddin who called after him lazily, "That was a close one, Golden Boy."

He got out into the middle of the arcade road and stood facing the mosque at the centre of the city. He would not die. His mother would not be shamed. He would not lose his job. The prostitute and the herbalist would suffer, whether they did it or not. He had harmed so many and there was no justice. Why was he not permitted to be martyred like Hurr to pay for what he'd done? He felt sick again. He stumbled back to the side of the road and squatted, feeling himself close to retching. A pain struck him in the side of the head as if he'd been stabbed straight through and what little he'd eaten that day came up at his feet.

He felt a hand on his back but couldn't look. Then the hand reached in and grabbed him by the collar of his cuirass and lifted him up. Lifted him so that his feet left the ground. He flailed trying to turn around to fight, to break free but couldn't. He looked around wildly.

Why isn't anyone stopping this! And only then he realized he wasn't in the Round City anymore. He was dangling above the centre of a great expanse of marble floor with empty marble benches surrounding it, each row higher than the one before it. The hand let go and he fell hard, hitting his elbow on the stone. He grabbed his arm, touching his elbow then extending it. Pain shot through it, but he could move it. It wasn't broken. He could fight.

He scrambled up to standing and turned in circles, feeling his scabbard at his side, ready for him. Where the benches had just been empty, he now saw jinn of every type taking up a seat, surrounding him. A woman in a red gown and a gazelle's head sat at the feet of a black eagle with human eyes and twitched her ears at him. A man with a monstrous chest and a human head with two faces kept turning around and around so both sets of eyes could get a look at him. An animal with an armoured back and long nose, curled over on itself and grasped red berries from a basket next to it, feeding them one by one into the human mouth inset into its belly. Ammar touched his throat for his talisman of protection. It was gone.

At the far side stood an empty throne, large enough for ten men. An ostrich and a child with taloned feet stood on either side of it. A humming, twittering, and buzzing as if bird-bees were encircling him, filled his head. He saw the creatures coming to attention. The animal put aside its basket of berries and watched the throne. A whorl of sand and smoke hovered over the throne and slowly took shape into a man of vast stature. His skin was a purple, so dark it was nearly black, then it shimmered to the deepest red, then alabaster white, then purple again. His head carried a turban heavy with jewels of every size and colour, a great red ruby set in gold at its centre.

The Ostrich called out, "Sit in attendance. Sit in respect. The court of our King Mazin is open."

The jinn in the assembly slapped and clapped and pounded their benches and the marble floor creating a din so extraordinary Ammar's body shook from the sound of it.

King Mazin roared, "You have offended the jinn. What do you have to say in your defence!"

The hand that had grabbed him by the cuirass, threw him to the ground. He stared at the marble, afraid to look up, unable to speak, wanting to vomit.

The child with the taloned feet had crossed the vast distance between him and the throne and knocked his turban off his head, then whispered in his ear, "Don't throw up in our court, you beast. Answer our King!"

Ammar choked on the words, "What do I say?"

The assembly laughed, the laughter rolling through them like a wave that crashed onto him and knocked him flat to the ground. King Mazin roared again and the jinn fell quiet.

Ammar raised himself to all fours. He lifted his head to the King. "God forgive me for offending you and your court! Forgive this human. What have I done?" Then he dropped his head, "What have I not done?"

The King's voice whirred and thrummed, "Not knowing is part of the offence." He tipped his hand to the ostrich beside him, who craned its neck and shook its wings and feathers, until every feather had fallen to the ground revealing a woman with bumpy pink skin and white hair tipped in black, rising from her head like a fan. She wore loose leather pants, a leather tunic, and a leather cuirass. A sword was belted to her side. He saw the hilt of the sword, and immediately reached for his scabbard. It was empty. The woman had it.

Her voice was like honey spiked with shards of glass, "We will explain, so you will understand your suffering. That fool of a Turkmen woman, so like you, had power that she used in utter arrogance. She decided she would save the slave without listening to the girl's own desires. Throughout her life she refused to listen, serving only her own lowest interests and calling it justice. She thought she knew better than the master who took her under her wing! Oh, she got what she deserved, smeared in shit and her head smashed in." She sniggered, "We doubt she thought her prayer to free the slave girl would call us to address her suffering. Only God's forgiveness can save her now."

The ostrich woman gestured to King Mazin, her arm opening to him like a wing. "Our King graciously protects those vulnerable ones whom you fools have made to suffer." She folded in her arm and stepped down from beside the throne and strutted across the court to him. She craned her head down, close enough to peck his eyes out. He covered his head with his arm. She said directly to his face, "We tried Imam Hashim for his crimes and executed him. It was a surprise and a pleasure that the prostitute gave him the poison that made him witness the act. An even worse death matching his crimes!"

She stood up and unfolded her arm, in a slow wave to the cheering crowd. "You challenged our ruling and harmed the very one our King had guarded so jealously!"

The assembly slapped and pounded so hard the floor shook.

He asked in confused terror. "She is...she is one of your own? She consorts with jinn?"

"Oh, you fool." She laughed. "A girl loved by Lady Fatima herself, may God be well-pleased with her, 'consorting with jinn'?" The woman looked back to King Mazin who inclined his head to her. "On the contrary, we executed the imam in the Lady's honour."

Ammar lay his cheek on the cool marble floor, he trembled. "Lady Fatima asked you..."

King Mazin roared, "Ask us? She does not ask us. It is only that we hope she will be pleased." He gestured to the ostrich woman. "You may explain."

"Our people offered to sacrifice ourselves at Karbala and were declined. Imam Husayn turned down the offers of sorcerers and talisman makers. He stood on the plain, with his people, alone. We learned from that. We no longer ask. We only do what we can when the opportunity arises." The woman spread her arms out, her fingers extending one by one, and screeched, "Lift your head!"

He sat up shaking, his hands up, begging for mercy.

"You knew we had judged him, yet you pursued the girl. You were rightly afraid of us, but a blameless girl scared you even more!"

King Mazin laughed, the smooth purple of his skin shimmering into black with small scars down his nose and across his cheeks. "Do you fear me more now?" Then Tein's face shimmered over the King's own. "Or now?"

Ammar choked, "My friend..."

The woman hissed, "You are no friend to him."

Tears streamed down his cheeks. "What will you do to me?"

King Mazin sat back, relaxing into his throne. "You would be pleased to be executed for what you've done. You want the chance to martyr yourself for your deeds."

The ostrich woman laughed. "Like Hurr!"

The crowd joined her mocking him, "Like Hurr! Like Hurr!"

The King leaned forward. "You want martyrdom? No, not for the likes of you. You will pay by living."

The jinn stomped and slapped and screeched, barking, and yelling out in pleasure at his sentence. He looked around the court and it began to spin. He tried to sit down to stop the spinning, but he collapsed in a heap on the floor, hearing nothing.

A hand shook his shoulder. "Ammar! Ammar!"

He opened his eyes, afraid of what he would see. Trembling, his clothes were soaked through with sweat, but he saw he was back in the city. Tein was beside him.

Nuruddin was leaning in the doorway, unimpressed. "He lives." Then pushed himself off the frame and went back inside to his office.

Tein tried to help Ammar sit up.

"I can do it," he said as he got himself up to sitting against the wall. "I need a minute, then I can walk."

Tein said, "You fainted. What is your punishment?"

He didn't dare tell him what happened, instead he said, "I keep my job. I do not die. I've been punished by living with what I've done."

Tein leaned against the wall and slid down to sit beside him.

THE EIGHTH DAY

30

Nuri's shrouded body lay beside the wide grave. Tein helped Mustafa lift him from the bier and lower him down to Nuri's son, Husayn, and his nephew, Bariq, who stood inside the grave, waiting. Husayn took his father's shoulders out of Tein's hands and lay him down, while Mustafa lowered his legs to Bariq, who did the same. Husayn loosened his father's shroud to expose his face. He squatted as best he could and took his father's cheeks in both hands to kiss him for the last time.

Husayn turned his father's body on its side, leaning him against the grave wall, and laid Nuri's head on a brick for a pillow, facing the niche dug out as a qibla facing Mecca. He checked again that there were no sharp stones under him. Then he looked out of the grave, tears streaming.

Tein and Mustafa took him by his hands and pulled him up and out, then Bariq. The men did not brush off the dirt from the grave on their clothes, but wore it, instead, as if it were a cloak laid on their shoulders by Nuri himself.

Husayn took a handful of soil and laid the first blanket of earth over his father, reciting the verses of the Qur'an,

From earth We created you.

He grasped another handful of soil.

And We will return you to it,

Then a third.

And We will resurrect you from it.

Bariq followed, then Junayd. Junayd bent down and took a handful of soil, then Ibn Ata, then Sumnun, then Shibli, one by one all the men from the community came forward. All who knew him lined up, the beggars and shopkeepers, and those who nobody knew. Once covered, the men stamped down the grave so there was no perceptible mound.

Then his son stood forward. "God, he is your servant, the son of your servant, who testified that there is no god but You, and that Muhammad is your servant and Messenger, but you know best. If he was one who performed beautiful deeds, then increase them. If he was one who performed ugly deeds, then disregard them. God, do not refuse us his reward in kind nor try us as he was tried."

Winding his way back through the crowd, Tein pulled shaggy breaths, needing to get away from the sea of bodies. He heard Junayd reciting from the head of the grave, *Alif, Lam, Mim, this is the book in which there is no doubt.*

Tein looked out at the low, thick walls of the cemetery where the poorest of the poor had dug in small hovels to sleep and the makeshift lean-tos and tents of those just better off nearby. He wanted to pull his turban off his head and scream. He wanted to pour a jug of wine into the gaping hole within him. He wanted to grasp Saliha and pull her away from the cemetery and find someplace to love her until the world forgot about him.

He saw his mother's grave in the distance next to the two date palms they had planted and watered as children. He wanted to walk to her and tell her that Uncle Nuri was more of a mother to him than she ever was and now he was gone. He was sobbing and he didn't care. *What good were you to us?* As he thought the words, he wanted to pound the realization out of himself. He looked back toward the women in wild-eyed sorrow. Saliha was watching him, but he couldn't read her face He said from the emptiness within him, desperately, *I am yours.*

The crowd began to turn and move, the men walking around the women to pass first, Junayd and Husayn leading with Ibn Ata and Sumnun. As they passed him, the uncles put their hands over their heart to him, acknowledging each other's grief. He heard Junayd say to them, "Half of Sufism is gone."

Tein thought, *Half of me.*

Tein saw Mustafa walking just ahead of the women with YingYue's father. YingYue was not far behind them, walking apart from the men but keeping her father and Mustafa in sight. *That's that, then.* Zaytuna and Saliha had disappeared in the crowd. Mustafa caught sight of Tein and said something to YingYue's father. YingYue came running up to take his place. Mustafa left them for Tein, hitting him with an embrace so hard that Tein stumbled back half a step. Tein wanted to grab him by the arms and push him off. The warmth of his brother's love crowded his grief and he could barely breathe from it. Finally Mustafa let go of him and stepped back, in tears, "Tein. How are you holding up?"

"I'm not," he admitted.

"So much has happened."

Tein nodded, then asked, "How is Mu'mina? Is she settling in with Ibn Salah's sister?"

Mustafa's eyes opened wide. "Allah! After Uncle Nuri was injured, then this, I forgot to say! She's left! As soon as the papers were signed, the money paid for her freedom, she left without saying a word to anyone. Ibn Salah's sister said she wouldn't speak to her on the way home. Then she snuck out. No one saw her go. She only took the warm clothes and boots they had left for her."

Tein looked toward his mother's grave, a sinking feeling in his gut, and said, "She's freed and puts herself in more danger. Does she even know what will happen to her, alone on the road?"

"We don't know where she's gone."

The way of my mother.

Mustafa touched his arm. "I have to go."

Pushing him lightly, Tein said, "Go."

"I'm sorry."

Tein forced himself to nod and say, "I'm sorry, too."

He looked for Zaytuna and Saliha, but they were still lost in the crowd. Auntie Hakima broke out of the throng of women and came to him. He wanted to say to her, "Not now. I can't. It hurts too much."

She pushed past his resistance and put her hand on his arm, squeezing it, saying, "Come visit me tomorrow."

He said it, but did not mean it, "I will, Auntie."

She scolded him lightly, "You didn't come last week."

He took her hand off his arm and tried to kiss it. She pulled it away and patted him. "You come. Tomorrow."

He nodded. He looked up and finally saw Saliha and Zaytuna coming. Auntie Hakima followed his glance and said, "Oh, I'll be going, then." She laughed. "I'm sharing my silence with your sister. She needs to see just a bit more of the back of my hand."

"Anything I should know?"

She patted him on the arm again. "She's coming along nicely, actually, but she can't know that. Between us?"

He nodded again, knowing he was loved but it felt like being on fire.

She looked him in the eye. "Tein, you won't find what you need in a woman, or drink for that matter."

"Then I'm lost."

She pushed at him and said, "Never," then followed the rest of the women out.

He barely heard her. Saliha was walking just a bit ahead of Zaytuna. She was still holding up her injured arm but wasn't being so tender with it anymore. It was healing. He saw Zaytuna watch Auntie

Hakima walk off ahead of her, rather than wait to be greeted. Zaytuna's face fell, tears coming.

They reached him and Saliha said, "Assalamu alaykum, Tein," looking him straight in the eye.

He wanted to look away, not out of embarrassment, but because he wanted to hold her to him and live. He held himself still and answered, "Wa alaykum assalam."

He turned to Zaytuna. "How are you?"

Zaytuna took hold of his robe and rubbed her face in it, then laughed through her tears, saying, "I've dirtied your clothes."

"My clothes are your clothes." He pushed her back so he could breathe and asked again, "How are you?"

She gave him a smile meant to prove she was fine. "You?"

"Right as rain."

Zaytuna gestured to Auntie Hakima, now nearly out of the cemetery and heading back to Tutha, "Did she say anything about me?"

"No, only that she wants me to visit." Then he asked Saliha, "How is your arm?"

"Healing, Yulduz puts a fresh poultice on it every day." She turned to Zaytuna, "Can you walk on your own for a bit? I need to talk to Tein."

Zaytuna looked at one then at the other. "I wanted to visit mother before I left anyway. You two go on."

Tein and Saliha stood in silence as they watched her walk through the gravestones to a place where there was nothing but two date palms growing. There must have been dogs there. He saw her lean down to reach for stone.

"I heard what you said outside the surgery room."

The tone was clear. He was ruined.

She asked, "Can we walk?"

Sorrow caught in his throat, "Yes."

They walked side by side until they reached the edge of the cemetery.

Looking at the poor camped along the edges of the graveyard, she said, "You're a long way from the nights you slept here."

He frowned. "I feel like I'm at its edge."

"I won't marry you." She offered nothing to soften the blow.

He expected the words, but he didn't know what to do with them now he had them. He wanted to put them down someplace and walk away. Instead he made himself hold them. He forced himself to face her and say, "I understand." But then he followed up in a hurry, feeling like a fool, wanting to reassure her he wouldn't become a problem. "I won't bother you when I come to see Zaytuna. You don't have to worry."

"No." Her voice rose, insistent, "Stop. Tein. That's not what I want."

He stumbled, trying to fix it. "I don't have to come there to see Zaytuna at all, if it will bother you."

She reached out and took his hand. "No. Listen. Tein, I love you."

The embarrassment and sorrow he felt just a moment before exploded within him to complete joy. He had been dead and brought back to life. His fingers intertwined with hers and it felt like sparks would come from them and set the dry brush blowing through the cemetery on fire. Her beautiful mouth, her full lips, opened slowly into a wide beaming smile. She threw her head back and laughed joyfully.

He laughed with her and without thinking of where they were or who would see, he put his other hand on the small of her back and pulled her to him. Still smiling, she let go of his hand and placed it on his chest, pushing against him lightly, saying, "Not yet."

Recovering himself, he stepped back from her, breathing heavily.

She became serious again and repeated, "I won't marry you."

"I don't understand." His joy sank into his gut and soured.

"I want to be with you. I love you, but I will not marry ever again."

Then he realized what she was saying. He wanted it. The thought of having her so easily passed through him, but then made it to the other side. He didn't want it. He wanted her love to fill every crack in his life. He wanted to feel her against him in bed at night, holding him to sleep instead of wine. He wanted her wild spirit to bring him to life in the morning. He wanted the aunties to fuss over her. He wanted the uncles to love her like their daughter. He wanted Zaytuna's dearest friend to become her sister. But this? Zaytuna would scorn Saliha's plan and she would be right. They'd be sneaking in and out of rooms rented by the hour, or worse, she'd come to him openly and become a pariah. Men would slap him on the back for it. She'd be destroyed.

"We can't hide it, Saliha. You know what that would mean. Your reputation. Your work."

He saw her nearly respond, then bite back her words at the mention of "work." She knew as well as he did any hint of impropriety would end it. She wasn't picking through bits of garbage to find something to sell outside the marketplaces, but she would be if they got found out. There wouldn't be laundry for her to wash. There would be no going back unless her boss was willing to take her on like a daughter and answer to people for her sake. And why would she do that when anyone could work for her just as easily?

"It's a heavy burden on a woman." He shook his head, "I can't do it to you."

She took a step back and dug in. "That burden is mine, Tein." She looked away from him. "This is why I won't marry. You think you can make decisions about what is best for me because you love me. What happens after that? What other burdens will you want to carry for me? Will I have to obey you so you can turn me into a good woman?"

"You *are* a good woman," he said in a rising panic that she couldn't see the truth of what he was saying. "Saliha, it's your wildness that made me love you! It's not about me. It's about this cursed world!"

She turned back to face him and was between anger and tears. "Why do I have to choose!"

"We can marry. I don't want to own you. You heard me in the hospital. I wasn't lying." He looked at Nuri's grave in the distance, "I want to take care of you without asking anything in return."

"You can sacrifice for me, but I can't for you. Tein, you can't stop me from risking everything for you."

"Why? Why do you have to risk everything for me?"

She moved so closely to him he could smell the salty sweetness of her skin. She said so softly he could feel it move through him, "You need to know you are loved," and placed her hand on his heart.

Her touch filled him to overflowing and made everything worse. He knew in that moment, that he couldn't marry her even if she agreed and he got what he wanted. The emptiness she filled would only want more and more from her until she could no longer make up for what was missing in him. Then what would they become? What did Auntie Hakima say? A woman wasn't going to save him. He'd come home drunk in the end, if he came home at all. Drink wasn't going to save him either, but at least it made the stench of living more bearable and he couldn't ruin the life of a barrel of wine. He felt sick.

"No."

She begged him, "Why can't you just let this be good?"

"Because nothing ends up good in this world."

He looked at her with the sorrow and longing of a last goodbye. He wanted to drink and he wanted to get into a fight and he wanted to sleep in the graveyard with the lost and the dead where he belonged. He wouldn't fail her like he'd failed everyone else. It was done. "I can't do this. Married or not, I'd ruin you."

"Tein, Tein!" She reached out and tried to hold him there, grabbing a fist of his robe. She pulled at it desperately. "Tein, how do we love each other?"

He shook his head. "I don't know."

"You don't know how to love me?"

"I don't know how to be the man you want me to be."

"You *are* the man I want."

"You think you are going to love me out of this mess I'm in. Maybe you would, for a while, but it wouldn't last. I'd end up coming home to you drunk. You know how I am. Is that what you want?"

She shook her head. "Zaytuna thinks the same. I don't believe it."

It made him angry that Zaytuna had said it, but she was right. "Saliha, she knows me." It took everything he had to say it, "Let go of me. Let me go."

Instead of letting him go, she wept openly and fell against him. He put his arms around her and held her to him, feeling every bit of her body trembling against him. He did not cry. He stood firm and let her quiet down before whispering, "Saliha. Let me go."

Saliha pushed herself off of him. She pulled her wrap over her face, pulling it around herself as if it were a blanket she could hide underneath, took three steps back, turned and walked slowly through the break in the graveyard walls, never looking back.

He returned to Uncle Nuri's graveside and stood beside the flattened mound looking for his uncle. "I'm lost." There was no answer, no feeling, nothing. He yelled at the earth, "Uncle!" Nothing. Tein turned his back on his uncle's grave and looked to the clearing where his mother's body lay. Zaytuna was not there, and he was relieved. He didn't want to go anywhere near it. He walked among the graves marked and unmarked, finally seeing her sitting beside a mound carelessly left unflattened. A young man was at Zaytuna's feet and she was weeping with him. Tein drew close enough to hear her, but not so that she could see him.

Zaytuna's hands were out in supplication. "God, widen her grave. Open a light onto her from Paradise. Make her longing for the Last Day joyful."

The young man's wrap was filthy from graveyard dirt and pulled around him in a way Tein knew too well. He'd been sleeping beside the grave. His heart went out to his sister for the kindness she was offering him. He wanted to join them and lay his head in her lap, have her pray for him, even though he didn't believe in prayers.

"God, take Farzaneh into Your loving care."

Tein let out a sharp breath. Farzaneh, the woman Saliha washed who had to withstand the imam's horrors. This must be her brother who visited her every week, despite the shame she brought her family. He would not abandon her even in death. Her friend Chandi and the herbalist who stood up to help were in cells to rot for killing an excuse of a man who deserved to die. Mu'mina was free but alone and without protection. His uncle was dead. Saliha was lost to him. *Curse this world.*

Then Zaytuna's back began to arch and her arms raised as if of their own accord. The gesture gripped him. He knew what was coming because he grew up watching his mother do the same. Tein wanted to rush forward and grab her and pull her out of her coming ecstatic state, but he couldn't move.

She called out to the heavens, "Hold his sister, bring her enraptured into your arms. Take our hearts, shatter them with Your love." Her arms outstretched as if she were holding the world in them, as she recited,

> *I see love, an ocean without a shore.*
> *If you are love's worthy one, dive in!*
> *Stay there until you drown in its depths,*
> *for there is no existence without love.*
> *There a brave one who disappears attains eternal life,*
> *and wins the prize that he was once denied.*

Tein turned his face from her slowly, scanning the cemetery, watching for anyone who might harm her.

COMING IN 2021

The Unseen
The Third Sufi Mystery

One arrow pierced his eye. Blood soaked through his sleeves, but the fabric was whole. Ammar pulled open the robe and felt the wounds. There were deep cuts in the victim's arms. Another arrow pierced the water skin still in his hand. A still damp narrow trail of water that had seeped out of the skin led away from the body. Ammar touched the moist earth; it had all happened within the hour.

When a young man is found dead, killed in the exact manner as a martyr slain on the fields of Karbala some two hundred years before, there is no mistaking it as anything other than an attack on the Shia community of Baghdad. The city is on edge as religious and political factions are exposed sending the caliph's army into the streets. Ammar and Tein have to clear the case, one way or another, before violence erupts. But Zaytuna has had a visionary dream of the murder that holds the key to solving the case, if she can read its signs and if Tein and Ammar are willing to listen.

GLOSSARY

Adhan: The call to ritual prayer. See **Time.**

Alhamdulillah: "Praise God."

Ali: The cousin and son-in-law of the Prophet Muhammad, husband of **Fatima**, and father to Hasan and **Husayn.** He is known as the inheritor of the Prophet's knowledge of God for both Sunni Sufis and Shia. He is also famed for his extraordinary bravery and restraint. He refused to kill a man who spit on him in battle lest he harm the man out of petty anger. He is called "The Lion."

Allahu akbar: "God is great." This can be used in times of shock or distress to say, "God is greater than whatever is happening," in times of joy, "God is amazing," and affirming what another person is saying, "You said it," to "Wow."

Arbitration and mediation: Exactly as you might imagine. Parties were encouraged to meet with a suitable mediator to resolve issues rather than clog up the court system.

Assalamu alaykum, wa alaykum assalam, and wa alaykum assalam wa rahmatullahi wa barakatuhu: It means literally "peace to you" its reply is "and on you peace" but can basically mean "hi." Arab Muslims and non-Muslims alike use it. The long version ends with "and God's mercy and blessings," used sincerely, but also, sometimes, performatively to be extra-pious or even joking.

Bismillah: "In the name of God." Used to start any action.

Duha: About twenty minutes after sunrise is completed. Casually, it can refer to the time following as well, broadly early to mid-morning.

Fals: The smallest denomination of money. These and other coins could be chinked, meaning, hand-cut into pieces to make smaller denominations.

Fatima: The prophet's daughter, the wife of **Ali**, and the mother of Hasan and **Husayn**. Her representation in Shia literature is beautiful and diverse, spanning the naturalistic to the metaphysical. Here I call on her representation as a loving and protective mother.

Ghazi: One who fought on the frontier of the empire's expansion. They are held in high respect, unlike the troops who fight internal, civil battles.

Habibi: Masculine form of "my love," or "my dear one." Feminine is "habibti."

Hanafi: Ibn Salah and Ibn al-Zayzafuni follow the Hanafi school of law. When scholars look at the Qur'an and hadith to determine what God and the Prophet intended Muslims to do and not do, Hanafis are open to using any number of methods of interpretation, such as analogy or an individual scholar's informed reasoning on a matter.

Hanbali: Mustafa is a follower of the Hanbali school of law. He is not a legal scholar, but a scholar of hadith (see **Hadith**). He collects, memorizes, and transmits the reports about Muhammad. But hadith scholars were asked to give legal opinions in the early days, just as Mustafa is by the guard. The Hanbali legal school prefers to stick to the basics when it comes to interpreting law, believing that methods such as analogy or using one's own personal judgment, no matter how informed, could lead to a person straying too far from what Muhammad intended. They prefer to rely on the judgments of the earliest members of the Muslim community.

Hadith: These are individual reports of what Muhammad said, did, accepted, and rejected. There are major compilations of hadith.

These compilations may have several similar accounts of the same event or the same saying, or even contradictory accounts. The goal of very early Muslim Sunni scholars was to collect everything, not necessarily to resolve differences. Zaytuna and Mustafa's argument over the slaves and wives of the Prophet is an example of one set of contradictions and the kinds of committed arguments Muslims have over what story to tell about the Prophet's life and his intentions.

Hurr: Hurr was a commander in the Umayyad army who changed sides and fought alongside Husayn at **Karbala** after being called by angels to stand for him and embrace martyrdom. He came to Husayn with his hands out, ready to be bound for his wrongdoing, begging for Husayn's forgiveness. Husayn forgave him and he was martyred at Karbala.

Husayn: The grandson of the Prophet. See **Karbala**.

Ifrit: A hostile and vicious type of jinn.

Inshallah: "If God wills." It is used to mean "Yes," "No," and "Maybe," and "if God wills," also as a statement of humility in response to praise.

Jinn: The general category of creatures made of fire. They are many types. They can be friendly and helpful--but always tricky--to demonic. See @aaolami on Twitter for helpful categorizations and descriptions.

Karbala: After the third caliph, Uthman, was murdered and Ali was ultimately offered the position of caliph, several prominent companions of the Prophet, led by his wife Aisha, challenged Ali's authority. This challenge ended on the battlefield with Ali soundly defeating them. Nevertheless, his authority continued to be contested. After Ali's death, his son Hasan negotiated away his right to lead, and the caliphate came into the hands of the Umayyads under the leadership of Muawiyya. After Muawiyya's death, Ali's other son, Husayn, was encouraged by the people of Kufa to lead a rebellion against the hereditary designation of Muawiyya's son Yazid as caliph. Husayn answered the call, but before he could reach Kufa he was met on the plain of Karbala by Umayyad forces. The people of

Kufa, under threat from the Umayyads, failed to support Husayn in battle. Others argue that no rebellion was planned, and the tensions arose from Husayn's refusal to submit to Yazid at his behest. Whichever case, Husayn's party which included many members of the Prophet's family were brutally killed, including women and children, while survivors were marched away and taken into custody. The loss of the Prophet's family, the loss of the leadership of his family, and the sorrow of the people of Kufa haunt the Shia religious imagination, as we see Ammar often experiencing.

Mashallah: "God willed it." It can be used to mean "Well, that's a done deal," to "wonderful," to "God willed it, so nothing can harm it."

Mazalim High Court: The highest religious court "hosted" by the caliph. It saw appeals from lower religious courts, cases of heresy, political cases, or cases deemed too controversial for lower courts.

Marketplace Inspector: The marketplace inspector handled all petty crime in the marketplace, theft and weights and measures issues. The inspectors also policed public decency in the markets. My understanding is that this court was more in line with a "hearing," rather than a court proper.

Police Chief's court: All criminal cases, except for petty marketplace crime, was handled by this court.

Religious courts: Most cities had only one of these, but Baghdad had three for each major region of the city. They handled what we would think of as civil matters, family matters, and religious questions. While religious scholars discussed the adjudication of criminal matters in their legal writings, they did not often hear these cases in court.

Nahariyya: Literally a "day-time" marriage house, meaning a brothel.

Niqab: A face veil, typically the eyes can be seen. Only privileged women wore them, with the exception of prostitutes. Other women covered their faces with their wraps as needed.

Qamis: A tunic worn by men or women of different lengths.

Qadi: The religious court judge.

Qur'an: For Muslims, the Qur'an is the word of God in the Arabic language as received by Muhammad through the angel Gabriel over 23 years.

Re'ya: A kind of jinn or spirit that tells secrets.

Sama: A Sufi ritual involving music, recitation of prayers remembering God, praise of the Prophet, and meant to induce ecstasy.

Sayyid/Sayyida: Master or Mistress, in the vein of Lord or Lady, typically used to refer to the Prophet and his family by Shia and some Sunni Muslims. Sayyidi means "My Master." Versions of this can also be used as the equivalent of sir or ma'am, as well.

Shahada: The statement "There is no god but God and Muhammad is God's messenger." It can be use to convert to Islam. It is said in babies ears just after they are born to make them Muslim. It is used as a general exclamation as well as a daily act of remembrance that people find meditative.

Sharia: Meaning "Islamic Law" in the most general terms. In a general sense, it refers to God's legal intent for Muslims as expressed in the Qur'an. In a particular sense, it is what any scholar at any point in time and place argues is God's legal intent based on the textual sources and interpretive methods they use to determine that intent. Overall, legal scholars and schools agree to disagree on the details which allows for extraordinary diversity of rulings. The term for determining that intent is "fiqh," meaning jurisprudence.

Shaykh: In general, it can refer to any teacher of any sort. In these books, I use it to refer only to an established Sufi guide. It was not used by Sufis at this time, but since it is the accepted term later, I use it.

Shia: Those who would come to be known as Shia were those who believed that the Prophet and God, as articulated in certain verses of the Qur'an, had designated, Ali, his cousin and son-in-law to be his successor rather than Abu Bakr. Although Shia did not use this name at the time of the book, I use it for clarity's sake. Most believe that true leadership is spiritually invested (rather than primarily politically), inhering in those with unique spiritual gifts as Ali was known to have. Ali was passed over three times for the caliphate, and by the time he was offered the position, the young empire was on the brink of civil war. The civil war ended after his death with his adult son, Husayn, and other members of his family and companions, slaughtered at **Karbala** in Iraq, by opposing political forces. Although all Muslims find those events to have been an extraordinary tragedy, the Shia continue to see the world's injustices through the lens of that fateful day. For most Sunnis, it was a terrible wrong, but something best left in the past.

Sirwal: Loose pants worn under the qamis tunic.

Subhanallah: "God is glorious" can be used as a kind of secular "wow," to a state of spiritual awe and wonder.

Sunna: The Sunna is the "Way" of Muhammad characterized by which **Hadith** one accepts or rejects. Muslims seek to follow his Sunna in ways small and large, such as drinking water the way he did or being "a man," on his model. While a great deal is accepted and consistent across Muslim cultures and times, Muslims continue to argue--sometimes violently--over other matters. Sexual consent and marriage are important points of dispute.

Sunni: The Muslims who would ultimately call themselves "Sunni," were those who chose to follow Abu Bakr as the first caliph of the Muslim community after Muhammad died. They believe scholars are the inheritors of the Prophet's guidance. There are four main Sunni schools of law and several schools of theology **Hanbali, Hanafi,** Shafii, and Maliki.

Time: Although there were water clocks and sundials, most people kept time by looking at the sun and the stars, but also by the call to prayer (see **Adhan**). There were six calls daily. About an hour before dawn (for a supererogatory prayer). Dawn. Just after zenith. Mid-afternoon. Sundown. After dark.

Walla: "By God," an oath akin to "I swear."

Ya Rabb: "Oh Lord," used as a sincere calling to God to pure sarcasm.

Yazid: The son of Mu`awiyya and the second of the Umayyad caliphs. Husayn and the rest of the Prophet's family were slain at **Karbala** on his order. To say someone is "no better than Yazid" is to say they are not only unjust, but one who would betray humanity for worldly power.

Zunnar: A rope belt, sometimes with knots, used specifically by non-Muslim "dhimmis," protected religious minorities, to identify them. There were extensive laws delineating what protected minorities could wear, but with the exception of two caliphs in the Abbasid Period, these were not enforced. Please see my website, under "clothing," for more details and trustworthy resources.

CHARACTERS

Arab Naming Conventions

Umm Marwa [Mother of Marwa] Fatima [Personal Name] bint Fahim [Daughter of Fahim] al-Jarriri [Fahim, the Potter] al-Karkhi [From Karkh]

1. Parent of Child Name: Abu (Father) or Umm (Mother) of Marwa
2. Personal Name: Fatima
3. Child of Father/Mother's Name (then often a list of ancestry, Parent Child of Grandparents's Name, and so on): ibn (Son) or bint (Daughter) of Fahim
4. Nickname or Profession Name: "al-Jarriri," The Potter.
5. Tribe Name or Neighbourhood/City/Region Name. "al-Karkhi," from Karkh

Characters are mainly referred to by their parental name or their personal names in the book. The narrator uses short forms of nicknames or profession names, Nuri rather than "an-Nuri," or "Ibn Salah" instead of "Ibn as-Salah." Shortening is an English language convention of Arab names, but Arabs do it, too, in some regional dialects.

The pronunciation guide is an approximation for North American English speakers without strong regional accents.

Main Characters

Zaytuna [zay-TOON-ah]: Our heroine, Zaytuna is a twenty-seven year old clothes washer of Nubian and Arab descent. She is the daughter of a female mystic, unnamed in the story, but known as al-Ashiqa al-Sawda, the Black Lover of God.

Tein [teen]: Zaytuna's twin, a former frontier fighter, a ghazi. He finds work with Ammar in the Baghdadi Police's Grave Crimes section.

Mustafa [MOOS-tah-fah]: Zaytuna and Tein's childhood friend, twenty-six years old, sometimes called a cousin or a brother to them. He is a Hanbali hadith scholar of Persian and Arab descent.

Saliha [SAH-lee-hah]: Zaytuna's best friend, neighbour and a corpse washer. She is a twenty-five year old Arab who comes from the countryside.

Ammar [ahm-MAAR]: Tein's old friend from his days as a ghazi, the main investigator for the Grave Crimes Section, and Tein's boss.

Recurring Characters

Zaytuna and Tein's mother, known as *al-Ashiqa as-Sawda* [al-AH-shee-ka as-SOW-duh]: A Nubian woman who is overcome without warning by states of ecstasy in which her ego-self dissolves into the ocean of God's love. Her character is a composite of women from the early period, but most explicitly based on Shawana, a 1st H/7th CE mystic of African descent.

Junayd [joo-NAID]: This character is based on the famous historical Sufi of Baghdad, Abu al-Qasim al-Junayd ibn Muhammad ibn al-Junayd al-Khazzaz al-Qawariri. Junayd is seventy-two years old. He is called "Uncle Abu al-Qasim" in the book, al-Junayd in more formal form, or simply Junayd.

Nuri [NOOR-ee]: This character is also based on a famous historical Sufi, Ahmad ibn Abu al-Husayn an-Nuri. Nuri is sixty-seven years old. He is a loving father-figure to Zaytuna, Tein, and Mustafa. He is called "Uncle Nuri" in the book, or simply Nuri.

Layla [LAY-luh]: Layla, a ten year old Arab servant girl, indentured by her parents at a young age.

Yulduz [YOOL-duhz] and Qambar [KAHM-baar]: Zaytuna and Saliha's neighbours. Yulduz is a bold Turkmen woman, wife to Qambar. Qambar is an Arab Shia who fell madly in love with Yulduz when they were young.

YingYue [ying-yway]: YingYue is an eighteen year old Chinese mystic prodigy from Taraz, a city on the edge of the Muslim empire in the East.

Burhan [buhr-HAAN] and Abu Burhan: Burhan is a hadith scholar who grew up in an environment of privilege. His father, Abu Burhan is the judge for the Karkh district of Baghdad.

Marta: Marta is Yuduz's best friend. She is a widowed Syriac Christian who brings her children a bit of coin by selling cups of pre-soaked chickpeas, ready to cook, on the roadside, just outside the official vegetable marketplace.

Maryam [MARE-yam]: Imam Ibrahim's housekeeper, Layla's boss and mother figure.

Characters In This Book Alone

Imam [ee-MAAM] Hashim [hah-SHEEM]: The victim of the crime. A religious scholar of ill-repute.

Hanan [hah-NAAN]: The wife of Imam Hashim

Isam [e-SAAM]: The brother or Imam Hashim, brother-in-law to Hanan

Ta'sin [ta'-SIIN]: Imam Hashim's housekeeper

Hushang [hoo-shung]: Tavern Keeper at the Pomegranate Nahariyya

Chandi [CHAAN-dee] and **Agnes:** Prostitutes at the Pomegranate Nahariyya

Khalil [kha-LEEL]: Tein's old friend from frontier days who now threatens debtors.

Ibn Salah [sah-LAAH]: A jurist who follows the Hanafi school of religious law

Qadi [Qaw-DEE] Ibn al-Zayzafuni [ib-in al-zay-zaw-FOON-ee]: The judge of the Rusafa district of Baghdad

Tansholpan [tan-shohl-PAN]: A Turkmen talisman and curse writer, friend of Yulduz